Frommer's 96

Washington, D.C.

by Rena Bulkin

Macmillan • USA

ABOUT THE AUTHOR

Rena Bulkin began her travel-writing career in 1964 when she set out for Europe in search of adventure. She found it writing about hotels and restaurants for the *New York Times* International Edition. She has since authored dozens of magazine articles and 15 travel guides to far-flung destinations.

MACMILLAN TRAVEL

A Simon & Schuster Macmillan Company
1633 Broadway
New York, NY 10019

ISBN 0-02-860630-2
ISSN 0899-3246

Editor: Charlotte Allstrom
Map Editor: Doug Stallings
Design by Michele Laseau
Digital cartography by Ortelius Design and Jim Moore

SPECIAL SALES

Bulk purchases (10+ copies) of Frommer's Travel Guides are available to corporations at special discounts. The Special Sales Department can produce custom editions to be used as premiums and/or for sales promotion to suit individual needs. Existing editions can be produced with custom cover imprints such as corporate logos. For more information write to: Special Sales, Simon & Schuster, 8th floor, 1633 Broadway, New York, NY 10019.

Manufactured in the United States of America

Contents

6   Dining   91

7   What to See & Do in Washington, D.C.   142

8   Washington Scandals: A Walking Tour   205

List of Maps

AN INVITATION TO THE READER

In researching this book, I discovered many wonderful places—hotels, restaurants, shops, and more. I'm sure you'll find others. Please tell me about them, so we can share the information with your fellow travelers in upcoming editions. If you were disappointed with a recommendation, I'd love to know that, too. Please write to:

Rena Bulkin
Frommer's Washington, D.C. '96
Macmillan Travel
1633 Broadway
New York, NY 10019

AN ADDITIONAL NOTE

Please be advised that travel information is subject to change at any time—and this is especially true of prices. We therefore suggest that you write or call ahead for confirmation when making your travel plans. The authors, editors, and publisher cannot be held responsible for the experiences of readers while traveling. Your safety is important to us, however, so we encourage you to stay alert and be aware of your surroundings. Keep a close eye on cameras, purses, and wallets, all favorite targets of thieves and pickpockets.

WHAT THE SYMBOLS MEAN

✪ Frommer's Favorites

Hotels, restaurants, attractions, and entertainment you should not miss.

⑨ Super-Special Values

Hotels and restaurants that offer great value for your money.

The following abbreviations are used for credit cards:

AE	American Express	EU	Eurocard
CB	Carte Blanche	JCB	Japan Credit Bank
DC	Diners Club	MC	MasterCard
DISC	Discover	V	Visa
ER	enRoute		

Introducing Washington, D.C.

As home to one of the world's major powers, Washington, D.C., offers its own special brand of excitement. Here, visitors can linger in the halls and chambers where great leaders have engaged in the democratic process; listen to Senate debates; hear the Supreme Court in session; visit the National Archives, where the most cherished U.S. documents—the Declaration of Independence, the Constitution, and the Bill of Rights—are enshrined; find inspiration in magnificent monuments to the greatest American presidents and check out the palatial digs of the current chief executive; learn how the FBI works to thwart crime; and see dollar bills being churned out at the Bureau of Engraving and Printing. In short, visitors can experience firsthand just how the government of the United States works.

Edifices of gleaming marble are the background to Washington sightseeing. And surrounding the city's grand beaux-arts buildings are spacious boulevards and tranquil tree-lined streets, grassy malls and parks, and circular plazas with splashing fountains and statuary at the focal points. This is a lushly verdant city. Millions of flowers create a dazzling riot of color in spring and summer, and every April the famous Japanese cherry trees burst into bloom along the Tidal Basin, resembling a pink snowstorm. In almost every respect, the capital is a showplace, one of the most beautiful cities in the country. But that hasn't always been the case. . . .

1 Frommer's Favorite Washington Experiences

- **The C&O Canal:** Hike or bike along the scenic tree-lined canal towpath from Georgetown to Fletcher's Boat House (about 3 miles), where there are picnic tables and grills. Spend the day—bring kites, watercolors, a good book, whatever. Bikes can be rented from Big Wheels at 1034 33rd St. NW.
- **A Day in Alexandria:** Just a short distance (by Metro or car) from the District is George Washington's Virginia hometown. Roam the quaint cobblestone streets, browse charming boutiques and antique stores, visit the boyhood home of Robert E. Lee and other historic attractions, and dine in one of Alexandria's fine restaurants.

- **Afternoon Tea:** Nothing is more totally self-indulgent than lingering over things sweet and caloric in the middle of the day—fresh-baked scones with Devonshire cream, pastries, finger sandwiches, and more. See "Best Bets" in Chapter 6 for suggestions.

- **You Be the Judge:** If you're in town when the Supreme Court is in session (October through late April, call **202/479-3000** for details), you can observe a case being argued; it's thrilling to see this august institution at work.

- **The Lincoln Memorial After Dark:** During the day, hordes of rambunctious schoolchildren detract from this monument's grandeur; at night the experience is infinitely more moving.

- **A Monument and Memorials Walking Tour:** You'll need a good map for this one. Start out with a hearty breakfast at Palladin (in the Watergate Hotel, overlooking the Potomac). Explore the Kennedy Center across the street (save in-depth touring for another time); then double back to the Vietnam and Lincoln Memorials; follow the cherry blossom–lined Tidal Basin path to the Jefferson Memorial; and finish your tour at the Washington Monument. This is a long but beautiful hike; afterward, head to the Ebbitt Grill for a strength-restoring lunch.

- **The Library of Congress:** The magnificent Italian-Renaissance–style Thomas Jefferson Building of the Library of Congress—filled with murals, mosaics, sculptures, and allegorical paintings—is one of America's most notable architectural achievements. Be sure to take the tour detailed in Chapter 7.

- **Experience the Earth Revolving:** The Foucault Pendulum at the National Museum of American History provides empirical evidence that the earth is revolving; don't miss it.

- **The Mall in the Morning:** Arrive on the Mall at about 8:30am (take the Metro to Smithsonian), and you might see President Clinton jogging with his entourage. The Mall is magical and tourist-free at this hour; stroll behind the Smithsonian Information Center (the Castle) through the magnolia-lined parterres of the beautiful Enid A. Haupt Garden. Exit on Jefferson Drive, walk east to the Hirshhorn, and cross the street to its sunken Sculpture Garden, an enchanting outdoor facility. Then cross back on Jefferson Drive, walk past the Hirshhorn and turn left on the brick path that leads into the lovely Ripley Garden—yet another gorgeous green space on the Mall.

- **Union Station:** Noted architect Daniel H. Burnham's neoclassical monument to the great age of rail travel, modeled after the Baths of Diocletian and the Arch of Constantine in Rome, is majestic and awe-inspiring. If, like myself, you love great architecture, a visit here is *de rigueur*. Spend a few hours wandering about, browse the shops, and have lunch (see dining suggestions in Chapter 6).

- **The Phillips Collection:** This museum, housed in a turn-of-the-century Georgian-Revival mansion, is a gem, displaying many impressionist and modernist works in a charming residential setting. Plan your visit for the morning, have a relaxing tapas lunch at the elegant Gabriel nearby, and in the afternoon tour Anderson House, a palatial turn-of-the-century mansion at 2118 Massachussetts Ave. filled with Belgian tapestries woven for Louis XIII, Ming Dynasty jade trees, and other treasures. It's open Tuesday through Saturday from 1 to 4pm.

• **Embassy Row:** Head northwest on Massachusetts Avenue from Dupont Circle. It's a gorgeous walk along tree-shaded streets lined with beaux-arts mansions. Built by fabulously wealthy magnates during the Gilded Age, most of these palatial precincts today are occupied by foreign embassies.

2 Washington Past & Present

Probably no living American thinks of Washington as a capital in the wilderness. But back in 1800, when Congress moved from its temporary home in Philadelphia to its new permanent seat of government on the Potomac, that's precisely what it was.

The Continental Congress had decided as early as 1783 that a federal city should be established as a permanent locale for its meetings. But even then, the question of slavery created a gap between the North and the South. The northern states insisted that the new capital be in the North, while southerners championed a national seat of government in their precincts.

Wrangling about a location for the capital continued until 1790, when New Yorker Alexander Hamilton and Virginian Thomas Jefferson resolved the dispute (over dinner in a Manhattan restaurant) with a compromise. In return for the South's agreement to pay the national Revolutionary War debts, the capital would be located in the South. Furthermore, it would be named Washington after the first U.S. president and (probably more important) a resident of the Commonwealth of Virginia.

By Act of Congress, George Washington was given full authority to choose a site "not exceeding ten miles square on the River Potomac . . . for the permanent seat of the Government of the United States."

ENTER PIERRE L'ENFANT

Virginia and Maryland, by agreement, ceded land for the new capital. It was to be known as the Federal District and to include Georgetown in

Dateline

■ **1608** Capt. John Smith sails up Potomac River from Jamestown: for the next 100 years Irish-Scotch settlers colonize the area.

■ **1783** Continental Congress proposes new "Federal Town"; North and South vie for it.

■ **1790** A compromise is reached: If South pays off North's Revolutionary War debts, new capital will be situated in its region.

■ **1791** French engineer Pierre Charles L'Enfant designs capital city but is fired within year.

■ **1792** Cornerstone is laid for Executive Mansion.

continues

- **1793** Construction begins on Capitol.
- **1800** First wing of Capitol completed; Congress moves from Philadelphia; Pres. John Adams moves into Executive Mansion.
- **1801** Library of Congress established.
- **1812** War with England.
- **1814** British burn Washington.
- **1817** Executive Mansion rebuilt, its charred walls painted white: becomes known as White House.
- **1822** Population reaches 15,000.
- **1829** Smithsonian Institution founded for "increase and diffusion of knowledge."
- **1847** Cornerstone laid for first Smithsonian museum building.
- **1861** Civil War; Washington becomes North's major supply depot.
- **1865** Capitol dome completed; Lee surrenders to Grant April 8; Lincoln assassinated at Ford's

continues

Maryland and Alexandria in Virginia. In 1791 Pierre Charles L'Enfant was employed by George Washington to survey the land and plan the city. L'Enfant, a Frenchman, had distinguished himself as an engineer in the Revolutionary Army. He had also remodeled New York's City Hall to serve as the first seat for our federal government.

L'Enfant's master plan (which you can see in the Library of Congress) proposed a "presidential palace" linked to the "home of Congress" by a vast green mall. Asked how he happened to choose the hill at the west end of Jenkins Heights as the site for the Capitol, he responded, "It stands as a pedestal waiting for a monument."

Assisting L'Enfant in laying out the design was Benjamin Banneker, an African-American surveyor, inventor, and mathematician. He was specifically responsible for drawing up the District boundary that affected the state of Maryland.

L'Enfant, though a genius, was also temperamental. He had no patience for practical politics and refused to cooperate with building commissioners or Washington's appointed surveyor, Andrew Ellicott. And he ignored Washington's repeated requests to produce a preliminary blueprint so that fundraising could begin. His situation became increasingly difficult, and in 1792 he was fired. For the next few decades, the embittered L'Enfant was often seen "haunting the lobbies of the Capitol . . . pacing the newly marked avenues"—keeping a jaundiced eye on the developing city. Architect Benjamin Latrobe wrote in his diary: "Daily through the city stalks the picture of famine, L'Enfant and his dog."

When L'Enfant died in 1825, the fact that he had designed Washington was almost forgotten. His superb plans were gathering dust; the city that had begun with such a grandiose vision muddled along as a nondescript small town. L'Enfant was buried without fanfare, and it wasn't until 1909 that his grave was moved to Arlington National Cemetery to rest on a hill looking out over the city that owes him so much.

LAYING THE FOUNDATION

Back in 1792, a nationwide competition was held for the design of the Capitol Building to be erected on the hill L'Enfant had designated. The winner was a young physician, an amateur architect named William Thornton, who later founded the Patent Office. (Architects in those days had little professional standing.) In the words of Thomas Jefferson, another "amateur" architect, the Capitol plan "captivated the eye and judgment of all." George Washington noted that "grandeur, simplicity, and convenience appear to be . . . well combined in this plan." The cornerstone for the Capitol was laid September 18, 1793, beside the banks of what the Native Americans called "The River of Swans," the Potomac.

The competition to design the "presidential palace" was won by an Irishman, James Hoban, who received $500 for his plan. (Other entrants included Thomas Jefferson, who submitted his design anonymously.) Hoban hailed from North Carolina, where he had designed that state's capitol building. Because the White House cornerstone was laid in 1792, it holds the distinction of being the oldest public building in Washington. George Washington, however, never occupied the mansion and is, in fact, the only American president never to have resided there. John Adams, the second president, became the first tenant on November 1, 1800—before the house was fully completed.

A CITY RISES

In the considerable period before the public buildings were finished, it was suggested that Congress meet alternately in Trenton, New Jersey, and Annapolis, Maryland—that is, part of the time in the North, part of the time in the South. This idea of shifting meetings was rejected when Francis Hopkinson suggested, sardonically, that a federal town be built atop a platform on wheels and rolled back and forth between two places of residence.

By 1800 one wing of the Capitol Building was ready for the legislators. They moved down from Philadelphia, the last temporary capital, in the fall of that year.

As the first occupants of the White House, President and Mrs. Adams headed from Baltimore; close to Washington they got so hopelessly lost that they "wandered for two hours without finding a guide or path." When they finally arrived, however, Abigail Adams pronounced her new home "a beautiful spot, capable of any improvement." Mrs. Adams, a Yankee woman of grit and gumption, finding "not the

Theatre April 14.
- **1871** Alexander "Boss" Shepherd turns Washington into a showplace, using many L'Enfant plans.
- **1889** National Zoo established.
- **1900** Population reaches about 300,000.
- **1901** McMillan Commission plans development of Mall from Capitol to Lincoln Memorial.
- **1907** Union Station opens, largest train station in country.
- **1908** Federal Bureau of Investigation (FBI) created.
- **1912** Cherry trees, a gift from Japan, planted in Tidal Basin.
- **1914** World War I begins.
- **1922** Lincoln Memorial completed.
- **1941** National Gallery of Art opens; U.S. declares war on Japan.
- **1943** Pantheon-inspired Jefferson Memorial and Pentagon completed.
- **1949** Interior of White House rebuilt.

continues

- **1957** Helicopters first seen on White House lawn.
- **1960** Population reaches almost 800,000.
- **1961** John F. Kennedy becomes first Catholic president.
- **1971** John F. Kennedy Center for Performing Arts opens.
- **1976** Metro, city's first subway system, opens in time for Bicentennial.
- **1982** Vietnam Veterans Memorial erected in Constitution Gardens.
- **1987** Arthur M. Sackler Gallery, a new Smithsonian facility focusing on Asian art, opens on Mall; expanded Museum of African Art, also part of Smithsonian, moves to Mall.
- **1991** Population exceeds 3 million.
- **1993** U.S. Holocaust Memorial Museum, documenting the horror and tragedy of Nazi era, opens near Mall.
- **1995** Korean War Veterans Memorial is dedicated.

least fence, yard, or other convenience," took it upon herself to hang the laundry out to dry in the East Room.

Pennsylvania Avenue, on paper the principal boulevard between the Capitol and the presidential palace, was then a muddy morass of a pathway covered with alder bushes. Where the path reached Georgetown, "houses had been erected, which bore the name of *The Six Buildings,*" a put-down of those who harbored ideas that it was a blossoming megalopolis.

Never mind. The new federal capital was in business. And John Adams wasted no time in delivering his presidential address to the first joint session of Congress. Yet the grumbling continued.

John Cotton, a congressman from Connecticut, complained: "A sidewalk was attempted in one instance by a covering formed of the chips hewed from the Capitol. It extended but a little way and was of little value, for in dry weather the sharp fragments cut our shoes, and in wet weather covered them with white mortar."

Newspapers all over the country quipped about "the palace in the wilderness" and referred to Pennsylvania Avenue as "the great Serbonian bog." Georgetown was called "a city of houses without streets" and Washington "a city of streets without houses."

Speculation escalated land prices in the capital. Congress had agreed to purchase land for public building sites. Land surrounding these sites was to be sold, with half the proceeds from the sale of lots to go to the landowners, half to the government for the erection of government buildings.

But as land prices soared around the Capitol Building, many of those who would have liked to live in the area were forced to buy elsewhere. As a result, settlement shifted toward the northwest, and, even today, the most fashionable town houses and embassies are found in the Northwest section. The area along Pennsylvania Avenue remained a soggy swamp. And when the land speculation syndicate fell apart in 1796, financial support for constructing government buildings went down the drain, too.

Jefferson, when he assumed the presidency in 1801, had to obtain money from Congress for public buildings. He planted poplar trees along Pennsylvania Avenue, doing what he could to make the "Appian Way of the Republic" something better than a "slough of despond." The Library of Congress was also established at this time.

Thomas Moore, Ireland's national lyricist, on a visit in 1804 cracked:

> *And what was Goose Creek once is Tiber now.*
> *This fam'd metropolis, where fancy sees,*
> *Squares in morasses, obelisks in trees;*
> *Which second-sighted seers e'en now adorn,*
> *With shrines unbuilt and heroes yet unborn.*

Building went on slowly, but no sooner had the youthful Congress seen James and Dolley Madison installed in the White House than it became necessary to declare war. England had been impressing American seamen, and disputes over western land worsened the situation. The War of 1812 had begun.

A CITY BURNS

On August 24, 1814, the British fleet sailed into Chesapeake Bay and marched on the capital. Admiral George Cockburn (pronounced Co-burn by the British) was in charge of the attack.

Fortunately, everybody knew that they were coming. Dolley Madison stubbornly stayed on in the White House, determined to save all she could. She hustled important documents off to Lewisburg, 35 miles northwest of Washington, for protection. When friends insisted that she leave for her own safety, at the last minute she cut Gilbert Stuart's portrait of George Washington out of its frame, rolled it up, and hied off to a nearby army camp where she spent the night in a tent, a soldier guarding the entrance. This famous portrait, probably the oldest original possession in the White House, hangs today in the East Room. Dolley Madison knew George Washington well—her younger sister, Lucy, was married to Washington's nephew—and she considered the portrait a remarkable likeness. Dolley saved another painting, too—a portrait of herself—which also hangs in the White House.

Luckily for the budding nation, the rains came on that fateful night. A torrential storm halted the flames that might have destroyed the city completely.

When the Madisons moved back into town, they set up housekeeping at Octagon House, on the corner of 18th Street and New York Avenue. The gala parties Dolley threw helped relieve the pall over Washington left by the war.

The Madisons remained at Octagon House until 1815, when they moved to the northwest corner of Pennsylvania Avenue and 19th Street, to a place known simply as "The Seven Buildings," early housing for the Department of State. There they stayed until the executive mansion was rebuilt, its charred walls painted white in March 1817. Ever since, the "president's palace" has been called the White House.

A CITY REBUILDS

After the British withdrew, Congress first met in the Blodgett Hotel, then moved into a brick building across from the burned-out Capitol. James Monroe took the presidential oath on the porch of what became known as the "Brick Capitol," which stood where the Supreme Court now stands, beginning the tradition of taking the presidential oath in open air, sometimes a chilly event in January.

Monroe also refurnished the burned-out White House with some $15,000 worth of French-designed furniture. Jefferson, Madison, and Monroe all had a taste for things French, and it's still reflected throughout the White House. More recently, First Lady Jacqueline Kennedy, also a Francophile, was responsible for refurnishing and redecorating the White House to reveal its original French character.

Repair work on the Capitol Building was directed by Benjamin Latrobe, an Englishman who had taken over responsibility for its construction in 1803. Slowly he replaced the gutted wood with marble, brick, and metal. It was reoccupied by Congress in 1819.

By 1822, only 22 years after its founding and eight years after being burned, the capital city boasted a population of nearly 15,000 people.

In 1829 the Smithsonian Institution was created when an Englishman, James Smithson, left half a million dollars "to found at Washington, under the name of the Smithsonian Institution, an establishment for the increase and diffusion of knowledge. . . ." Smithson never visited the United States, but the cornerstone for his great legacy, the now-sprawling Smithsonian, was laid in 1847. The first building in the complex is a red sandstone castle of Norman inspiration. That original building is located on the Mall, and it was reopened to the public after undergoing considerable restoration in 1972. Today it serves as a visitor information center for the Smithsonian complex.

Government building continued to boom. By 1842 the present Treasury Building—blocking the vista from the White House to the Capitol and spoiling L'Enfant's original plan—was completed. Andrew Jackson had tired of waiting for the appointed Commission to choose a Treasury site, so he marched out of the White House one day, pointed to a spot, and said that the Treasury cornerstone would be laid there. His will was done . . . plunk in the middle of Pennsylvania Avenue!

MID-19TH-CENTURY WASHINGTON

From all this, you might assume that Washington was well on its way from villagehood to cityhood. Gas lights were lit on the Capitol grounds in 1847. But by 1860 no more than Pennsylvania Avenue had been lit. "Pigs roamed the principal thoroughfares, pavements but for a few patches were lacking, and open sewers carried off refuse." Visiting author Anthony Trollope declared Washington "as melancholy and miserable a town as the mind of man could conceive." Soon things would get even worse.

The Civil War turned the capital into an armed camp. It was the principal supply depot of the North and an important medical center.

The rotunda of the Capitol Building—its 9-million-pound cast-iron dome completed in 1865—was used as a barracks, referred to by the soldiers as "the big tent." Later it became a troop hospital, and here the American poet Walt Whitman wandered among the wounded, helping where he could. Altogether, 3,000 troops were billeted in the Capitol, and basement committee rooms were converted into bakeries.

The Civil War ended when Lee surrendered to Grant on April 8, 1865. The greatest parade in the capital's history celebrated this event. To the tune of fife and drums, troops marched down Pennsylvania Avenue for two full days and nights. Less than a week later, on April 14, Pres. Abraham Lincoln was shot at Ford's Theatre by John Wilkes Booth, and the city went into mourning.

The war's legacy was poverty, unemployment, and disease. Washington's population swelled with uneducated, agrarian ex-slaves, and tenement slums arose within a stone's throw of the Capitol.

SUDDEN EXPANSION

In 1870 several factions attempted to transfer the national capital to another city. St. Louis bid several million dollars for the honor, and Horace Greeley suggested that the capital go west. But the move was never considered seriously, and Congress went ahead and voted $500,000 to build the Departments of State and War and the Navy Building.

Enter "Boss" Shepherd and a new era. Gov. Alexander R. Shepherd was chosen to head a territorial government established in the District of Columbia from 1871 to 1874. Shepherd was a handsome, strapping man with blustery charm. He'd been a successful plumber, an alderman, a newspaper owner, and president of the City Reform Association. He was a natural to become leader of the territorial government. Once installed in office, though, he ignored budgets and followed a bankruptcy course to beautify his domain. Under his guidance, the L'Enfant plan was finally executed in earnest. Three hundred miles of half-laid streets were improved. Nearly every thickly populated thoroughfare was paved with wood, concrete, or macadam. Some 128 miles

Impressions

I know of no other capital in the world which stands on so wide and splendid a river. But the people and the mode of life are enough to take your hair off!   —Henry Adams

My God! What have I done to be condemned to reside in such a city!
                —A French diplomat in the early days

The whole aspect of Washington is light, cheerful, and airy; it reminds me of our fashionable watering places.   —Mrs. Frances Trollope

Washington . . . enormous spaces, hundreds of miles of asphalt, a charming climate, and the most entertaining society in America.
                —Henry James

of sidewalks were built, and 3,000 gas lamps and a system of sewers were installed. Old Tiber Creek was filled in. Scores of new parks were graded and beautified with fountains. A special park commission planted 6,000 trees.

Soon there were more paved streets in Washington than in any other city in the country. And Pres. Ulysses S. Grant declared in a message to Congress, "Washington is rapidly becoming a city worthy of the nation's capital." Grant temporarily swept a few facts about the grand public works under the rug—like the whopping $20-million bill for the improvements.

Before long Congress reacted, and Shepherd was nearly booed out of town. In 1874 the territorial form of government gave way to a trio of commissioners. Shepherd took his family to Mexico. But when he returned to the United States in 1887, he was acclaimed as the man who had made Washington a showplace. And he certainly had.

The nation's Centennial Celebration of 1876 in Philadelphia and the Chicago Exposition of 1893 brought about a cultural awakening throughout the country. Following that period, the Corcoran Art Gallery was built in Washington, the Metropolitan Museum in New York, and the Museum of Fine Arts in Boston. In 1884 the Washington Monument was completed. And in 1897 the Library of Congress, which took 11 years to build, was completed. During the following year, 1898, L'Enfant's plan was dusted off again, and adjustments were made to tailor the District to the motor age.

But the capital of the United States was 100 years old and home to 300,000 before the plan for development and improvement drawn up by the McMillan Commission was enacted in 1901. At his own expense, James McMillan, a senator from Michigan, sent an illustrious committee—New York's Central Park landscapist Frederick Law Olmsted, sculptor Augustus Saint-Gaudens, and noted architects Daniel Burnham and Charles McKim—to Europe on a seven-week study tour to observe the architecture and landscaping of the world's great capitals. It was a committee worthy of L'Enfant's vision and backed by the necessary political clout to get the job done.

The principal thrust of the commission's plan was to develop the Mall, which, at the turn of the century, was little more than a pasture traversed by the tracks of the Pennsylvania Rail Road. The company agreed to remove its tracks in return for funding to construct Union Station.

The Mall, in addition to housing the National Gallery of Art and the Smithsonian Institution, was to become the site for the Department of Agriculture and other important structures. When finished, it would extend 1 mile in length, 300 feet in width, from the Capitol to the Lincoln Memorial. Projected plans also included several public buildings—office buildings for members of the House, Senate, and the Supreme Court (which had met in the Capitol until then).

Aesthetics came into play in 1910, when the National Commission of Fine Arts was created by President Taft. Its duty was to advise on fountains, statues, and monuments in public squares, streets, and parks throughout the District of Columbia. Thanks to Mrs. Taft, the famous cherry trees presented to the United States by the Japanese in 1912 were planted in the Tidal Basin. And thanks to Taft's commission, neoclassic architecture and uniform building height became the order of the day. The commission fixed a 110-foot maximum rooftop height for buildings in the downtown district, so that the Capitol dome might be seen from miles around.

WASHINGTON TODAY

During the Great Depression in the 1930s, FDR's Works Progress Administration—WPA, *We Do Our Part*—put the unemployed to work erecting public buildings and artists to work beautifying them.

More recently (1971), the John F. Kennedy Center for the Performing Arts, on the Potomac's east bank, filled a longtime need for a cultural haven.

In 1974 the opening of the new Hirshhorn Museum and Sculpture Garden on the Mall met the need for a major museum of modern art. Another storehouse of art treasures is the magnificent East Building of the National Gallery of Art, which opened in 1978. It was designed to handle the overflow of the gallery's burgeoning collection and to accommodate traveling exhibits of major importance.

In time for the Bicentennial, the National Air and Space Museum opened in splendid new quarters, and the first leg of the capital's much-needed subway system, Metro, was completed. The 45 acres between the Washington Monument and the Lincoln Memorial were transformed into Constitution Gardens, and in 1982 the park became the site of the Vietnam Veterans Memorial.

In 1987 Washington got a new $75-million Smithsonian complex on the Mall; it houses the Arthur M. Sackler Gallery of Art, the relocated National Museum of African Art, the International Center, and the Enid A. Haupt Garden. In 1989 renovation of the city's magnificent Union Station (inspired by the Baths of Diocletian) was completed. In 1993 the United States Holocaust Memorial Museum, adjoining the Mall, opened, and in 1995 the Korean War Veterans Memorial was dedicated.

As the millennium approaches, Washington, like other American cities, faces some fairly serious problems, including one of the highest urban crime rates, homelessness, a disintegrating school system, and a $700 million deficit, not to mention a "perpetual" mayor whose previous administration was instrumental in creating the current budget crisis. Furthermore, in 1995, it was deemed necessary to close a section of Pennsylvania Avenue to vehicular traffic after a plane crashed onto the White House lawn and gunfire twice hit the presidential mansion.

However, none of these problems is likely to affect you as a tourist. Almost all of the city's attractions are in safely serene parts of town, and, budget crunch aside, they're operating normally and being beautifully maintained. Few cities can vie with Washington in its offerings of quality theater, sophisticated dining, treasure-filled major museums, and other metropolitan pleasures.

It's no wonder Washington attracts more than 20 million visitors each year. History and heritage, art and politics, cuisine and culture combine to make this a vital and beautiful city—a fitting capital for a great nation.

3 Famous Washingtonians

Benjamin Banneker (1731–1806)   When Pierre L'Enfant left Washington in 1792, Banneker, a black mathematician, astronomer, and surveyor, re-created his maps and city plans from memory.

Art Buchwald (b. 1925)   Pulitzer Prize–winning syndicated columnist and political satirist.

Frederick Douglass (1818–95)   Born in slavery, he escaped and fled north to become a driving force in the abolitionist movement and its most impassioned voice.

Edward (Duke) Ellington (1899–1974)   Native Washingtonian, bandleader, pianist, and songwriter, he composed "Mood Indigo" and "Sophisticated Lady."

Helen Hayes (1900–93)   The First Lady of the American Theater was well known for her roles in *Long Day's Journey into Night* and *The Glass Menagerie.*

Pierre Charles L'Enfant (1754–1825)   Brilliant French military engineer who, invited by George Washington, laid out plans for the national capital in 1791.

Dolley Madison (1769–1849)   President Madison's wife and capital society's first queen, she rescued Gilbert Stuart's famous portrait of George Washington from the British in the War of 1812.

Perle Mesta (1891–1975)   Official Washington's "hostess with the mostest," especially during the Truman years. She was the inspiration for the musical *Call Me Madam.*

James Smithson (1765–1829)   Although he never set foot in the United States, he should be considered an honorary Washingtonian because he left his fortune to this country for the museum complex that, bearing his name, has become the largest in the world.

John Philip Sousa (1854–1932)   America's bandmaster, known as "The March King," composer of "Semper Fidelis," "Stars and Stripes Forever," and "The Washington Post."

Walt Whitman (1819–92)   American poet, author of *Leaves of Grass* and *O Captain, My Captain,* the latter a tribute to Lincoln, whom he greatly admired. He thought of himself as the great poet of democracy.

4 Recommended Books & Films

BOOKS

As the capital of the United States, Washington probably is better documented than any other American city. The following list is a good starting point for further reading.

ECONOMIC, POLITICAL & SOCIAL HISTORY
Adler, Bill. *Washington, a Reader.* Meredith Press, 1967.
Arnebeck, Bob. *Through a Fiery Trial: Building Washington, 1790–1800.* Madison, 1991.

Bishop, Jim. *The Day Lincoln Was Shot*. Harper & Row, 1955.

Cooke, Alistair. *One Man's America*. Knopf, 1952.

Duncan, Don. *Washington: The First One Hundred Years*. Seattle Times, 1989.

Kite, Elizabeth S. *L'Enfant and Washington, 1791–92*. Ayer Co., 1970.

Loftin, T. L. *Contest for a Capital*. TL Loftin, 1989.

Schlesinger, Arthur M., Jr. *The Birth of the Nation*. Houghton Mifflin, 1968.

Terrell, John Upton. *The Key to Washington*. JB Lippincott, 1962.

ARCHITECTURE & THE ARTS

Aylesworth, Thomas, and Virginia Aylesworth. *Washington, the Nation's Capital*. Gallery Books, a division of WH Smith, 1986.

Carter, Edward C., et al. *Latrobe's View of America, 1795–1820* (Selections from the Watercolors and Sketches). Yale University Press, 1985.

Reed, Robert. *Old Washington, D.C., in Early Photographs*. Dover, 1980.

FICTION & MYSTERY

Drury, Allen. *Advise and Consent*. Doubleday, 1959.

McCarthy, Abigail. *Circles, a Washington Story*. Doubleday, 1977.

Roosevelt, Elliott. *The White House Pantry Murder* and others in the Eleanor Roosevelt as sleuth series. St. Martin's Press, 1987.

Truman, Margaret. *Murder at the Smithsonian, . . . at the FBI, . . . at the CIA, . . . in Georgetown*; and six others in the Capital Crimes Series. Fawcett, 1985–1990.

HUMOR

Adler, Bill. *The Washington Wits*. Macmillan, 1967.

Pitch, Anthony S. *Exclusively Washington Trivia*. Mino, 1989.

Rash, Bryson B. *Footnote Washington*. EPM, 1983.

FOR KIDS

Krementz, Jill. *A Visit to Washington, D.C.* Scholastic, 1987.

Loewen, N. *Washington, D.C.* Rourke, 1989.

Petersen, Anne. *Kidding Around Washington, D.C.: A Young Person's Guide to the City*. John Muir, 1989.

Weston, Marti, and Florri DeCell. *Washington! Adventures for Kids*. Vandemeer, 1989.

FILMS

Hundreds of film companies have used the streets and famous interiors of Washington, D.C., as a setting for films for some 80 years. Some of the more memorable include *Birth of a Nation* (1915), *Mr. Smith Goes to Washington* (1939), *Born Yesterday* and *Magnificent Yankee* (1950), *The FBI Story* (1959), *Advise and Consent* (1962), *Seven Days in May* (1964), *The Last Detail* (1974), *All the President's Men* (1976), *The Seduction of Joe Tynan* (1978), *Heartburn* (1985), *No Way Out* (1986), and *Broadcast News* (1987).

2

Planning a Trip to Washington, D.C.

A lot of what you'll want to see and do in the capital can be arranged after you arrive, but some things should be planned in advance, while you're still home.

1 Visitor Information & Money

Before you leave, contact the **Washington, D.C., Convention and Visitors Association,** 1212 New York Ave. NW, Washington, DC 20005 (☎ **202/789-7000**), and ask them to send you a free copy of the *Washington, D.C., Visitors Guide,* which details hotels, restaurants, sights, shops, and more. They'll also be happy to answer specific questions.

Also write or call the **D.C. Committee to Promote Washington,** P.O. Box 27489, Washington, DC 20038-7489 (☎ **202/724-4091** or 800/422-8644), and request a free copy of *Discover Washington, D.C.* It lists low weekend rates at dozens of Washington hotels.

SPECIAL TICKETS FOR VIP CONGRESSIONAL TOURS

Based on availability, senators and/or congressional representatives can provide their constituents with tickets for VIP tours of the Capitol, the White House, the FBI, the Bureau of Engraving and Printing, and the Kennedy Center. This is no secret. Thousands of people know about it and do write, so make your request as far in advance as possible—even six months ahead is not too early—specifying the dates you plan to visit and the number of tickets you need. Their allotment of tickets for each sight is limited, so there's no guarantee you'll secure them, but it's worth a try.

Address requests to representatives as follows: U.S. House of Representatives, Washington, DC 20515; and to senators: U.S. Senate, Washington, DC 20510. Don't forget to include the exact dates of your Washington trip. When you write, also request tourist information and literature.

Note: Before writing, you might try calling a senator or congressperson's local office; in some states you can obtain passes by phone.

THE CAPITOL   There are special, more comprehensive, tours of the Capitol departing at intervals between 8 and 8:45am, Monday to Friday, for those with tickets.

What Things Cost in Washington	U.S. $
Taxi from National Airport to downtown	10.00–12.00
Bus from National Airport to downtown	8.00 (14.00 round-trip)
Local telephone call	.25
Double at the Jefferson Hotel (very expensive)	245.00–265.00
Double at the Barceló Washington Hotel (expensive)	155.00–180.00
Double at the Channel Inn (moderate)	110.00–135.00
Double at the Days Inn Downtown (inexpensive)	79.00–99.00
Three-course dinner at the Willard Room (very expensive)	55.00
Three course dinner at Petitto's (expensive)	35.00
Three-course dinner at Jaleo (moderate)	18.00–22.00
Three-course dinner at Scholl's Cafeteria (inexpensive)	7.00–8.00
Bottle of beer (restaurant)	2.75
Coca-Cola (restaurant)	1.50
Cup of coffee (restaurant)	1.25
Roll of ASA 100 Kodacolor film, 36 exposures	4.50
Admission to all Smithsonian museums	Free
Theater ticket at the National	22.50–60.00

THE WHITE HOUSE   Between 8 and 8:45am the doors of the White House are open for special VIP tours to those with tickets. Once again, write far, far in advance, because each senator receives only 15 tickets a week to distribute, and each representative only 10. These early tours ensure your entrance during the busy tourist season when thousands line up during the two hours daily that the White House is open to the public. They're also more extensive than later tours, with guides providing explanatory commentary as you go; on later tours, attendants are on hand to answer questions but don't give formal talks in each room.

THE FBI   The line for this very popular tour can be extremely long. One way to beat the system is to ask a senator or representative to make a reservation for you for a scheduled time.

BUREAU OF ENGRAVING & PRINTING   Guided VIP tours are offered weekdays at 8am, except on holidays.

THE KENNEDY CENTER   VIP tours departing Monday through Saturday at 9:30am and 9:45am enable you to avoid a long wait with the crowds who did not take the trouble to write to a senator or representative.

2 When to Go

THE CLIMATE

Probably you'll visit when you have vacation time or when the kids are out of school, but if you have a choice, I'd recommend the fall. The weather is lovely, Washington's scenery is awash in fall foliage colors, and the tourists have thinned out.

If you really hate crowds and want to get the most out of Washington sights, winter is your season. It's not that cold (see chart below), there are no long lines or early-morning dashes to avoid them, and hotel prices are lower.

Spring weather is delightful, and of course there are those cherry blossoms. Along with autumn, it's the nicest time to enjoy D.C.'s outdoor attractions, to get around to museums in comfort, and to laze away an afternoon or evening at the ubiquitous Washington street cafés. But the city is also crowded with millions of tourists.

The throngs remain in summer, and anyone who's ever spent a summer in D.C. will tell you how hot and steamy it is. Though there's occasional relief, those 90° days do seem to arrive with amazing frequency. The advantage: This is the season (especially June and July) to enjoy hundreds of outdoor events—free concerts, festivals, parades, Revolutionary War reenactments, and more. There's something doing almost every night and day. And, of course, Independence Day (July 4th) in the capital is a spectacular celebration. But no matter when you visit, you can be sure there will be plenty going on around town.

Average Temperatures (°F) in Washington, D.C.

	Jan	Feb	Mar	Apr	May	June	July	Aug	Sept	Oct	Nov	Dec
Avg. High	44	44	53	64	75	83	87	84	78	68	55	45
Avg. Low	24	28	35	44	55	64	68	66	60	48	38	30

WASHINGTON CALENDAR OF EVENTS

The District is the scene of numerous daily special events, fairs, and celebrations. Listed below are the major annual events. When in town, check the *Washington Post,* especially the Friday "Weekend" section, and pick up an events calendar at the Washington Visitor Information Center, 1455 Pennsylvania Ave. (☎ **202/789-7038**). The Smithsonian Information Center, 1000 Jefferson Dr. SW (☎ **202/ 357-2700**), is another good source. For annual events in Alexandria, see Chapter 10.

January

- **Washington Antique Show,** Omni Shoreham Hotel, 2500 Calvert St. NW, at Connecticut Avenue (☎ **202/234-0700**). About 50 outstanding East Coast dealers display their wares. Admission is charged, and the profits go to charities. Catalogs include articles by scholars and museum curators, and there are guest speakers—for example, George Plimpton, J. Carter Brown, and Henry Kissinger. Early January.

- **Presidential Inauguration,** on the Capitol steps. After the swearing-in, the crowd lines the curbs as the new president proceeds down Pennsylvania Avenue to the White House. The event is heralded by parades, concerts, parties, plays, and other festivities. For details, call **202/789-7038.** January 20 in years following a national election.
- **Martin Luther King, Jr.'s Birthday.** Events include speeches by prominent civil-rights leaders and politicians; readings; dance, theater, and choral performances; prayer vigils; a wreath-laying ceremony at the Lincoln Memorial; and concerts. Many events take place at the Martin Luther King Memorial Library, 901 G St. NW (☎ **202/727-1186**). Call **202/789-7000** for further details. Third Monday in January.

February

- **Chinese New Year celebration.** A friendship archway, topped by 300 painted dragons and lighted at night, marks Chinatown's entrance at 7th and H streets NW. The celebration begins the day of the Chinese New Year and continues for 10 or more days, with traditional firecrackers, dragon dancers, and colorful street parades. Some area restaurants offer special menus. For details, call **202/789-7000.** Late January or early to mid-February.
- **Black History Month.** Features numerous events, museum exhibits, and cultural programs celebrating contributions of African Americans to American life. For details check the *Washington Post* or call **202/357-2700** or 202/727-1186.
- **Abraham Lincoln's Birthday,** Lincoln Memorial. Marked by the laying of a wreath and a reading of the Gettysburg Address at noon. Call **202/426-6895.** February 12.
- **George Washington's Birthday,** Washington Monument. Similar celebratory events. Call **202/426-6841** for details. Both president's birthdays also bring annual citywide sales. February 22.

March

- **Spring Antiques Show,** D.C. Armory, 2001 E. Capitol St. Features close to 200 dealers from the United States, Canada, and Europe. Admission (about $5) is charged. Call **301/738-1966** for details. Usually Friday through Sunday the first weekend in March.
- **St. Patrick's Day,** on Constitution Avenue NW from 7th to 17th streets. A big parade that's all you'd expect—floats, bagpipes, marching bands, and the wearin' o' the green. Past grand marshals have included Tip O'Neill, John Hume, Redskins' "player of the decade" John Riggins, and political comic Mark Russell. For parade information, call **301/879-1717** or 202/789-7000. The Sunday before March 17 (unless March 17 falls on a Sunday as it will in 1996).

✪ **Smithsonian Kite Festival.** A delightful event if the weather cooperates—an occasion for a trip in itself. Throngs of kite enthusiasts fly their unique creations and compete for ribbons and prizes.

Where: On the Washington Monument grounds. **When:** A Saturday in mid- or late March. **How:** If you want to compete, just show up with your kite and register between 10am and noon. Call **202/357-2700** or 202/357-3030 for details.

✪ **Cherry Blossom Events.** Washington's best-known annual event—the blossoming of the famous Japanese cherry trees. Festivities include a major parade (marking the end of the festival) with princesses, floats, and celebrity guests, not to mention bands, clowns, fireworks, fashion shows, concerts, a Japanese lantern-lighting ceremony, a ball, and a marathon race. There are also special ranger-guided tours departing from the Jefferson Memorial.

Where: The trees bloom by the Tidal Basin in Potomac Park. Related events take place all around town. **When:** Late March or early April (national news programs monitor the budding). **How:** For parade information, call the DC Downtown Jaycees (☎ **202/728-1135**). For other cherry-blossom events, check the Washington Post or call **202/789-7038.**

April

Cherry blossom events continue (see above).

- **Easter Sunrise Services,** Memorial Amphitheater at Arlington National Cemetery Easter Sunday. There are free shuttle buses to the site from the visitor center parking lot. Call **202/475-0856** or 202/789-7000 for details.

✪ **White House Easter Egg Roll.** The biggie for little kids. In past years, entertainment has included clog dancers, clowns, storytellers, Easter bunnies, Ukrainian egg-decorating exhibitions, puppet and magic shows, military drill teams, an egg-rolling contest, and a hunt for 1,000 or so hidden wooden eggs, many of them signed by celebrities (e.g., Tom Hanks and Barbra Streisand), astronauts, or the Clintons. *Note:* Attendance is limited to children ages 3 to 6.

Where: The White House South Lawn and the Ellipse; enter at the southeast gate on East Executive Avenue. **When:** Easter Monday between 10am and 2pm; arrive early. **How:** In past years participants just had to show up, but there has been talk of issuing tickets. Call **202/208-1631** for details.

- **Thomas Jefferson's Birthday,** Jefferson Memorial. Celebrated with a wreath-laying, speeches, and a military ceremony. Call **202/462-6822** for time and details. April 13.

- **White House Gardens.** These beautifully landscaped creations are open to the public for special free tours between 2 and 5pm. Call **202/456-2200** for details. Two days only, in mid-April.

- **Georgetown House Tour.** The interiors of beautiful old George-town homes can be seen. Admission ($20 per person per day) is charged, and includes tea and light fare at St. John's Georgetown Parish Church. Participants visit six houses per day between noon and 5pm. Call **202/338-1796** for details. Late April.
- **Justice Douglas Reunion Hike,** C&O Canal. If you love hik-ing, don't miss this event. Douglas, bless him, once walked the entire 184½-mile towpath in protest against a plan to build a scenic parkway along the canal. The annual hike covers about 12 miles, on a different section each year. A buffet banquet wraps up the day's activities, and there's a bus to take you back to town. For details and tickets (there's a charge for the bus and buffet), contact the C&O Canal Association, P.O. Box 366, Glen Echo, MD 20812 (☎ **703/356-1809** for reservations). Usually the last Saturday in April.

May

- **Georgetown Garden Tour.** View the remarkable private gardens of one of the city's loveliest neighborhoods. Admission (about $18) includes light refreshments. Some years there are related events such as a flower show at a historic home. Call **202/333-6896** for details. Early to mid-May.
- **Washington National Cathedral Annual Flower Mart,** on the cathedral grounds. Includes displays of flowering plants and herbs, decorating demonstrations, ethnic food booths, children's rides and activities (including an old-fashioned carousel), cos-tumed characters, puppet shows, and other entertainments. Admission is free. Call **202/537-6200** for details. First Friday and Saturday in May.
- **Asian Pacific American Heritage Festival,** Freedom Plaza, on Pennsylvania Avenue between 13th and 14th streets NW. Honors the contributions of Asian Americans to this country and presents their varied cultural heritages. All of Washington's Asian communities participate. There are cultural displays, crafts booths, ethnic foods, dragon dances, and martial arts exhibitions. For information, call **703/354-5036.** First weekend in May.
- **Memorial Day.** At 11am, a wreath-laying ceremony takes place at the Tomb of the Unknowns in Arlington National Cemetery, followed by military band music, a service, and an address by a high-ranking government official (sometimes the president); call **202/475-0856** for details. There's also a ceremony at 1pm at the Vietnam Veterans Memorial—wreath-laying, speakers, and the playing of taps; call **202/619-7222** for details. On the Sunday before Memorial Day, the National Symphony Orchestra performs a free concert at 8pm on the West Lawn of the Capi-tol; call **202/619-7222** for details.

June

- **Spirit of America Pageant,** USAir Arena, Landover, Maryland. This 3rd U.S. Infantry and U.S. Army Band concert program traces the history of the American soldier from the birth of the nation into the 21st century with music and skits. Call **202/ 475-0685** for details. Early June.

✪ **Smithsonian Festival of American Folklife.** A major event with traditional American music, crafts, foods, games, concerts, and exhibits. Past performances have ranged from Appalachian fiddling to Native American dancing, and demonstrations from quilting to coal mining. All events are free.

  Where: Most events take place on the Mall. **When:** For 5 to 10 days, always including July 4th weekend. **How:** Call **202/ 357-2700,** or check the listings in the *Washington Post,* for details.

July

✪ **Independence Day.** There's no better place to be on the Fourth of July than Washington, D.C. The festivities include a massive National Independence Day Parade down Constitution Avenue, complete with lavish floats, princesses, marching groups, and military bands. Other events include baseball games, a jazz festival, dances, arts-and-crafts exhibits, celebrity entertainers, concerts, and food booths. A morning program in front of the National Archives includes military demonstrations, period music, and a reading of the Declaration of Independence. In the evening the National Symphony Orchestra plays on the west steps of the Capitol with guest artists (for example, Leontyne Price). And big-name entertainment also precedes the fabulous fireworks display over the Washington Monument. *Note:* You can also attend an 11am free organ recital at Washington's National Cathedral.

  Where: Most events take place on the Washington Monument grounds. **When:** July 4, all day. **How:** Just show up. Check the *Washington Post* or call **202/789-7000** for details.

- **Men's Tennis Classic,** Rock Creek Park at 16th and Kennedy streets NW. Top-seeded players such as Andre Agassi and Pete Sampras compete. Call **703/276-3030** for details, 202/ 432-SEAT for tickets. Mid-month.

August

- **Tchaikovsky's *1812* Overture,** Sylvan Theatre on the Washington Monument grounds. The U.S. Army Band gives a free performance of this famous work, complete with roaring cannons. For details, call **703/696-3399.** Sometime during the month.

✪ **Smithsonian Birthday Party.** In 1996, the Smithsonian will celebrate its 150th anniversary with a big party including music, crafts, family activities, an outdoor evening concert, and fireworks—all free. There will be other celebratory events, both in Washington and nationwide, throughout the year.

Where: The party will take place on the Mall. **When:** August 10 and 11. **How:** For details call **202/357-2700** or check listings in the *Washington Post.*

September

- **National Frisbee Festival,** on the Washington Monument grounds. See world-class Frisbee champions and their disk-catching dogs at this noncompetitive event. For details, call **301/645-5043.** Weekend.
- **International Children's Festival,** Wolf Trap Farm Park in Vienna, Virginia. At this three-day arts celebration, the entertainment—all of it outdoors—includes clowns, musicians, mimes, puppet shows, and creative workshops from 10am to 4:30pm each day. Admission is charged. For details, call **703/642-0862.** Late September
- **Washington National Cathedral's Open House.** Celebrates the anniversary of the laying of the foundation stone in 1907. Events include demonstrations of stone carving and other crafts utilized in building the cathedral; carillon and organ demonstrations; and performances by dancers, choirs, strolling musicians, jugglers, and puppeteers. This is the only time visitors are allowed to ascend to the top of the central tower to see the carillon; it's a tremendous climb, but you'll be rewarded with a spectacular view. For details, call **202/537-6200.** A Saturday in late September or early October.
- **Rock Creek Park Day.** A birthday party for Washington's largest park (1990 was its centennial). The celebration includes music, folk dancing, balloons, pony rides, international crafts and food booths, children's activities, and environmental exhibits. Activities take place at the Nature Center (☎ **202/426-6829**), Pierce Mill (☎ **202/426-6908**), and the Old Stone House in Georgetown (☎ **202/426-6851**).
- **Annual Kennedy Center Open House Arts Festival.** A day-long festival of the performing arts in late September or early October, featuring local and national artists on all of the Kennedy Center stages and outdoors. Admission free; no tickets required. Call **202/467-4600** for details.

October

- **Taste of D.C. Festival,** Pennsylvania Avenue between 9th and 14th streets. Dozens of Washington's restaurants offer international food-tasting opportunities, along with live entertainment, dancing, storytellers, and games. Admission is free; purchase tickets for tastings. Call **202/724-4091** for details. Columbus Day weekend.
- **White House Fall Garden Tours.** For two days visitors have an opportunity to see the famed Rose Garden and South Lawn.

Admission is free. A military band provides music. For details, call **202/456-2200.** Mid-October.

- **Washington International Horse Show,** USAir Arena, 1 Harry S Truman Dr., Landover, Md. This is one of the nation's most important equestrian events, featuring a hunt night, Jack Russell terrier races, international team show jumping, and dressage. Admission (about $18) is charged. Call **301/840-0281** for details, 202/432-SEAT for tickets. Eight days in late October.

- **Halloween.** Never officially organized, but with costumed revels on the increase every year. Giant block parties take place in the Dupont Circle area and Georgetown. Check the *Washington Post* for special parties and activities. October 31.

- **Marine Corps Marathon.** Over 16,000 runners compete in this 26-mile race (the fourth-largest marathon in the U.S.). It begins at the Marine Corps Memorial (the Iwo Jima statue) and passes major monuments. Call **703/690-3431** or 800/RUN-USMC for details. A Sunday late in the month.

November

- **Veterans Day.** The nation's war dead are honored with a wreath-laying ceremony at 11am at the Tomb of the Unknowns in Arlington National Cemetery followed by a memorial service. The President of the United States or a very high-ranking government personage officiates. Military music is provided by a military band. Call **202/475-0856** for information. At the Vietnam Veterans Memorial (☎ **202/619-7222**), observances include speakers, a wreath-laying, a color guard, and the playing of taps. November 11.

December

- **St. Nicholas Festival,** at the Washington National Cathedral. An evening for families that includes a visit from St. Nicholas, dancers, choral groups, crafts, caroling, bell ringing, and much more. Call **202/537-6200** for more information, or to inquire about other Christmas concerts, pageants, services, and children's activities. First week of December.

- **Christmas Pageant of Peace/National Tree Lighting,** at the northern end of the Ellipse. On a selected Wednesday or Thursday in early December at 5pm, the president lights the national Christmas tree to the accompaniment of orchestral and choral music. The lighting inaugurates the three-week Pageant of Peace, a tremendous holiday celebration with seasonal music, caroling, a Nativity scene, 50 state trees, and a burning Yule log. Call **202/619-7222** for details. Early December.

- **White House Candlelight Tours.** On three evenings from 6 to 8pm, visitors can see the president's Christmas holiday decorations by candlelight. String music enhances the tours. Call **202/456-2200** for dates and details.

3   Tips for Special Travelers

FOR TRAVELERS WITH DISABILITIES

Two helpful travel organizations, **Accessible Journeys** (☎ 610/521-0339 or 800/TINGLES) and **Flying Wheels Travel** (☎ 507/451-5005 or 800/535-6790), offer tours, cruises, and custom vacations worldwide for people with physical disabilities; Accessible Journeys can also provide nurse/companions for travelers. **The Guided Tour Inc.** (☎ 215/782-1370 or 800/783-5841) offers tours for people with physical or mental disabilities, the visually impaired, and the elderly.

Mobility International USA, P.O. Box 10767, Eugene, OR 97440 (☎ 503/343-1284), provides accessibility and resource information to its members and sponsors many interesting travel programs for the disabled. Membership ($25 a year) includes a quarterly newsletter called *Over the Rainbow.*

There's no charge for help via telephone (accessibility information and more) from the **Travel Information Service** (☎ 215/456-9600). Another organization, the **Society for the Advancement of Travel for the Handicapped** (SATH), 347 Fifth Ave., Suite 610, New York, NY 10016 (☎ 212/447-7284), charges $5 for sending requested information.

Recommended books: A publisher called **Twin Peaks Press,** Box 129, Vancouver, WA 98666 (☎ 360/694-2462), specializes in books for people with disabilities. Write for their *Disability Bookshop Catalog,* enclosing $5.

Finally, a Washington phone number to keep on hand is **202/966-8081,** the **Information, Protection, and Advocacy Center for People with Disabilities.** This organization publishes a series of pamphlets called *Access Washington: A Guide to Metropolitan Washington for the Physically Disabled,* which cover everything from hotels to restaurants to sightseeing attractions. There's a nominal fee for mailing, but it's well worth it. The center can help make your stay in Washington a worry-free, enjoyable experience.

SIGHTSEEING ATTRACTIONS   Washington, D.C., is one of the most accessible cities in the world for the disabled. The **White House** has a special entrance on Pennsylvania Avenue for visitors arriving in wheelchairs. For details, call **202/456-2322.**

All **Smithsonian museum buildings** (and the National Gallery) are accessible to wheelchair visitors. A comprehensive free publication called *Smithsonian Access* lists all services available to visitors with disabilities, including parking, building access, and more. To obtain a copy, write to the Smithsonian Institution, SI Building, Rm. 153, MRC 010, Washington, DC 20560 (☎ 202/357-2700 or TTY 202/357-1729).

The **Lincoln and Jefferson memorials** and the **Washington Monument** are also equipped to accommodate disabled visitors. The last-named keeps a wheelchair on the premises and allows disabled visitors to go to the head of the waiting line.

Call ahead to other sightseeing attractions for accessibility information and special services.

SHOPPING   For shoppers, places well equipped with wheelchair ramps and other facilities for the disabled include the Shops at National Place, the Pavilion at the Old Post Office, and Georgetown Park Mall.

THEATER   The **John F. Kennedy Center for the Performing Arts** provides headphones to hearing-impaired patrons at no charge, allowing them to adjust the volume as needed. There are also special signed performances for the hearing impaired. All theaters in the complex (except the Terrace) are wheelchair accessible. Also inquire (in advance) about cassettes for the visually impaired, offering audio descriptions at select performances. For details call **202/416-8340;** for other questions regarding patrons with disabilities call **202/416-8727.** The TTY number is **202/416-8525.**

The **Arena Stage** has a wheelchair lift and is otherwise accessible. It offers audio description and sign interpretation at designated performances as well as infrared assistive listening devices for the hearing-impaired; program books in braille, large-print, and on audiocassette; and a TTY box office line (☎ **202/484-0247**).

Ford's Theatre is handicapped-accessible and offers listening devices as well as special signed and audio-described performances. Call **202/347-4833** for details.

The **National Theatre** features special performances of its shows for visually and hearing-impaired theatergoers. To obtain earphones for narration, simply ask an usher before the performance. The National also offers a limited number of half-price tickets to disabled patrons. For details, call **202/628-6161.**

GETTING AROUND TOWN   Each **Metro** station is equipped with an elevator (complete with braille number plates) to train platforms, and rail cars are fully accessible. Conductors make station and on-board announcements of train destinations and stops. The TTD number for Metro information is **202/638-3780.**

Regular **Tourmobile** trams are accessible to physically impaired visitors. The company also operates special vans for immobile travelers, complete with wheelchair lifts. For information, call **202/544-5100.**

TRAVELING BY BUS, TRAIN & PLANE   A companion can accompany a disabled person at no charge aboard a **Greyhound** bus (you must inform Greyhound in advance). Call **800/752-4841** at least 48 hours in advance to discuss other special needs.

Amtrak (☎ **800/USA-RAIL**) provides redcap service (at all major stations), wheelchair assistance, and special seats with 72 hours' notice. The disabled are also entitled to a 25% discount on one-way regular coach fares. Documentation from a doctor or an ID card proving your disability is required. Amtrak also provides wheelchair-accessible sleeping accommodations on long-distance trains, and guide dogs are permissible and travel free of charge. Write for a free booklet called *Amtrak's America* from Amtrak Distribution Center, P.O. Box 7717, Itasca, IL 60143, which has a section detailing services for passengers with disabilities.

Note: Washington offers redcap service, but check your own departure station.

When making your flight reservations, ask the airline or travel agent where your wheelchair will be stowed on the plane and if seeing or hearing guide dogs can accompany you.

FOR SENIORS

Bring some form of photo ID that includes your birth date since many city attractions, theaters, transportation facilities, hotels, and restaurants grant special senior discounts.

If you haven't already done so, consider joining the **American Association of Retired Persons** (AARP), 601 E St. NW, Washington, DC 20049 (☎ 202/434-2277). Annual membership costs $8 per person or per couple. You must be at least 50 to join. Membership entitles you to many discounts. Write to Purchase Privilege Program, AARP Fulfillment, 601 E St. NW, Washington, DC 20049, to receive AARP's *Purchase Privilege* brochure—a free list of hotels, motels, and car-rental firms nationwide that offer discounts to AARP members.

Another good source of reduced-price information is *The Discount Guide for Travelers Over 55* by Caroline and Walter Weinz (EP Dutton).

Elderhostel, a national organization that offers low-priced educational programs for people over 55 (your spouse can be any age, a companion must be at least 50), sponsors frequent week-long residential programs in Washington. Some of these focus on government and American history, others on art, literature, and other subjects. Cost averages about $355 per person, including meals, room, and classes. For information, call **410/830-3437** or contact Elderhostel headquarters at 75 Federal St., Boston, MA 02110 (☎ **617/426-7788**).

Saga International Holidays, 222 Berkeley St., Boston, MA 02116 (☎ **617/262-2262** or 800/343-0273), offers tours in the U.S. and abroad designed for travelers over 60. These include "Road Scholar" educational programs, resort holidays, cruises, escorted motorcoach tours, and special-interest tours. Prices are moderate.

Amtrak (☎ **800/USA-RAIL**) offers a 15% discount off the lowest available coach fare (with certain travel restrictions) to people 62 or over.

Greyhound also offers discounted fares for senior citizens. Call your local Greyhound office for details.

FOR SINGLE TRAVELERS

Of major interest to single travelers is the opportunity to meet others. There is, of course, the bar scene (see Chapter 10). Another good way to meet people is to go on a hike, river-rafting trip, or other such excursion, many of which are listed in the *Washington Post* Friday "Weekend" section. You'll find other people-meeting activities listed there as well.

Another tip: Choose a bed-and-breakfast facility; it's easy to meet people over coffee and muffins in the communal dining room.

FOR FAMILIES

Contact **Travel With Your Children, (TWYCH),** 45 W. 18th St., New York, NY 10011 (☎ 212/206-0688), to subscribe to the *Family Travel Times,* a newsletter about traveling with children. It's packed with useful information, and readers can call in for advice during certain periods each week.

FOR GAYS & LESBIANS

The complete source for the gay and lesbian community is *The Washington Blade,* a comprehensive weekly newspaper distributed free at about 700 locations in the District. Every issue provides an extensive events calendar and a list of hundreds of resources, such as crisis centers, health facilities, switchboards, political groups, religious organizations, social clubs, and student activities; it puts you in touch with everything from groups of lesbian birdwatchers to the Asian Gay Men's Network. Gay restaurants and clubs are, of course, also listed and advertised. You can subscribe to the *Blade* for $40 a year or pick up a free copy at: Olsson's Books/Records, 1307 19th St. NW; Annie's Paramount Steak House, 1609 17th St. NW; Kramerbooks, 1517 Connecticut Ave. NW, in the Dupont Circle area; the Biograph Theatre, 29th and M streets NW, in Georgetown; and Chesapeake Bagel Bakery, 215 Pennsylvania Ave. SE, on Capitol Hill. Call the *Blade* office at **202/797-7000** for other locations.

4 Getting There

BY PLANE

Washington is served by three major airports—**Washington National Airport,** just across the Potomac in Virginia and a 15-minute drive from downtown; **Dulles International Airport,** about 45 minutes from downtown, also in Virginia; and **Baltimore-Washington International Airport,** between Baltimore and Washington, about 45 minutes from downtown. Most visitors come in via National, which is served by American, America West, Continental, Delta, Northwest, TWA, United, and USAir. The major foreign airlines that are served by Dulles Airport include: Air France, British Airways, KLM, and Swissair.

BEST-FOR-THE-BUDGET FARES   When evaluating airline fares, take into consideration bus and/or taxi fares to and from departure and arrival airports. The taxi and bus fares listed below will help you make these computations.

As we go to press, there's a major airline price restructuring going on throughout the country. With everything up in the air (so to speak), quoting specific fares here would be meaningless. Always remember, however, that it pays to book flights as far in advance as possible, since advance-purchase fares are often substantially lower.

When you call, also inquire about money-saving packages that include essentials like hotel accommodations, car rentals, and tours with your airfare. Some of the best are offered by **Delta Dream Vacations** (☎ 800/872-7786 for details).

SHUTTLES TO & FROM NEW YORK   The **Delta Shuttle,** which flies out of LaGuardia's Marine Air Terminal in New York and Washington National Airport's Main Terminal (between Gates 15 and 17), has flights departing New York every hour on the half hour Monday to Friday, 6:30am to 8:30pm, with an extra departure at 9pm. Saturday flights are offered every hour on the half hour between 7:30am and 8:30pm. Sunday flights are scheduled every hour on the half hour between 8:30am and 8:30pm, with an extra departure at 9pm. The first weekday flight leaves Washington National at 6:45am, with flights every hour on the half hour after that until 9:30pm. Saturday flights depart every hour on the half hour between 7:30am and 8:30pm. Sunday flights are offered every hour on the half hour between 8:30am and 9:30pm. At press time, the price was $150 each way Monday to Friday and Sunday after 2:30pm, and $75 all day Saturday and through 2:30pm Sunday. Since it's possible for prices and/or flight schedules to change, double-check the above by calling Delta (☎ **800/ 221-1212**).

The same prices are offered by the **USAir Shuttle,** which departs from the USAir terminal at LaGuardia. Flights to Washington National Airport leave New York Monday to Saturday every hour on the hour from 7am to 9pm, and Sunday on the hour from 9am to 9pm. Washington–New York flights leave at the same hours. You can call USAir at **800/428-4322.**

At either airline, inquire about special fares for seniors, children, and youth (up to age 24), as well as 7- and 14-day advance-purchase fares.

GETTING DOWNTOWN FROM THE AIRPORT   Washington National Airport is right on the Blue and Yellow **Metro** lines from which you can reach just about any point in town. There is a courtesy van service between the airport terminal and the Metro station.

The **Washington Flyer** (☎ **703/685-1400**) operates buses between the very centrally located Airport Terminal Building at 1517 K St. NW and both Dulles and National airports. Fares to/from Dulles are $16 one way, $26 round-trip; to/from National, $8 one way, $14 round-trip. Children 6 and under ride free. There are departures in each direction about every 30 minutes. At the K Street Terminal Building you can board a free loop shuttle that goes to eight Washington hotels—the Sheraton Washington, Omni Shoreham, Washington Hilton, Mayflower, Washington Renaissance, Grand Hyatt, J. W. Marriott, and Harrington. The Harrington alone requires an advance reservation, since it's not on the loop unless someone requests it.

The **Airport Connection II** (☎ **301/261-1091,** 301/441-2345, or 800/284-6066) runs buses between the Airport Terminal Building at 1517 K St. NW and Baltimore-Washington International Airport, with departures about every hour or two in each direction; call for exact times. The fare is $14 one way, $25 round-trip, free for children 5 and under.

Taxi fares come to about $9 between National Airport and the White House, $42 to $45 between the White House and Dulles or BWI. (From National, take a D.C. rather than a Virginia cab—it's cheaper.)

Note: There have been price-gouging incidents in which tourists going from the airports into town have been overcharged by taxi drivers. If you think you're being ripped off, make sure to write down the company name and number of the cab (they're on the door), get an accurate receipt for the fare, and, if possible, the license plate number of the cab and the driver's name. Call **202/331-1671** to report any problems.

BY TRAIN

Amtrak trains arrive at historic **Union Station,** 50 Massachusetts Ave. NE, a turn-of-the-century beaux-arts masterpiece that was magnificently restored in the late 1980s at a cost of more than $180 million. Offering a three-level marketplace of shops and restaurants, this stunning depot is conveniently located and connects with Metro service. There are always lots of taxis available there. For rail reservations, contact Amtrak (☎ **800/USA-RAIL**). (For more on Union Station, see Chapters 6, 7, and 9.)

Like the airlines, Amtrak offers several discounted fares; although not all are based on advance purchase; you have more discount options by reserving early. Be sure to inquire exactly when the discount tickets can be used. At this writing, regular round-trip coach fares and discount fares are as follows between Washington's Union Station and five selected cities:

Standard Fares

	Regular Fare	Discount Fare
N.Y.–D.C.	$166	$102
Chicago–D.C.	$242	$128
Atlanta–D.C.	$238	$108
L.A.–D.C.	$494	$254
Boston–D.C.	$172	$110

I also suggest that you inquire about money-saving packages that include hotel accommodations, car rentals, tours, etc., with your train fare. Call **800/321-8684** for details.

Metroliner service—which costs a little more but provides faster transit and roomier, more comfortable seating—is available between New York and Washington, D.C., and points in between. The round-trip Metroliner fare between New York and D.C. at this writing is $206. *Note:* Metroliner fares are substantially reduced on weekends.

The most luxurious way to travel is **First Class Club Service,** available on all Metroliners and some other trains as well. For an additional $53 each way, passengers enjoy roomier, more upscale seating in a private car; complimentary meals and beverage service; and Metropolitan Lounges (in New York, Chicago, Philadelphia, and Washington) where travelers can wait for trains in a comfortable, living room–like setting while enjoying free snacks and coffee.

BY BUS

Greyhound buses connect almost the entire United States with Washington, D.C. They pull in at a terminal at 1005 1st St. NE at L Street (☎ **800/231-2222**). The closest Metro station is Union Station, four blocks away. The bus terminal area is not what you'd call a showplace neighborhood, so if you arrive at night, it's best to take a taxi.

The fare structure on buses is not necessarily based on distance traveled. The good news is that when you call Greyhound to make a reservation, the company will always offer you the lowest fare options. Call in advance and know your travel dates, since some discount fares require advance purchase.

BY CAR

Major highways approach Washington, D.C., from all parts of the country. The District is 240 miles from New York City, 40 miles from Baltimore, and 600 miles from Chicago and Atlanta.

If you're driving from New York or other points north, you'll probably take I-95 south to U.S. 50 west, which becomes New York Avenue in D.C. This avenue will be on your map, so you can easily figure out how to reach your hotel.

If you start elsewhere, your best bet, if you're a member of AAA, is to call for exact directions. Otherwise, the Convention and Visitors Association (☎ **202/789-7000**) can help you find the way; have a map in front of you when you call.

3

For Foreign Visitors

Although American fads and fashions have spread across Europe and other parts of the world so that America may seem like familiar territory before your arrival, there are still many peculiarities and uniquely American situations that any foreign visitor will encounter.

1 Preparing for Your Trip

The **Services of Meridian International Center** (☎ 202/939-5566 or 202/939-5538) is a nonprofit, community volunteer organization that provides special services to D.C.'s many visitors from abroad. It has a language bank of volunteers on call who speak dozens of languages, and provides assistance (by phone) with accommodations, sightseeing, dining, and other traditional tourist needs. Phones are answered seven days a week around the clock.

ENTRY REQUIREMENTS

DOCUMENT REGULATIONS Canadian citizens may enter the United States without visas; they need only proof of residence.

Citizens of the United Kingdom, New Zealand, Japan, and most Western European countries traveling on valid passports may not need a visa for fewer than 90 days of holiday or business travel to the United States, providing that they hold a round-trip or return ticket and enter the United States on an airline or cruise line participating in the visa waiver program.

(Note that citizens of these visa-exempt countries who first enter the United States may then visit Mexico, Canada, Bermuda, and/or the Caribbean islands and then reenter the United States, by any mode of transportation, without needing a visa. Further information is available from any U.S. embassy or consulate.)

Citizens of countries other than those stipulated above, including citizens of Australia, must have two documents:

- a valid **passport,** with an expiration date at least six months later than the scheduled end of the visit to the United States; and
- a **tourist visa,** available without charge from the nearest U.S. consulate. To obtain a visa, the traveler must submit a completed application form (either in person or by mail) with a $1^1/2$-inch square photo and demonstrate binding ties to a residence abroad.

Usually you can obtain a visa at once or within 24 hours, but it may take longer during the summer rush from June to August. If you cannot go in person, contact the nearest U.S. embassy or consulate for directions on applying by mail. Your travel agent or airline office may also be able to provide you with visa applications and instructions. The U.S. consulate or embassy that issues your visa will determine whether you will be issued a multiple- or single-entry visa and any restrictions regarding the length of your stay.

MEDICAL REQUIREMENTS   No inoculations are needed to enter the United States unless you are coming from, or have stopped over in, areas known to be suffering from epidemics, particularly cholera or yellow fever.

If you have a disease requiring treatment with medications containing narcotics or drugs requiring a syringe, carry a valid signed prescription from your physician to allay any suspicions that you are smuggling drugs.

CUSTOMS REQUIREMENTS   Every adult visitor may bring in free of duty: 1 liter of wine or hard liquor; 200 cigarettes or 100 cigars (but no cigars from Cuba) or 3 pounds of smoking tobacco; and $100 worth of gifts. These exemptions are offered to travelers who spend at least 72 hours in the United States and who have not claimed them within the preceding six months. It is altogether forbidden to bring into the country foodstuffs (particularly cheese, fruit, cooked meats, and canned goods) and plants (vegetables, seeds, tropical plants, and so on). Foreign tourists may bring in or take out up to $10,000 in U.S. or foreign currency with no formalities; larger sums must be declared to Customs on entering or leaving the country.

INSURANCE

There is no national health system in the United States. Because the cost of medical care is extremely high, I strongly advise every traveler to secure health insurance coverage before setting out.

You may want to take out a comprehensive travel policy that covers (for a relatively low premium) sickness or injury costs (medical, surgical, and hospital); loss or theft of your baggage; trip-cancellation costs; guarantee of bail in case you are arrested; costs of accident, repatriation, or death. Such packages (for example, "Europe Assistance" in Europe) are sold by automobile clubs at attractive rates, as well as by insurance companies and travel agencies.

MONEY

CURRENCY & EXCHANGE   The U.S. monetary system has a decimal base: one American **dollar** ($1) = 100 **cents** (100¢).

Dollar bills commonly come in $1 ("a buck"), $5, $10, $20, $50, and $100 denominations (the last two are not welcome when paying for small purchases and are not accepted in taxis or at subway ticket booths). There are also $2 bills (seldom encountered).

There are six denominations of coins: 1¢ (one cent or "a penny"), 5¢ (five cents or "a nickel"), 10¢ (ten cents or "a dime"), 25¢ (twenty-five cents or "a quarter"), 50¢ (fifty cents or "a half dollar"), and the rare $1 piece.

TRAVELER'S CHECKS   Traveler's checks denominated in U.S. dollars are readily accepted at most hotels, motels, restaurants, and large stores. But the best place to change traveler's checks is at a bank. Do not bring traveler's checks denominated in other currencies.

CREDIT & CHARGE CARDS   The methods of payment most widely used are credit and charge cards: VISA (BarclayCard in Britain), MasterCard (EuroCard in Europe, Access in Britain, Chargex in Canada), American Express, Diners Club, Discover, and Carte Blanche. You can save yourself trouble by using credit cards in most hotels, motels, restaurants, and retail stores (many food and liquor stores now accept credit/charge cards). You must have a credit or charge card to rent a car. It can also be used as proof of identity or as a "cash card," enabling you to draw money from banks and automated teller machines (ATMS) that accept it.

Note: The "foreign-exchange bureaus" so common in Europe are rare even at airports in the United States, and nonexistent outside major cities. It is best not to change foreign money (or traveler's checks denominated in a currency other than U.S. dollars) at a small-town bank, or even a branch in a big city; in fact, leave any currency other than U.S. dollars at home—it may prove a greater nuisance to you than it's worth.

SAFETY

GENERAL   While tourist areas are generally safe, crime is on the increase everywhere, especially in large U.S. cities. It is wise to ask the city's or area's tourist office if you're in doubt about which neighborhoods are safe.

Remember that hotels are open to the public, and in a large hotel, security may not be able to screen everyone entering. Always lock your room door—don't assume that once inside your hotel you are automatically safe and no longer need be aware of your surroundings.

DRIVING   Safety while driving is particularly important. Question your rental agency about personal safety, or ask for a brochure of traveler safety tips when you pick up your car. Obtain written directions, or a map with the route marked in red, from the agency showing how to get to your destination. If possible, arrive and depart during daylight hours.

If you see someone on the road who indicates a need for help, do *not* stop. Take note of the location, drive on to a well-lighted area, and telephone the police by dialing **911.**

Park in well-lighted, well-traveled areas if possible. Always keep your car doors locked, whether attended or unattended. Look around before you get out of your car, and never leave any packages or valuables in sight. If someone attempts to rob you or steal your car, do *not* try to resist the thief/carjacker—report the incident to the police department immediately.

You may wish to contact the local tourist information bureau in Washington, D.C., before you arrive. They may be able to provide you with a safety brochure.

2 Getting To & Around the U.S.

Travelers from overseas can take advantage of the **APEX (Advance Purchase Excursion) fares** offered by all the major U.S. and European carriers. Aside from these, attractive values are offered by **Icelandair** on flights from Luxembourg to New York and by **Virgin Atlantic Airways** from London to New York/Newark.

Some large American airlines (for example, TWA, American Airlines, Northwest, United, and Delta) offer travelers on their transatlantic or transpacific flights special discount tickets under the name **Visit USA,** allowing travel between any U.S. destinations at minimum rates. They are not on sale in the United States, and must, therefore, be purchased before you leave your foreign point of departure. This system is the best, easiest, and fastest way to see the United States at low cost. You should obtain information well in advance from your travel agent or the office of the airline concerned, since the conditions attached to these discount tickets can be changed without advance notice.

The visitor arriving by air should make very generous allowance for delay in planning connections between international and domestic flights—an average of two to three hours at least.

In contrast, travelers arriving by car or by rail from Canada will find border-crossing formalities streamlined to the vanishing point. And air travelers from Canada, Bermuda, and some places in the Caribbean can sometimes go through Customs and Immigration at the point of departure, which is much quicker and less painful.

For information on transportation to Washington, D.C., from elsewhere in the United States, see "Getting There" in Chapter 2.

International visitors can also buy a **USA Railpass,** good for 15 or 30 days of unlimited travel on Amtrak. The pass is available through many foreign travel agents. Prices in 1995 for a 15-day pass are $229 off-peak, $340 peak; a 30-day pass costs $339 off-peak, $425 peak. (With a foreign passport, you can also buy passes at some Amtrak offices in the United States, including locations in San Francisco, Los Angeles, Chicago, New York, Miami, Boston, and Washington, D.C.) Reservations are generally required and should be made for each part of your trip as early as possible.

With a few notable exceptions (for instance, the Northeast Corridor line between Boston and Washington, D.C.), train service is rarely up to European standards: Delays are common, routes are limited and often infrequently served, and fares are rarely significantly lower than discount airfares. Thus, cross-country train travel should be approached with caution.

The cheapest way to travel around the United States is by **bus.** Greyhound, the nation's nationwide bus line, offers an **Ameripass** for unlimited travel for 7 days (for $259), 15 days (for $459), and 30 days (for $559). Bus travel in the United States can be both slow and uncomfortable, so this option is not for everyone.

FAST FACTS: For the Foreign Traveler

Automobile Organizations   Auto clubs will supply maps, suggested routes, guidebooks, accident and bail-bond insurance, and emergency road service. The major auto club in the United States, with 955 offices nationwide, is the **American Automobile Association (AAA).** Members of some foreign auto clubs have reciprocal arrangements with the AAA and enjoy its services at no charge. If you belong to an auto club, inquire about AAA reciprocity before you leave. The AAA can provide you with an **International Driving Permit** validating your foreign license. You may be able to join the AAA even if you are not a member of a reciprocal club. To inquire, call **800/AAA-HELP.** In addition, some automobile rental agencies now provide these services, so you should inquire about their availability when you rent your car.

Automobile Rentals   To rent a car you need a major credit or charge card. A valid driver's license is required, and you usually need to be at least 25 years old. Some companies do rent to younger people but add a daily surcharge. Be sure to return your car with the same amount of gas you started out with; rental companies charge excessive prices for gasoline. For car-rental companies in Washington, D.C., see "Getting Around" in Chapter 4.

Business Hours   Banks are open weekdays 9am to 3 or 4pm, although there's 24-hour access to the automatic tellers (ATMs) at most banks and other outlets. Generally, offices are open weekdays 9am to 5pm. Stores are open six days a week, with many open on Sunday, too; department stores usually stay open until 9pm at least one day a week.

Climate   See "When to Go" in Chapter 2.

Currency Exchange   You will find currency exchange services in major airports with international service. Elsewhere, they may be quite difficult to come by. In New York, a reliable choice is **Thomas Cook Currency Services, Inc.** They sell commission-free foreign and U.S. traveler's checks, drafts, and wire transfers; they also do check collections (including Eurochecks). Their rates are competitive and the service excellent. They maintain several offices in New York City (☎ **212/757-6915** for Manhattan locations and office hours), and at the JFK Airport International Arrivals Terminal (☎ **718/656-8444**). In Washington, there are Thomas Cook offices at 1800 K St. NW (☎ **202/872-1233**) and at Union Station opposite Gate G on the train concourse (☎ **202/371-9219**).

Drinking Laws   See "Liquor Laws" in "Fast Facts: Washington, D.C." in Chapter 4.

Electricity   The United States uses 110–120 volts, 60 cycles, compared to 220–240 volts, 50 cycles, as in most of Europe. In addition to a 100-volt converter, small appliances of non-American manufacture, such as hair dryers or shavers, will require a plug adapter, with two flat, parallel pins.

Embassies/Consulates   All embassies are located in Washington, D.C., since it's the nation's capital, and many consulates are located here as well. Here are several embassy addresses: **Australia,** 1601 Massachusetts Ave. NW (☎ **202/797-3000**); **Canada,** 501 Pennsylvania Ave. NW (☎ **202/682-1740**); **France,** 4101 Reservoir Rd. NW (☎ **202/944-6000**); **Germany,** 4645 Reservoir Rd. NW (☎ **202/298-4000**); **Ireland,** 2234 Massachusetts Ave. NW (☎ **202/462-3939**); **Netherlands,** 4200 Wisconsin Ave. NW (☎ **202/244-5300**); **New Zealand,** 37 Observatory Circle, NW (☎ **202/328-4800**); and the **United Kingdom,** 3100 Massachusetts Ave. NW (☎ **202/462-1340**). You can obtain the telephone numbers of other embassies and consulates by calling "Information" in Washington, D.C. (dial **411** within D.C.'s 202 area code; elsewhere, dial **202/555-1212**). Or consult the phone book in your hotel room.

Emergencies   In all major cities you can call the police, an ambulance, or the fire brigade through the single emergency telephone number **911.** Another useful way of reporting an emergency is to call the telephone-company operator by dialing **0** (zero, *not* the letter "O").

If you encounter such travelers' problems as sickness, accident, or lost or stolen baggage, call the **Travelers Aid Society,** 512 C St. NE (☎ **202/546-3120**), an organization that specializes in helping distressed travelers, whether American or foreign. See "Orientation," in Chapter 4, for further details.

Gasoline (Petrol)   One U.S. gallon equals 3.75 liters, while 1.2 U.S. gallons equals one Imperial gallon. You'll notice there are several grades (and price levels) of gasoline available at most gas stations. And you'll also notice that their names change from company to company. The unleaded ones with the highest octane are the most expensive (most rental cars take the least expensive "regular" unleaded) and leaded gas is the least expensive, but only older cars can take this now, so check if you're not sure.

Holidays   On the following legal national holidays, banks, government offices, post offices, and many stores, restaurants, and museums are closed: January 1 (New Year's Day), third Monday in January (Martin Luther King, Jr., Day), third Monday in February (Presidents Day, Washington's Birthday), last Monday in May (Memorial Day), July 4 (Independence Day), first Monday in September (Labor Day), second Monday in October (Columbus Day), November 11 (Veterans Day/Armistice Day), fourth Thursday in November (Thanksgiving Day), December 25 (Christmas).

Finally, the Tuesday following the first Monday in November is Election Day, and is a legal holiday in presidential-election years.

Languages   Major hotels often have multilingual employees. Unless your language is obscure, they can usually supply a translator on request.

Legal Aid   The foreign visitor, unless positively identified as a member of the Mafia or of a drug ring, will probably never become involved with the American legal system. If you are pulled up for a minor infraction (for example, of the highway code, such as speeding), never attempt to pay the fine directly to a police officer; you may wind up arrested on the much more serious charge of attempted bribery. Pay fines by mail, or directly into the hands of the clerk of the court. If accused of a more serious offense, it's wise to say and do nothing before consulting a lawyer. Under U.S. law, an arrested person is allowed one telephone call to a party of his or her choice. Call your embassy or consulate.

Mail   If you want your mail to follow you on your vacation and you aren't sure of your address, your mail can be sent to you, in your name, **c/o General Delivery** at the main post office of the city or region where you expect to be. The addressee must pick it up in person and produce proof of identity (for example, driver's license, credit or charge card, or passport).

Generally to be found at intersections, mailboxes are blue with a red-and-white stripe and carry the inscription U.S. MAIL. If your mail is addressed to a U.S. destination, don't forget to add the five-figure postal code, or ZIP (Zone Improvement Plan) Code, after the two-letter abbreviation of the state to which the mail is addressed (CA for California, FL for Florida, NY for New York, and so on).

In Washington, the **main post office** is located opposite Union Station at Massachusetts Avenue and North Capitol Street (☎ **202/ 523-2628**). It's open Monday to Friday 7am to midnight, Saturday and Sunday until 8pm.

Newspapers/Magazines   National newspapers include the *New York Times, USA Today,* and the *Wall Street Journal.* There are also a great many national newsweeklies including *Newsweek, Time,* and *U.S. News & World Report.* For information on local Washington, D.C., periodicals, see "Newspapers/Magazines" in "Fast Facts: Washington, D.C.," Chapter 4.

Radio/Television   Audiovisual media, with four coast-to-coast networks—ABC, CBS, NBC, and Fox—joined in recent years by the Public Broadcasting System (PBS) and the cable network CNN, play a major part in American life. In big cities, televiewers have a choice of about a dozen channels (including the UHF channels), most of them transmitting 24 hours a day, without counting the pay-TV channels showing recent movies or sports events. All options are usually indicated on your hotel TV set. You'll also find a wide choice of local radio stations, each broadcasting particular kinds of talk shows and/or music—classical, country, jazz, pop, gospel—punctuated by news broadcasts and frequent commercials.

Safety   See "Safety" in "Preparing for Your Trip," above.

Taxes   In the United States there is no VAT (value-added tax) or other indirect tax at a national level. Every state, and each city in it, has the right to levy its own local tax on all purchases, including hotel and restaurant checks, airline tickets, and so on.

Telephone/Telegraph/Telex   The telephone system in the United States is run by private corporations, so rates, especially for long-distance service, can vary widely—even on calls made from public telephones. Local calls in the United States usually cost 25¢.

Generally, hotel surcharges on long-distance and local calls are astronomical. You are usually better off using a **public pay telephone,** which you will find clearly marked in most public buildings and private establishments as well as on the street. Outside metropolitan areas, public telephones are more difficult to find. Stores and gas stations are your best bet.

Most **long-distance** and **international** calls can be dialed directly from any phone. For calls to Canada and other parts of the United States, dial **1** followed by the area code and the seven-digit number. For international calls, dial **011** followed by the country code, city code, and the telephone number of the person you wish to call.

For **reversed-charge or collect calls,** and for **person-to-person calls,** dial **0** (zero, *not* the letter "O") followed by the area code and number you want an operator will then come on the line, and you should specify that you are calling collect, or person-to-person, or both. If your operator-assisted call is international, ask for the overseas operator.

For local **directory assistance** ("information"), dial **411;** for **long-distance information,** dial **1,** then the appropriate area code and **555-1212.**

Like the telephone system, **telegraph** and **telex** services are provided by private corporations like ITT, MCI, and above all, Western Union, the most important. You can bring your telegram in to the nearest Western Union office (there are hundreds across the country), or dictate it over the phone (☎ **800/325-6000**). You can also telegraph money, or have it telegraphed to you, very quickly over the Western Union system.

Telephone Directory   There are two kinds of telephone directories available to you. The general directory is the so-called **white pages,** in which private and business subscribers are listed in alphabetical order. The inside front cover lists the emergency number for police, fire, and ambulance, and other vital numbers (like the Coast Guard, poison-control center, crime-victims hotline, and so on). The first few pages are devoted to community-service numbers, including a guide to long-distance and international calling, complete with country codes and area codes.

The second directory, printed on yellow paper (hence its name, **yellow pages**), lists all local services, businesses, and industries by type of activity, with an index at the back. The listings cover not only such obvious items as automobile repairs by make of car, or drugstores (pharmacies), often by geographical location, but also restaurants by type of cuisine and geographical location, bookstores by special subject and/or language, places of worship by religious denomination, and other information that the tourist might otherwise not readily find. The yellow pages also include city plans or detailed area maps, often showing postal ZIP Codes and public transportation routes.

Time   The United States is divided into four **time zones** (six, if Alaska and Hawaii are included). From east to west, these are: Eastern Standard Time (EST), Central Standard Time (CST), Mountain Standard Time (MST), Pacific Standard Time (PST), Alaska Standard Time (AST), and Hawaii Standard Time (HST). Always keep changing time zones in mind if you are traveling (or even telephoning) long distances in the United States. For example, noon in New York City (EST) is 11am in Chicago (CST), 10am in Denver (MST), 9am in Los Angeles (PST), 8am in Anchorage (AST), and 7am in Honolulu (HST).

   Daylight Saving Time   is in effect from the first Sunday in April through the last Saturday in October (actually, the change is made at 2am on Sunday) except in Arizona, Hawaii, part of Indiana, and Puerto Rico. Daylight Saving Time moves the clock one hour ahead of standard time.

Tipping   This is part of the American way of life, based on the principle that one should pay for any special service received. Here are some rules of thumb: bartenders, 10% to 15%; bellhops, at least 50¢ per piece, $2 to $3 for a lot of baggage; cab drivers, 15% of the fare; cafeterias, fast-food restaurants, no tip; chambermaids, $1 a day; checkroom attendants (restaurants, theaters), $1 per garment; cinemas, movies, theaters, no tip; doormen (hotels or restaurants), not obligatory; gas-station attendants, no tip; hairdressers, 15% to 20%; redcaps (airport and railroad station), at least 50¢ per piece, $2 to $3 for a lot of baggage; restaurants, nightclubs, 15% to 20% of the check; sleeping-car porters, $2 to $3 per night to your attendant; valet parking attendants, $1.

Toilets   Visitors can usually find a toilet in a bar, restaurant, hotel, museum, department store, service station, or train station.

AMERICAN SYSTEM OF MEASUREMENTS
Length

1 inch (in.)	=	2.54cm					
1 foot (ft.)	=	12 in.	=	30.48cm	=	.305m	
1 yard	=	3ft.			=	.915m	
1 mile (mi.)	=	5,280 ft.					= 1.609km

To convert miles to kilometers, multiply the number of miles by 1.61 (for example, 50 mi. × 1.61 = 80.5km). Note that this conversion can be used to convert speeds from miles per hour (m.p.h.) to kilometers per hour (kmph).

To convert kilometers to miles, multiply the number of kilometers by .62 (for example, 25km × .62 = 15.5 mi.). Note that this same conversion can be used to convert speeds from kilometers per hour to miles per hour.

Capacity

1 fluid ounce (fl. oz.)			=	.03 liters	
1 pint	=	16 fl. oz.	=	.47 liters	
1 quart	=	2 pints	=	.94 liters	
1 gallon (gal.)	=	4 quarts	=	3.79 liters	=	.83 Imperial gal.

To convert U.S. gallons to liters, multiply the number of gallons by 3.79 (example, 12 gal. × 3.79 = 45.58 liters).

To convert U.S. gallons to Imperial gallons, multiply the number of U.S. gallons by .83 (example, 12 U.S. gal. × .83 = 9.95 Imperial gal.).

To convert liters to U.S. gallons, multiply the number of liters by .26 (example, 50 liters × .26 = 13 U.S. gal.).

To convert Imperial gallons to U.S. gallons, multiply the number of Imperial gallons by 1.2 (example, 8 Imperial gal. × 1.2 = 9.6 U.S. gal.).

Weight

1 ounce (oz.)			=	28.35g			
1 pound (lb.)	=	16 oz.	=	453.6g	=	.45kg	
1 ton			=	2,000 lb.	=	907kg	=	.91 metric tons

To convert pounds to kilograms, multiply the number of pounds by .45 (example, 90 lb. × .45 = 40.5kg).

To convert kilograms to pounds, multiply the number of kilos by 2.2 (example, 75kg × 2.2 = 165 lb.).

Area

1 acre			=	.41ha		
1 square mile	=	640 acres	=	259ha	=	2.6km^2

To convert acres to hectares, multiply the number of acres by .41 (example, 40 acres × .41 = 16.4ha).

To convert square miles to square kilometers, multiply the number of square miles by 2.6 (example, 80 sq. mi. × 2.6 = 208km^2).

To convert hectares to acres, multiply the number of hectares by 2.47 (example, 20ha × 2.47 = 49.4 acres).

To convert square kilometers to square miles, multiply the number of square kilometers by .39 (example, 150km^2 × .39 = 58.5 square miles).

Temperature

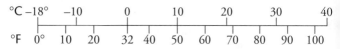

To convert degrees Fahrenheit to degrees Celsius, subtract 32 from °F, multiply by 5, then divide by 9 (example, 85°F − 32 × $^5/_9$ = 29.4°C).

To convert degrees Celsius to degrees Fahrenheit, multiply °C by 9, divide by 5, and add 32 (example, 20°C × $^9/_5$ + 32 = 68°F).

Getting to Know
Washington, D.C.

Washington is one of America's most delightful cities—a fitting show-place for the nation's capital. It's a city designed for strolling, offering both natural beauty and stunning architecture. Learning your way around is quick and easy.

1 Orientation

VISITOR INFORMATION

There are two excellent tourist-information centers in town, and though each focuses on a specific attraction they also can provide information about all other Washington sights.

The **Smithsonian Information Center,** 1000 Jefferson Dr. SW (☎ 202/357-2700), is open daily 9:30am to 5:30pm.

The **White House Visitor Center,** Pennsylvania Avenue between 14th and 15th Streets NW (☎ **202/208-1631,** 202/456-7041 for recorded information), is open Memorial Day to Labor Day 7am to 5pm Tuesday through Saturday, 8am to 5pm Sunday and Monday; the rest of the year it is open 8am to 5pm daily. Try to visit both facilities when you're in town to garner information and see interesting on-site exhibits. Further details are provided in Chapter 7.

The **Travelers Aid Society** is a nationwide network of voluntary nonprofit social-service agencies providing help to travelers in difficulty. This might include anything from crisis counseling to straightening out ticket mix-ups, not to mention reuniting families accidentally separated while traveling, locating missing relatives (sometimes just at the wrong airport), and helping retrieve lost baggage (also sometimes at the wrong airport).

In Washington, Travelers Aid has a central office in the Capitol Hill area at 512 C St. NE (☎ **202/546-3120**), where professional social workers are available to provide assistance. It's open only on weekdays 9am to 5pm.

There are also Travelers Aid desks at Washington National Airport (open Sunday to Friday 9am to 9pm, Saturday 9am to 6pm; ☎ **703/419-3972**), on the lower concourse at the west end of Dulles International Airport (open Monday to Friday 10am to 9pm, Saturday and

Sunday 10am to 6pm; ☎ **703/661-8636**), and at Union Station (open Monday to Saturday 9:30am to 5:30pm, Sunday 12:30 to 5:30pm; ☎ **546-3120**); TTY or TDD (telecommunications device for the deaf) are provided at the above-mentioned locations.

CITY LAYOUT

Pierre Charles L'Enfant designed Washington's great sweeping avenues crossed by numbered and lettered streets. At key intersections he placed spacious circles. Although the circles are enhanced with monuments, statuary, and fountains, L'Enfant also intended them to serve as strategic command posts to ward off invaders or marauding mobs. After what had happened in Paris during the French Revolution—and remember, that was current history at the time—his design views were quite practical.

MAIN ARTERIES & STREETS   The primary artery of Washington is **Pennsylvania Avenue,** scene of parades, inaugurations, and other splashy events. Pennsylvania runs northwest in a direct line between the Capitol and the White House, continuing on a northwest angle to Georgetown from the White House.

Constitution Avenue, paralleled to the south most of the way by **Independence Avenue,** runs east–west flanking the Capitol and the Mall.

Washington's longest avenue, **Massachusetts Avenue,** runs north of and parallel to Pennsylvania. Along the way you'll find Union Station and Dupont Circle, central to the area known as Embassy Row. Farther out are the Naval Observatory (the vice-president's residence is on the premises), Washington National Cathedral, American University, and, finally, Maryland.

Connecticut Avenue, which runs more directly north, starts at Lafayette Square directly opposite the White House. It's the city's Fifth Avenue—the boulevard with elegant eateries, posh boutiques, and expensive hotels.

Wisconsin Avenue, from the point where it crosses M Street, is downtown Georgetown. Antiques shops, trendy boutiques, discos, restaurants, and pubs all vie for attention. Yet somehow Georgetown manages to keep its almost European charm.

FINDING AN ADDRESS   Once you understand the city's layout, it's easy to find your way around. You'll find it helpful, when reading this, to have a map handy.

The city is divided into four basic quadrants—**northwest, northeast, southwest,** and **southeast.** If you look at your map, you'll see that some addresses—for instance, the corner of G and 7th streets—appear in four different places. There's one in each quadrant. Hence you must observe the quadrant designation (NW, NE, SW, or SE) when looking for an address.

The **Capitol** dome is the center of the District of Columbia—the dividing point for the four quadrants: Each of the four corners of the District of Columbia is exactly the same distance from the dome. The White House and most government buildings and important monuments are west of the Capitol (in the northwest and southwest quadrants); so are important hotels and tourist facilities.

Numbered streets run north–south, beginning on either side of the Capitol with East 1st Street and West 1st Street. **Lettered streets** run east–west.

Avenues, named for U.S. states, run at angles across the grid pattern and often intersect at traffic circles. For example, New Hampshire, Connecticut, and Massachusetts avenues intersect at Dupont Circle.

With this in mind, finding an address is a cinch. On **lettered streets,** the address tells you exactly where to go. For instance, 1776 K Street NW is between 17th and 18th streets (the first two digits of 1776 tell you that) in the northwest quadrant (NW). *Note:* I Street is often written Eye Street to prevent confusion with 1st Street.

To find an address on **numbered streets** you'll probably have to use your fingers. For instance, 623 8th Street SE is between F and G streets (the sixth and seventh letters of the alphabet; the first digit of 623 tells you that) in the southeast quadrant (SE). One thing to remember though—there's no J Street (skipping the letter J was meant as a slap in the face to unpopular Chief Justice John Jay). So when counting, remember that K becomes the 10th letter, L the 11th, and so on.

As you go farther out—beyond Washington's original layout—the letter alphabetical system ends and a new one begins—two-syllable names in alphabetical order: Adams, Bryant, Channing, and so forth. When the two-syllable alphabet is used up, the system begins anew with three-syllable names—Albemarle, Brandywine, Chesapeake, and so on.

NEIGHBORHOODS IN BRIEF

The Mall   This lovely tree-lined stretch of open space between Constitution and Independence avenues, extending for $2^1/_2$ miles from the Capitol to the Lincoln Memorial, is the hub of tourist attractions. It includes most of the Smithsonian Institution museums, and many other visitor attractions are close by. The 300-foot-wide Mall is used by natives as well as tourists—joggers, food vendors, kite-flyers, and picnickers among them.

Downtown   The area roughly between 7th and 22nd streets NW going east to west, and P Street and Pennsylvania Avenue going north to south, downtown is a mix of Federal Triangle's government office buildings, K Street and Connecticut Avenue restaurants and shopping, F Street department stores, and much more. Too large an area to have a consistent character, it includes lovely Lafayette Park, Washington's tiny porno district, its ever expanding Chinatown, the convention center, and a half dozen or so sightseeing attractions.

Capitol Hill   Everyone's heard of "the Hill," the area crowned by the Capitol. When people speak of Capitol Hill, they refer to a large section of town, extending from the western side of the Capitol to RFK Memorial Stadium going east, bounded by H Street NE and the Southwest Freeway north and south. It contains not only the chief symbol of the nation's capital, but the Supreme Court building, the

Washington, D.C., at a Glance

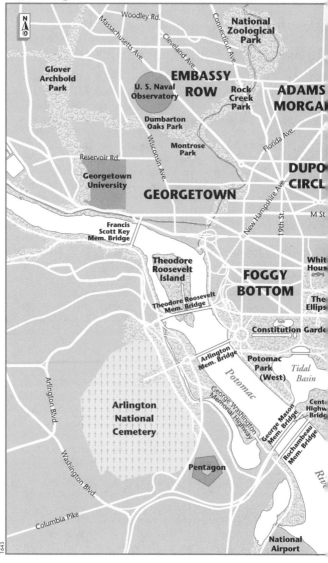

Library of Congress, the Folger Shakespeare Library, Union Station, and the U.S. Botanic Garden. Much of it is a quiet residential neighborhood of tree-lined streets and Victorian homes. There are many restaurants in the vicinity.

Foggy Bottom   The area west of the White House to the edge of Georgetown, Foggy Bottom was Washington's early industrial center. Its name comes from the foul fumes emitted in those days by a coal

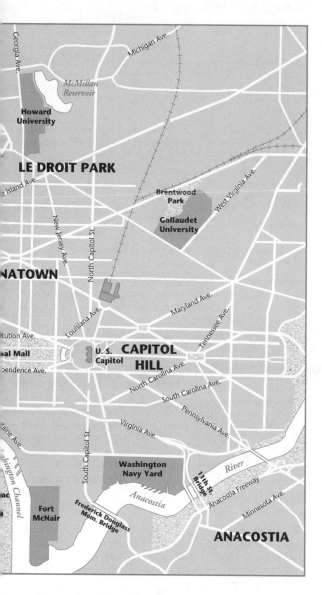

depot and gasworks, but its original name, Funkstown (for owner Jacob Funk), is perhaps even worse. There's nothing foul about the area today. The Kennedy Center and George Washington University are located here. Constitution and Pennsylvania avenues are Foggy Bottom's southern and northern boundaries, respectively.

Dupont Circle Generally, when Washingtonians speak of Dupont Circle they don't mean just the park, they mean the area around it.

The park itself, named for Rear Adm. Samuel Francis Dupont of the U.S. Navy, is centered around D.C.'s most famous fountain, at the intersection of Connecticut and Massachusetts avenues, and is a popular rendezvous spot. Dupont Circle is one of the liveliest sections in town, rivaled only by Georgetown and Adams-Morgan for nightspots, movie theaters, and restaurants. It is also the hub of D.C.'s gay community.

Georgetown   This historic community dates back to colonial times. It was a thriving tobacco port long before the District of Columbia was formed, and one of its attractions, the Old Stone House, dates back to pre-Revolutionary days. Georgetown action centers on M Street and Wisconsin Avenue NW, where you'll find numerous boutiques (see Chapter 9 for details), chic restaurants, and popular pubs. But do get off the main drags and see the quiet tree-lined streets of restored colonial row houses, stroll through the beautiful gardens of Dumbarton Oaks, and check out the C&O Canal. One of the reasons so much activity flourishes in Georgetown is because of Georgetown University and its students.

Adams-Morgan   This increasingly trendy multiethnic neighborhood is popular for its restaurants serving Jamaican, Ethiopian, Spanish, and other international cuisines. Try to plan at least one meal up here; it's a good opportunity to see an authentic, untouristy area of Washington. Adams-Morgan centers around Columbia Road and 18th Street NW.

2   Getting Around

Washington is one of the easiest U.S. cities in which to get around. Only New York rivals its comprehensive transportation system, but Washington's clean, efficient subways put the Big Apple's underground nightmare to shame. There's also a complex bus system with routes covering all major D.C. arteries, and it's easy to hail a taxi anywhere at any time. Finally, Washington—especially the areas of interest to tourists—is pretty compact, and often the best way to get from one place to another is on foot.

BY METRO

The Metrorail stations are immaculate, cool, and attractive, with terra-cotta floors and high, vaulted ceilings; the sleek subway cars are air-conditioned, carpeted, furnished with upholstered seats, and fitted with picture windows; the tracks are rubber-cushioned so the ride is quiet; the service is frequent enough so you usually get a seat; and the system is so simply designed that a 10-year-old can understand it.

Metrorail's 74 stations and 89 miles of track (83 stations and 103 miles of track are the eventual goal) include locations at or near almost every sightseeing attraction and extend to suburban Maryland and northern Virginia. If you're in Washington even for a few days you'll probably have occasion to use the system, but if not, I suggest you create one—perhaps dinner at a Union Station or Dupont Circle restaurant. The Metro is a sightseeing attraction in its own right.

There are five lines in operation—**Red, Blue, Orange, Yellow,** and **Green**—with extensions planned for the future. The lines connect at several points, making transfers easy. All but Yellow and Green Line trains stop at Metro Center; all but Red Line line trains stop at L'Enfant Plaza; all but Blue and Orange Line trains stop at Gallery Place.

Metro stations are indicated by discreet brown columns bearing the station's name and topped by the letter M. Below the M is a colored stripe or stripes indicating the line or lines it serves. When entering a Metro station for the first time, go to the kiosk and ask the station manager for a free "Metro System Pocket Guide." It contains a map of the system, explains how it works, indicates parking lots at Metrorail stations, and lists the closest Metro stops to points of interest. The station manager can also answer questions about routing or purchase of farecards.

To enter or exit a Metro station you need a computerized **farecard,** available at vending machines near the entrance. The minimum fare to enter the system is $1.10, which pays for rides to and from any point within 7 miles of boarding during nonrush hours; during rush hours (Monday to Friday from 5:30 to 9:30am and 3 to 8pm) $1.10 only takes you for 3 miles. The machines take nickels, dimes, quarters, and bills from $1 to $20; they can return up to $4.95 in change (coins only). If you plan to take several Metrorail trips during your stay, put more value on the farecard to avoid having to purchase a new card each time you ride. Otherwise you might waste time standing in long lines. There's a 10% discount on all farecards of $20 or more. Up to two children under 5 can ride free with a paying passenger.

When you insert your card in the entrance gate, the time and location are recorded on its magnetic tape and your card is returned. Don't forget to snatch it up, and keep it handy—you have to reinsert it in the exit gate at your destination, where the fare will automatically be deducted. The card will be returned if there's any value left on it. If you arrive at a destination and your farecard doesn't have enough value, add what's necessary at the Exitfare machines near the exit gate.

If you're planning to continue your travel via Metrobus, pick up a **transfer** *at the station where you enter the system* (not your destination station) from the transfer machine on the mezzanine. It's good for a discount on bus fares in D.C. and Virginia. There are no bus-to-subway transfers.

Impressions

If Washington should ever grow to be a great city, the outlook from the Capitol will be unsurpassed in the world. Now at sunset I seemed to look westward far into the heart of the continent from this commanding position.   —Ralph Waldo Emerson

Like a city in dreams, the great white capital stretches along the placid river from Georgetown on the west to Anacostia on the east.
                                                              —Allen Drury

Metrorail operates Monday to Friday from 5:30am to midnight and on weekends (and most holidays) from 8am to midnight. Call **202/637-7000** for information on Metro routes.

BY BUS

While a 10-year-old can understand the Metrorail system, the Metrobus system is considerably more complex. The 15,800 stops on the 1,489-square-mile route (it operates on all major D.C. arteries and in the Virginia and Maryland suburbs) are indicated by red, white, and blue signs. However, the signs tell you only what buses pull into a given stop, not where they go. For **routing information,** call **202/637-7000;** a transit information agent can tell you the most efficient route from where you are to where you want to go (using bus and/or subway) almost instantly. Calls are taken Monday to Friday from 6am to 11:30pm, weekends from 8am to 11:30pm; the line is often busy, so don't wait until the last minute to call.

If you travel the same route frequently and would like a free map and time schedule, ask the bus driver or call **202/637-7000.** Information about parking in Metrobus fringe lots is also available from this number.

Base fare in the District is $1.10 and transfers 10¢. There are additional charges for travel into the Maryland and Virginia suburbs. Bus drivers are not equipped to make change, so be sure to *carry exact change or tokens.* The latter are available at 375 ticket outlets (☎ **202/637-7000** for locations and hours of operation). If you'll be in Washington for a while and plan to use the buses a lot, consider a two-week pass, also available at ticket outlets.

Most buses operate daily almost around the clock. Service is quite frequent on weekdays, especially during rush hours. On weekends and late at night, your wait will be longer.

There's a full bus information center/sales office at Metro Center Station (12th and F streets), where tokens and special bus passes are available. It's open 7:30am to 6:30pm weekdays.

Up to two children under 5 ride free with a paying passenger on Metrobus, and there are reduced fares for senior citizens (☎ **202/962-1179**) and people with disabilities (☎ **202/962-1245**).

If you should leave something on a bus, on a train, or in a station, call Lost and Found at **202/962-1195.**

BY CAR

Within the District a car is a luxury, since public transportation is so comprehensive. Having a car can even be an inconvenience, especially during spring and summer, when traffic jams are frequent, parking spaces almost nonexistent, and parking lots ruinously expensive. But there's a great deal to see in the D.C. vicinity, and for most attractions in Virginia and Maryland you will want a car.

All the major car-rental companies are represented here. Some handy phone numbers: **Budget** (☎ **800/527-0700**), **Hertz** (☎ **800/654-3131**), **Thrifty** (☎ **800/367-2277**), **Avis** (☎ **800/331-1212**), and **Alamo** (☎ **800/327-9633**)

Taxicab Zones

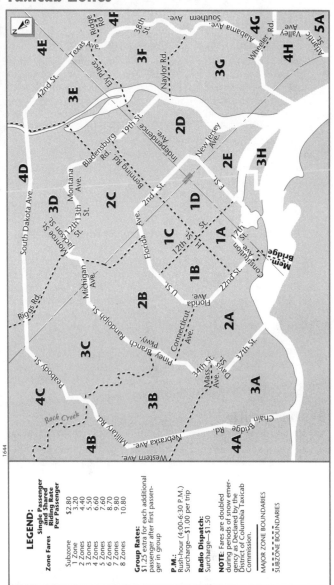

BY TAXI

Surprise! You can take taxis in Washington without ruining your budget—at least in some cases. District cabs have a zone system. If you take a trip from one point to another in the same zone, you pay just $3.20 ($2.80 within a subzone of Zone 1), regardless of the distance traveled.

So it would cost you $3.20 to travel a few blocks from the U.S. Botanic Garden to the Museum of American History, but the same $3.20 would take you from the Botanic Garden all the way to Dupont Circle. They're both in Zone 1. Also in Zone 1 are most other tourist attractions: the Capitol, the White House, most of the Smithsonian, the Washington Monument, the FBI, the National Archives, the Supreme Court, the Library of Congress, the Bureau of Engraving and Printing, the Old Post Office, and Ford's Theatre. If your trip takes you into a second zone the price is $4.40, $5.50 for a third zone, $6.60 for a fourth, and so on. You're unlikely to travel more than three zones unless you're staying in some remote section of town.

So far, the fares are pretty low. Here's how they can add up: There's a $1.25 charge for each additional passenger after the first, so a $3.20 Zone 1 fare can become $6.95 for a family of four (though one child under 6 can ride free). There's also a rush-hour surcharge of $1 per trip between 4 and 6:30pm weekdays. Surcharges are also added for large pieces of luggage and for arranging a pickup by telephone ($1.50).

The zone system is not used when your destination is an out-of-District address (such as an airport); the fare is then based on mileage covered—$2 for the first half mile or part thereof and 70¢ for each additional half mile or part. You can call **202/331-1671** to find out the rate between any point in D.C. and an address in Virginia or Maryland. Call **202/645-6018** to inquire about fares within the District.

It's generally easy to hail a taxi. There are about 7,500 cabs, and drivers are allowed to pick up as many passengers as they can comfortably fit. Expect to share. You can also call a taxi, though there's that $1.50 charge. Try **Diamond Cab Company** (☎ **202/387-6200**) or **Yellow Cab** (☎ **202/544-1212**).

BY TOURMOBILE

You can save on shoe leather and see most Washington landmarks in comfort aboard Tourmobiles (☎ **202/544-5100**)—open-air blue-and-white sightseeing trams that run along the Mall and as far out as Arlington National Cemetery and even (with coach service) Mount Vernon.

WASHINGTON/ARLINGTON CEMETERY TOUR   You can take the Washington and Arlington Cemetery tour or tour Arlington Cemetery only. The former stops at 15 different sights on or near the Mall and three sights at Arlington Cemetery: the Kennedy gravesites, the Tomb of the Unknowns, and Arlington House.

Here's how the system works. You can board a Tourmobile at 15 different locations: the White House, the Washington Monument, the Arts and Industries Building/Hirshhorn Museum, the National Air and Space Museum, Union Station, the Capitol, the National Gallery of Art, the Museum of Natural History, the Museum of American History, the Bureau of Engraving and Printing/U.S. Holocaust Memorial Museum, the Jefferson Memorial, West Potomac Park, the Kennedy Center, the Lincoln Memorial/Vietnam Veterans Memorial, and Arlington National Cemetery.

Tourmobile

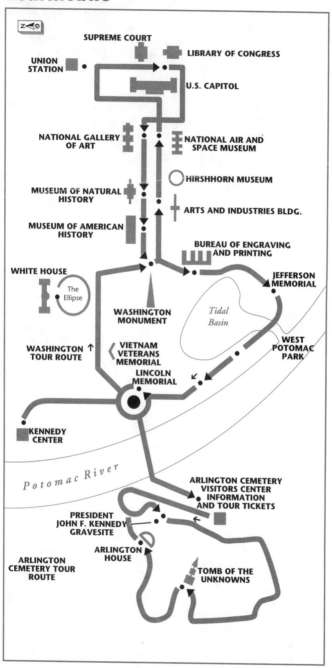

SUPREME COURT

LIBRARY OF CONGRESS

UNION STATION

U.S. CAPITOL

NATIONAL GALLERY OF ART

NATIONAL AIR AND SPACE MUSEUM

HIRSHHORN MUSEUM

MUSEUM OF NATURAL HISTORY

ARTS AND INDUSTRIES BLDG.

MUSEUM OF AMERICAN HISTORY

BUREAU OF ENGRAVING AND PRINTING

WHITE HOUSE

The Ellipse

JEFFERSON MEMORIAL

WASHINGTON MONUMENT

Tidal Basin

WASHINGTON TOUR ROUTE

VIETNAM VETERANS MEMORIAL

WEST POTOMAC PARK

LINCOLN MEMORIAL

KENNEDY CENTER

Potomac River

ARLINGTON CEMETERY VISITORS CENTER INFORMATION AND TOUR TICKETS

PRESIDENT JOHN F. KENNEDY GRAVESITE

ARLINGTON HOUSE

ARLINGTON CEMETERY TOUR ROUTE

TOMB OF THE UNKNOWNS

You pay the driver when you first board the bus. Along the route, you may get off at any stop to visit monuments or buildings. When you finish exploring each area, you step aboard the next Tourmobile that comes along without extra charge. The buses travel in a loop, serving each stop every 20 to 30 minutes. One **fare** allows you to use the buses for a full day. The charge for the Washington/Arlington Cemetery tour is $10 for adults, $5 for children 3–11. For Arlington Cemetery only, adults pay $3, children $1.50. Children under 3 ride free. Buses follow "figure-8" circuits from the Capitol to Arlington Cemetery and back, Between June 15 and Labor Day you can also buy a ticket after 4pm good for the rest of the afternoon and the following day ($12 for adults, $6 for children), the rest of the year the same offer is available after 2pm. Well-trained narrators give commentaries about sights along the route and answer questions.

Tourmobiles operate daily year-round on the following schedules. From June 15 to Labor Day, they ply the Mall between 9am and 6:30pm. After Labor Day, the hours are 9:30am to 4:30pm. From Arlington Cemetery, between October and March, they start at 8am and end at 4:30pm. April to September, the hours are 8:30am to 6:30pm.

OTHER TOURS   Tourmobiles also run round-trip to **Mount Vernon** from April to October. Coaches depart from the Arlington National Cemetery Visitors Center and the Washington Monument at 10am and 2pm. The price is $17 for adults, $8.25 for children, including admission to Mount Vernon. A combination tour of Washington, Arlington Cemetery, and Mount Vernon is $31 for adults, $15.50 for children—cheaper than the Gray Line equivalent. Another offering (June 15 to Labor Day) is the **Frederick Douglass National Historic Site Tour,** including a guided tour of Douglass's home, Cedar Hill. Departures are from Arlington National Cemetery and the Washington Monument at noon. Adults pay $5; children, $2.50. A two-day **Combination Frederick Douglass Tour and Washington–Arlington National Cemetery Tour** is also available at $20 for adults, $10 for children. For both the Mount Vernon and Frederick Douglass tours you must reserve at least an hour in advance.

BY OLD TOWN TROLLEY

A service similar to Tourmobile's is Old Town Trolley Tours of Washington (☎ **301/985-3020**). For a fixed price, you can get on and off these green-and-orange vehicles as often as you like within one loop at 16 locations in the District plus Arlington National Cemetery. Most stops are at or near major sightseeing attractions, including Georgetown. The trolleys operate seven days a week: Memorial Day to Labor Day hours are 9am to 5pm; the rest of the year, 9am to 4pm. The cost is $16 for adults, $8 for ages 5 to 12, free for children under 5. The full tour, which is narrated, takes two hours, and trolleys come by every 20 to 30 minutes. Stops are made at Union Station, the Hyatt Regency Hotel (near the National Gallery), the Pavilion at the Old Post Office, the Grand Hyatt (Chinatown), the FBI Building, the

J. W. Marriott (near the Renwick and Corcoran), the Hotel Washington (near the White House), the Capital Hilton (near the National Geographic Society), the Washington Hilton (near the Phillips Collection and Adams-Morgan restaurants), the Park Gourmet Washington (near the National Zoo), Washington National Cathedral, the Georgetown Park Mall, Washington Harbour, Lincoln Memorial, Arlington National Cemetery, the Washington Monument/ U.S Holocaust Memorial Museum, the Holiday Inn Capitol Hill (near Mall museums), and the Library of Congress.

You can board without a ticket and purchase it en route.

FAST FACTS: Washington, D.C.

Airports/Airport Transportation   See "Getting There" in Chapter 2.

Ambulances   See "Emergencies," below.

American Express   There's an American Express Travel Service office at 1150 Connecticut Ave. NW (☎ 202/457-1300).

Area Code   Within the District of Columbia, it's 202. In suburban Virginia, it's 703. In suburban Maryland, it's 410 or 301.

Baby-sitters   Most hotels provide child-care services. If yours does not, contact Mother's Aides Inc. (☎ 703/250-0700). In business since 1979, this company uses only licensed and bonded sitters whose qualifications and personal history have been carefully checked. Rates are $8 per hour for one child, $1 per hour for each additional sibling, $2 per hour for any other child. There's a four-hour minimum, a one-time $15 booking fee, and a $5 round-trip transportation charge. Call weekdays between 8:30am and 4:30pm.

Car Rentals   See "Getting Around," earlier in this chapter.

Climate   See "When to Go" in Chapter 2.

Crime   See "Safety," below.

Congresspersons   To locate a senator or congressional representative, call the Capitol switchboard (☎ 202/224-3121).

Convention Center   The Washington, D.C., Convention Center, 900 9th St. NW, between H Street and New York Avenue (☎ 202/789-1600), is a vast multipurpose facility with 381,000 square feet of exhibition space and 40 meeting rooms.

Doctors/Dentists   George Washington Medical Center (☎ 202/994-4112) can refer you to any type of doctor you need. Its roster includes just about every specialty. Phones are answered 24 hours a day. You can also call the Dental Referral Service (☎ 202/547-7615 Monday to Friday 8am to 4pm).

Drugstores   CVS, Washington's major drugstore chain (with about 40 stores), has two 24-hour locations: 14th Street and Thomas Circle NW, at Vermont Avenue (☎ 202/628-0720), and at Dupont Circle (☎ 202/785-1466), both with round-the-clock pharmacies. These drugstores also carry miscellaneous goods ranging from frozen food and basic groceries to small appliances. Check your phone book for other convenient locations.

Embassies   See "Fast Facts: For the Foreign Traveler" in Chapter 3.

Emergencies   Dial **911** to contact the police or fire department or to call an ambulance. See also "Hospital Emergency Wards," below.

Hairdressers/Barbers   The Hair Cuttery, 1645 Connecticut Ave., near Dupont Circle (☎ **202/232-9685**), is an inexpensive unisex hair salon offering trendy cuts, hair coloring, and styling on a walk-in, no-appointment-necessary basis. It's open Monday to Friday 8am to 8:30pm, Saturday 8:30am to 6:30pm, Sunday 11am to 4:30pm.

Holidays   See "When to Go" in Chapter 2.

Hospital Emergency Wards   Georgetown University Hospital, 3800 Reservoir Rd. NW (make a left off Wisconsin Avenue; ☎ **202/784-2118**), and George Washington University Hospital, 901 23rd St. NW (entrance on Washington Circle; ☎ **202/994-3884**), are both excellent.

Hotel Tax   In addition to your hotel rate, in the District you'll have to pay about 15% in taxes, in Virginia and Maryland it will be about 10%.

Libraries   The Martin Luther King Memorial Library, 901 G St. NW (☎ **202/727-1186**), is an extensive facility. It's open daily; hours vary seasonally, so call ahead.

Liquor Laws   Minimum drinking age is 21. Establishments can serve alcoholic beverages from 8am to 2am Monday to Thursday, until 2:30am Friday and Saturday, and 10am to 2am Sunday. Liquor stores are closed on Sunday.

Newspapers/Magazines   The major newspaper is, of course, the renowned *Washington Post.* The city's other daily is the *Washington Times.* Also informative are *Washingtonian* magazine and *The City Paper,* the latter a free newspaper available at restaurants, in bookstores, and other places around town.

Poison Control Center   A 24-hour emergency hotline is **202/625-3333.**

Post Office   The city's main post office (☎ **202/523-2628**) is located opposite Union Station at 2 Massachusetts Ave. NE (at G and North Capitol streets). It's open Monday to Friday 7am to midnight, and on weekends until 8pm.

Religious Services   Every hotel keeps a list of places of worship for all faiths. Inquire at the front desk.

Safety   In Washington, you're quite safe throughout the day in all the major tourist areas described in this book, and you can also safely visit the Lincoln Memorial after dark. None of the restaurants listed here will take you into dangerous or sparsely populated areas at night. Also riding the Metro in Washington is quite safe.

Taxis   See "Getting Around," earlier in this chapter.

Tickets   A service called TICKETplace (☎ **202/TICKETS**) sells half-price tickets—on the day of performance only—to most major Washington-area theaters and concert halls. It also functions as a Ticketmaster outlet. See Chapter 10 for details.

Time   Call **202/844-2525.**

Tourist Information   Two major sources are the **White House Visitor Center,** Pennsylvania Ave, NW between 14th and 15th Sts. (☎ **202/208-1631**) and the **Smithsonian Information Center,** 1000 Jefferson Dr. SW (☎ **202/357-2700**). Details on both above and in Chapter 7.

You can also call **Dial-a-Museum** (☎ **202/357-2020**), the Smithsonian's number for recorded daily information on all its museum programs and activities, and **Dial-a-Park** (☎ **202/ 619-PARK**) to find out about events in the National Capital Region parks.

Transit Information   See "Getting There" in Chapter 2 and "Getting Around" earlier in this chapter.

Weather   Call **202/936-1212.**

5

Accommodations

Your first priority on a Washington visit is finding a place to stay. Luckily, with more than 63,600 hotel and motel rooms in the District and surrounding metropolitan area, there's no shortage of rooms. They exist in every category, from luxurious accommodations to budget guesthouses—with many more, alas, in the upper bracket than in the lower. Presented below are those establishments in all price categories that offer the best value for your money.

HOW TO READ THE LISTINGS

The hotels listed below are divided first by location, then alphabetized by price category within a given district. Hotels categorized as **very expensive** charge $200 or more for a double room, those charging $150 to $200 are listed as **expensive,** $100 to $149 as **moderate,** and $99 or less as **inexpensive.** Most of the recommendations in all price categories are located in the northwest sector, where you will also find a number of major sightseeing attractions and good restaurants. If you have a car, inquire about the cost of parking when you make your reservation; some hotels charge as much as $22 a night!

Taxes   In addition to your hotel rate, in the District you'll have to pay about 15% in taxes, in Virginia and Maryland it will be about 10%.

GETTING THE MOST FOR YOUR DOLLAR

WEEKEND, OFF-SEASON & SPECIAL RATES   In Washington, the majority of hotels in all price categories slash their rates by almost half on the weekends, and sometimes weekdays as well during the off-season (generally July through August and late December through January). When telephoning to make arrangements, be sure to verify that your reservation is at weekend rates before you hang up, and check on it again when you register. At many hotels, you must register in advance to obtain weekend rates. *Note:* Weekend rates listed for hotels in this chapter are, generally, subject to availability.

Contact the **D.C. Committee to Promote Washington,** P.O. Box 27489, Washington, D.C. 20038-7489 (☎ **202/724-4091** or 800/ 422-8644), and request a copy of "Discover Washington, D.C." It lists weekend rates at more than 90 hotels in all price ranges.

Taj International Hotels, 1315 16th St. NW, Washington, D.C. 20036 (☎ **202/462-7104** or 800/DC-VISIT), owns four centrally located Washington, D.C. hotels—the Hampshire Hotel, the

Canterbury Hotel, the Quality Hotel, and Howard Johnson's Hotel & Suites—all of which are described in this chapter. Their weekend rates, also available sometimes on weekdays November to February and July and August, range from $65 to $89 per room per night. They also offer marvelous weekend packages with extras such as champagne and chocolates upon arrival. Write or call for details.

Also inquire about special packages. Many hotels offer special rates as a matter of course to senior citizens, families, active-duty military personnel, and government workers.

A RESERVATIONS SERVICE   Make use of a free service offered by **Capitol Reservations,** 1730 Rhode Island Ave. NW, Suite 506, Washington, D.C. 20036 (☎ **202/452-1270** or 800/VISIT-DC). They'll find you a hotel that meets your specific requirements and is within your price range, and they'll do the bargaining for you. "Because of the high volume of room nights we book," explains owner Thom Hall, "many properties offer discounts available only through this service." Capitol Reservations listings begin at about $55 a night for a double. Hotels are screened for cleanliness and other desirability factors, and they're all in safe neighborhoods.

GROUPS   If you're planning a meeting, convention, or other group function requiring 10 rooms or more, you should know about a free service called **U.S.A. Groups** (☎ **202/861-1900** or 800/872-4777). Representing hotel rooms at almost every hostelry in the Washington, D.C., and suburban Virginia/Maryland region—in categories from expensive to low cost—this organization works hard to find accommodations that fit your group's needs perfectly; this service will save you from having to make dozens of phone calls.

BED & BREAKFASTS

One of the most enjoyable ways to travel on a budget is to stay at B&B accommodations. Prices are reasonable, rooms are often charming, and you have an opportunity to meet local people and other travelers.

In addition to specific B&B accommodations, I've listed two services that represent numerous homes that rent out rooms on this basis. Call as far in advance as possible so that you will have the largest choice of locations and the lowest rates, and be sure to specify your needs and preferences: For instance, discuss children, pets, smoking policy, preferred locations (do you require convenient public transportation?), parking, availability of TV and/or phone, preferred breakfast, and choice of payment.

The **Bed and Breakfast League/Sweet Dreams and Toast,** P.O. Box 9490, Washington, D.C. 20016 (☎ **202/363-7767**), is a reservation service representing more than 70 B&Bs in the District. Through them, you might find a room in a mid-1800s Federal-style Capitol Hill mansion, a Georgetown home with a lovely garden, or a turn-of-the-century Dupont Circle town house filled with Victorian furnishings. Those are just a few of the many possibilities. The accommodations are all screened, and guest reports are given serious consideration. Hosts are encouraged, though not required, to offer such niceties as fresh-baked muffins at breakfast. All listings are convenient to public transportation. Rates for most range from $40 to $120 for a single, $50 to $135 for a double, and $10 to $25 per additional person. There's a two-night minimum-stay requirement and a booking fee of $10 (per reservation, not per night). AE, DC, MC, V.

A similar service, **Bed & Breakfast Accommodations Ltd.,** P.O. Box 12011, Washington, D.C. 20005 (☎ **202/328-3510;** fax 202/ 332-3885), has more than 80 homes, inns, guesthouses, and unhosted furnished apartments in its files. Most are in historic districts. Its current roster offers, among many others, a Georgian-style colonial brick home on a tree-lined avenue in Tenley Circle; an 1899 Victorian home on Capitol Hill owned by a network news producer (a well-stocked library is a plus); and a Dupont Circle Victorian town house with a two-level deck. Rates are $45 to $100 single, $55 to $110 double, $15 for an extra person, and from $65 for a full apartment. At guesthouses and inns, rates run the gamut from $68 to $180 single, $78 to $250 double. AE, DC, MC, V.

1 Best Bets

- **Best for Business Travelers:** Several Washington hotels cater largely to a business and convention clientele and are fully equipped to meet your business needs, notably: the **J.W. Marriott,** 1331 Pennsylvania Ave. NW (☎ **202/393-2000**), which also has very pretty rooms and connects to a vast shopping mall; the **Washington, D.C., Renaissance Hotel,** 999 9th St. NW (☎ **202/898-9000**), closest to the Convention Center; and the **Washington Hilton and Towers,** 1919 Connecticut Ave. NW (☎ **202/483-3000**), which combines a full business center with extensive resort facilities.
- **Best for a Romantic Getaway:** The posh **Four Seasons,** 2800 Pennsylvania Ave. NW (☎ **202/342-0444**), at the edge of Georgetown, pampers guests with every luxury and sets a sumptuous stage for romance. For less well-heeled lovers, there's the **Georgetown Dutch Inn,** 1075 Thomas Jefferson St. NW (☎ **202/337-0900**), on a quaint tree-lined street and a block from the C&O Canal, which is great for romantic towpath strolls.
- **Best for Families:** A swimming pool, plus accommodations with full kitchens and dining areas, make the **Howard Johnson's Hotel & Suites,** 1430 Rhode Island Ave. NW (☎ **202/462-7777**), a good—and fairly inexpensive—choice. **Marriott's Residence Inn,** 1000 29th St. NW (☎ **202/298-1600**), doesn't have a pool, but its accommodations provide full kitchens, and facilities include outdoor barbecue grills.
- **Best Inexpensive Hotel:** The superbly located **Quality Hotel Downtown,** 1315 16th St. NW (☎ **202/232-8000**), delivers solid comfort at low prices. Spacious accommodations have full kitchens.
- **Best Location:** I love to stay in beautiful, historic Georgetown at the **Latham,** 3000 M St. NW (☎ **202/726-5000**), or the **Georgetown Dutch Inn** (see address and telephone above), which is close to great shopping, restaurants, and the C&O Canal.

- **Best Service.** The aristocratic **Hay-Adams,** 16th and H Sts. NW (☎ 202/638-6600), and **Jefferson,** 1200 16th St. NW (☎ **202/ 347-2200**), offer the kind of service that harks back to the days when people traveled with steamer trunks.

- **Best (Most Breathtaking) Interior:** The **Willard Inter- Continental,** 1401 Pennsylvania Ave. NW (☎ **202/628-9100**), is an architectural masterpiece and a national landmark that has been painstakingly restored to its original opulence (it's worth a look even if you don't stay here). Another neoclassic beauty is the **Mayflower,** 1127 Connecticut Ave. NW (☎ **202/347-3000**), grande dame of Washington hotels; stop by for afternoon tea and a look at its pa- latial marble-floored and crystal-chandeliered lobby promenade.

- **Best Trendy Hotel:** The **Four Seasons** (see address and telephone above) is the glamorous choice of many visiting celebrities; Michael Jackson had a special dance floor set up in his room, Richard Simmons did jumping jacks in the lobby, and Billy Joel once took over the Garden Terrace piano and entertained delighted guests for an hour.

- **Best Resort Hotel:** The **Omni Shoreham,** 2500 Calvert St. NW (☎ 202/234-0700), bordering beautiful Rock Creek Park, offers biking, hiking, and jogging trails (including a Perrier parcourse with exercise stations); tennis courts; an Olympic-size swimming pool; complete health club; and more.

2 Downtown

VERY EXPENSIVE

Henley Park

926 Massachusetts Ave. NW (at 10th St.), Washington, D.C. 20001. ☎ **202/ 638-5200** or 800/222-8474. Fax 202/638-6740. 90 rms, 6 suites. A/C MINIBAR TV TEL. Weekdays $185–$235 double. Summer and weekends $89 double (includ- ing parking). Extra person $20. Children under 14 stay free in parents' room. AE, CB, DC, DISC, ER, MC, V. Parking $15. Metro: Metro Center or Gallery Place.

Named for the quaint British town Henley-on-Thames, this intimate, English-style hotel is housed in a converted 1918 Tudor-style apart- ment house with 119 gargoyles on its facade. The lobby, with its exquisite Tudor ceiling, archways, and leaded windows, is particularly evocative of the period. Room decor is in the English country house mode, with Hepplewhite-, Chippendale-, and Queen Anne–style fur- nishings, including lovely period beds. Floral-print bedspreads and drapes are colorful, walls are hung with framed botanical prints, and crown moldings harmonize with carpet hues. Baths offer phones, makeup mirrors, and luxury toiletries, and in-room amenities include remote-control cable TVs with pay-movie options.

Dining/Entertainment: The hotel's posh restaurant, **Coeur de Lion** (for Richard the Lion-Hearted, an English king of French descent), serves classic continental cuisine; the menu highlights seafood, and the wine list is excellent. Adjoining the Coeur de Lion is **Marley's,**

Georgetown & Downtown Accommodations

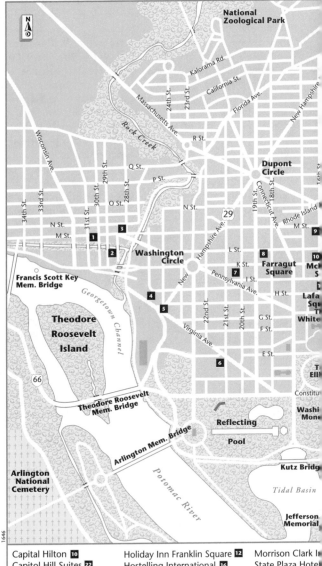

National Zoological Park

Kalorama Rd.

California St.

Florida Ave.

Massachusetts Ave.

24th St.
23rd St.

New Hampshire

Rock Creek

R St.

Wisconsin Ave.

Q St.

P St.

O St.

N St.

M St.

29th St.
30th St.
28th St.
31st St.

34th St.
33rd St.

Dupont Circle

19th St.

Connecticut Ave.

Rhode Island

16th St.

M St.

9

N St.

M St.

1

3

2

Washington Circle

New Hampshire Ave.

29

L St.

8

10

Mc
S

K St.

Farragut Square

Francis Scott Key Mem. Bridge

Georgetown Channel

7

I St.

Pennsylvania Ave.

22nd St.
21st St.
20th St.

H St.

4

Lafa
Squ

5

G St.

White

Theodore Roosevelt Island

Virginia Ave.

F St.

E St.

6

66

T
Ell

Theodore Roosevelt Mem. Bridge

Constitu

Arlington Mem. Bridge

Reflecting Pool

Washi
Mon

Arlington National Cemetery

Kutz Bridg

1646

Potomac River

Tidal Basin

Jefferson
Memorial

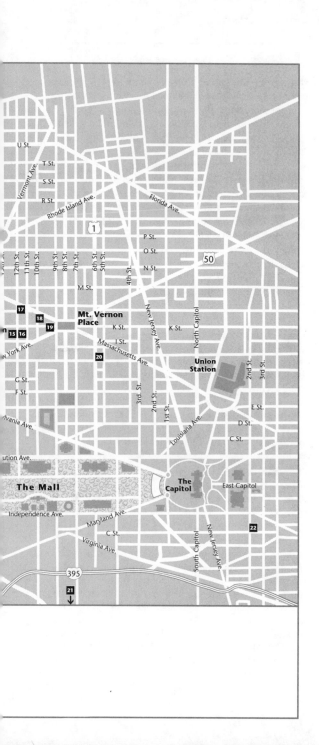

Concierge Levels

If you travel a lot, you're probably aware of the concierge-level phenomenon—a hotel-within-a-hotel concept, which usually occupies one or more upper floors of a luxury property. Guests on these floors enjoy scenic views as well as upgraded room amenities and private registration and checkout. They're pampered with nightly bed turndown and other special services—including a private concierge—and have access to a plushly furnished lounge where complimentary continental breakfast is served. Some hotels also offer a spread of afternoon hors d'oeuvres (in some cases a lavish meal that obviates the need for dinner) and late-night petit fours in these lounges. Although concierge floors (sometimes also called "tower floors" or "club floors") cater primarily to business travelers, vacationers will also enjoy the extra cosseting. In Washington, D.C., you'll find concierge-level accommodations at the J. W. Marriott, The Washington, D.C., Renaissance, The Capital Hilton, The Ritz-Carlton, and the Washington Hilton and Towers.

---

a delightful cocktail lounge, the setting for piano bar entertainment (and complimentary hors d'oeuvres) weekdays 5 to 8pm and live jazz on weekend nights. Afternoon tea is served daily in the octagonal **Wilkes Room,** a charming and comfortably furnished parlor with a working fireplace.

Services: 24-hour concierge and room service, *Washington Post* delivery each weekday morning, complimentary shoeshine, nightly bed turndown with gourmet chocolate, complimentary weekday limo service to downtown and Capitol Hill locations.

Facilities: Access to a full health club a block away.

✪ J. W. Marriott

1331 Pennsylvania Ave. NW (at E St.), Washington, D.C. 20004. ☎ **202/393-2000** or 800/228-9290. Fax 202/626-6991. 721 rms, 51 suites. A/C MINIBAR TV TEL. Weekdays $199–$209 double, $219–$229 concierge level double. Weekends $119–$159 double with full breakfast. Extra person free. AE, DC, DISC, ER, JCB, MC, V. Parking $16. Metro: Metro Center.

This flagship property, opened in 1984 as part of the master plan to renovate historic Pennsylvania Avenue, is adjacent to the National and Warner theaters. It's stunning, combining futuristic architecture with warm color schemes and lush plantings to create an exciting but very livable environment.

Rooms are decorated in pleasing color schemes (sage and rose or celadon and apricot) and furnished with cherrywood pieces in traditional styles. They're equipped with remote-control TVs with cable and HBO. Floors 14 and 15 comprise a concierge level.

Dining/Entertainment: The hotel's most elegant facility is **Celadon,** wherein Chinese Chippendale chairs and Oriental vases and screens create an Eastern ambience. Dinner menus offer American/

continental fare. The very pretty **National Café** has a pink-and-peach Victorian/art nouveau interior, and, in warm weather, seating at umbrella-shaded tables. Lunch or dinner, the fare ranges from simple burgers and salads to heartier entrées. An "early-bird" dinner here costs under $15. Alfresco dining is also a feature of **SRO** (for Standing Room Only), a friendly pub. And for piano entertainment and jazz bands nightly there's the skylit **Garden Terrace.**

Services: 24-hour room service.

Facilities: A connecting mall with 85 shops and restaurants, complete health club (with indoor swimming pool and, hydrotherapy pool), video-game arcade, full business center, gift shop.

Washington, D.C., Renaissance Hotel

999 9th St. NW (at K St.), Washington, D.C. 20001. ☎ **202/898-9000** or 800/ 228-9898. Fax 202/789-4213. 779 rms, 21 suites. A/C MINIBAR TV TEL. Weekdays $205–$225 double; club level $245 double. Weekends $99 double. Extra person free. AE, CB, DC, DISC, MC, V. Parking $14. Metro: Gallery Place.

Directly across the street from the D.C. Convention Center, this hotel is part of the $340-million World Technology Trade Center Complex. Although catering primarily to conventioneers and business travelers, it also delivers a lot of luxury and convenience to tourists.

For openers, the spiffy rooms are well equipped and attractive. Done up in teal/mauve or sage/sienna color schemes, with oak furnishings and Southwest-look bedspreads and drapes, they offer remote-control TVs (with cable stations, pay-movie options, and video message retrieval/checkout) and phones with voice mail and computer jacks. An entire 15-story tower with 166 rooms constitutes the Renaissance Club, a concierge-level concept.

Dining/Entertainment: Mahogany-paneled and crystal-chandeliered, **The Tavern** features American regional cuisine; a bar adjoins. Less formal is the cheerful **Café Florentine,** off the lobby, offering reasonably priced buffets and à la carte meals. Surrounded by lush tropical plantings, the skylit **Marco Polo** piano bar resembles a Chinese pagoda. And the **Plaza Gourmet & Pastry Shop** offers take-out sandwiches, salads, and fresh-baked pastries.

Services: 24-hour room service, concierge.

Facilities: Gift shop, hairdresser, full business center, full health club.

✪ Willard Inter-Continental

1401 Pennsylvania Ave. NW, Washington, D.C. 20004. ☎ **202/628-9100** or 800/ 327-0200. Fax 202/637-7326. 304 rms, 37 suites. A/C MINIBAR TV TEL. Weekdays $295–$395 double. Weekends $199 double. Extra person $30. Children under 12 stay free in parents' room. AE, DC, DISC, JCB, MC, V. Parking $15.75. Metro: Metro Center.

Billed as the "crown jewel of Pennsylvania Avenue," the Willard Inter-Continental is actually the crown jewel of all Washington hotels.

Originally built in 1850, its history is inextricably intertwined with the history of the nation's capital. In the 1860s, Nathaniel Hawthorne said of the Willard, "You exchange nods with governors of sovereign States; you elbow illustrious men, and tread on the toes of generals. . . ."

Lincoln spent the eve of his inaugural here, and it was at the Willard that Julia Ward Howe penned the words to the "Battle Hymn of the Republic."

In 1901 Henry Janeway Hardenbergh—architect of New York's Waldorf-Astoria and Plaza hotels—was hired to design the French Second Empire beaux-arts palace that occupies the hotel's original site today. The hotel continued as a "residence of presidents" for decades. By the time the Willard closed its doors in 1968, however, it had deteriorated considerably.

Saved as a national landmark in 1974, restoration began in the 1980s, and a new building, designed to harmonize with the old, was constructed. In the original building, the exquisite plasterwork and scagliola marble were repaired or replicated, along with marble mosaic tile floors, carpeting, and chandeliers. The main lobby today is again an awesome entranceway, with massive marble columns ascending to a lofty ceiling decorated with 48 state seals and hung with huge globe chandeliers. Alaska and Hawaii seals are in Peacock Alley, a plush potted-palmed promenade.

Rooms are suitably sumptuous, furnished in Edwardian and Federal-period reproductions and adorned with beautiful gilt-framed French prints. Phones have dual lines, and cable TVs (with remote control, pay-movie channels, video messaging, and video checkout) are concealed in armoires. In the bath you'll find a hair dryer, scale, phone, and TV speaker.

Dining/Entertainment: The **Willard Room** (the term "power lunch" originated here) is simply stunning (see Chapter 6 for details). The circular **Round Robin Bar** is where Henry Clay mixed the first mint julep in Washington. The **Café Espresso** offers croissant sandwiches, pastas, pastries, and vintage wines by the glass, along with more substantial grilled entrées; full afternoon teas are served here weekdays from 3 to 5pm. And the **Nest Lounge** offers afternoon tea and live jazz on weekends.

Services: Twice-daily maid service, nightly bed turndown, complimentary shoeshine, 24-hour room service, concierge, currency exchange, airline/train ticketing.

Facilities: Full business center, complete fitness center.

MODERATE

Comfort Inn

500 H St. NW, Washington, D.C. 20001. ☎ **202/289-5959** or 800/228-5150. Fax 202/682-9152. 195 rms. A/C TV TEL. Weekdays $89–$139 double. Weekends $89 double. Extra person $10. Children under 18 stay free in parents' room. 30% senior-citizen discount with a 30-day advance booking (call number above to obtain this rate). AE, CB, DC, DISC, JCB, MC, V. Parking $10. Metro: Gallery Place.

A lower-priced offshoot of the Quality Inn chain, this hotel is within walking distance of many attractions—including Smithsonian museums. Rooms are attractively decorated and offer remote-control cable TVs. The **Café Comfort** offers buffet breakfasts and reasonably priced and à la carte lunches. On-premises facilities include a coin-op washers/dryers, a sunny exercise room, and a gift shop.

Newspapers are free at the front desk. Reserve early. This popular hotel is close to Chinatown restaurants and just three blocks from the convention center.

✪ State Plaza Hotel

2117 E. St. NW, Washington, D.C. 20037. ☎ **202/861-8200** or 800/424-2859. Fax 202/659-8601. 221 suites. A/C MINIBAR TV TEL. Weekdays $125–$150 efficiency suite for one or two people. $175–$225 a large one-bedroom suite (with dining room) for up to four people. Weekend (also, subject to availability, off-season weeknights) $69–$109. Extra person $20. Children under 18 stay free in parents' room. AE, DC, ER, MC, V. Parking $12. Metro: Foggy Bottom.

I was charmed by the State Plaza from the moment I entered its antique-furnished lobby—a setting enhanced by beautiful floral arrangements and the soft strains of classical music. This all-suite hotel is deservedly popular with performers (including many ballet troupes) from the nearby Kennedy Center.

The spacious accommodations are just lovely, done up in pastel hues and pretty chintz fabrics, with Federal-style mahogany beds, Queen Anne chests, and framed botanical prints embellishing the walls. Fully equipped kitchens have been fitted with shuttered windows and louver doors. Remote-control cable TVs offer Spectravision movie options. Amenities here include coin-op washers/dryers and a fully equipped fitness center. Services include complimentary shoeshine, complimentary newspapers delivered to your room weekday mornings, and nightly turndown.

The pristinely pretty **Garden Café** has an awning-covered patio for alfresco dining. Light and cheerful during the day, it's elegantly candlelit at night. The menu features American regional cuisine, highlighting market-fresh fare.

INEXPENSIVE

Days Inn Downtown

1201 K St. NW, Washington, D.C. 20005. ☎ **202/842-1020,** 800/562-3350, or 800/325-2525. Fax 202/289-0336. 220 rms. A/C TV TEL. Weekdays $79–$99 double. Weekends $59–$79 double. Extra person $10. Children under 18 stay free in parents' room. Lower "Super Saver" rates (about $49) are sometimes available if you reserve in advance (the earlier the better) via the toll-free number, 800/325-2525—it's worth a try. AE, CB, DC, DISC, MC, V. Parking $11. Metro: McPherson Square.

This hotel is conveniently located near the Convention Center. Newly renovated rooms with attractive blond-wood furnishings are cheerfully decorated and equipped with remote-control satellite TVs (with free and pay-movie channels), hair dryers, and coffeemakers; some also offer kitchenettes and/or cafes.

Savannah's, a pleasant on-premises restaurant, specializes in reasonably priced steak, seafood, and pasta dishes. The adjoining lounge airs sporting events on TVs over the bar. A small rooftop pool and a video-game arcade make this a good choice for families with young children. Additional amenities: room service, a small fitness center, and a car-rental agency just across the street. City tours depart from the lobby. Inquire about special packages when you reserve.

ⓢ Hostelling International—Washington, D.C.

1009 11th St. NW (at K St.), Washington, D.C. 20001. ☎ **202/737-2333.** 250 beds. A/C. $17 for AYH members, $20 for nonmembers. MC, V. Metro: Metro Center.

The best bet among budget hotels is this spiffy youth hostel, which opened in late 1987. Situated in a fully renovated eight-story brick building, it offers freshly painted dorm rooms (with 4 to 14 beds) and clean baths down the hall. Though the accommodations are basic, the facility itself provides a lot of features you won't find at a hotel. These include a huge self-service kitchen where you can cook your own meals (a supermarket is two blocks away), a dining room, a comfortable lounge, coin-op washers/dryers, storage lockers, and indoor parking for bicycles. HIW offers special activities for guests—volleyball games, cookouts, lectures, movies, travel seminars, and more. And knowledge-able volunteers staff a comprehensive information desk to help guests with sightseeing and other travel questions.

The hostel's location is excellent—just three blocks from the Metro, six blocks from the Mall. And the clientele is monitored, so it's a per-fectly safe place to send your college-age kids or, for that matter, your mother.

All age groups are welcome, but since the dorms are for men or women only, couples are separated. (Subject to availability, there are a limited number of rooms for families and couples October to March; reserve them early.) Maximum stay is six nights, but that limit may be extended with permission, subject to available space. You must supply your own towels and soap (blankets, linens, and pillows are provided); sleeping bags are not allowed. Call as far in advance as possible to reserve (there are only 250 beds and they go fast), and assure your reservation with a 50% deposit.

BED & BREAKFAST

✪ Morrison Clark Inn

Massachusetts Ave. NW (at 11th St.), Washington, D.C. 20001. ☎ **202/898-1200** or 800/332-7898. Fax 202/289-8576. 40 rms (all with bath), 14 suites. A/C TV TEL. Weekdays $125–$195 double. Weekends $85 double. (Rates include continental breakfast.) Extra person $20: children under 12 stay free in parents' room. AE, CB, DC, DISC, MC, V. Parking $15. Metro: Metro Center.

This magnificent inn, occupying twin 1865 Victorian brick town houses—with a newer wing in converted stables across an interior courtyard—is on the National Register of Historic Places. Its arresting Victorian/Chinois facade features Shanghai porches with Chinese Chippendale railings and a pagodalike mansard roof. Guests enter via a turn-of-the-century parlor, with velvet-lace-upholstered Victorian furnishings, lace-curtained bay windows, and a large floral centerpiece on a piecrust table under a converted gaslight chandelier. Continental breakfast—oven-fresh cakes, muffins, danish, and croissants—is served in the adjoining Club Room with 13-foot windows flanking gold-leafed mahogany-framed pier mirrors on either side of the room; ornate white marble fireplaces, large potted palms in Chinese cachepots, and a 19th-century carved rosewood screen with Chinese paintings on silk in glass panels are further adornments.

Exquisite, high-ceilinged guestrooms are individually decorated. Some are furnished in antique wicker pieces with floral chintz balloon shades on the windows and matching bed ruffles. Others have floral swag friezes and/or decorative fireplaces. Color schemes utilize delicate hues like rose, muted gray/blue, and cream. Four rooms have private porches, a few are octagonal with bay windows, and many have plant-filled balconies (with umbrella tables) overlooking a fountained courtyard garden with flower beds. In-room amenities include remote-control cable TVs housed in handsome armoires, and two phones (bed and bath) equipped with computer jacks.

Room service is available from the inn's highly acclaimed restaurant (see Chapter 6). Other amenities here include twice-daily maid service with Belgian chocolates at bed turndown, complimentary daily newspapers, overnight shoeshine, a concierge, many business services, and fresh flowers in every room. A fitness center is on the premises.

3 Near the White House

VERY EXPENSIVE

The Capital Hilton

16th St. NW (between K and L sts.), Washington, D.C. 20036. ☎ **202/393-1000** or 800/HILTONS. Fax 202/639-5784. 517 rms, 32 suites. A/C MINIBAR TV TEL. Weekdays $210–$290 double; tower $235–$315 double. Weekends (including continental breakfast) $119–$135 double. Extra person $25. Children of any age stay free in parents room. AE, CB, DC, DISC, JCB, MC, V. Parking $22. Metro: Farragut West or McPherson Square.

This longtime Washington resident has hosted every American president since FDR, and the annual Gridiron Club Dinner and political roast is held in the ballroom each year.

During a five-year $55-million renovation in the late 1980s, the public areas were upgraded (note the gorgeous cherrywood paneling in the lobby). And in 1993 the rooms were redecorated in Federal-period motif with Queen Anne– and Chippendale-style furnishings. Each has three phones equipped with call waiting and a remote-control cable TV featuring pay-movie stations. In the bath you'll find a small TV and hair dryer. Floors 10 to 14 house the Towers accommodations.

Dining/Entertainment: Fran O'Brian's Steakhouse, an upscale sports-themed restaurant named for its former Redskin owner, features steak and seafood. Another fine Hilton dining room is **Twigs,** a sunny gardenlike setting with lots of plants, white trelliswork, and seating amid potted palms; the more elegant **Twigs Grill** adjoins. Fare is American regional. Complimentary hors d'oeuvres are served in **The Bar,** a plushly furnished lobby lounge, weekdays from 5 to 7pm and a pianist entertains throughout the evening.

Services: 24-hour room service, 24-hour concierge, full business center, tour and ticket desk.

Facilities: Unisex hairdresser, gift shop, facial salon, shoeshine stand, jeweler, airline desks (American, Continental, Northwest), fitness center.

✪ Hay-Adams

16th and H sts. NW, Washington, D.C. 20006. ☎ **202/638-6600** or 800/424-5054. Fax 202/638-3803. 117 rms, 19 suites. A/C MINIBAR TV TEL. Weekdays $210–$360 double. Weekends $135–$210 per room. Extra person $30. Children under 12 stay free in parents' room. AE, CB, DC, JCB, MC, V. Parking: $19. Metro: Farragut West or McPherson Square.

In 1927, famed Washington builder Harry Wardman created the Hay-Adams (on the site of the 19th-century homes of Theodore Roosevelt's secretary of state, John Hay, and noted historian Henry Adams) "to provide for the socially elite as well as men who loom large in the country's life." Its architecture evokes an Italian Renaissance palazzo with Doric, Ionic, and Corinthian orders and intricate ceiling motifs. Among the early guests were Amelia Earhart, Sinclair Lewis, Ethel Barrymore, and Charles Lindbergh. In the 1990s, the hotel is as elegant as ever—still a haunt of visiting royalty and powerful business leaders.

Rooms are individually furnished with antiques and appointments far superior to those usually found in today's hotels. A typical accommodation might feature 18th-century–style furnishings, silk-covered walls hung with botanical prints and fine art, a gorgeous molded plaster ceiling, and French silk floral-print bedspreads, upholstery, and curtains. Many have ornamental fireplaces and/or French doors that open onto views of Lafayette Square and the White House. Amenities include fine toiletries, hair dryers, cosmetic mirrors, and phones in the bathrooms; terry-cloth robes; and remote-control cable TVs equipped with HBO, On-Command pay movies, and Nintendo.

Dining/Entertainment: The sunny **Lafayette Restaurant,** overlooking the White House, is an elegant venue with comfortable mahogany chairs upholstered in Scalamandré silk and French Empire crystal candelabra chandeliers. Fare is contemporary American/

🏠 Family-Friendly Hotels

Channel Inn *(see p. 90)*   This lovely hotel has a swimming pool, and adults will love the rooms with views of the boat-filled Washington Channel.

Howard Johnson's Hotel & Suites *(see p. 76)*   Close to sightseeing attractions, it has a rooftop pool and video-game arcade. And most accommodations have kitchens, so you can prepare meals in your room—a big money-saver. Coin-op washers/dryers here, too.

Omni Shoreham *(see p. 85)*   Adjacent to Rock Creek Park, close to the zoo, and equipped with two outdoor pools—a large one for swimming laps and a kiddie pool—the Shoreham offers an extensive program of children's activities. Three lighted tennis courts are an additional attraction.

Washington Hilton and Towers *(see p. 86)*   A large heated outdoor pool, a wading pool, video-game arcade, three tennis courts, shuffleboard, and bike rental. What more do you need?

continental; it's open for all meals, including Sunday brunch and afternoon tea. The adjoining lounge features nightly piano-bar entertainment.

Services: 24-hour room and concierge service, nightly bed turndown, complimentary shoeshine.

Facilities: Guest access to a local health club, secretarial and business services, in-room fax available.

✪ The Jefferson

1200 16th St. NW (at M St.), Washington, D.C. 20036. ☎ **202/347-2200** or 800/ 368-5966. Fax 202/223-9039. 70 rms, 30 suites. A/C MINIBAR TV TEL. Weekdays $245–$265 double. Weekends $175 double. Extra person $25. Children under 12 stay free in parents' room. AE, CB, DC, JCB, MC, V. Parking $20. Metro: Farragut North.

Opened in 1923 just four blocks from the White House, The Jefferson has served as the Washington home of political personages, royalty, actors, writers, and other notables. Among those who've enjoyed its discreet small-hotel hospitality over the years are Edward R. Murrow, Helen Hayes, Robert Frost, Leonard Bernstein, and H. L. Mencken (his books are still in the room he occupied). With a very high staff-to-guest ratio, The Jefferson puts utmost emphasis on service; if you like, a butler will unpack your luggage and press clothes wrinkled in transit.

The Jefferson is impressive from the minute you set foot in the sedately elegant lobby, where beautiful Persian rugs adorn marble floors, Chippendale armchairs face a Georgian-reproduction fireplace, and a Thomas Jefferson grandfather clock chimes the hour. A very fine art collection graces public areas, rooms, and hallways. Each room is uniquely decorated. Yours might have a four-poster bed with plump eyelet-trimmed comforter and pillow shams (many are topped with canopies), a cherrywood bibliothéque from the Napoleonic period filled with rare books, a French Empire Louis XVI bureau, or a red lacquer chinoiserie case filled with objets d'art. In-room amenities include multiline phones with speaker-phone option plus fax and computer jacks, remote-control cable TVs with VCRs, CD players, and, in the baths, terry robes, hair dryers, and phones.

Dining/Entertainment: Off the lobby is one of the city's premier dining venues (see Chapter 6). A marvelous high tea is served daily from 3 to 5pm in the reading room, its walls hung with framed original Thomas Jefferson letters and documents. Classical music enhances the ambience. There's also a cozy bar/lounge with a working fireplace, the setting for live jazz on Saturday night.

Services: 24-hour butler service, overnight shoeshine, nightly bed turndown with Godiva chocolate, morning newspaper delivery, 24-hour room and multilingual concierge service.

Facilities: Business/secretarial services; for a fee, guests have access to full health club facilities at the University Club across the street.

MODERATE

Holiday Inn Franklin Square

1155 14th St. NW (at Massachusetts Ave.), Washington, D.C. 20005. ☎ **202/ 737-1200** or 800/HOLIDAY. Fax 202/783-5733. 208 rms. A/C TV TEL. Weekdays $129–$149 double. Weekends $109 double. Extra person $15. Children under 18 stay free in parents' room. (For discount information, see below.) AE, CB, DC, DISC, JCB, MC, V. Parking $10 (valet only). Metro: McPherson Square.

Just five blocks from the White House, this centrally located, 14-story Holiday Inn is a good choice in the moderately priced category. Spacious rooms are equipped with remote-control cable TVs offering free HBO plus Civil Command Video; phones feature call waiting and modem jacks. There's a fairly large rooftop swimming pool and sundeck offering nice city views.

The hotel's restaurant/lounge, **Filibusters,** serves buffet breakfasts and dinners. Other amenities include coin-op washer/dryer and a special parking lot for oversize vehicles.

At this writing, all Holiday Inns are featuring a "Great Rates" promotion, offering discounts of 10% to 50%, depending on the season and space availability. Be sure to inquire via the above toll-free number.

ⓢ Lincoln Suites Downtown

1823 L St. NW, Washington, D.C. 20036. ☎ **202/223-4320** or 800/424-2970. Fax 202/223-8546. 99 suites. A/C TV TEL. Weekdays $129–$149 suite for one person, $15 for each additional person. Weekends $69–$99 suite for two, extra person $15. Children under 16 stay free in parents' suite. AE, CB, DC, DISC, JCB, MC, V. Parking $10 (at nearby garage). Metro: Farragut North or Farragut West.

Fronted by an elegant gray canopy, the hotel offers suite accommodations in the heart of the downtown business/shopping/restaurant area, just five blocks from the White House. The large, comfortable suites—some with full kitchens, others with refrigerators, wet bars, coffeemakers, and microwaves—were completely refurbished in 1995 during a multimillion-dollar renovation. They're delightfully decorated in forest green/sienna color schemes, with traditional mahogany furnishings and attractive striped wallpapers. In-room amenities include remote-control cable TVs with free HBO, Water Pik shower massagers, hair dryers, and irons and ironing boards..

Samantha's, a delightful plant-filled eatery with an outdoor cafe, offers tasty and reasonably priced American fare. Equally charming and affordable is the stone-walled **Beatrice,** a rather elegant grotto-like Italian restaurant open for all meals.

Room service is provided during restaurant hours; complimentary copies of the *Washington Post* are available every morning; there is a unisex hair salon; and guests can enjoy free use of the well-equipped Bally's Holiday Spa nearby.

4   Dupont Circle

VERY EXPENSIVE

ⓞ Mayflower

1127 Connecticut Ave. NW (between L and M sts.) Washington, D.C. 20036. ☎ **202/347-3000** or 800/HOTELS-1. Fax 202/466-9082. 581 rms. 78 suites. A/C MINIBAR TV TEL. Weekdays $275–$335 double. Weekends $125–$170 double. Extra person $25. Children under 18 stay free in parents' room. Inquire about

Adams-Morgan & Dupont Circle Accommodations

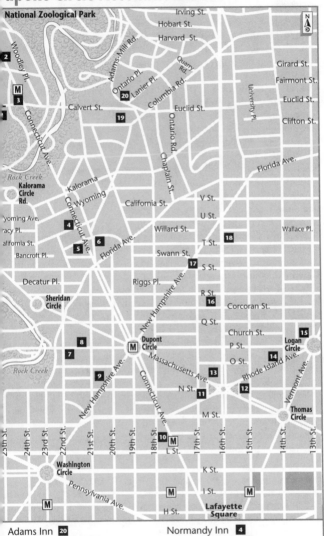

Adams Inn **20**	Normandy Inn **4**
Canterbury Hotel **12**	Omni Shoreham **3**
Carlyle Suites **17**	Quality Inn Downtown **11**
Connecticut Avenue Days Inn **2**	Radisson Barceló **7**
Embassy Inn **16**	Reeds' Bed & Breakfast **15**
Hampshire Hotel **9**	Ritz-Carlton **8**
Holdiay Inn Central **13**	Savoy Suites Georgetown **1**
Howard Johnson's Hotel & Suites **14**	Washington Courtyard **5**
Kalorama Guest House **19**	Washington Hilton & Towers **6**
Mayflower **10**	Windsor Inn **18**

"summer value rates." AE, CB, DC, DISC, ER, JCB, MC, V. Parking $12. Metro: Farragut North.

Designed by the architectural firm whose masterpieces include Grand Central Terminal in New York, the Stouffer Renaissance–owned Mayflower (opened in 1925) is the grande dame of Washington hotels. FDR penned the words "The only thing we have to fear is fear itself" in Suite 776.

A major restoration in the 1980s uncovered large skylights and renewed the lobby's pink marble bas-relief frieze and the spectacular block-long promenade. Ceilings and columns were regilded and Italianate murals rediscovered.

In the graciously appointed guestrooms, hardwood crown moldings adorn high ceilings. Cream moiré wall coverings are complemented by accents of claret and teal, mahogany furnishings are period reproductions (Queen Anne, Sheraton, Chippendale, Hepplewhite), 25-inch remote-control TVs are discreetly concealed in handsome armoires, and amenities include three phones; in the bath you'll find a terry robe, hair dryer, fine toiletries, and a small color TV.

Dining/Entertainment: The hotel's much-acclaimed premier restaurant, **Nicholas,** features superb seafood meals in a plush setting.

Washington lawyers and lobbyists gather for power breakfasts in the **Café Promenade.** Under a beautiful domed skylight, the restaurant is adorned with Edward Laning's murals, crystal chandeliers, ficus trees, marble columns, and lovely flower arrangements. A full English tea is served here afternoons Monday to Saturday.

The clubby, mahogany-paneled **Town & Country** is the setting for light buffet lunches and complimentary cocktail-hour hors d'oeuvres. And the **Lobby Court,** a Starbucks espresso bar just opposite the front desk, features coffee and fresh-baked pastries each morning, piano bar and cocktails later in the day.

Services: Coffee and newspaper with wake-up call, 24-hour room service, twice-daily maid service, complimentary overnight shoeshine, complimentary limo within a 3-mile radius of the hotel, concierge.

Facilities: Business center, full on-premises fitness center, florist, hair salon, gift shop, Cartier jeweler.

✪ The Ritz-Carlton

2100 Massachusetts Ave. NW, Washington, D.C. 20008. ☎ **202/293-2100** or 800/241-3333. Fax 202/293-0641. 206 rms, 32 suites. A/C MINIBAR TV TEL. Weekdays $215–$285 double, $335 Club double. Weekends $190 double. Extra person free. Inquire about lower-priced packages, especially in summer. AE, CB, DC, MC, V. Parking $16 (valet only). Metro: Dupont Circle.

Built in 1924, The Ritz-Carlton is a gem, from its richly walnut-paneled lobby to its pristine Oriental-carpeted hallways and lovely residential rooms. The latter—decorated in muted tones (champagne or cream, with willow green, wheat, gray, and rose accents)—are handsomely furnished with traditional dark-wood pieces. Windows are framed by elegant tasseled draperies, walls hung with French architectural watercolor renderings. In-room amenities include remote-control cable TVs (with HBO movie stations) concealed in armoires, safes, three phones, and terry robes. Gorgeous marble baths are equipped with hair dryers and upscale toiletries (some also have small black-and-white TVs). The seventh and eight floors comprise the Club level, a concierge floor.

Dining/Entertainment: The **Jockey Club** has long been one of Washington's most prominent restaurants (see details in Chapter 6). The **Fairfax Bar,** with a working fireplace and glossy knotty-pine walls hung with equestrian art, offers intimate seating for cocktails. The adjoining **Potomac Room,** with a dance floor in front of another working fireplace, features piano-bar entertainment Wednesday to Saturday nights. (*Note:* Michael Feinstein got his start playing piano at The Ritz-Carlton.)

Services: Complimentary morning newspaper delivery and shoeshine, nightly turndown with imported chocolates, 24-hour concierge and room service.

Facilities: Fitness room, business center.

EXPENSIVE

Canterbury Hotel

1733 N St. NW, Washington, D.C. 20036. ☎ **202/393-3000** or 800/424-2950. Fax 202/785-9581. 99 junior suites. A/C MINIBAR TV TEL Weekdays $160–$195 suite for two. Weekends and off-season weekdays $109–$129 per room. Extra person $20. Children under 12 stay free in parents' room. AE, CB, DC, DISC, MC, V. Parking $13. Metro: Dupont Circle.

The Canterbury Hotel is a small, European-style hostelry. Its prestigious address was once the home of both Theodore Roosevelt and Franklin D. Roosevelt. And though the hotel building is not the actual town house the Roosevelts occupied, it does attempt to recapture the elegance of an earlier era. It's entered via a graciously appointed lobby hung with hunting prints, a tranquil setting in which to plan your day's itinerary. Classical music is played in public areas.

Each room is actually a junior suite, with a sofa/sitting area, dressing room, and kitchenette or full kitchen. Attractively decorated in residential style, these spacious accommodations offer 18th-century mahogany English-reproduction furnishings (a few have four-poster beds). Among the amenities: remote-control cable TVs with HBO movies, coffeemakers, and multifeature phones; baths are supplied with cosmetic mirrors, hair dryers, phones, and baskets of fine toiletries.

Dining/Entertainment: Intimate and charming, the richly oak-paneled and beam-ceilinged **Chaucer's** features British specialties such as cock-a-leekie soup, shepherd's pie, and prime rib with Lancashire pudding. And the Tudor-beamed **Union Jack Pub,** complete with dart board and a menu featuring fish-and-chips, is the perfect place to relax after a busy day on the town. English beers on tap are served in pint mugs.

Services: Nightly turndown with fine chocolate, room service, morning delivery of the *Washington Post,* complimentary *Wall Street Journal* available in lobby and restaurant.

Facilities: Guests enjoy gratis use of the nearby YMCA/National Capital Health Center's extensive workout facilities, including an indoor lap pool.

Radisson Barceló Hotel

2121 P St. NW, Washington, D.C. 20037. ☎ **202/293-3100** or 800/257-5432.
Fax 202/331-9719. 208 rms, 92 suites. A/C MINIBAR TV TEL. Weekdays $155–$180
double. Weekends $79–$109 double. Extra person $10. Children under 12 stay free
in parents' room. AE, CB, DC, DISC, MC, V. Parking $13. Metro: Dupont Circle.

The Spanish-owned Barceló (affiliated here with Radisson) opened
with great fanfare in January 1994 when 11 Hispanic ambassadors
joined Spain's ambassador Jaime de Ojeda and former D.C. Mayor
Sharon Pratt Kelly for a gala ribbon-cutting ceremony. The first American venture for this Mallorca-based firm, the Barceló offers friendly
European-style service and an unbeatable location about midway
between Dupont Circle and Georgetown. Its art deco marble-floored
lobby is inviting, and its residential-look accommodations (formerly
apartments) are enormous. Decorated in neutral tones with soft green
accents (celadon and melon), they're furnished with traditional
mahogany pieces. All offer workspaces with desks and living room
areas containing sofas and armchairs. In-room amenities include
remote-control cable TVs with free HBO and more than 200 pay-
movie options, three phones with voice-mail and modern jacks, and
marble baths with hair dryers.

Dining/Entertainment: Gabriel, features first-rate Spanish cuisine
and tapas (details in Chapter 6). Its simpatico bar/lounge, popular with
Washingtonians, is a big plus. Guests receive a coupon for a complimentary tapas appetizer or dessert upon registration.

Services: Concierge, room service, complimentary *Washington Post*
mornings at front desk.

Facilities: Rooftop swimming pool and sundeck, sauna, small fitness
room, coin-op washers/dryers, gift shop.

MODERATE

Hampshire Hotel

1310 New Hampshire Ave. NW (at N St.), Washington, D.C. 20036. ☎ **202/
296-7600** or 800/368-5691. Fax 202/293-2476. 82 junior suites. A/C MINIBAR
TV TEL. Weekdays $119 suite for two. Weekends and off-season weekdays $79–$89
per suite. Inquire, too, about low summer rates. Extra person $15. Children under 12
stay free in parents' room. AE, CB, DC, DISC, ER, JCB, MC, V. Parking $10. Metro:
Dupont Circle.

Though it's on a quiet tree-lined street, the Hampshire is within easy
walking distance of Georgetown and two blocks from Dupont Circle—
convenient to numerous restaurants and nightspots.

Spacious junior-suite accommodations, furnished with 18th-century
mahogany reproductions, are residentially decorated and offer lots of
closet space, big dressing rooms, couches and coffee tables, desks, and
fully equipped kitchenettes. There's a hair dryer in the bathroom. You'll
find chocolates on arrival. Multifeature phones (offering push-button
access to everything from sports statistics to pizza delivery), and remote-
control TVs with HBO movies are additional amenities.

The acclaimed and pleasantly elegant **J. Sung Dynasty** serves
first-rate Manchurian/Hunan specialties; it's open for all meals, and
offers terrace seating, weather permitting. A bar/lounge adjoins.

Complimentary copies of the *Washington Post* are provided and room service is available during restaurant hours. Guests can enjoy free use of extensive workout facilities at the YMCA/National Capital Health Center nearby.

Holiday Inn Central

1501 Rhode Island Ave. NW, Washington, D.C. 20005. ☎ **202/483-2000,** 800/248-0016, or 800/HOLIDAY. Fax 202/797-1078. 205 rms, 8 suites. A/C TV TEL. Weekdays $97–$129 double. Weekends $79–$99 double. Extra person $13. Children under 18 stay free in parents' room. Note also Holiday Inns' "Great Rates" program (see the Holiday Inn Franklin Square, above). AE, CB, DC, DISC, JCB, MC, V. Parking $7. Metro: McPherson Square or Dupont Circle.

This very well located hotel underwent a major renovation in 1991 and it sparkles. It's the typical "no surprises" hotel the Holiday Inn chain prides itself on offering. You'll find a souvenir shop and video-game room off the lobby and a pool and sundeck on the roof. A pleasant restaurant features competitively priced American fare, and guests can relax over cocktails in an adjoining lounge.

Smartly decorated rooms offer remote-control cable TVs with free movie stations, coffeemakers, in-room irons and ironing boards, and phones with multilingual voice mail and computer hook-ups. Other pluses here are a coin-op washers/dryers, room service (from 6am to 11:30pm), and an exercise room.

Washington Courtyard by Marriott

1900 Connecticut Ave. NW (at Leroy Pl.), Washington, D.C. 20009. ☎ **202/332-9300** or 800/842-4211. Fax 202/328-7039. 147 rms. A/C TV TEL. Weekdays $120–$155 double. Weekends $69–$120 double. Extra person $15. Children under 18 stay free in parents' room. AE, CB, DC, DISC, MC, V. Parking: $10. Metro: Dupont Circle.

The Courtyard has the well-heeled look of a much more expensive hostelry with the amenities to match. You'll be pleased from the minute you step into the chandeliered lobby, where classical music is always playing. Very nice residentially furnished guestrooms—off charming hallways—are equipped with remote-control cable TVs (with pay-movie options) concealed in mahogany armoires, coffeemakers, and phones with modem jacks. Accommodations on higher floors offer panoramic views, and some rooms have stocked minibars.

In addition to an outdoor pool and sundeck, facilities include **Claret's,** a rather elegant restaurant with Waterford-crystal chandeliers overhead. It serves moderately priced American fare at breakfast and dinner. **Bailey's,** a clubby bar, adjoins. *USA Today* is available gratis at the front desk. For a fee, guests can use the very well-equipped Washington Sports Club just across the street. Sightseeing tours can be picked up across the street at the deluxe Washington Hilton and Towers.

INEXPENSIVE

Carlyle Suites

1731 New Hampshire Ave. NW (between R and S sts.), Washington, D.C. 20009. ☎ **202/234-3200** or 800/964-5377. Fax 202/387-0085. 176 suites. A/C TV TEL. Weekdays $79–$139 studio suite for two; $150–$180 one-bedroom suite.

Weekends $69 suite for two. Extra person $10. Children under 18 stay free in parents' suite. AE, CB, DC, MC, V. Free limited parking. Metro: Dupont Circle.

On a quiet residential street near Dupont Circle—the kind of street with a neat little garden and a shade tree in front of each house— Carlyle Suites occupies a converted landmark building. Its exterior art deco elements are complemented by similarly styled interior silver moldings, light fixtures, and cove ceilings.

Only the suites eschew the art deco motif. Cheerfully decorated in pastel hues, they have oak beds and cheerful print bedspreads with matching pillow cushions on the sofa. All accommodations are equipped with huge closets, remote-control TVs with pay-movie choices, small but complete kitchens (a huge Safeway is two blocks away), cozy seating areas with sofas, and dining nooks.

The **Neon Cafe,** its art deco ambience enhanced by background music from the 1930s/1940s, serves moderately priced American/ continental fare and features live music (a singer and combo) weekend nights. Carry-out food is available from the cafe; there are coin-op washers/dryers and free access to a well-equipped health club nearby.

ⓢ Howard Johnson's Hotel & Suites

1430 Rhode Island Ave. NW, Washington, D.C. 20005. ☎ **202/462-7777** or 800/ 368-5690. Fax 202/332-3519. 168 minisuites. 18 one-bedroom suites. A/C MINIBAR TV TEL. Weekdays $89–$109 minisuite for two, $99–$119 one-bedroom suite. Weekends (and off-season weekdays) $65 suite for two. Extra person $10. Children under 18 stay free in parents' room. AE, CB, DC, DISC, MC, V. Parking $8. Metro: Dupont Circle.

Set on a tranquil tree-lined street close to Mall attractions, Dupont Circle, and the White House, this hotel is popular with government employees, businesspeople, and families. It has a handsome marble-floored lobby and attractive residential-style rooms, all but 20 of them with dining areas and full kitchens. In-room amenities include remote-control cable TVs (with HBO and Spectravision movies) and safes. Eighteen one-bedroom suites additionally offer a full living room with a sofabed plus a bedroom with a king-size bed, with phones and TVs in each. Among the on-premises facilities are coin-op washers/dryers, a small video-game room, and a rooftop pool and sundeck. Guests enjoy complimentary use of the well-equipped YMCA/National Capital Health Center nearby.

Off the lobby is the cozy **Kitchen Cabinet,** featuring moderately priced American fare and a special menu for children. Cocktails are served in the **Civil Servant Lounge,** an inviting low-ceilinged pub with shelves of books and a pool table.

✪ Normandy Inn

2118 Wyoming Ave. NW (at Connecticut Ave.), Washington, D.C. 20008. ☎ **202/ 483-1350** or 800/424-3729. Fax 202/387-8241. 75 rms. A/C TV TEL. Weekdays $107 double. Weekends $79 double. Extra person $10. Children under 12 stay free in parents' room. AE, CB, DC, MC, V. Parking $10. Metro: Dupont Circle.

This gracious small hotel blends in perfectly with neighboring embassies. Pristinely charming rooms have tapestry upholstered mahogany furnishings in 18th-century styles. Hunter-green and white floral-print bedspreads harmonize nicely with lemon-colored walls hung with gilt-framed botanical prints. Amenities include refrigerators, coffee-makers, and remote-control cable TVs.

Continental breakfast (juices, tea or coffee, croissants, English muffins, toast, and cold cereals) is available in your room or in the comfortable **Tea Room** off the lobby for $5. Coffee and tea are served throughout the day from an antique oak sideboard in the Tea Room, and cookies are put out at 3pm. In nice weather you can take these snacks outside to umbrella tables on a garden patio. Tuesday nights, complimentary wine and cheese are served to guests. Numerous restaurants are located nearby, and guests enjoy access to a large swimming pool a block away.

Quality Hotel Downtown

1315 16th St. NW (between Rhode Island Ave. and O St.), Washington, D.C. 20036. ☎ **202/232-8000** or 800/368-5689. Fax 202/667-9827. 125 rms, 10 suites. A/C TV TEL. Weekdays $89–$109 double. $99–$129 one-bedroom suite. Weekends $69 double. Extra person $15. Children under 18 stay free in parents' room. AE, CB, DC, DISC, ER, JCB, MC, V. Parking $8.50. Metro: Dupont Circle.

The very central and pleasantly plush-looking Quality offers a lot of bang for your buck. For openers, each of the rooms here is actually a large suite, with a fully equipped kitchen. Done up, for the most part, in shades of muted teal and pale rose/mauve, the rooms feature French country pine or dark-wood furnishings in traditional styles. Most contain dining areas and sofas, and all have cable TVs with free HBO (plus pay movies) and dressing rooms. Baths offer hairdryers and baskets of fine toiletries. A few rooms feature Murphy beds—an innovation appreciated by people who conduct business in their hotel rooms.

The Quality's restaurant, **Wondi's Cafe,** is pleasant and pretty, with numerous plants flourishing in the sunlight. At night **Scott's** is cozily candlelit. Open for all meals, it serves (in addition to American fare), Asian and Ethiopian specialties. **Bleeker's Lounge,** a cozy pub off the lobby, has a billiards table.

Guests enjoy gratis use of the extensively equipped YMCA/National Capital Health Center nearby. Room service, coin-op washers/dryers, a full-service business center, and free use of the swimming pool at a nearby hotel are additional pluses. Gray Line tours depart from the lobby.

Note: Bill Clinton attends Sunday services at the Baptist church across the street and often greets guests outside the hotel.

BED & BREAKFASTS

Embassy Inn

1627 16th St. NW (between Q and R sts.), Washington, D.C. 20009. ☎ **202/234-7800** or 800/423-9111. Fax 202/234-3309. 38 rms (all with bath). A/C TV TEL. Weekdays $79–$99 double. Weekends $55 double. Rates include continental breakfast. Extra person $10, Children under 14 stay free in parents' room. AE, CB, DC, MC, V. Metro: Dupont Circle.

This four-story brick building, built in 1922 and an inn for two decades (1940–62), was rescued from demolition some years back, spruced up, and transformed once more into a quaintly charming small hotel. Its Federal-style architecture harmonizes with other town houses on the block, some of which were actually designed by Thomas Jefferson. The comfortably furnished pale-lemon lobby, with its plushly upholstered sofas and armchairs, doubles as a parlor. Breakfast (fresh blueberry muffins, croissants, cold cereals, juice, and coffee) is served here daily, and fresh coffee brews all day; it's complimentary, along with tea, cocoa, and evening sherry. You can buy Tourmobile tickets here, too, pick up maps and brochures, read a complimentary *Washington Post,* or request sundries you may have forgotten (toothbrush, razor, and the like). Soft classical music is piped into the lobby. There's also a basement lounge with a cable TV featuring HBO movies, ice machines, a small refrigerator, and a supply of books.

The rooms are furnished with 18th-century-style mahogany pieces. Bedspreads and curtains in attractive floral prints, pale-lemon walls hung with turn-of-the-century lithographs and historic prints of Washington, and new carpeting combine to create a homey atmosphere. Everything is freshly painted, pristine, and neat. Baths have showers only (no tubs). *Note:* There is no elevator, and there's street parking only.

○ The Reeds' Bed & Breakfast

P.O. Box 12011, Washington, D.C. 20005. ☎ **202/238-3510.** 5 rms (with shared bath), 1 apt (with bath). A/C TV TEL. $70–$85 double with breakfast. Apt (no breakfast) $75–$85 for two. Extra person $15. Children 18 and under $10; crib $5 extra. AE, DC, MC, V. Parking $5. Metro: McPherson Square or Dupont Circle (about six blocks from either).

Even by the most exacting standards, the Reeds' restored Victorian mansion is a masterpiece of good taste. It was built in 1887 by notable Washington builder John Shipman. When Charles and Jackie Reed bought it in 1975, it was in such disrepair that they spent nine years on a renovation they say "took on the appearance of a Pentagon cost overrun." They combed antiques shops and auction houses for period/reproduction furnishings and art, landscaped the garden, and added fountains. Today, the house is a gorgeous Victorian/art nouveau showplace with carved fireplace mantels, shuttered bay windows, leaded glass, and rich oak and mahogany paneling. The living room is furnished with a velvet Chesterfield, a Jacobean oak armchair, Oriental carpet, and a turn-of-the-century player piano. Breakfast is served at a Victorian banquet table in a formal dining room complete with 19th-century stained-glass windows and a working fireplace.

The rooms, reached by a grand carved-oak staircase with intricate fretwork and a leaded-glass skylight above, are charmingly decorated in period styles. All are supplied with books and magazines. Completely separate from the main building is a one-bedroom apartment with a private bath and a fully equipped kitchen; it easily accommodates five people. There's no maid service, however, and you'll have to get your own breakfast.

Guests are encouraged to use the gorgeous Victorian-style lattice porch, fountained patio, and barbecue facilities. Breakfast is continental (featuring fresh-baked breads and muffins, cereals, fruit, and juice) on weekdays, a full bacon-and-eggs meal on weekends. A computer and a treadmill are available on request, and there's a washer and dryer for guest use. No charge for local calls here.

Because the Reeds' doesn't take walk-ins, the address above is a P.O. Box. You must call to reserve.

❾ Windsor Inn

1842 16th St. NW (at T St.), Washington, D.C. 20009. ☎ **202/667-0300** or 800/ 423-9111. Fax 202/667-4503. 44 rms (all with bath), 2 suites. A/C TV TEL. Weekdays $79–$99 double; $125–$150 suite accommodating up to five people. Weekends $55 double. Rates include continental breakfast. Extra person $10. Children under 14 stay free in parents' room. AE, CB, DC, MC, V. Metro: Dupont Circle.

The Windsor Inn, a neat brick building on a tree-lined residential street, was built in the 1920s as a boarding house, then renovated and run as an inn through 1963. A wealthy owner subsequently let the property stand empty until the Windsor folks discovered and purchased it in 1985, along with an adjacent building fronted by a neoclassic portico. Accommodations are located in both. Some of the public areas are done up in art deco motif, and hallways are especially nice, lit by sconces and hung with lovely gilt-framed lithographs. Rooms are neat as a pin and handsomely furnished. Some have floral wall friezes, many are adorned with botanical prints or silk flower arrangements, and you may get a sofa and/or decorative fireplace. Suites are worthy of a first-class hotel—but much cheaper. Lower-level rooms face a skylit terrace with lawn furnishings, but I prefer the sunnier upstairs accommodations. A continental breakfast—croissants and muffins, cold cereals, fruit juices, and tea or coffee—is served in the comfy lobby. During the day, complimentary coffee, tea, and hot chocolate are available, and sherry is offered evenings from 5 to 9pm. There are ice machines and a refrigerator for guest use. A very friendly multilingual staff is a big plus. Guests also enjoy free use of a beautiful small conference room that seats 10. *Note:* There is no elevator, and parking is on the street.

5 Foggy Bottom/Georgetown

VERY EXPENSIVE

❖ The Four Seasons

2800 Pennsylvania Ave. NW, Washington, D.C. 20007. ☎ **202/342-0444** or 800/ 332-2442. Fax 202/944-2076. 166 rms, 30 suites. A/C MINIBAR TV TEL. Weekdays $325–$370 double. Weekends $230–$250 double. Extra person $30. Children under 18 stay free in parents' room. AE, CB, DC, ER, JCB, MC, V. Parking $20. Metro: Foggy Bottom.

Since it opened in 1979, this most glamorous of Washington's haute hotels has hosted everyone from Billy Joel (who took over the Garden Terrace piano and entertained delighted guests for an hour) to King Hussein of Jordan. Open the front door and you enter a plush setting where thousands of plants and palm trees grow, and large floral arrangements enhance the gardenlike ambience. Classical music is played throughout the public areas.

Exceptionally pretty accommodations, many of them overlooking Rock Creek Park or the C&O Canal, offer contrasting traditional dark-wood furnishings and charming print fabrics. Textured white walls are hung with gilt-framed antique prints, and the bedding is embellished with dust ruffles and scalloped spreads. Large desks and plump cushioned armchairs with hassocks contribute to the residential atmosphere. In-room amenities include remote-control cable TVs with free HBO and Spectravision pay-movie options, VCRs (movies and video games are available), CD players (the concierge stocks CDs), three phones, bathrobes, and, in the baths, hair dryers, lighted cosmetic mirrors, and upscale toiletries.

Dining/Entertainment: The elegant and highly acclaimed **Seasons** is detailed in Chapter 6. Paneled in Australian ash, the delightful **Garden Terrace** is bordered by tropical plants, ficus trees, and flower beds and has a wall of windows overlooking the canal. It's open for lunch, a lavish Sunday jazz brunch, and classic English-style afternoon teas. And guests are given temporary membership at the warmly intimate **Desirée,** a private on-premises nightclub.

Services: Twice-daily maid service, 24-hour room service and concierge, complimentary limousine service weekdays within the District, gratis newspaper of your choice, car windows washed when you park overnight, complimentary shoeshine.

Facilities: Beauty salon, gift shop, jogging trail, business facilities, children's programs, extensive state-of-the-art fitness club (the best in town).

The Watergate Hotel

2650 Virginia Ave. NW, Washington, D.C. 20037. ☎ **202/965-2300** or 800/424-2736. Fax 202/337-7915. 90 rms, 145 suites. A/C MINIBAR TV TEL. Weekdays $285–$310 double. Weekends $155 double. Suites from $410 double, with greatly reduced weekend rates. Extra person $25. Children under 18 stay free in parents' room AE, CB, DC, DISC, JCB, MC, V. Parking $10 (valet only). Metro: Foggy Bottom.

Everyone associates the Watergate with the notorious 1972 break-in that brought down the Nixon administration (actually it happened in the adjoining Watergate apartment complex). But you'll forget that sordid scandal the minute you step into the Watergate's lavish marble-floored and Doric-columned lobby, where antique furnishings and objets d'art grace intimate lamp-lit sitting areas amid potted palms and ficus trees; classical music enhances the upscale ambience. Spacious rooms and suites are exquisitely appointed in the residential mode. Traditional furnishings are complemented by lovely gilt-framed botanical prints and floral-print bedspreads, dust ruffles, and drapes. Each accommodation is equipped with a remote-control TV offering free Showtime movies and more than 50 cable stations, an umbrella, and a terry robe; in the bath you'll find a well-equipped toiletries package, cosmetic mirror, hair dryer, scale, and phone. Fax machines, VCRs, and dozens of movies can be rented. Many accommodations have balconies overlooking the Potomac. Suites—some with full living rooms and dining areas—may offer extra phones, entertainment centers with

VCRs and cassette players, and shelves of books. Many celebrity entertainers—Carol Channing, Richard Chamberlain, Itzhak Perlman, Jessye Norman—have stayed here when performing at the adjacent Kennedy Center.

Dining/Entertainment: Celebrated French chef Jean-Louis Palladin oversees the kitchens of the eponymous **Jean-Louis** (one of Washington's top restaurants) and **Palladin** (both detailed in Chapter 6). The softly lit **Potomac Lounge** off the lobby is a sedately elegant setting for cocktails, light gourmet fare, and daily afternoon tea.

Services: 24-hour room service and concierge, full business services, nightly turndown, complimentary shoeshine, delivery of your choice of seven newspapers to your room daily.

Facilities: Indoor lap pool and sundeck, Jacuzzi, steam, sauna, state-of-the-art health club offering massage and spa treatments, barber/beauty salon, gift shop, jewelers (numerous shops incluing a supermarket, drugstore, and post office are in the adjacent complex).

EXPENSIVE

The Latham

3000 M St. NW, Washington, D.C. 20007. ☎ **202/726-5000** or 800/368-5922. Fax 202/342-1800. 121 rms, 22 suites. A/C TV TEL. Weekdays $155–$175 double. Weekends $119–$139. $245–$290 suite. Extra person $15. Children under 12 stay free in parents' room. AE, CB, DC, DISC, JCB, MC, V. Parking $14 (valet only).

The Latham is at the very hub of Georgetown's trendy nightlife/restaurant/shopping scene, but since its accommodations are set back from the street none of the noise of nighttime revelers will reach your room. It's also the only Georgetown hotel with a swimming pool. You'll enter an upscale marble-floored lobby, with comfortable furnishings amid potted palms. Charming earth-toned rooms are decorated in French-country motif, with multipaned windows that open, pine furnishings, and gilt-framed works of art adorning striped wallpapers. Remote-control cable TVs (offering free HBO plus pay-movie selections) are housed in forest-green armoires; VCRs and rental movies are available. All rooms are equipped with large desks, hair dryers, terry robes, irons, and ironing boards. Tenth-floor rooms offer gorgeous river views, and third-floor accommodations—all two-room suites—have windows facing a hallway designed to replicate a quaint Georgetown street. Most luxurious are two-story carriage suites with cathedral ceilings, full living rooms, and stocked minibars.

Dining/Entertainment: The highly acclaimed Citronelle—one of D.C.'s hottest dining venues under the auspices of famed French chef Michel Richard—is on the premises, serving all meals (see Chapter 6 for details).

Services: Room service during restaurant hours, concierge, nightly turndown, complimentary shoeshine, delivery of a choice of three newspapers to your room daily.

Facilities: Small outdoor pool and bilevel sundeck; guests enjoy free use of an adjacent fully equipped health club.

Inside Washington: Hotel Stories

Washington hotels have seen a lot of history (not to mention gossip-column fodder), from pre–Civil War days when the **Willard** maintained separate entrances for pro-Union and secessionist factions . . . to pre-Trump wedding days when Marla Maple's flung a shoe—and a $7^1/_2$-carat engagement ring—at The Donald in the lobby of the **Four Seasons.**

Washington Mayor-for-Life Marion Barry experienced a brief power outage—in the form of a 6-month jail sentence—when he was lured to the **Vista Hotel** by former girlfriend Rasheeda Moore, arrested for smoking crack cocaine, and led off in handcuffs muttering curses.

FDR lived at the **Mayflower,** the grande dame of Washington hotels, between his election and inauguration, and both Lyndon Johnson and John F. Kennedy called the Mayflower home while they were young congressmen. For 20 years before his death, J. Edgar Hoover ate the same lunch at the same table in the hotel's Grille Room every day—chicken soup, grapefruit, and cottage cheese (one wonders what he ate for dinner to maintain his portly frame). One day he spotted Public Enemy No. 3 at an adjoining table and nabbed him!

Back at the **Willard:** Brought to the capital by her lover and manager, P. I. T. Barnum, the "Swedish Nightingale" Jenny Lynd received a steady stream of visitors during her stay, among them Daniel Webster and President Millard Fillmore. Ulysses S. Grant, who often partook of cigars and brandy at the Willard, coined the

MODERATE

✪ The Georgetown Dutch Inn

1075 Thomas Jefferson St. NW (just below M St.), Washington, D.C. 20007. ☎ **202/337-0900** or 800/388-2410. Fax 202/333-6526. 47 suites. A/C TV TEL. Weekdays $120–$160 one-bedroom suite for two; $195–$300 two-bedroom duplex penthouse quad (sleeps six). Weekends $99 one-bedroom suite for two, $180–$220 penthouse suite. (Rates include continental breakfast.) Extra person $20. Children under 14 stay free in parents' room. AE, CB, DC, DISC, MC, V. Free parking. Metro: Foggy Bottom. Bus: M Street buses go to all major Washington tourist attractions.

The Dutch Inn is superbly located in the heart of Georgetown, just half a block from the C&O Canal (many rooms offer water views), on a charming brick-paved street lined with maple trees. Thomas Jefferson once lived on this street. Accommodations are rather spacious one- and two-bedroom suites, nine of them ultra-luxurious duplex penthouses with $1^1/_2$ baths. Staying here is like having your own Georgetown apartment. You'll have a full living room with a comfy queen-size convertible sofa, dining area, and desk, plus a complete kitchen (the maid does your dishes, and the hotel offers food-shopping service). Decor is classic residential—handsome mahogany furnishings, textured beige walls hung with gilt-framed botanicals and architectural prints of

term "lobbyists" to describe people who pestered him there seeking to influence government business. Thomas Marshall, vice president under Woodrow Wilson, also liked to smoke cigars at the Willard, but found the prices scandalous, commenting, "What this country needs is a good five-cent cigar."

General John F. Pershing lived at **The Sheraton Carlton** during Prohibition; often he would bring his own flask to the dining room and openly mix an old-fashioned at his table.

During JFK's inaugural festivities Frank Sinatra and his Rat Pack cronies took over a dozen rooms on the 10th floor of the **Capital Hilton** so they could visit each other without being bothered by autograph-seekers in the halls.

Speaking of JFK, he courted Jackie over drinks in the Blue Room at the **Shoreham**—a famous nightclub where Rudy Vallee, Lena Horne, Bob Hope, Maurice Chevalier, Judy Garland, and Frank Sinatra performed; today the room is a meeting facility. In its heyday, the Shoreham entertained the rich and the royal, but its most ostentatious guest ever was Saudi Arabian King Ibn-Saud who, traveling with a full complement of armed guards and 32 limos, dispensed solid gold watches as tips.

And returning once again to the Kennedys, the **Ritz-Carlton's** Jockey Club was a major Kennedy-clan hangout during the JFK years; in this posh precinct an exuberant Ethel smashed a cake in Andy Williams's face on his birthday.

Washington, a forest green sofa, a burgundy wing chair, and attractive striped bedspreads and drapes in the same Ralph Lauren–like color scheme. Amenities include remote-control cable TVs with free HBO, full-size irons and ironing boards, coffeemakers, and three phones (bedside, living room, and bath). You'll also find upscale toiletries, a cosmetic mirror, and a hair dryer in the bathroom.

There's no on-premises restaurant; however, an extensive room-service menu is available, and there are dozens of eating places within a block or two. Complimentary continental breakfast is served in the charming lobby each morning, and free newspaper delivery is available on request. Guests also enjoy free use of the West End Fitness Center at 24th and M streets, a state-of-the-art health club. The Canal towpath is ideal for jogging and cycling.

Hotel Lombardy

2019 Pennsylvania Ave. NW, Washington, D.C. 20006. ☎ **202/828-2600** or 800/424-5486. Fax 202/872-0503. 85 rms, 41 suites. A/C MINIBAR TV TEL. Weekdays $130 double; $165 suite for two. Weekends (and sometimes off-season weekdays) $69–$89 double; $109–$129 suite for two. Extra person $20. Children under 16 stay free in parents' room. AE, CB, DC, MC, V. Parking $15. Metro: Farragut West or Foggy Bottom.

From its rich wood-paneled lobby with carved Tudor ceilings to its appealing restaurant and rooms, the Lombardy offers a lot of luxury for the price—and the location, about five blocks west of the White House. Rooms are charmingly residential, all but 20 with fully equipped kitchens, large walk-in closets, and dining nooks. Entered via pedimented louver doors, they have fine cherrywood furnishings (including large desks), cotton chintz floral bedspreads and drapes, dusty-rose carpeting, and Casablanca fans overhead. Cream-colored walls are hung with gilt-framed mirrors and well-chosen works of art. All offer remote-control cable TVs with pay-movie options. The *Washington Post* is delivered to your room weekday mornings, beds are turned down nightly, shoes are shined gratis overnight, and coin-op washers/dryers are located in the basement.

The **Café Lombardy,** a sunny glass-enclosed restaurant and lounge (with open-air seating, weather permitting), serves delicious and authentic northern Italian fare. Yummy desserts here, too.

✪ Marriott's Residence Inn

1000 29th St. NW (between K and M sts.), Washington, D.C. 20007. ☎ **202/ 298-1600** or 800/331-3131. Fax 202/333-2019. 78 suites. A/C TV TEL. Rates include extended continental breakfast. $139 studio suite (for two), $149 one-bedroom suite (for up to four). Weekends $99 studio suite, $109 one-bedroom suite. Rates for Rollaways or sleep sofa $10 extra. Discounts for stays of seven days or more. AE, CB, DC, DISC, JCB, MC, V. Parking $13 (limited). Metro: Foggy Bottom.

This home-away-from-home concept was designed to meet the needs of business travelers making extended visits, but it's marvelous even if you're spending only one night. Residence Inn accommodations are luxurious apartments, with fully-equipped kitchens, living rooms, and dining areas. This particular inn, in the heart of Georgetown, is entered via a brick courtyard with flowering plants in terra-cotta pots and Victorian white wooden benches. Inside, off the lobby, is a comfortable lounge equipped with a cable TV, games, books, magazines, and daily newspapers. Here, tea and coffee are available throughout the day, and a substantial continental breakfast is served daily. Monday to Thursday afternoons, complimentary beer, wine, and soft drinks are offered to guests between 5:30 and 7pm, along with snacks such as nachos or sloppy joes. Wednesday afternoon that snack is a full dinner—perhaps spaghetti and salad or barbecue.

Attractive resortlike accommodations are equipped with large desks, remote-control cable TVs with HBO, hair dryers, and irons and ironing boards. On-premises facilities include an outdoor barbecue grill for guest use, occasional organized parties and activities, coin-op washers/dryers, and a small exercise room. Hotel services include complimentary grocery shopping and food delivery from nearby restaurants. M Street buses (a block away) will take you to most major D.C. attractions.

INEXPENSIVE

Howard Johnson's Lodge

2601 Virginia Ave. NW (at New Hampshire Ave.), Washington, D.C. 20037. ☎ **202/ 965-2700** or 800/I-GO-HOJO. Fax 202/965-2700, ext. 7910. 192 rms. A/C TV TEL.

Weekdays $84–$112 double. Weekends $57 double. Extra person $5. Children under 18 stay free in parents' room. AE, DC, DISC, JCB, MC, V. Free parking (maximum height 6'2"). Metro: Foggy Bottom.

Just two blocks from the Kennedy Center is a HoJo with a nicely landscaped entrance where rose bushes bloom in season. Attractively furnished modern rooms have desks, small refrigerators, and VCRs (movies can be rented). Some rooms feature sofas, and half are balconied. A **Bob's Big Boy** on the premises offers typical American fare, including inexpensive all-you-can-eat buffets at breakfast and lunch. Coin-op washer/dryers, sightseeing bus tours, a large L-shaped rooftop pool with sundeck and Ping-Pong room, a gift/sundry shop, and video games are additional amenities.

6 North Washington/Adams-Morgan

VERY EXPENSIVE

Omni Shoreham

2500 Calvert St. NW (at Connecticut Ave.), Washington, D.C. 20008. ☎ **202/234-0700** or 800/228-2121. Fax 202/265-5333. 745 rms, 55 suites. A/C TV TEL. Weekdays $205–$285 double. Off-season and weekends $89 double. Extra person $20. Children under 18 stay free in parents' room. AE, CB, DC, DISC, ER, JCB, MC, V. Parking $12. Metro: Woodley Park-Zoo.

Set on 11 acres adjacent to verdant Rock Creek Park, the Shoreham is a resort hotel right in the heart of the city. Built in 1930, this deluxe hostelry has been the scene of inaugural balls for every president since FDR. In the early years, prominent socialites such as Perle Mesta and Alice Roosevelt Longworth threw private parties here. And Truman held poker games in Room D-106 while his limousine waited outside. Some years ago, the hotel's public areas were restored to their original grandeur. In the vast Renaissance lobby, Chinese carpets were laid on marble floors, exquisite stenciled artwork was restored on vaulted ceilings, clerestory windows were fitted with new glass and opulent crystal chandeliers made to sparkle. Spacious guest rooms are beautifully decorated and equipped with remote-control cable TVs (with pay-movie options).

Dining/Entertainment: The hotel's excellent restaurant, the **Monique Café et Brasserie,** is reminiscent of the famed La Coupole in Paris—a convivial enclave of polished brass, dark woodwork, simulated marble columns, potted palms, and Oriental mirrors. It specializes in continental/American fare with an emphasis on steak and seafood. The delightful **Garden Court,** under a 35-foot vaulted ceiling, is lushly planted with ficus trees and tropical foliage, all of it reflected in beveled-mirror walls; Rock Creek Park provides a fitting backdrop for this popular cocktail lounge. The hotel's nightlife centers on the art deco **Marquee Cabaret** (details in Chapter 10).

Services: Room service, concierge.

Facilities: Shops; travel/sightseeing desk; business center; extensive children's activity programs; 10 miles of jogging, hiking, and bicycle trails (winding off into Rock Creek Park), plus a 1¹/₂-mile Perrier parcourse with 18 exercise stations; three lighted Har-Tru tennis courts; Olympic-size swimming pool and kiddie pool; extensive health club.

Washington Hilton and Towers

1919 Connecticut Ave. NW (at T St.), Washignton, D.C. 20009. ☎ **202/483-3000** or 800/HILTONS. Fax 202/797-5755. 1,203 rms, 82 suites. A/C MINIBAR TV TEL. Weekdays $230–$270 double; Towers rooms $265–$305 double. Weekends (and selected weekdays and holidays) $97 per room, $122 for Towers rooms. Extra person $20. Children of any age stay free in parents' room. AE, CB, DC, DISC, JCB, MC, OPT, V. Parking $12. Metro: Dupont Circle.

This is a kind of super-hotel/resort offering every imaginable amenity. The Hilton hosts numerous conventions and functions—inaugural balls, debutante cotillions, state banquets, and society shindigs. Rooms are cheerful, attractively furnished, and equipped with bathroom scales and remote-control cable TVs with pay-movie stations; many offer panoramic views of Washington. The 10th floor comprises a concierge level called the Towers.

Dining/Entertainment: The handsome mahogany-paneled **1919 Grill,** embellished with sporting gear and equestrian art, specializes in steaks, seafoods, and pasta dinners. The cheerful **Capital Café,** for buffet meals and coffee shop fare, has a wall of windows overlooking the pool. The **Gazebo,** an alfresco poolside eatery, serves light fare under a striped tent top in season. The sports-themed **McClellan's,** a clubby lounge with a handsome brass-railed mahogany bar and commodious leather chairs, offers pool tables, pinball, and electronic darts; sporting events are aired on four TV monitors. And **Capital Court,** an elegant lobby lounge, features nightly piano bar entertainment.

Services: Room service during restaurant hours, nightly bed turn-down, transportation/sightseeing desk.

Facilities: Extensive health club facilities, a large nightlit heated outdoor pool, children's pool, three nightlit tennis courts, shuffleboard, bike rental, jogging path, lobby shops, comprehensive business center, shoeshine stand, car-rental desk.

INEXPENSIVE

Connecticut Avenue Days Inn

4400 Connecticut Ave. NW (between Yuma and Albemarle sts.), Washington, D.C. 20008. ☎ **202/244-5600,** 800/325-2525, or 800/952-3060. Fax 202/244-6794. 150 rms, 5 suites. A/C TV TEL. Weekdays $59–129 double, $99–139 suite. Weekends $59–$79 double, $99–$139 suite. Extra person $10: children under 18 stay free in parents' room. Inquire about senior-citizen rates. Lower "Super Saver" rates are sometimes available if you reserve at least 29 days in advance via the corporate toll-free number, 800/325-2525. AE, CB, DC, DISC, MC, V. Parking $5. Metro: Van Ness.

If you don't mind a 10- to 15-minute Metro or bus ride into the heart of town, you can do very nicely here. This Days Inn is located in a very pleasant neighborhood, and its recently refurbished rooms are in tip-top condition. Furnished in teak Danish modern pieces, with brass-framed art prints on grass-cloth-covered walls, they offer remote-control cable TVs with HBO, in-room safes, and refrigerators. Families can book a parlor suite that includes an extra room (and an extra

TV). There's a gift shop in the rather charming Queen Anne–style lobby.
A coin-op Laundromat and several restaurants are close by.

Savoy Suites Georgetown

2505 Wisconsin Ave. NW (above Calvert St.), Washington, D.C. 20007. ☎ **202/337-9700** or 800/944-5377. Fax 202/337-3644. 150 rms. A/C TV TEL. Weekdays $79–$139 double. Weekends $69 double. Extra person $10. Children under 18 stay free in parents' room. AE, CB, DC, MC, V. Free parking. Even-numbered buses stop in front of the hotel and connect to Georgetown, Dupont Circle, and the Mall.

This inexpensive luxury hotel is in a sedate embassy district, just five
minutes from the heart of Georgetown by bus or car. Many restaurants
are within walking distance, and Washington National Cathedral is just
four blocks away.

The accommodations, half of them suites with fully stocked kitchens and dining areas, are decorated with French provincial pieces,
marble-topped bureaus, and faux malachite desks with cabriole legs.
Grass-cloth–covered walls are hung with gilt-framed 18th-century color
lithographs. All rooms offer remote-control cable TVs with pay-movie
stations. Many have in-room steam baths or Jacuzzis, and about half
offer panoramic city views over the treetops.

The owner hired a set designer to liven up the hotel's public areas.
A stunning art nouveau lobby is set against a garden-motif restaurant
called **On Wisconsin,** which features reasonably priced American/
continental fare. In warm weather the Savoy also has a tree-shaded
outdoor cafe serving light fare.

Other on-premises amenities include a small sundeck and coin-op
washers/dryers. The front desk proffers conciergelike hospitality, and
there's a complimentary shuttle bus to and from the Woodley Park
Metro stop. Guests also enjoy free use of a well-equipped nearby health
club with an Olympic-size pool.

By the way, note the ornate fence fronting the Savoy Suites. Made
in 1890, it's from the original lion's cage of the National Zoo.

BED & BREAKFASTS

Adams Inn

Lanier Place NW (between Calvert St. and Ontario Rd.), Washington, D.C. 20009. ☎ **202/745-3600** or 800/578-6807. 25 rms (12 with bath). A/C. $55 double without bath, $70–$95 double with bath. (Rates include continental breakfast.) Extra person $10. Weekly rates available on some rooms. AE, CB, DC, DISC, MC, V. Parking $7. Metro: Woodley Park–Zoo (seven blocks away).

While many B&B accommodations are decorator homey with rooms
in *Architectural Digest* good taste, the Adams is down-to-earth, for-real
homey—like your Aunt Edna's house. It occupies three turn-of-the-
century brick town houses on a residential tree-lined street fronted by
small gardens and porches. All have cozily furnished Victorian parlors
or lounges with decorative fireplaces and lace-curtained windows;
they're stocked with books, games, and magazines for guests.

Accommodations, furnished with flea market and auction finds,
have a kitschy charm. They're all very clean and freshly painted or

D.C. with Dogs

If you take your dog along when you travel, you're always grateful to find a hotel that accepts pets—let alone one that actually welcomes them with open arms. Well, Fido has a home in Washington at the **Loew's L'Enfant Plaza Hotel,** 480 L'Enfant Plaza SW, Washington, D.C. 22024 (☎ **202/484-1000**). It's conveniently located for a game of fetch on the Mall (and for you to do some sightseeing at the Smithsonian). Actually, it's a wonderful choice for anyone: its rooms are comfortable and have nice views; there are terrific amenities for kids and for business travelers; and the hotel restaurant is really outstanding, for those nights when you're just too tired to venture out. The service was truly exceptional during my recent stay here—the doorman took a shine to my dog and remembered us each time we came and went, offering tips on where she was welcome and grabbing up extra towels to protect my car seat when she headed off for a swim.

So what's a good outing for you and your dog? My recommendation is to head for the C&O Canal. I had a wonderful scenic stroll here with Lucy, my Golden Retriever (I walked along the towpath and she swam alongside me up the canal). After your walk, you can head for Georgetown, where there are lots of outdoor cafes that don't mind having a well-behaved dog tied up at your sidewalk table. We also enjoyed Rock Creek Park, though Lucy had to be leashed there for much of the time.

Two terrific resources for your trip are *Frommer's America on Wheels: Mid-Atlantic Region* (Macmillan Travel), which uses easily spotted dog icons to indicate which accommodations throughout the region accept pets; and *Frommer's On the Road Again with Man's Best Friend: Mid-Atlantic States* (Macmillan Travel), which has extensive reviews of select dog-friendly hotels and inns.

—Lisa Renaud

papered, and some have bay windows or handsome oak paneling. No phones or TVs here, but you do get a clock radio. Rooms that share baths have in-room sinks. A substantial continental breakfast (including fresh-baked breads and muffins) is served each morning in the dining room; in warm weather you can take your breakfast out to the front porch or a small garden patio. Tea, coffee, and doughnuts are available throughout the day.

A coin-op washer/dryer is available in the basement, there are pay phones in the lobby, and the desk takes incoming messages. Other pluses: a refrigerator, microwave oven, iron/ironing board, and TV lounge. The location is close to Adams-Morgan eateries and a Safeway supermarket. Anne Owens is your genial host.

Note: No smoking is permitted on the premises. No pets, but children are welcome.

⑤ Kalorama Guest House

1854 Mintwood Place NW (between 19th St. and Columbia Rd.), Washington, D.C.
20009. ☎ **202/667-6369.** 31 rms (12 with bath). A/C. $45–$75 double with
shared bath, $60–$100 double with bath; $95 two-room suite ($5 each additional
occupant). AE, CB, DC, DISC, MC, V. Parking $7 (limited). Metro: Woodley Park-Zoo.

This San Francisco–style B&B guesthouse was so successful it expanded
in a short time from a six-bedroom Victorian town house (at 1854
Mintwood) to include four houses on Mintwood Place and two on
Cathedral Avenue NW. A great effort was made to create charming
rooms and public areas. Owner Roberta Pieczenik regularly haunts
antique stores, flea markets, and auctions to find beautiful furnishings.

Many rooms are furnished with brass beds and perhaps lovely
floral-print bedspreads and matching ruffled curtains. Whatever you
find will be a delight. Live plants and/or fresh flowers grace the rooms,
and you're likely to get a dish of candy, too.

Over at 1854 is the cheerful breakfast room with plant-filled windows and park benches at marble tables. Breakfast consists of bagels,
croissants, English muffins, orange juice, and tea or coffee. Adjoining
amenities include a seldom-used TV, a phone (local calls are free), a
phone for long-distance credit- or charge-card calls, a vending machine
for soft drinks, a washing machine and dryer, and a refrigerator.
Upstairs in the parlor, which has a working fireplace, there's a decanter
of sherry on the buffet for complimentary evening apéritifs; magazines,
games, and current newspapers are provided. There's a garden behind
the house with umbrella tables. At 1859 Mintwood (also a Victorian
town house) is another cozy parlor with two working fireplaces. A
lower level here has additional laundry and ironing facilities and a
refrigerator. Though the rooms have no phones, incoming calls are
answered around the clock, so people can leave messages for you. Maid
service is provided daily.

The Mintwood Place location is very good—near Metro stations,
dozens of restaurants, nightspots, and Connecticut Avenue shops. And
the Cathedral Avenue houses (☎ **202/328-0860**), even closer to the
Metro, provide similarly wonderful amenities and facilities. *Note:* Some
of the houses are nonsmoking.

7   Capitol Hill/Mall

EXPENSIVE

⑤ Capitol Hill Suites

200 C St. SE, Washington, D.C. 20003. ☎ **202/543-6000** or 800/424-9165.
Fax 202/547-2608. 152 suites. A/C TV TEL. Weekdays $144–$164 double. Weekends
and the month of August $89–$109 double. Extra person $15. Children under 18 stay
free in parents' room. AE, CB, DC, DISC, MC, V. Parking $12 (valet only). Metro:
Capitol South.

This well-run all-suite property comprises two contiguous converted
apartment houses on a residential street close to the Library of Congress, the Capitol, and Mall attractions. Hence, its popularity with
numerous congresspeople whose photographs are displayed in the

pleasant lobby. Spacious accommodations offer full kitchens or kitchenettes and dining areas—complete living and dining rooms in one-bedroom units. Decor is residential, featuring 18th-century mahogany reproduction furnishings, sofas or sofabeds, pretty floral-print bedspreads and drapes, and white stucco walls hung with museum art prints. All suites are equipped with remote-control cable TVs with Showtime and pay-movie options. The hotel provides a very helpful guide to local shops and services.

There's no on-premises restaurant, but dozens of local establishments deliver, a food market is close by, and the charming Le Bon Café around the corner bakes fresh pastries and croissants each morning and offers French cafe luncheon fare (pâtés, quiches, sandwiches on baguettes). Weekdays, gratis drinks and snacks are served in the hotel lobby at cocktail hour. The *Washington Post* is delivered to your door Monday to Saturday. There are coin-op washers/dryers, and guests enjoy free use of extensive facilities at the nearby Washington Sports Club.

MODERATE

✪ Channel Inn

650 Water St. SW (at 7th St. and Maine Ave.), Washington, D.C. 20024. ☎ **202/554-2400** or 800/368-5668. Fax 202/863-1164. 100 rms. A/C TV TEL. Weekdays $110–$135 double. Weekends $80–$90 double. Extra person $10. Children under 12 stay free in parents' room. Call toll-free number for best rates. AE, CB, DC, DISC, JCB, MC, V. Free parking. Metro: Waterfront.

This is Washington's only waterfront hotel, built in 1973 as part of a redevelopment project that brought a marina and a row of seafood restaurants to the area. Its rooms, most offering wonderful views of the boat-filled Washington Channel, are beautifully decorated in rich shades of teal and mauve, with floral chintz bedspreads and drapes, 18th-century-style mahogany furnishings, brass lamps, and plush velvet-upholstered armchairs. Some have high cathedral ceilings; all have balconies.

Pier 7, an inviting nautically themed continental/seafood restaurant, serves moderately priced fare. Mahogany paneled and under a lofty beamed ceiling, it offers comfortable seating with park and marina views. Across the way is a sunny glass-walled coffee shop serving cafeteria-style breakfasts. The immense **Engine Room** lounge, featuring a cozy nautical decor and beautiful water views, offers a happy hour buffet of free hors d'oeuvres and a low-priced raw bar; stop by for live jazz and dancing Monday to Saturday until 1am.

There is a concierge and room service (during restaurant hours). You can also enjoy complimentary access to the fully equipped Waterside Fitness Club and outdoor pool/sundeck; a golf course and indoor/outdoor tennis courts are within walking distance; and the waterfront is an ideal place for jogging.

6

Dining

In the 1980s, Washington, like many other American cities, discovered food. Once a culinary boondocks, today it is on a par with major American cities and European capitals. The District supports dozens of first-rate restaurants, whose chefs are not only up-to-date on the latest culinary trends but in the vanguard. And in a city filled with foreign embassies, numerous eateries cater to the international contingent, offering everything from Spanish tapas to Ethiopian zilzil wat. Here, too, you can join the rich and powerful at select spots where historic decisions are made over gravlax and champagne or perhaps rub elbows with a justice at the Supreme Court cafeteria or with your senator in a Capitol restaurant. Fresh seafood comes in from Chesapeake Bay, hence crabcakes are a staple of Washington menus. And because this is also a southern town, biscuits are on many breakfast menus, and it's not too hard to find greens and grits. It all adds up to an excitingly diverse dining scene.

HOW TO READ THE LISTINGS

The restaurants listed below are divided first by location, then alphabetically by price. I've used the following price categories: **very expensive** (dinner typically costs more than $50 per person for a full meal, including a glass of wine, tip, and tax), **expensive** (main courses at dinner average $13 to $19), **moderate** (a full dinner can be had for about $20 to $25 per person), and **inexpensive** (main courses at dinner are under $10).

Keep in mind that the above categories refer to *dinner* prices, but some very expensive restaurants offer affordable lunches and/or early-bird dinners. Also, I'm assuming that you're not going to stint when you order. Some restaurants, for instance, offer entrées ranging from $12 to $20. In most cases you can dine for less if you order carefully.

Note: A Metro station is indicated when it's within walking distance of a restaurant. If you need bus-routing information, call **202/ 637-7000.**

Although my favorite restaurants are marked with a star, I must admit that every restaurant listed here is actually a favorite of mine, and I wish I could star them all. I guarantee a marvelous dining experience at all of these establishments. Bon appétit!

1 Best Bets

- **Best Spot for a Romantic Dinner:** When the weather is balmy, enjoy a tête-à-tête under the grape and wisteria arbor at the **Iron Gate,** 1734 N St. NW (☎ 202/737-1370,) if it's cold snuggle by the blazing fireplace within.

- **Best Spot for a Business Lunch:** Few restaurants convey the ambience of success and affluence as does the **Willard Room,** 1401 Pennsylvania Ave. NW (☎ 202/637-7440), where, in fact, the term "power lunch" was coined. Large tables are well spaced for privacy. The food's great, too.

- **Best Spot for a Celebration: Citronelle,** 3000 M St. NW (☎ 202/625-2150), where every dish is an exquisite little culinary celebration, is fancy enough for special occasions but casual enough to be fun. For a more exuberant—and less expensive—celebration, dine to a Brazilian rhythm at **Coco Loco,** 810 7th St. NW (☎ 202/ 289-2626), and stay on to dance the night away.

- **Best Decor: B. Smith's** (☎ 202/289-6188), occupying the opulent Presidential Suite of Union Station takes the prize for beaux-arts magnificence. I also love the Wild West whimsicality of **Red Sage,** 605 14th St. NW (☎ 202/638-4444), and the rustic elegance of **Vidalia,** 1900 M St. NW (☎ 202/659-1990), and **Provence,** 2401 Pennsylvania Ave. NW (☎ 202/296-1166).

- **Best View:** Washington Harbour, with its stunning flower-bedded esplanade, is the setting for **Sequoia's,** 3000 K St. NW (☎ 202/944-4200), multilevel garden terrace overlooking the Potomac and verdant Theodore Roosevelt Island beyond; if you're dining inside, ask for the bar-level alcove that overlooks the Harbour's spectacular fountain as well as the Potomac–best seat in the house. River vistas are also a feature of Jean-Louis's superb **Palladin,** 2650 Virginia Ave. NW (☎ 202/298-4455)—best food with a good view—and the **Roof Terrace Restaurant** (☎ 202/ 416-8555) at the Kennedy Center. And **Sea Catch,** 1054 31st St. NW (☎ 202/337-8855), features alfresco seating right on the C&O Canal.

- **Best Wine List:** At the opulent **Jean-Louis,** 2650 Virginia Ave. NW (☎ 202/298-4488), dazzling culinary creations are complemented by a vast and recherché wine cellar; consult the sommelier for suggestions with each course.

- **Best Italian Cuisine: Petitto's,** 2653 Connecticut Ave. (☎ 202/ 667-5350), luscious pastas, marinated seafood salads, pan-fried herbed breads, and seafood dishes—even its desserts—are inspired.

- **Best Pizza: Pizzeria Paradiso's,** 2029 P St. NW (☎ 202/ 223-1245), peerless chewy-crusted pies are baked in an oak-burning oven and crowned with delicious toppings; great salads and sandwiches on fresh-baked foccacia here, too.

- **Best Southern Cuisine: Vidalia,** 1990 M St. NW (☎ **202/ 659-1990**). Chef Jeff Buben calls his cuisine "Provincial American," a euphemism for fancy fare that includes cheese grits and biscuits in cream gravy.

- **Best Southwestern Cuisine:** It doesn't get more exciting than **Red Sage** (see address and telephone above), where superstar chef Mark Miller brings contemporary culinary panache to traditional southwestern cookery; keep his **Cafe and Chili Bar** in mind for Red Sage cuisine and ambience at lower prices.

- **Best Tapas: Coco Loco's** (see address and telephone above) tapas are brilliantly innovative, running the gamut from plump silver-dollar-size crabcakes with roasted pumpkin seed/crème fraîche sauce to chihuahua cheese-stuffed shrimp wrapped in bacon and served on chipotle chili/key lime sauce. The ambience is Brazilian sizzle; a noteworthy contrast is the more tranquilly elegant **Gabriel,** 2121 P St. NW (☎ **202/293-3100**), also dishing up terrific tapas.

- **Best Steakhouse: Morton's of Chicago,** 3251 Prospect St. NW (☎ **202/342-6258**), serves up prime succulent steaks in a convivial often celebrity-studded setting.

- **Best Desserts:** Hot chocolate cake with orange ginger sauce at **Citronelle** (see address and telephone above)—or any dessert at Citronelle—domain of award-winning patissier Michel Richard; **Pizzeria Paradiso's** (see address and telephone above) robustly flavorful homemade ice creams; **Patisserie Café Didier's,** 3206 Grace St. NW (☎ **202/342-9083**), fluffy maple syrup–flavored lemon soufflé pancake on fresh berry purée.

- **Best Late-Night Dining:** Washington's not a late-night town unless you count the action at 5 or 6am when the workaholic population gets into gear for early office arrival. The causal **Kramerbooks & Afterwords, A Café,** 1517 Connecticut Ave. NW (☎ **202/ 387-1462**), stays open 7:30am to 1am Monday through Thursday and around the clock on the weekend. D.C.'s top chefs hang out after hours at **Bistro Français,** 3124 M St. in Georgetown (☎ **202/ 338-3830**), exchanging culinary gossip over coquilles St. Jacques; it's open to 3am Sunday through Thursday, 4am Friday and Saturday.

- **Best for Families:** Take the kids to the **Dirksen South Buffet Room** (☎ 202/224-4249) which involves a subway ride inside the Capitol; the affordable fixed-price buffet includes a make-your-own-sundae bar.

- **Best Brunch:** (*Note:* Reservations are suggested at buffets.) Combine a Kennedy Center tour or Sunday matinee with a lavish brunch at its on-premises **Roof Terrace Restaurant** (see telephone number above). This ornate establishment invites guests into the kitchen where a stunning array of food is laid out. Your meal includes a glass of champagne or a mimosa, and musicians (flute and guitar) entertain while you dine. Price is $22.95, hours Sunday 11:30am to 3pm. An à la carte menu is also available.

A similarly opulent buffet is featured Sundays from 11am to 2:30pm at the Mayflower Hotel's **Café Promenade** (☎ **202/ 347-3000**) a delightful gardenlike setting under a domed skylight. Price is $28 for adults, $14 for children.

Café Petitto, 1724 Connecticut Ave. NW (☎ **202/462-8771**), has an all-you-can-eat antipasto buffet brunch for just $10.75, served Saturday and Sunday from 11:30am to 3pm. It includes sausages with peppers, bruschetta, stuffed grape leaves, dozens of salads, cheeses, cold cuts, pizzettes, frittatas, poached and deviled eggs, calzones, fried cauliflower, breads, pastries, and more.

Gabriel (see address and telephone above), the exciting Spanish restaurant at the Radisson Barceló Hotel, offers tapas, a quesadilla bar, and suckling pig, along with the usual carving and waffle stations, salads, cheeses, cold cuts, and desserts that make up a traditional brunch buffet. Served Sundays from 11:30am to 3pm, it includes a glass of champagne or a mimosa. Price is $16.75 for adults, $12.50 for children under 12.

The **Old Ebbitt Grill,** 675 15th St. NW (☎ **202/347-4801**), a stunning reconstructed 19th-century saloon, serves à la carte Sunday brunches from 9:30am to 4pm. Entrées are $5.95 to $9.95. Very elegant.

Or try an Indian buffet at **Bombay Palace,** 2020 K St. NW (☎ **202/331-4200**)—tandoori chicken, curries, rice pilaf, and more—Saturday and Sunday from noon to 2:30pm for just $9.95.

- **Best Afternoon Tea:** The **Café Promenade** at the Mayflower Hotel (described above under brunch listings) features à la carte afternoon teas Monday to Saturday from 3 to 5 pm. Prices range from $8 to $12.50, the latter for a selection of tea sandwiches, English pound cake, raisin scones, toasted crumpets, Devonshire cream and preserves, a fruit tartlet, and a pot of fresh-brewed tea.

  Equally divine, and also gardenlike with lush plantings and windowed walls overlooking the C&O Canal, the **Garden Terrace** at the Four Seasons Hotel (☎ **202/342-0444**), provides soothing piano music during afternoon tea Monday through Saturday from 3 to 5pm and Sunday from 3:30 to 5pm. For $12.25 you can enjoy a selection of finger sandwiches, fresh fruit tartlets, assorted English tea breads and biscuits, a Scottish sultana scone with double Devonshire cream and homemade preserves, and a pot of fresh-brewed tea. Vintage ports, sherries, and champagne are also available.

- **Best Breakfast:** The plush **Old Ebbitt Grill** (see address and telephone above) opens for breakfast at 7:30am weekdays, 8am Saturday featuring reasonably priced items ranging from cranberry muffins to thick slabs of French toast with sausage and maple syrup. Luxury hotel restaurants such as the Ritz Carlton's **Jockey Club** (☎ **202/659-8000**), the Latham's **Citronelle** (see address and telephone above), and the **Willard Room** (see address and telephone above) also serve as elegant breakfast venues. At the other end of the price scale, stuff yourself at an all-you-can-eat buffet at **Reeve's,** 1306 G St. NW (☎ **202/628-6350**), just $4.95 weekdays, $5.95 Saturdays. Marie Antoinette would opt for cake—or fresh-baked croissants and breakfast pastries—at **Patisserie Café Didier** (see address and telephone above) in Georgetown (*moi aussi*).

Palladin (see telephone number above), in the Watergate hotel, offers an $18 prix-fixe Japanese breakfast (miso soup, seaweed, grilled salmon, coddled egg, and more; American breakfasts are also available). And finally, there's **Mixtec,** 1792 Columbia Rd. (☎ **202/332-1011**), where authentic regional breakfast specialties include a Mayan dish called huevos motuleños—a tortilla sandwich layered with fried egg and served with tomato sauce, peas, and crumbled añego cheese; it comes with sautéed tomatoes or potatoes or a vegetable tamale. Also on the menu: cafe olla flavored with brown sugar, cinnamon, and lime peel.

- **Best Picnic Fare/Picnic Places:** I like to buy gourmet picnic fare at **Dean & Deluca,** 3276 M St. NW (☎ **202/342-2500**), in Georgetown and hike the C&O Canal to tables at Fletcher's Boathouse, an easy 3.2-mile hike along the towpath.
- **Best Rainy Day Restaurant:** The **Iron Gate's** (see address and telephone above) cobblestoned carriageway entrance, lined with tables, offers a delightful open-air setting for long, leisurely lunches on rainy days.

2 Restaurants by Cuisine

AMERICAN

America (Inexpensive, Union Station)
Café des Artistes at the Corcoran (Inexpensive, the Corcoran)
Cafeteria (Inexpensive, Library of Congress)
Center Cafe (Inexpensive, Union Station)
Clyde's (Moderate, Foggy Bottom/Georgetown)
Concourse Buffet (Inexpensive, National Gallery of Art)
Dirksen Senate Office Building South Buffet Room (Inexpensive, the Capitol)
Encore Cafe (Inexpensive, Kennedy Center)

Flight Line (Inexpensive, National Air and Space Museum)
Houston's (Moderate, Foggy Bottom/Georgetown)
House of Representatives Restaurant (Inexpensive, the Capitol)
The Jefferson (Very Expensive, Near the White House)
Kramerbooks & Afterwords, A Café (Moderate, Dupont Circle)
Montpelier Room (Inexpensive, Library of Congress)
Morrison Clark Inn (Very Expensive, Downtown)
Old Ebbitt Grill (Expensive, Downtown)
Reeve's Restaurant and Bakery (Inexpensive, Downtown)

Refectory (Inexpensive,
the Capitol)
Roof Terrace Restaurant
(Expensive, Kennedy
Center)
Sequoia (Expensive, Foggy
Bottom/Georgetown)
1789 (Very Expensive, Foggy
Bottom/Georgetown)
Sholl's Cafeteria
(Inexpensive, Near
the White House)
Supreme Court Cafeteria
(Inexpensive, Supreme
Court)
Trio (Inexpensive,
Dupont Circle)
The Tombs (Inexpensive,
Foggy Bottom/
Georgetown)
Vidalia (Very Expensive,
Dupont Circle)
The Willard Room (Very
Expensive, Downtown)
The Wright Place
(Inexpensive, National
Air and Space Museum)

ASIAN

Asia Nora (Expensive,
Dupont Circle)

CHINESE

City Lights of China
(Moderate, Dupont Circle)
Sichuan Pavilion (Moderate,
Near the White House)

CONTINENTAL/INTERNATIONAL

Cities (Expensive,
Adams-Morgan)
Dean & Deluca (Inexpensive,
Foggy Bottom/
Georgetown)
National Gallery Restaurants
(Inexpensive, National
Gallery of Art)

Seasons (Very Expensive,
Foggy Bottom/
Georgetown)

ETHIOPIAN

Zed's (Inexpensive,
Foggy Bottom/
Georgetown)

FRENCH

Citronelle (Very Expensive,
Foggy Bottom/
Georgetown)
Jean-Louis (Very Expensive,
Foggy Bottom/
Georgetown)
The Jockey Club (Very
Expensive, Dupont Circle)
La Ruche (Moderate, Foggy
Bottom/Georgetown)
Le Lion d'Or (Very
Expensive, Near the
White House)
Palladin (Expensive, Foggy
Bottom/Georgetown)
Provence (Very Expensive,
Foggy Bottom/
Georgetown)

INDIAN

Aditi (Moderate, Foggy
Bottom/Georgetown)
Bombay Palace (Moderate,
Near the White House)

ITALIAN

Café Petitto (Moderate,
Dupont Circle)
Obelisk (Expensive,
Dupont Circle)
Panevino Ristorante
(Moderate, Dupont Circle)
Paolo's (Expensive, Foggy
Bottom/Georgetown)
Patisserie Café Didier
(Inexpensive, Foggy
Bottom/Georgetown)

Petitto's (Expensive,
   Adams-Morgan)
Pizzeria Paradiso
   (Inexpensive, Dupont
   Circle)
Sfuzzi (Inexpensive,
   Union Station)

MEDITERRANEAN

Iron Gate Restaurant &
   Garden (Expensive,
   Dupont Circle)

MEXICAN

Coco Loco (Moderate,
   Downtown)
Mixtec (Inexpensive,
   Adams-Morgan)

ORGANIC

Nora (Very Expensive,
   Dupont Circle)

SANDWICHES/SALADS/PASTRY

Chesapeake Bagel Bakery
   (Inexpensive, Capitol Hill/
   Union Station)
Georgetown Bagelry
   (Inexpensive, Foggy
   Bottom/Georgetown)

Uptown Bakers (Inexpensive,
   Near the National Zoo)

SEAFOOD

The Sea Catch (Expensive,
   Foggy Bottom/
   Georgetown)

SOUTHWESTERN/SOUTHERN

B. Smith's (Expensive,
   Union Station)
Peyote Cafe (Moderate,
   Adams-Morgan)
Red Sage (Very Expensive,
   Downtown)
Roxanne/On the Rox
   (Moderate,
   Adams-Morgan)

SPANISH

Gabriel (Expensive,
   Dupont Circle)
Jaleo (Moderate, Downtown)

STEAKS/CHOPS

Morton's of Chicago (Very
   Expensive, Foggy Bottom/
   Georgetown)
Prime Rib (Very Expensive,
   Near the White House)

3 Downtown

VERY EXPENSIVE

✪ Morrison Clark Inn

Massachusetts Ave. NW (at 11th St.). ☎ **202/898-1200.** Reservations recommended. Main courses $10.50–$13.75 at lunch, $16.75–$21.50 at dinner; three-course Sun brunch (including unlimited champagne) $19.50. AE, CB, DC, MC, V. Mon–Fri 11:30am–2:30pm, nightly 6–9pm; Sun 11:30am–2pm. Metro: Metro Center. AMERICAN REGIONAL.

The dining room at the Morrison Clark, an exquisite upscale accommodation (see Chapter 5), is one of the District's most fashionable restaurants. During the Bush years, Barbara celebrated a birthday at the inn, and Newt Gingrich recently hosted a breakfast here. The dining room has floor-to-ceiling mahogany- and gilt-valenced lace-curtained windows flanking pier mirrors at either end; also paired are ornately carved white marble fireplaces. At night soft lighting emanates from

Georgetown & Downtown Dining

National Zoological Park

Kalorama Rd.

Massachusetts Ave.

24th St.
23rd St.
California St.

Florida Ave.

New Hampshire

Rock Creek

R St.

Wisconsin Ave.

Dupont Circle

Q St.

P St.

30th St.
29th St.
28th St.

31st St.

33rd St.
34th St.

N St.

M St.

O St.

N St.

18th St.
17th St.
16th St.

Connecticut Ave.

Rhode Island

M St.

29

Washington Circle

New Hampshire Ave.

L St.

K St.
I St.

Pennsylvania Ave.

Farragut Square

McP S

Francis Scott Key Mem. Bridge

Georgetown Channel

H St.

Lafa Squ T

White

Theodore Roosevelt Island

22nd St.
21st St.
20th St.

G St.
F St.

Virginia Ave.

E St.

66

Constitu

Theodore Roosevelt Mem. Bridge

T Elli

Reflecting Pool

Washi Monu

Arlington Mem. Bridge

Potomac River

Kutz Bridg

Arlington National Cemetery

Tidal Basin

Jefferson Memorial

1648

Victorian brass candelabras, crystal chandeliers, and candles. During the day, sunlight streams in through those massive windows. A smaller adjoining area has trellised walls hung with plants, and, weather permitting, you can dine outdoors at courtyard umbrella tables.

Chef Richard Mahan's seasonally changing menus are elegant and inspired. Recently, appetizers varied from Thai noodle salad tossed with chunks of lobster, minced pork, and roasted peanuts in cilantro-lime dressing to sautéed duck foie gras served on a bed of hoppin' John (a mixture of rice and black-eyed peas) in aged balsamic vinegar. An entrée of sautéed red snapper in a citrusy pan sauce (lemon, blood oranges, and extra virgin olive oil) was served with marinated black olives, tomato marmalade, and crispy-creamy pommes Lyonnaises. Another choice was grilled leg of lamb in a Merlot/lamb jus reduction accompanied by a goat cheese fritter and caramelized pearl onions. Similar fare is available at lunch. A reasonably priced wine list offers a variety of premium wines by the glass, plus a good choice of champagnes and sparkling wines. Desserts—such as a Belgian chocolate silk brioche bread pudding with a blood orange/zabaglione sauce—are fittingly fancy.

✪ Red Sage

605 14th St. NW. ☎ **202/638-4444.** Reservations recommended. Main courses $12.50–$16 at lunch, $17.25–$27 at dinner; Cafe/Chili Bar items all under $10. AE, CB, DC, MC, V. Restaurant Mon–Fri 11:30am–2:15pm and 5:30–10:30pm, Sat 5:30–10:30pm, Sun 5–10pm. Cafe/Chili Bar Mon–Sat 11:30am–11:30pm, Sun 4:30–11:30pm. Metro: Metro Center. SOUTHWESTERN/CONTEMPORARY AMERICAN.

One of the brightest stars in Washington's culinary galaxy, Red Sage is the creation of renowned chef Mark Miller, who brings brilliant inspiration to southwestern-nuanced American cuisine. His dynamic setting is an elegantly whimsical Wild West fantasy. Down a curved stairway, the main dining room comprises a warren of cozy, candlelit alcoves under a curved ponderosa log-beamed ceiling. Zapotec rugs are strewn on flagstone floors, and adobe-peach fresco walls are hand-rubbed to a sheen with beeswax. Diners are comfortably ensconced in butter-soft burgundy-leather booths or roomy chairs. Special dining areas include an exhibition kitchen, a wine bar, a hogan (Native American hut), and a library where "bookshelves" in arched niches are used to display wines. Upstairs are the more casual (albeit gorgeous) Cafe and high-ceilinged Chili Bar, the latter with a large white cloud (emitting bolts of blue lightning) overhead.

Miller's food presentations are exquisite. An appetizer of pan-fried softshell crab arrived tented over a tower of lemon-basil couscous with saffron aïoli sauce. Cubes of seared ahi tuna carpaccio were centered on a bouquet of summer onion sprouts drizzled with mango scotch bonnet oil. An entrée of pan-roasted squab came artistically arranged on a bed of morels and roasted corn and asparagus, embellished with grilled sea scallops in a balsamic vinegar sauce. Another standout—roasted rack of lamb—was coated with mint pistachio pesto and served with raviolis stuffed with goat cheese, spinach, and artichokes in a roasted red pepper sauce. Red Sage desserts—such as a moist, warm chocolate cake with hazelnut caramel and honey-spiced bananas—are sublime, and the wine list is extensive and well researched. The Chili Bar and Cafe offer inexpensive light fare ranging from barbecued brisket quesadillas to a sandwich of grilled chicken, smoked prosciutto, sun-dried tomato spread, mozzarella, and Monterey Jack on roast garlic/herb foccacia.

The Willard Room

In the Willard Inter-Continental Hotel, 1401 Pennsylvania Ave. NW. ☎ **202/ 637-7440.** Reservations recommended. Main courses $8.25–$16 at lunch, $17.50–$23 at dinner; three-course prix-fixe lunch $22; prix-fixe dinners $33–$42 ($46–$62 with wine). AE, DC, DISC, JCB, MC, V. Mon–Fri 7:30–10am and 11:30am–2pm, nightly 6–10pm. Metro: Metro Center. AMERICAN REGIONAL/CLASSIC EUROPEAN.

An 1880 guidebook to the city described the Willard Room as "a most agreeable and pleasing spectacle where refined people enjoy an unequaled table." Today that "refined" clientele includes upper-crust Washingtonians, visiting presidents and premiers, movie and sports stars, and often a king or two. To ensure an ongoing "unequaled table," the restaurant shops the markets of the world to stock its larders, from the pâtés of Strasbourg to West Virginia's finest mountain brook trout. And the room itself has been re-created to reflect its original turn-of-the-century splendor in every detail—the gorgeous carved oak paneling, towering scagliola columns, brass and bronze torchères and chandeliers, and faux-bois beamed ceiling have all been restored or faithfully reproduced. "The Willard Room is so elegant," said *Dossier* magazine, "that one could eat a hot dog here and still think it was the dining experience of a lifetime."

Chef Guy Reinbolt, like many great *cuisiniers,* trained in Alsace; he added créole and southern dishes to his repertoire during stints in Memphis and New Orleans. His menus change seasonally. At a recent dinner, a companion and I shared appetizers of sautéed duck foie gras (served atop a corn-flour tart with a dice of smoked duck breast in a light jus) and a light potato custard with chopped tomatoes and spinach in a cabernet sauvignon reduction sauce (garnished with waffled potato chips). An entrée of sautéed goujonettes (diamonds) of Maryland black sea bass came with buttery sautéed leeks and watercress in a port wine reduction sauce. And a stunning combination of seared veal médaillon and sautéed lobster tail was accompanied by a medley of grapes, tiny cocotte potatoes, and chanterelles in cream sauce. For dessert, a feuilleté of Asian pear (served on crème anglaise marbelized with fruit confit and drizzled with kirsch sauce) was exquisite. A list of more than 250 fine wines mentions Thomas Jefferson's notes from his voyages in the vineyards of France.

EXPENSIVE

⑤ Old Ebbitt Grill

675 15th St. NW (between F and G sts.). ☎ **202/347-4801.** Reservations recommended. Main courses $4.50–$6.95 at breakfast, $5.95–$9.95 at brunch, $6.95–$10.95 at lunch, $9.95–$14.95 at dinner; burgers and sandwiches $6.25–$10.95. AE, DC, DISC, MC, V. Mon–Fri 7:30am–midnight, Sat 8am–midnight, Sun 9:30am–midnight. Bar Sun–Thurs to 2am, Fri–Sat to 3am. Metro: McPherson Square or Metro Center. AMERICAN.

Located two blocks from the White House is the city's oldest saloon, founded in 1856. Presidents Grant, Johnson, McKinley, Cleveland, Theodore Roosevelt, and Harding were patrons, and among its artifacts are Alexander Hamilton's wooden bears—one with a secret compartment in which it's said he hid whiskey bottles from his wife. However, don't expect to find a fusty old tavern. The existing facility is a plush reconstruction loosely based upon the original. Fronted by a grandiose beaux-arts facade, it has Persian rugs on beautiful oak and marble floors, beveled mirrors, gas lighting, etched-glass panels, and other elements evocative of turn-of-the-century Washington saloons. Old Ebbitt heirlooms are scattered throughout, including animal trophies bagged by Teddy Roosevelt. The street level comprises a dining area and three bars, plus a glassed-in atrium dining room with umbrella tables amid much greenery. The main dining room, hung with period oil paintings, has lace-curtained windows and forest-green velvet banquettes and booths. Other areas include the Old Bar (where the Ebbitt's famed collection of antique beer steins is displayed), the Oyster Bar, and Grant's Bar, complete with a classic gilt-framed bar nude. The Ebbitt is a stunning setting for meals, cocktails, or a romantic rendezvous.

Menus change daily, but lunch entrées might include anything from a fried oyster sandwich to fettuccine tossed with spinach and walnuts in cream sauce. Typical dinner entrées: a half chicken (roasted with lemon, herbs, and honey, and served with rice and fresh vegetables) and straw and hay pasta tossed with prosciutto, peas, onions, mushrooms, olive oil, and fresh-grated Parmesan. At either meal you can order a sandwich or hamburger, thus enjoying the luxe ambience at low cost. For dessert, there's toll house pie studded with chocolate morsels and walnuts, spiked with bourbon, and served warm with vanilla ice cream.

MODERATE

✪ Coco Loco

810 7th St. NW (between H and I sts.). ☎ **202/289-2626.** Reservations recommended. Tapas mostly $3.95–$7.95; churrascaria with antipasti bar $15.95 lunch, $24.95 dinner; antipasti bar only $9.95 lunch, $15.95 dinner. AE, DC, MC, V. Mon–Fri 11:30am–2:30pm; Sun–Wed 5:30–10pm, Thurs–Sat 5:30–11pm. Valet parking $4 evenings. Metro: Gallery Place. CONTEMPORARY MEXICAN (TAPAS)/BRAZILIAN CHURRASCARIA.

Superbly talented and endlessly innovative French chef Yannick Cam (see Provence in the "Foggy Bottom/Georgetown" section, below) is one of the owners of—and the culinary inspiration behind—this large (6,000 square feet) and festive Washington restaurant. Its exuberant interior—with massive columns and bamboo lighting fixtures in variegated tropical hues—focuses on a daily-changing buffet table where cheese, fresh fruit, salads (ranging from roasted tomatoes with mozzarella to garbanzos with figs), olives, cold cuts, and other antipasti are temptingly arranged on palm fronds and banana leaves. Coco Loco crackles with excitement, especially at night. Much of the action emanates from a colorful mosaic-tiled and copper-hooded double exhibition kitchen (one part for meat, the other for tapas). Also a lively precinct is the U-shaped bar. Brazilian music provides an appealing audio backdrop. If you want a quieter setting, sit in the window-walled front room or at an umbrella-shaded table in the walled garden patio.

Coco Loco's tapas combine diverse textures and subtle flavors. Pan-roasted shrimp, for instance, is served on a bed of chewy black Chinese jasmine rice (infused with squid ink) and flavored with smoked bacon and minuscule cubes of pork; a garnish of fried garlic and parsley adds delicate crunch. And red snapper is served with sweet fried plaintains in a rich coconut milk sauce nuanced with caramelized onions, red pepper strips, and green and yellow jalapeños. Another dining choice here is Brazilian churrascaria (a mixed grill of succulent rotisseried beef, lamb, pork, sausages, and chicken) served with salsa, fried potatoes, coconut-flavored rice, and farofa (a buttery/bacony yucca flour season-ing); this mixed-grill meal includes antipasti bar offerings. All this and tira misu for dessert, too. The wine list is small but well chosen; the service warm and competent.

✪ Jaleo

480 7th St. NW (at E St.). ☎ **202/628-7949.** Reservations accepted before noon for lunch and before 6:30pm for dinner only. Main courses $6.95–$9.75 at lunch, $10.50–$14.50 at dinner; paellas $17–$18. AE, DC, DISC, MC, V. Mon–Sat 11:30am–2:30pm (with a limited tapas menu served 2:30–5:30pm) Sun 11:30am–3pm; Sun–Mon 5:30–10pm. Tues–Thurs 5:30–11:30pm, Fri–Sat 5:30pm–midnight. Metro: Archives or Gallery Place. SPANISH REGIONAL/TAPAS.

The exuberantly colorful Jaleo, specializing in tapas (little dishes) "reflective of the diversity of classical and contemporary Spanish cuisine," is housed in the Civil War–era Lansburgh building. Its cor-ner location allows light to stream in through cafe-curtained windows on two sides. The casual-chic interior focuses on a large mural of a flamenco dancer based on John Singer Sargent's painting *Jaleo,* which inspired the restaurant's name. There's a large bar area, and background music ranges from the Gypsy Kings to classical Spanish guitar.

Peruse the menu over a gratis dish of Spanish olives and roasted almonds. Zesty tapas include mild but savory warm goat cheese served with toast points, a skewer of grilled chorizo sausage atop garlic mashed potatoes, and delicious eggplant flan served with roasted red pepper sauce. The humble potato reaches an apogee in patatas bravas—crisp fried chunks of red potato topped with a piquant tomato-chili sauce and aïoli. There are heartier entrées such as grilled lamb steak served with roasted garlic oil and grilled asparagus, and four varieties of paella are offered at night. Spanish wines, sangrías, and sherries selected to comple-ment these items are available by the glass, and fresh-baked chewy bread comes in handy for soaking up tangy sauces. For dessert try a rum- and butter-soaked apple charlotte encrusted in a bread pastry and topped with Mexican Vanilla ice cream, or, alternatively, a plate of Spanish cheeses.

INEXPENSIVE

⑤ Reeve's Restaurant and Bakery

1306 G St. NW. ☎ **202/628-6350.** Main courses $4.90–$7.45; sandwiches $3–$5.95; buffet breakfast $4.95 Mon–Fri, $5.95 Sat and holidays. MC, V. Mon–Sat 7am–6pm. Metro: Metro Center. AMERICAN.

There's no place like Reeve's, a Washington institution since 1886. J. Edgar Hoover used to send a G-man to pick up chicken sandwiches, and Lady Bird Johnson and daughter Lynda Bird worked out the latter's wedding plans over lunch here. Closed for a few years when its former building was demolished, Reeve's reincarnated at a new address in 1992 offering the identical famous fare and retaining something of its vintage ambience. It's still fronted by a long bakery counter filled with scrumptious pies and cakes. One exultant reviewer compared the strawberry pie—Bess Truman's favorite, by the way—to desserts at Maxim's in Paris. And the familiar brass-railed counter seating on both floors utilizes the original 19th-century wooden stools. The ambience is cheerful. Oak-wainscoted cream walls are hung with pictures of the city, and soft lighting emanates from wall sconces. Much of the seating is in cozy booths and banquettes.

Everything is homemade with top-quality ingredients—the turkeys, chickens, salads, breads, desserts, even the mayonnaise. At breakfast, you can't beat the all-you-can-eat buffet—scrambled eggs, home fries, French toast, pancakes, cinnamon buns, corned-beef hash, grits, bacon, sausage, stewed and fresh fruit, biscuits with sausage gravy, and more. At lunch, try a roast turkey sandwich on fresh-baked bread, perhaps with an order of homemade potato salad. Hot entrées run the gamut from golden-brown Maryland crabcakes to country-fried chicken with mashed potatoes and gravy. And leave room for one of those fabulous pies—strawberry, peach, chocolate cream, key lime, coconut custard . . . you name it. No alcoholic beverages are served.

4 Near the White House

VERY EXPENSIVE

The Jefferson

1200 16th St. NW (at M St.). ☎ **202/347-2200.** Reservations recommended. Main courses $13.25–$16.50 at lunch, $18.50–$25 at dinner; Sun brunch $20–$23.50. AE, CB, DC, JCB, MC, OPT, V. Daily 6:30–10:30am, 11am–3pm, and 6–10:30pm. Metro: Farragut North. AMERICAN REGIONAL/FRENCH.

Built in 1923 as a residence for Washington's social elite, The Jefferson remains one of the city's most exclusive hotels, discreetly catering to royalty and other distinguished visitors. Its dining room is, of course, fittingly elegant, offering the kind of exquisite fare and impeccable service you'd expect in such a prestigious establishment. Cozy, rather than intimidatingly plush, it has bare oak floors and flower-bedecked tables covered with brown-and-cream tattersall-plaid cloths. Walls and ceiling are handsomely painted in faux tortoiseshell, the former adorned with intricately carved moldings and hung with 1830s hand-colored lithographs by Charles Bird King, James Otto Lewis, and other notable American artists. Seating is in deep-brown tufted-leather banquettes.

American chef Andrew Roche was trained in the French tradition. His menus change seasonally. I last visited in the spring, when he offered a silky roasted-garlic soup replete with plump poached oysters and an appetizer of grilled jumbo scallops with stewed fennel in a vivid blood orange sauce. An entrée of spice-crusted tuna was accompanied by couscous and cumin-flavored carrots. And duck breast was fanned in thin pink and juicy slices and served with duck/celery root hash. The napoleon—feuilleté layered with thick chocolate mousse and fresh raspberries—is a signature dessert here. An extensive wine list includes many by-the-glass selections, and the brunch menu adds such breakfast items as blueberry pancakes with Bourbon maple syrup and link sausage.

✪ Le Lion d'Or

1150 Connecticut Ave. NW (at M St.). ☎ **202/296-7972.** Reservations required. Main courses $20–$32. AE, CB, DC, MC, V. Mon–Sat 6–10pm. Metro: Farragut North. FRENCH.

Under the creative and skillful direction of owner/chef Jean Pierre Goyenvalle, Le Lion d'Or is one of Washington's most highly esteemed bastions of haute cuisine. It opened in 1976 to immediate acclaim, Goyenvalle having previously garnered a loyal following in a decade of classic cookery at other noted area restaurants. Though the restaurant is down a flight of steps from the street, you'll quickly forget you're underground because of delightful French country setting with seating in dark-brown tufted-leather banquettes under tented silk canopies. Ecru silk walls are adorned with provincial French Faience platters, copper cooking implements, and gilt-framed oil paintings of pastoral scenes.

The food is classic French cuisine at its best, beautifully presented and graciously served. A not-to-be-missed hors d'oeuvre is the petit soufflé de homard, a feather-light hot lobster mousse, delicately pink and lightly browned on top in lobster-cream sauce flavored with a soupçon of tarragon and parsley. Another excellent beginning: ravioli de foie gras—a large poached pasta pocket stuffed with fresh duck foie gras marinated in white port wine and served in a canard glaze with small diced vegetables. A red snapper entrée "aux senteurs de Provence" (with the aroma of Provence) comes lightly roasted in extra-virgin olive oil and served on a bed of fennel with a side dish of new potatoes and a colorful garnish of julienned tomatoes and spinach. And tender, juicy roast rack of lamb is coated just before completion with a Dijon-mustard meringue, crushed green peppercorns, and herbed breadcrumbs; it's served with an array of fresh seasonal vegetables. Dessert options range from soufflés (orange, raspberry, chocolate, and passionfruit) to scrumptious pastry cart selections, though a dish of cookies or miniature pastries is complimentary. Le Lion d'Or offers an extensive wine list, primarily French and Californian, and house wines are bottled with the restaurant's own label.

Prime Rib

2020 K St. NW. ☎ **202/466-8811.** Reservations recommended. Main courses $10–$16.50 at lunch, $18–$26 at dinner. AE, CB, DC, MC, V. Mon–Fri 11:30am–3pm; Mon–Thurs 5–11pm, Fri–Sat 5–11:30pm. Free parking (valet) after 6pm. Metro: Farragut West. STEAKS/CHOPS/SEAFOOD.

Washington Post restaurant critic Phyllis Richman calls the Prime Rib "Washington's most glamorous setting for plain old steak and roast beef." Modeled after Central Park South hotel restaurants, it is indeed glamorous—in a substantial, well-heeled fashion—with gold-trimmed black walls, comfortable black leather chairs and banquettes, white-linened tables softly lit by shaded brass lamps, swagged white curtains, and large floral displays. Waiters are in black tie, a pianist at the baby grand plays show tunes, and the art on the walls includes dozens of gilt-framed Louis Icart art deco lithographs.

As for that "plain old" steak and roast beef, they are thick, tender, juicy, and prepared from meat of the best grain-fed steers that has been aged for four to five weeks. And it's served exactly the way you ordered it. For less carnivorous diners there are about a dozen seafood entrées. A bountiful basket of fried potato skins with a big bowl of sour cream is a must. Lunch or dinner might begin with an appetizer of smoked fresh trout with Dijon-mustard sauce or creamy lobster bisque and end with a gorgeous hot-fudge sundae over amaretto pound cake. Bar drinks here, by the way, are made with fresh-squeezed juices and Evian water.

MODERATE

Bombay Palace

2020 K St. NW. ☎ **202/331-4200.** Reservations recommended. Main courses $6.50–$16.95 (most are under $12), prix-fixe three-course lunch (Mon–Fri) $10.95–$13.95, lunch buffet (Sat–Sun) $9.95. AE, MC, V. Mon–Fri 11:30am–2:30pm, Sat–Sun noon–2:30pm; Sun–Thurs 5:30–10pm, Fri–Sat 5:30–10:30pm. Metro: Farragut North or Farragut West. NORTH INDIAN.

Bombay Palace features the Mughlai cooking of northern India, famous for its subtle mélanges of full-flavored spices and creamy yogurt-based marinades. Many senators (for example, Al D'Amato, Pat Moynihan, Bob Dole) and ambassadors are regulars here. Beautifully decorated in burgundy-accented soft tones of mauve and beige, with gleaming etched-mirror walls and columns, the ambience is both restful and plush. Recessed lighting casts a rosy glow over crisp, linen-covered tables; and comfortable upholstered banquettes and armchairs comprise most of the seating. Soft Indian music and bas-relief sculptures of Indian deities provide the requisite exotic note.

Start off with a selection of appetizers such as aloo papri chat (a medley of chick-peas and potato and flour crisps topped with chutney-yogurt dressing) and samosas (flaky pastries stuffed with lightly spiced potatoes and peas). Tandoori (clay oven–baked) specialties range from large juicy prawns to an Afghani version of lamb chops marinated with ginger and herbs (ask for curry sauce with it). One of my favorite dishes here is Makhani (butter) chicken, tandoor-baked and served in a fragrant tomato cream sauce spiced with coriander, ginger, garlic, and chili. If you're sharing dishes with a companion, order it along with an entrée of Hyderabadi biryani (tender lamb cubes marinated in yogurt and fried spices tossed with steam-baked long-grain basmati rice). Make sure to order one of the tandoor-baked breads with your meal—perhaps chewy naan stuffed with cashews and dried fruits. For dessert try gulab jamun (milk dumplings flavored with rose water and green cardamom). There's a full bar, and the wine list recommends selections for specific dishes.

Sichuan Pavilion

1820 K St. NW. ☎ **202/466-7790.** Reservations recommended. Main courses
$6.95–$14.95 at lunch, $7.95–$15.95 at dinner; prix-fixe brunch (Sat–Sun) $10.95.
AE, DC, DISC, MC, V. Mon–Fri 11:30am–3pm, Sat–Sun noon–4pm, dinner nightly
5–10:30pm. Metro: Farragut North or Farragut West. SZECHUAN.

The Sichuan Pavilion is unique in several ways. Though it's American-
owned, its chefs are recruited from the highest ranks of the People's
Republic of China's Chengdu Service Bureau, which operates luxurious
hotels and restaurants for visiting dignitaries and prepares sumptuous
state banquets. These chefs, supplied from home with special season-
ings and spices not otherwise available in the United States, are
masters of Szechuan cuisine.

The setting is unpretentious but elegant, with white-linen-covered
tables, crystal chandeliers, and walls hung with paintings and calligraphy from the Chungking Institute of Fine Arts. And the food is beautifully presented (since these chefs are also trained in food sculpture,
they adorn platters with exquisite carrot and leek flowers). It's also
light—never greasy—low in salt, and prepared without MSG.

Do begin with an appetizer of tangy dumplings in spicy red hot
sauce or crispy but feather-light spring rolls. And keep in mind that
though some of the dishes sound familiar—moo shu pork, Kung Pao
chicken, twice-cooked shredded duck—their subtle flavors distinguish
them from Szechuan fare you've had elsewhere. The chef's specialties
include tinkling bells with 10 ingredients (sliced shrimp, crab, beef, and
chicken sautéed with vegetables and topped with Sichuan dumplings)
and crispy fried sea bass in Sichuan sauce. Each dish is a revelation;
dining here is like discovering new colors in the culinary spectrum.

INEXPENSIVE

◉ Sholl's Cafeteria

In the Esplanade Mall, 1990 K St. NW. ☎ **202/296-3065.** Main courses $1.65–
$5.25. No credit cards. Mon–Sat 7am–8pm, Sun 8:30am–6pm. Metro: Farragut West.
AMERICAN.

In March 1928, Pennsylvania Dutchman Evan A. Sholl opened this
Washington cafeteria, offering fresh, wholesome, inexpensive fare,
prayers, and patriotism. Though Mr. Sholl died in 1984, the current
owner, his nephew, upholds his uncle's traditions. On every table is a
sheet announcing the weekly special (for example, baked ham with
peach half), along with a biblical quote or prayer, the slogan "We pray
together. . . . We stay together," Sholl's motto ("Live well for less
money with quality food at more reasonable prices"), and perhaps an
inspirational poem as well. Sholl's is a homey environment, with soft
lighting, carpeted floors, and photographs of the President and Pope
John Paul II prominently displayed on cream-colored walls.

Everything served here is prepared on the premises. All vegetables are
fresh, pies and cakes are homemade, and chopped meat is ground daily.
And the prices are not to be believed. At breakfast, load up your tray
with scrambled eggs, bacon, biscuits, coffee, orange juice, and home
fries for under $3.50. Lunch or dinner entrées might include braised
beef and rice, roast turkey and dressing, or beef stew with potatoes,

carrots, celery, and onions. Add a vegetable or a scoop of mashed potatoes for another 75¢ to 85¢, a piece of homemade peach or pumpkin pie for $1.05.

5 Dupont Circle

VERY EXPENSIVE

The Jockey Club

In The Ritz-Carlton hotel, 2100 Massachusetts Ave. NW. ☎ **202/659-8000.** Reservations required. Main courses $12–$23 at lunch, $24–$30 at dinner. AE, CB, DC, ER, MC, V. Daily 11:30am–3pm, 6–11pm. Metro: Dupont Circle. FRENCH/CONTINENTAL.

The Jockey Club, Washington's longest-running power-dining enclave, opened in 1961 and immediately became a Kennedy-clan favorite. JFK once quipped that when he wanted to reach a staff member, he first called their office, then their home, then the Jockey Club. During the Reagan years Nancy was a regular, as was Barbara during the Bush years. Humorist Art Buchwald has a designated table, as do notables ranging from Boutros Boutros-Ghali to Princess Michael of Kent.

The big surprise when you first visit this society-page tableau-vivant is its total lack of pomp and crystal-chandeliered pretension. Instead it is cheerful and pubby, with red-leather banquettes, a random-plank oak floor, lanterns suspended from a low beamed ceiling (the subdued amber lighting is as cozy as the glow of a fireplace), and walls of stucco or aged oak paneling hung with English equestrian prints. Tables are covered in red-and-white tattersall check and bedecked with single red roses.

Chef Hidemasa Yamamoto brings Eastern nuance to classic continental cookery. For instance, an appetizer of sautéed quail with California artichokes and green lentils is garnished with oba (Japanese basil). And an entrée of truffle-studded sautéed Dover sole, in a white wine–infused pale-pink lobster cream sauce, comes with bok choy as well as artichokes, julienne roast peppers, and puréed truffled potatoes. Big fluffy crabcakes meunière comprise the restaurant's signature dish. And there's also a marvelous pan-fried lobster entrée with a trinity of *boules*—avocado, mango, and red beets—in a sauterne beurre blanc sauce with fresh ginger and cilantro. I'm listing a lot of seafood, but you could also order a New York strip steak here. Crusty sun-dried tomato, cheese, and basil breads are served warm. And for dessert there are silky smooth soufflés dusted with powdered sugar. After dinner, enjoy piano-bar music and a cognac by the fireplace in the adjoining Fairfax Bar.

✪ Nora

2132 Florida Ave. NW (at R St.). ☎ **202/462-5143.** Reservations recommended. Main courses $19.95–$24.95. MC, V. Dinner Mon–Thurs 6–10pm, Fri–Sat 6–10:30pm. Metro: Dupont Circle. ORGANIC/MULTIETHNIC.

This charming Washington restaurant, where owner-chef Nora Pouillon brings haute panache to healthful organic cookery, is a favorite

Adams-Morgan & Dupont Circle Dining

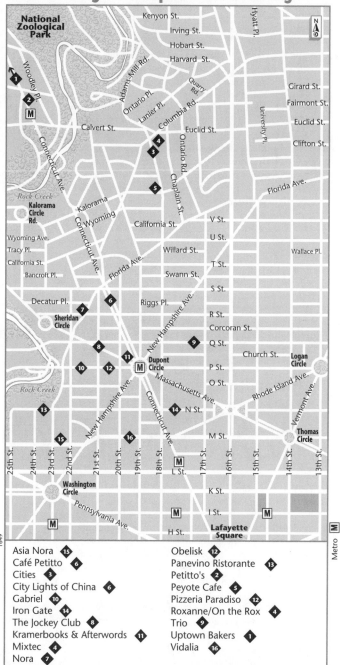

Asia Nora
Café Petitto
Cities
City Lights of China
Gabriel
Iron Gate
The Jockey Club
Kramerbooks & Afterwords
Mixtec
Nora

Obelisk
Panevino Ristorante
Petitto's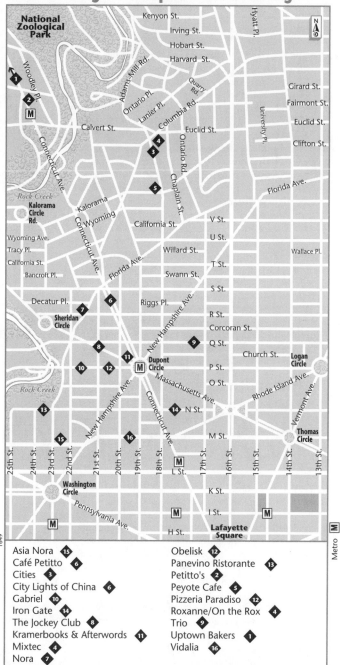
Peyote Cafe
Pizzeria Paradiso
Roxanne/On the Rox
Trio
Uptown Bakers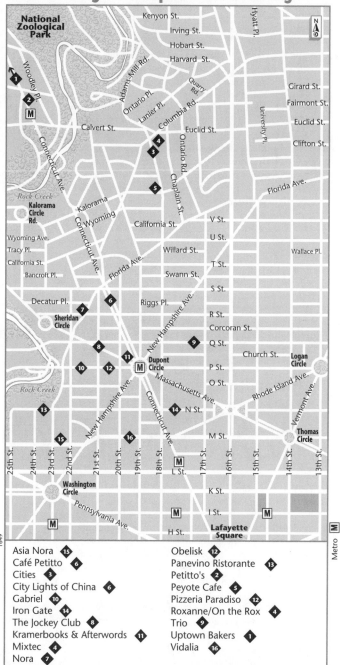
Vidalia

of the Clintons and the Gores (who celebrated Tipper's 45th birthday here). The ever fit Jane Fonda comes in when she's in town, and fit wannabee Ted Kennedy is a regular. Actor Harrison Ford once quipped of the free-range chicken, "it's free, but it's dead." Housed in a turn-of-the-century building, the restaurant is entered via a cozy bar. The skylit main dining room is a converted stable, with a weathered-looking beamed pine ceiling, damask-covered tables lit by shaded paraffin lamps, and a display of Amish and Mennonite patchwork crib quilts on pale-gray brick walls. Handmade Windsor chairs enhance the Early American feel. Especially lovely is the intimate brick-walled patio with its vast window box of dried flowers and a large shade tree creating leafy shadows over the skylight.

The chemical-free, organically grown, free-range fare is extremely healthful, but not of the brown-rice-and-bean-sprout variety. Menus vary nightly. Salads here make good beginnings—perhaps young lettuce tossed with spicy pecans and chunks of mango in a piquant citrus vinaigrette. Or you might start your meal with grilled portobello mushroom in picada sauce (garlicky herbed olive oil) with creamy semolina and greens. Entrées on my recent visit included grilled Copper River king salmon (served with tomato-onion relish, sweetcorn succotash, and fiddlehead ferns) and roasted free-range chicken stuffed with goat cheese and toasted pumpkin seeds and served with fresh-baked cornbread and grilled zucchini in ancho chili sauce. Most desserts are light and utilize fruits and nuts, for instance, a banana-nut upside-down cake served with vanilla ice cream, grilled pineapple, and caramel sauce. An extensive wine list includes—but is not limited to— selections made with organically grown grapes. I promise you won't miss any of the bad-for-you ingredients at Nora, and you will experience the vivid and earthy flavors of natural foods.

✪ Vidalia

1990 M St. NW. ☎ **202/659-1990.** Reservations recommended. Complimentary valet parking at dinner. Main courses $9.50–$13.50 at lunch, $16–$20 at dinner. AE, DC, MC, V. Mon–Fri 11:30am–2:30pm; Mon–Sat 5:30–10:30pm. Onion Bar, Mon–Sat to midnight. Metro: Dupont Circle. PROVINCIAL AMERICAN.

Down a flight of steps from the street is the charmingly country-cozy Vidalia, named for a variety of sweet Georgia onion. It's entered via a foyer where an oak table displays baskets overflowing with fresh flowers, breads, and onions. The oak-floored bi-level dining room has a similar display table. Its cream stucco walls are hung with gorgeous dried-flower wreaths and works by local artists, soft lighting emanates from graceful Georgian-style brass chandeliers and sconces, and seating is in sturdy oak chairs or tapestried banquettes. It's a lovely setting, enhanced by exquisite flower arrangements, big terra-cotta pots of chrysanthemums, and bowls of fruit.

Chef Jeff Buben's "provincial American" menus (focusing on southern-accented regional specialties) change frequently, but his highly recommended crisp East Coast lump crabcakes (the lightest, fluffiest ever, with a piquant dash of capers and cayenne) are a constant among appetizer choices; they're served with a mound of celery seed–studded pepper slaw and coriander mayonnaise. On a recent visit, I had a choice of various tempting entrées including a scrumptious platter of sautéed shrimp on a mound of creamed grits and caramelized onions in a chopped tomato and fresh thyme sauce. At lunch, there are hearty sandwiches such as seared tuna on sourdough bread with arugula, bacon and saffron aïoli. Meals here include an assortment of fresh-baked breads such as wheatberry, onion focaccia, and moist cornbread studded with chewy creamed-corn niblets. Either meal, save room for a dessert of buttery-crusted lemon chess pie with strawberry sauce—or pig out over a dessert sampler plate. Tapas are served in the very simpatico adjoining Onion Bar. A carefully chosen wine list highlights American vintages.

EXPENSIVE

Asia Nora

2213 M St. NW. ☎ **202/797-4860.** Reservations recommended. Main courses $18–$22.50. MC, V. Mon–Thurs 5:45–10pm, Fri–Sat 5:45–10:30pm. Metro: Dupont Circle or Foggy Bottom. ASIAN FUSION.

Long-time gourmet-organic restaurant queen Nora Pouillon (see Nora above) expanded her food concept in 1994 with Asia Nora. Although her new cuisine remains healthful and organic, the setting evokes the adventure-movie glamour of the 1930s. Gold-flecked jade walls display Asian artifacts (Philippine rice baskets, Japanese teashop signs, Balinese puppets, kimonos, coolie hats) framed in mahogany paneling and the waitstaff is attired in black silk pajamas. Like Nora, this is a big celebrity haunt where you might spot stars (Jane Fonda and Ted Turner, Steven Spielberg and Kate Capshaw) and Washington notables (Tipper Gore, Janet Reno, George Stephanopoulos) at adjoining tables.

The Asian fusion concept implies an intermingling of diverse Asian cuisines. Hence, appetizers run the gamut from grilled scallops (marinated in Japanese peppers, ginger, and olive oil, topped with cilantro chutney, and served atop Asian greens and raita) to paper-thin slices of salmon sashimi dotted with wasabi sauce and served with crunchy Thai cucumber/peanut salad. An entrée of sake-sauced teriyaki salmon is accompanied by Chinese sticky rice and served on a "mountain" of summer vegetables. More geographically unified is a thali tray of chicken curry, basmati rice, chutney, dahl, vegetables, raita, and Indian breads. Although the wine list has been constructed to complement boldly flavored Asian dishes, I find hot sake goes well with everything. Desserts—such as a grilled banana with coconut sorbet, passionfruit ice cream, and chocolate and caramel sauces—maintain the Asian theme.

✪ Gabriel

In the Radisson Barceló Hotel, 2121 P St. NW. ☎ **202/293-3100.** Reservations recommended. Main courses $7.25–$13.50 at lunch, $13.25–$18.50 at dinner. AE, CB, DC, DISC, MC, V. Mon–Sat 11:30am–2:30pm, Sun–Thurs 6–10:30pm; Fri–Sat 6–11pm; Sun 11:30am–3pm; tapas and bar daily 11:30am–midnight. Metro: Dupont Circle. SPANISH/MEDITERRANEAN.

Gabriel, opened in 1994, brought an exciting new cuisine and a sophisticated setting to the Washington dining scene. Its warmly inviting interior, in sienna and turquoise, offers seating in roomy upholstered mahogany armchairs, booths, and banquettes. Cafe-au-lait stucco walls are hung with colorful prints, cafe curtains adorn high windows, and soft lighting flatters diners. A large rectangular mahogany bar is the centerpiece of a convivial lounge area. Noted Washington chef Greggory Hill, who years ago honed his craft as sous-chef at the French embassy, spent months studying with major chefs in various parts of Spain and Mexico before creating Gabriel's dazzlingly innovative—and ever-changing—menu.

You can graze on tapas at the bar or begin a meal with them—perhaps Salvadorean pupusas (chili-flavored corn/potato pancakes) served with large grilled scallops and chunks of hot and spicy chorizo sausage in a smoked garlic/cilantro cream sauce; they come with a side of cayenne slaw. And many dishes can be ordered in appetizer or entrée portions—among them flour tortillas filled with rotisserie shredded duck and sweet corn mushrooms, served with tomatillo/smoked-jalapeño salsa and feta cheese garnish. Less exotic but equally satisfying is rotisserie free-range chicken with lemony-herb gravy, grilled eggplant slices, and garlic mashed potatoes. Resist the temptation to fill up on crusty-chewy fresh-baked sourdough bread dipped in rosemary/garlic-infused olive oil. There's a good wine list, with several by-the-glass selections including dry and sweet sherries—the ideal complement to tapas. Incredible desserts here include a phyllo purse stuffed with custard, papaya, pineapple, berries, and pistachio nuts; it's poised atop cinnamon custard marbleized with apricot raspberry coulis.

○ Iron Gate Restaurant & Garden

1734 N St. NW. ☎ **202/737-1370.** Reservations recommended. Main courses $8.50–$13.50 at lunch, $15.50–$19 at dinner. AE, MC, V. Mon–Fri 11:30am–5pm; Mon–Sat 5–10pm, Sun 5–9pm. Closed Sun July–Aug. Metro: Dupont Circle. MEDITERRANEAN.

Housed in a converted 19th-century stable, the Iron Gate is probably Washington's most romantic dining venue. In winter, it's the coziest place in town: A big fire blazes in an immense brick fireplace hung with gleaming copper pots, and the smell of burning wood is as alluring as the aromas emerging from the kitchen. Exposed brick walls are hung with exquisite dried flower arrangements and wreaths. There's additional seating upstairs in a room with another working fireplace. And spring through fall, you can dine alfresco under a grape-and-wisteria arbor in an enchanting brick-walled garden with a splashing fountain and lovingly tended flower beds.

Everything is prepared with finesse using the freshest and finest possible ingredients. An excellent beginning is a baked goat-cheese torte with charred-pepper coulis. There are fantastic soups such as potato-leek topped with lebne (rich, creamy drained yogurt) and parsley. And the mesclun salad is a refreshing mix of greens with chopped tomato and crumbled goat cheese in a tasty balsamic vinaigrette. Entrées are served with fresh-baked focaccia breads (herb, parmesan, walnut, sun-dried tomato). A totally satisfying pasta dish is tagliatelle tossed with grilled shrimp, pancetta, and sugar peas. Crisp-skinned roast free-range chicken (you'll taste the difference) is served with fresh veggies and garlic mashed potatoes. And there's also a savory vegetable tajine with couscous. Divine desserts include a chocolate-truffle pie with dark cookie crust on a raspberry coulis topped with fresh whipped cream. There's a full bar, a good choice of wines, even fresh-squeezed lemonade. Keep the Iron Gate in mind not only for meals, but as the perfect place for leisurely afternoon tea/espresso/cappuccino or cocktails.

Obelisk

2029 P St. NW. ☎ 202/872-1180. Reservations recommended. Prix-fixe four-course dinners only: $38. DC, MC, V. Mon–Sat 6–10pm. Metro: Dupont Circle. ITALIAN REGIONAL.

Charming and intimate (there are only 17 tables), Obelisk occupies the second floor of a former town house. Coffee-hued walls with cream crown moldings are hung with beautiful gilt-framed 19th-century French botanical prints and Italian lithographs. A wine rack cupboard occupies one wall, and a central table is used for an aesthetically appealing display of wines, biscotti, breadsticks, and beautifully arranged flowers.

Here owner/chef Peter Pastan prepares his small prix-fixe menus nightly, using the freshest possible ingredients and baking scrumptious breads and desserts daily. "My culinary philosophy," says Pastan is to "get the best stuff we can and try not to screw it up." In this quest, he is markedly successful. Each night's menu offers diners two or three choices for each course, all of them expertly prepared. Recently I began dinner here with an antipasti of grilled semolina bread topped with a garlicky ratatouille-like eggplant confit/tomato stew and skewers of grilled shrimp. This was followed by a large bowl of homemade noodles tossed with fresh peas (both perfectly al dente), shavings of prosciutto, and freshly grated Parmesan. The main course was a flavorful grilled pompano in parsley/anchovy sauce, served with haricots verts (grilled lamb loin with pan-fried artichokes and potatoes in rosemary balsamic vinaigrette was another option). A small cheese course was comprised of a slice of hot-pepper pecorino with an almond-stuffed dried fig. And for dessert there was a rich, moist, flourless hazelnut-chocolate torte topped with whipped cream. Pastan's carefully crafted wine list, like his menu, encompasses varied regions of Italy.

MODERATE

⑤ Café Petitto

1724 Connecticut Ave. NW (between R and S sts.). ☎ 202/462-8771. Reservations not accepted. Main courses $7.95–$12.95 at lunch, $8.95–$12.95 at dinner, $5.95–$9.25 at brunch; buffet lunch/brunch $8.95, buffet dinner $9.95; pizzas from $5.25; sandwiches and hoagies $5–$6.50; AE, DC, MC, V. Mon–Thurs 11:30am–midnight, Fri–Sat 11:30am–1am, Sun 11:30am–11pm. Metro: Dupont Circle. ITALIAN.

Café Petitto lures diners inside with an exquisite antipasto display in the front window—about 50 items including stringbean and fava-bean salads, marinated eggplant, snow peas with oil-cured olives, creamy egg salad, stuffed grape leaves, cold fried eggplant, pasta salads, escarole and pancetta, homemade potato salad, rice/peas/pepper salad, and much more. It's always changing, always fabulous, and you can eat all you want. Then there are the scrumptious Calabrian pizzas, on flavorful bread dough that's lightly fried in olive oil before toppings (more than 30 choices ranging from baby clams to sun-dried tomatoes) are added and the whole thing grilled.

A third menu category is sandwiches (for example, grilled eggplant, fresh mozzarella, pepper, and tomato on toasted peasant bread) served with roasted potatoes. Daily specials always include great pasta dishes. Italian wines are reasonably priced and available by the glass. And fresh-baked desserts—such as ricotta cheesecake and pecan spice cake with caramel sauce—change daily. Additional breakfast items such as eggs Benedict are offered at brunch, but you can't beat the lavish all-you-can-eat buffet for value and quality.

The original dining room here has pine-wainscoted walls hung with a veritable Petitto family photo album. A gorgeous adjoining bar (open till 3am nightly and a good choice for happy hour) and a sunken dining room were added in 1993. Arrive off-hours to avoid waiting in line.

⑤ City Lights of China

1731 Connecticut Ave. NW (between R and S sts.). ☎ **202/265-6688.** Reservations recommended. Main courses mostly $5.95–$9.95 at lunch, $6.95–$11.95 at dinner (a few are pricier). AE, CB, DC, DISC, MC, V. Mon–Thurs 11:30am–10:30pm, Fri 11:30am–11pm, Sat noon–11pm, Sun noon–10:30pm (dinner from 3pm daily). Metro: Dupont Circle. CHINESE.

George McGovern, Jesse Jackson, Bruce Babbitt, and political commentator Martin Agronsky are just a few of the many Washington insiders who make City Lights a regular stop on their dining itinerary. Even Mick Jagger came in several times while playing D.C. Like myself, they're hooked on the irresistible Mandarin/Cantonese/Szechuan dishes prepared by talented Taiwanese chef (and part owner) Kuo-Tai Soug. The setting is pretty but unpretentious—a three-tiered dining room with much of the seating in comfortable pale-green leather booths and banquettes. Neat white-linen-covered tables set with peach napkins, cloth flower arrangements in lighted niches, and green neon track lighting complete the picture.

There are wonderful appetizers such as crisp-fried Cornish hen prepared in a cinnamon-soy marinade and served with a tasty dipping sauce, garlicky Chinese eggplant with a hot red-pepper tang, sesame noodles tossed with shreds of cucumber and scrambled eggs, and plump, delicious dumplings (steamed or pan-fried) stuffed with artfully seasoned pork, chives, scallions, and green peppers. As for entrées, the pièce de résistance (listed under "chef's specialties") is the crisp fried shredded beef—a delicate mix of finely julienned beef, carrot, scallion, and celery in a crunchy peppercorn hot-caramel sweet glaze. Also exemplary here: stir-fried spinach (richly flavored with sesame and garlic) and pan-fried noodles (a crunchy Chinese kugel topped with shrimps, scallops, and vegetables). There's a full bar.

Kramerbooks & Afterwords, A Café

1517 Connecticut Ave. NW, (between Q St. and Dupont Circle). ☎ **202/387-1462.** Reservations not accepted. Main courses $7.75–$13.25. AE, DISC, MC, V. Mon–Thurs 7:30am–1am, around the clock Fri 7:30am–Mon 1am. Metro: Dupont Circle. AMERICAN.

This schmoozy bookstore-cum-cafe is the kind of congenial place you go for cappuccino after the movies, for an intense discussion of your love life over a platter of fettuccine, or to linger over a good book and a cognac (both of which can be purchased here) on a sunny afternoon. There's cozy seating indoors under a low beamed ceiling, at the bar (scene of monthly changing art exhibits), upstairs on a balcony, in a two-story glassed-in solarium, and at outdoor cafe tables.

The cafe opens early serving such items as cream cheese and Nova on a bagel. At Sunday brunch—served from 9:30am to 3pm—a glass of champagne or a Bloody Mary is just $1.25. Fare at lunch or dinner includes salads; hot entrées such as cheese-filled tortellini tossed with pancetta and field mushrooms in creamy basil Parmesan sauce; and sandwiches such as sliced chicken breast with hickory bacon, grilled sweet peppers, and onion on a sourdough bun. Meats are roasted on the premises, fish are fresh, and there are many vegetarian dishes. Other options include margaritas ($17.50 for a large pitcherful) served with nachos, banana splits and ice-cream sundaes, luscious desserts like chocolate/coconut/sour cream blackout cake, and rum-spiked ice-cream drinks, as well as a selection of premium wines offered by the glass. Wednesday through Saturday nights there's live entertainment—piano, folk, jazz, or blues.

⑤ Panevino Ristorante

In the Embassy Suites Hotel, 23rd and N sts. NW. ☎ **202/223-0747.** Reservations recommended. Main courses $6.75–$12.50 at lunch, $9.75–$14.95 at dinner (pizzas $6.75–$9.95); antipasti table $9.95; three-course early-bird dinner (5–8pm daily) $12.95; Fri night four-course seafood dinner $19.95; three-course Sun brunch $16.95. AE, CB, DC, JCB, MC, V. Daily 11am–11pm. Metro: Foggy Bottom or Dupont Circle. CONTEMPORARY TUSCAN.

Under a ceiling painted to look like sky, Panevino's Tuscan farmhouse decor features country cabinets filled with colorful Italian pottery, twig wreaths, displays of bread, and a large rustic oak table overflowing with antipasti. On a more whimsical note, the walls are covered with inter-nationally commissioned woodcuts, paintings, and collages—hung like schoolchildren's art—that combine the restaurant's robbiana (wreath) theme with fruit, vegetables, food, and wine. At lunch Panevino is sedate, filled with local businesspeople; during the tourist season great food at low prices attracts scores of families for early dinners; arrive after 7:30pm to avoid the hubbub.

Hard to pass up is the sumptuous daily-changing antipasti table, laden with platters of tomato and mozzarella salad, bean salads, pasta salads, baked stuffed peppers, cold cuts, cheeses, marinated mushrooms, mussels, endives stuffed with couscous, olives, sausages, and much more—including extra-virgin olive oils and balsamic vinegars. With fresh-baked herbed focaccia and a pitcher of chianti, this makes for quite a meal. Other recommendables: pizzas (most notably the quattro formaggi), pastas (such as spinach and ricotta-stuffed ravioli), and calzizza—a half calzone stuffed with chopped arugula, fontina and fresh mozzarella cheeses, basil, and chopped tomatoes. Or you could choose a full entrée (served with soup or salad) such as salmon grilled in seasoned olive butter with seasonal vegetables. Focaccia sandwiches are another choice at lunch. The specialty dessert is sogno nero (black dream)—a chocolate/almond cake filled with chocolate mousse and served atop raspberry coulis. A comfortable bar/lounge adjoins.

INEXPENSIVE

✪ Pizzeria Paradiso

2029 P St. NW. ☎ **202/223-1245.** Reservations not accepted. Pizzas $6.50–$15.75, sandwiches and salads $3.95–$5.95. DC, MC, V. Mon–Thurs 11am–11pm, Fri–Sat 11am–midnight, Sun noon–10pm. Metro: Dupont Circle. ITALIAN REGIONAL PIZZA AND PANINI

Another Peter Pastan establishment (see Obelisk above), Pizzeria Paradiso is also housed on the second floor of a Dupont Circle town house. Pristinely charming, its arched trompe l'oeil ceiling is painted to suggest blue sky peeping through ancient stone walls. An exhibition kitchen at the far end of the room basks in the rosy glow of an oak-burning pizza oven.

Since there are only about 16 tables, it is best to come either early or late to avoid waiting for a table. Everything served here is exceptional, and the secret is out. Even before you order, your server will bring a small dish of delicious mixed olives, and you'll find herbed extra-virgin olive oil on the table. You can order two types of toppings on a single pizza if you wish; I like the combination of Genovese (thin slices of redskin potatoes drizzled with pesto and fresh Parmesan) and quattro formaggi studded with chunks of fresh garlic. Also on the menu are panini (sandwiches) such as homemade focaccia stuffed with chilled garlic- and oregano-marinated roast lamb, roasted vegetables (eggplant, red peppers, tomatoes, onions), and fresh spinach leaves. And there are great salads such as tuna and white bean or Tuscan bread and vegetables (ask for balsamic vinegar on the side, grated parmigiano reggiano, and fresh-baked focaccia to soak up the dressing). For dessert, the tira misu is excellent, but even better are the baked pears marsala topped with crumbled biscotti and the creamy flavorful homemade ice creams. There's a small Italian wine list, and the coffee here is rich and freshly brewed.

❸ Trio

1537 17th St. NW (at Q St.). ☎ **202/232-6305.** Reservations not accepted. Main courses $4.25–$8.50 at lunch and dinner; burgers and sandwiches $1.75–$5; full breakfasts $2.75–$5.95. AE, MC, V. Daily 7:30am–midnight. Metro: Dupont Circle (Q Street exit). AMERICAN.

The Trio is a real find. Its comfortable and roomy red leather booths (the kind with coathooks) are filled each morning with local residents checking out the *Washington Post* over big platters of bacon and eggs. There are fresh flowers on every table, and in warm weather, the awning-covered outdoor cafe is always packed. The Trio has been around for four decades—originally Pete and Helen Mallios's mom-and-pop business, now run by son George; it's something of a Washington legend.

The food is fresh and you can't beat the prices. The same menu is offered throughout the day, but there are very low-priced lunch specials such as crabcakes with tartar sauce, grilled pork chops with applesauce, turkey with cornbread dressing and cranberry sauce, and fried oysters—all served with two side dishes (perhaps baked macaroni au gratin and buttered fresh carrots) and a beverage. The same kind of specials are featured at dinner, when they also include fabulous home-made soups and a dessert such as homemade rice pudding. In addition, an extensive menu features such typical coffee-shop fare as a chef's salad, chili con carne, and a turkey-salad sandwich. There's a full bar, so a glass of wine with your meal is an option. In fact, there's a surprisingly extensive wine list. A soda fountain turns out hot-fudge sundaes and milkshakes. And that's not all—specialty drinks (Irish coffee topped with whipped cream, a Fuzzy Navel, and others) are also available at this eclectic eatery.

6 Foggy Bottom/Georgetown

VERY EXPENSIVE

✪ Citronelle

In the Latham hotel, 3000 M St. NW. ☎ **202/625-2150.** Reservations recommended. Main courses mostly $10.50–$14.95 at lunch/brunch, $23–$29 at dinner; three-course pretheater dinner (until 6:30pm) $30, five- and six-course prix-fixe dinners $50 and $60, respectively (for $100 the latter dinner includes wines and a tour of the kitchen). AE, CB, DC, DISC, JCB, MC, V. Daily 6:30–10:30am, 11am–3pm, and 5:30–10:30pm. Complimentary valet parking at dinner. CONTEMPORARY FRENCH.

Citronelle is an East Coast branch of Los Angeles's famed Citrus—the creation of exuberant French chef Michel Richard. A Richard meal is like no other: Each dish provides a wondrous explosion of tastes and crispy-crunchy textures; the dazzling presentations enhance the taste sensation. The bilevel atrium setting is charming—vaguely French country, with oak plank floors, a stone wall, and a rustic pine table displaying wines and a lavish flower arrangement. The gallery-white walls are hung with a changing art show, and candlelit tables—some in intimate alcoves—are set amid potted palms and other greenery.

A signature appetizer is sautéed foie gras with translucently thin slices of warm poached beets and fresh figs in a port wine balsamic sauce. Another, of pan-seared cognac-spiked crabcakes came enfolded in crisp Moroccan spring-roll skins on a bed of crunchy Savoy cabbage slaw drizzled with mint vinaigrette. An entrée of peppered and piquantly sauced tuna steak quick-sautéed and served rare, was poised atop a sunburst of kataifi (a kind of Mediterranean shredded wheat) on a bed of potato-leek salad vinaigrette. And most sublime was a fan of pan-seared and roasted Muscovy duck surrounding a feuilleté cornucopia anchored in a dollop of garnished mashed potatoes and filled with couscous and sun-dried fruits; it was served with a crisp-skinned duck leg and garnished with plump Bing cherries cooked in port wine. The dessert of choice: sumptuous, velvety hot chocolate cake enhanced with orange/ginger sauce. Citronelle's extensive wine list offers 17 premium by-the-glass selections.

✪ Jean-Louis

In the Watergate Hotel, 2650 Virginia Ave. NW. ☎ **202/298-4488.** Reservations required. Pretheater four-course dinner $45; five-course dinner $85, six-course dinner $95, not including wine, tax, or gratuity. AE, CB, DC, DISC, MC, V. Tues–Sat 5:30–10pm; pretheater seating from 5:30–6:15pm, second seating 8–8:30pm. Free valet parking. Metro: Foggy Bottom. FRENCH.

One of Washington's most prestigious restaurants—under the auspices of one of America's most brilliant imported French chefs, Jean-Louis Palladin—occupies an unlikely precinct—the basement of the Watergate Hotel. This intimate dining room (it seats only 42) is entered via a glass-walled corridor where the restaurant's extensive wine offerings (750 labels, most of them French) are displayed. Its interior decor features an arrangement of back-lit gold and copper silk banners, flower-bedecked tables covered in white napery and lit by hurricane lamp candles, a mirrored tile ceiling, and soft green carpeting. Its most notable feature, however, is a panel of mirrors that girds the room at eye level, allowing diners to scope the crowd without being conspicuous.

Jean-Louis began his culinary apprenticeship at the age of 12 in his native Gascony, and, by the time he was 28, he had his own Michelin two-star establishment there. Enticed by an American ambassador, he came to Washington in 1979 to open his eponymous Watergate restaurant. He defines his "instinctive" cuisine as grounded in rich classical gastronomy but seasoned with the magic of inspiration and spontaneity.

His prix-fixe menus change nightly. What comprises a typical $95 six-course dinner? Let me tantalize you with one I recently enjoyed. After we had been seated, a complimentary nugget of smoked salmon arrived at our table, followed by a quail egg nestled in toasted brioche with ossetra caviar garnish. The first actual course was chestnut soup (a rich chicken-broth-based purée of chestnuts, ham, shallots, and foie gras) afloat with chicken wings stuffed with wild mushrooms and delicate quenelles filled with chestnut meat and black truffles. Next came a plate of lightly smoked halibut gravlax atop a mélange of seaweeds in ginger dressing. Duck foie gras came on a sweetish quince–duck jus purée with poached quince garnish. This was followed by broiled fresh rouget (red mullet) seasoned with thyme and rosemary and served with a julienne of pumpkin sautéed with cardamom and cumin and spiced pumpkin coulis. Roasted noisettes of Texas venison in a red wine–venison reduction sauce were accompanied by a gratin de pommes. And dessert was a napoleonlike almond feuilleté layered with dried, sweetened pineapple and served on blueberry coulis with a dollop of pineapple sherbet. Like the wines recommended for each course by friendly sommelier Vincent Feraud, the breads also change with each course (anchovy-buttered brioches, country French breads, and others).

○ Morton's of Chicago

3251 Prospect St. NW. ☎ **202/342-6258.** Reservations recommended. Main courses $15.95–$29.95. AE, CB, DC, JCB, MC, V. Mon–Sat 5:30–11pm, Sun 5–10pm. Free valet parking. STEAKS/CHOPS/SEAFOOD.

Part of a national restaurant empire created by Arnie Morton, a flamboyant former Playboy Enterprises executive, this superb steak house attracts a celebrity-studded clientele: You might spot James Carville and Mary Matalin, Janet Reno, CNN's Larry King, or Sen. Ted Kennedy among the beef eaters. It's also a favorite of athletes; the Washington

Redskins once served as waiters for a Special Olympics fundraiser here. And National Symphony Orchestra conductor Mstislav Rostropovich dined here one night with a famous classical pianist, both wearing headphones! But, basically, one comes to eat, not gawk at the glitterati.

Huge portions of succulent USDA prime midwestern beef and scrumptious side dishes are the real attraction. Start off with an appetizer such as smoked Pacific salmon or a lump-crabmeat cocktail served with rémoulade sauce. Steaks (rib eye, double filet mignon, porterhouse, or New York sirloin) are perfectly prepared to your specifications. Other entrée choices include prime rib, fresh swordfish steak, and baked Maine lobster. Side orders of flavorfully fresh al dente asparagus served with hollandaise or hash browns are highly recommended. A loaf of onion bread on every table is complimentary. Consider taking home a doggy bag if you want to leave room for dessert—perhaps a soufflé Grand Marnier or rich and creamy cheesecake.

Morton's plush interior is cozy and convivial. Large framed LeRoy Nieman sports prints adorn wainscoted stucco walls, and seating is in comfortable cream-colored leather booths at white-linened tables lit by pewter oil lamps in the shape of donkeys or elephants.

✪ Provence

2401 Pennsylvania Ave. NW. ☎ **202/296-1166.** Reservations recommended. Main courses $10.50–$18 at lunch, $13.50–$24 at dinner. AE, CB, DC, MC, V. Mon–Fri noon–2pm; Mon–Wed 6–10pm, Thurs–Sat 5:30–11pm. Complimentary valet parking evenings. Metro: Foggy Bottom. FRENCH.

For more than a decade French chef Yannick Cam reigned over the peerless Le Pavillon, where his ultra-haute multicourse meals were once described as "evolving poetry." Ever versatile, he's now created two exciting (but, in the spirit of the '90s, decidedly less pricey and formal) new establishments—this and the exuberant Coco Loco (details in "Downtown" section, above). Not that Provence isn't elegant; Washington insiders will immediately note the presence of distinguished former Jockey Club maître d' Martin Garbisu, who was dubbed "the city's real chief of protocol" by Pat Buchanan. Enhanced by an exhibition kitchen arrayed with gleaming copperware, Provence's interior is country French, with terra-cotta floors, cafe-curtained windows lined with flowering potted plants, dried-flower arrangements, and grapevine-motif iron-grillwork dividers. Panels of rough-hewn stone are framed by rustic shutters, antique hutches display provincial pottery, and delicate chandeliers and shaded sconces provide a soft amber glow.

Cam's provençale cuisine "personalisée" refers to his unique interpretations of traditional Mediterranean recipes, which lose nothing in the way of regional integrity. An appetizer of pan-roasted young squid—stuffed with finely ground scallops and shrimp, sautéed shallots and garlic, wild mushrooms, parsley, toasted pine nuts, and lavender blossoms—was complemented by buttery pan juice. An entrée of escalloped Alaskan sockeye salmon—grilled over oak, apple, and cherry woods to tender, smoky perfection—was served over spinach in a dill sauce. And crisp-skinned organic roast chicken—perfumed with bay leaf, rosemary, sweet garlic, and a soupçon of anchovy—was accompanied by roasted potatoes and artichoke hearts sauced with a superb mélange of flavors—red wine, citrus, tomato concassé, garlic, chopped olives, and rosemary-infused olive oil. Cam's chewy herbed breads are perfect for soaking up sauces. For dessert, two large dollops of praline-studded white chocolate mousse were sandwiched between delicate crunchy almond waffles. The knowledgeable waitstaff can suggest appropriate wines from the 90%-French list.

✪ Seasons

In the Four Seasons hotel, 2800 Pennsylvania Ave. NW. ☎ **202/944-2000.** Reservations recommended. Main courses $12.75–$18 at lunch, $16–$29 at dinner. AE, CB, DC, ER, JCB, MC, V. Mon–Fri noon–2:30pm; nightly 6–10:30pm. Free valet parking. CONTINENTAL.

Seasons, the signature restaurant of one of Washington's most upscale hotels, has replaced posh dining room formality with a more casual approach. Although the room is gorgeous, the atmosphere is relaxed, there's no dress code, and the waitstaff and wine captains are friendly and unintimidating. Diners are comfortably ensconced in plush booths, neoclassic-design club chairs, or boardroom chairs regally upholstered in hunter green, burgundy, or black velvet. Elegantly appointed tables—adorned with orchids, white freesia, or flowering plants in small clay pots—are draped in white linen over black-and-white table skirts depicting scenes of ancient Rome. Slate floors are strewn with black wool carpets abloom with red and white roses on a green trellis. And glossy hunter-green lacquer walls display Italian engravings of birds from an 18th-century text. Seasons is candlelit at night; during the day light streams in from a wall of windows overlooking the C&O Canal.

Scottish chef William Douglas McNeill's cuisine focuses on fresh market fare. In search of the highest quality ingredients, he plucks baby lettuces from the garden just hours before serving, raises free-range venison on a 600-acre Texas ranch, and has fresh fish flown in from Maine and Florida within hours of the catch. And his passion for wine is behind Seasons' extensive and *recherché* list encompassing major wine-growing regions of France and California as well as vintage ports.

The menu changes seasonally. A recent dinner offered an appetizer of seared raw tuna médaillons in a spicy pocket of saffroned raw and smoked salmon on a julienne of snow peas and Japanese seaweed. Another choice was ravioli stuffed with julienned wild mushrooms and a nugget of goose foie gras on a truffle-infused tomato-butter sauce. An entrée of crisp-fried sea bass was served on a bed of julienned and gingered Oriental vegetables. And roast rack of lamb encrusted with Indian spices came with saffroned rice studded with raisins, pine nuts, morsels of dried apricot, pistachios, and slivered almonds. Meals are accompanied by a basket of scrumptious fresh-baked breads—rosemary flat bread, sun-dried tomato bread drizzled with Parmesan, and others. Desserts might range from ambrosial mango crème brûlée garnished with mint and crème fraîche to a warm apple tart on caramel sauce marbleized with crème anglaise and topped with homemade honey ice cream.

✪ 1789

1226 36th St. NW (at Prospect St.). ☎ **202/965-1789.** Reservations recommended. Main courses $18–$29, prix-fixe pretheater menu $25. AE, DC, DISC, MC, V.

Sun–Thurs 6–10pm, Fri 6–11pm, Sat 5–11pm. Complimentary valet parking.
AMERICAN REGIONAL.

The restaurant 1789 (its name commemorates not the French Revolution but the year the village of Georgetown was incorporated) is as cozy as a country inn. Housed in a Federal town house, its intimate dining areas are typified by the John Carroll Room, where walls are hung with Currier and Ives prints and old city maps, a log fire blazes in the hearth, and a gorgeous flower arrangement is displayed atop a hunting-themed oak sideboard. Throughout, silk-shaded brass oil lamps provide romantic lighting at crisp, white-linened tables set with Limoges china; 1789 is a virtual decorative arts museum of period furnishings and museum-quality paintings, prints, and objets d'art. It's also one of the city's prime see-and-be-seen dining venues, where you might spot anyone from Bill and Hillary Clinton to Stacy Keach at the next table.

The menus change seasonally. A recent one offered appetizers of basil-potato stuffed dumplings (garnished with julienned Petrossian smoked salmon in a light and lemony cream sauce) and grilled Gulf Coast shrimp coated with bourbon-pecan barbecue sauce and served on a bed of fresh sweet corn purée. An entrée of roast rack of lamb with garlicky Napa goat-cheese crust was served au jus on an array of sautéed mixed southern greens with potatoes au gratin. Also notable were lumpmeat crabcakes (with zesty infusions of garlic, cayenne, and Dijon mustard) served with fire-roasted tomato sauce, grilled ratatouille, and Cheddar-cheese grits. Homemade breads such as basil Parmesan and whole-wheat walnut accompany entrées, desserts might range from tira misu to pecan-crusted lemon soufflé pie with raspberry sauce, and the wine list is long and distinguished. A great bargain here: The pretheater menu offered nightly through 6:45pm includes appetizer, entrée, dessert, and coffee for just $25!

EXPENSIVE

✪ Palladin

In the Watergate Hotel, 2650 Virginia Ave NW. ☎ **202/298-4455.** Reservations recommended. Main courses $18–$32.50 at lunch or dinner (most under $22); sandwiches and salads $9.50–$14.50 at lunch; buffet brunch $35; three-course pretheater dinner $35. AE, CB, DC, DISC, MC, V. Daily 7–10:30am, 11:30am–2:30pm, 5:30–10:30pm (pretheater dinner till 7pm). Free valet parking. Metro: Foggy Bottom. FRENCH/MEDITERRANEAN.

This lovely dining room bears the name of Washington's famed French chef Jean-Louis Palladin (see Jean-Louis above), who oversees its kitchen. But the room's executive chef is Jean-Louis's sous-chef of many years, Moroccan Larbi Dahrouch, who adds a North African touch to his mentor's French menus. It's a gorgeous setting. Large windows provide beautiful views of the Potomac River and verdant Theodore Roosevelt Island beyond. Outside, a surrounding fence adorned with colorful planters of geraniums creates a pristine garden ambience; inside, the room is carpeted in forest green and crisply linened tables are flower-bedecked and elegantly appointed. At night pin-spot lighting envelops diners in a flattering rosy glow.

A recent menu (they change seasonally) included coconut and crab soup richly flavored with Thai kafir (lime) leaves, ginger, and lemongrass. A Moroccan appetizer of b'astilla combined layers of shredded free-range chicken, crushed almonds, and a hint of cilantro in brick-leaf pastry, the top dusted with powdered sugar and cinnamon. Dahrouch's entrée presentations are magnificent. Deep-fried turbot came wrapped in a crisp sculpted "potato net" with chive coulis. And tajine of lamb—flavored with orange flower water, saffron, and 25 Moroccan spices—with apricots spilled out from a feuilleté cornucopia filled with very fine couscous studded with morsels of carrot, zucchini, raisins, pearl onions, yellow squash, and turnips. The largely French wine list is extensive. Desserts range from a Grand Marnier soufflé to a rich Belgian chocolate tart served on marbleized crème anglaise. Keep Palladin in mind when you're attending performances at the Kennedy Center, and for breakfast or lunch if you're touring the facilities. A lavish buffet Sunday brunch here includes unlimited champagne.

Paolo's

1303 Wisconsin Ave. NW (at N St.). ☎ **202/333-7353.** Reservations accepted at lunch and brunch only. Pastas $8.25–$16.95, pizzas $6.95–$9.95, main courses $12.95–$16.95. AE, CB, DC, DISC, MC, MOST, V. Sun–Thurs 11:30am–midnight, Fri–Sat 11:30am–12:30am. Bar open (pizza is served) Sun–Thurs till 1am, Fri–Sat till 2am. CALIFORNIA-STYLE ITALIAN.

Restaurateur Paul Cohn is a virtuoso when it comes to creating a scene that crackles with excitement. "It's the closest thing to show business," he says. "You're on every night." I never tire of the show at Paolo's. For one thing, the setting is *molto simpático*. The tables spill out onto the street from an open-air patio, and the front room, with a stunning peach-hued Italian marble floor and black marble bar, basks in the warm glow of a pizza-oven fire. The back room, richly paneled in cherrywood and agleam with copper mirrors, also has an exhibition kitchen. Paolo's is a major D.C. see-and-be-seen celebrity haunt. Ted Kennedy, Tipper Gore, and Jack Kent Cooke come in often; Muhammed Ali signed autographs here one night; and when they were in town, Alec Baldwin and Kim Basinger ate lunch and dinner here for two days in a row!

A delightful surprise arrives as soon as you're seated—a bowl of tapenade (a Mediterranean spread of puréed olives, eggplant, chickpeas, and roasted red peppers) along with oven-fresh sesame-studded chewy breadsticks made from pizza dough. The same menu is offered all day. You can dine lightly on a pizza with toppings running the gamut from oak-grilled chicken to goat cheese. Pastas include such temptations as grilled garlic-fennel sausage served with peppers and onions over saffron fettuccine in marinara sauce. Among the nonpasta entrées is a mixed grill of jumbo shrimp wrapped around a sea scallop, médaillon of beef tenderloin, and marinated chicken breast, served with garlicky whipped potatoes and roasted vegetables. Wines, many available by the glass, are *de rigueur* with this food. Desserts include a white-chocolate banana-cream pie. Paolo's takes no reservations at dinner, so plan a before-dinner drink in the bar. There's live jazz Sundays from noon to 3pm.

The Sea Catch

1054 31st St. NW (just below M St.). ☎ **202/337-8855.** Reservations recommended. Main courses $7.75–$13.95 at lunch, mostly $15.75–$19.95 at dinner. AE, CB, DC, MC, V. Mon–Sat noon–3pm and 5:30–10:30pm. SEAFOOD.

Since I love the C&O Canal, I was especially thrilled when this stunning restaurant opened in 1988 offering canalside seating. Outside on the long awning-covered wooden deck, mulberry and ailanthus trees form a verdant archway over the canal. The marble-topped tables are romantically candlelit in the evening; by day, watch ducks, punters, and mule-drawn barges glide by while you dine. But don't pass up Sea Catch on days that are less than ideal for alfresco meals; the restaurant, housed in a historic Georgetown stone-and-brick building, is as beautiful within as without. There's a white Carrara-marble raw bar adorned with exquisite floral and food displays and backed by a rustic stone wall. A deluxe brasserie under a low inn-style beamed ceiling adjoins; large windows overlook the canal, and there's a working fireplace. And the main dining room—with its rift-sawn white oak ceiling, random-plank oak floor, and rough-hewn walls made of fieldstone dug from Georgetown quarries is also warmed by a working fireplace. Classic jazz tapes provide a fine acoustical background.

A dinner here might begin with an appetizer of white calamari rings marinated in lime juice and herbs served with grilled eggplant. Of course, plump farm-raised oysters, fresh Florida jumbo stone crabs with mustard sauce, and other raw-bar offerings also merit consideration. The entrée focus is on daily-changing fresh fish and seafood specials, such as big, fluffy jumbo lump crabcakes served with crunchy Oriental-style Napa cabbage slaw and pickled ginger mayonnaise. The kitchen willingly prepares fresh fish and seafood dishes to your specifications, including live lobster from the tanks. Don't miss the softshell crab amandine when it's in season here. At lunch seafood salads are a recommendable option. An extensive wine list highlights French, Italian, and American selections and features five premium wines by the glass each day. Fresh-baked desserts usually include an excellent key lime pie.

Sequoia

3000 K St. NW (at the Washington Harbour). ☎ **202/944-4200.** Reservations recommended (not accepted for outdoor seating). Main courses $10.95–$20.95, salads and sandwiches $7.95–$14.95. AE, DISC, MC, V. Sun–Thurs 11:30am–midnight, Fri–Sat 11:30am–1am. Paid parking available at the Harbour, discounted to restaurant patrons at dinner. AMERICAN REGIONAL.

In the Washington-restaurant-with-a-view category, no setting is more spectacular than Sequoia's terrace, where umbrella-shaded tables overlook the boat-filled Potomac between two bridges. It's especially magical at night, when London plane trees in large flower beds twinkle with hundreds of tiny lights. If the weather precludes alfresco dining, you can enjoy the same river vista from the soaring window-walled interior, an elegant balconied setting where Brazilian cherrywood floors and Frank Lloyd Wright–look mahogany chairs evoke redwood (can't chop down those sequoias anymore), and candlelit white-linened tables are adorned with sprays of fresh flowers. Although the view outshines the food, this is one of Washington's most popular restaurants; even the

Clintons often come in with Chelsea, and movie premiere parties are frequent events. It's a casual place; feel free to come in jeans. *Note:* The ambience is decidedly more romantic after 8pm, when families with rambunctious children have returned home.

The varied and extensive menu runs the gamut from burgers and fries to a warm grilled Thai chicken salad served over rice noodles tossed with bean sprouts, julienned carrots, scallions, and shredded cabbage in a spicy peanut dressing. I prefer the less complicated items here, such as grilled chicken brushed with basil oil and served with mashed potatoes and sautéed vegetables. Do save room for one of Sequoia's excellent desserts—perhaps southern-style cheesecake with brandy-soaked dried cherries and pecans in a graham-cracker/toasted-pecan crust. Many wines are offered by the glass, and regional beers and ales are featured. At Saturday and Sunday brunch the menu also includes omelets, smoked fish platters, brioche French toast, and other breakfast fare.

MODERATE

Aditi

3299 M St. NW. ☎ **202/625-6825.** Reservations recommended. Main courses $4.95–$7.50 at lunch, $6.95–$13.95 at dinner. AE, DC, DISC, MC, V. Mon–Sat 11:30am–2:30pm, Sun noon–2:30pm; Sun–Thurs 5:30–10pm, Fri–Sat 5:30–10:30pm. INDIAN.

This pristinely charming restaurant provides a serene setting in which to enjoy first-rate Indian cookery—the kind where everything is made from scratch and each dish is uniquely spiced and sauced. You enter a small, red-carpeted, cream-walled front room, where the tables are set with white linen, fresh flowers, and candles. Above the bar is a display of Kathakali figurines, representing the classic dance forms of India. A staircase spirals its way past niches filled with plants to the larger second-level dining space. Soft Indian music sets the tone for your meal.

A "must" here is the platter of assorted appetizers—bhajia (a deep-fried vegetable fritter), deep-fried cheese and shrimp pakoras, and crispy vegetable samosas stuffed with spiced potatoes and peas. Favorite entrées include lamb biryani, an aromatic saffron- and rosewater-flavored basmati rice pilaf tossed with savory pieces of lamb, cilantro, raisins, and almonds. I also love the chicken pasanda (in a mild yogurt-cream sauce seasoned with onion, cumin, fresh cilantro, and almond paste) and the skewered jumbo tandoori prawns, chicken, lamb, or beef—all fresh and fork tender—barbecued in the tandoor (clay oven). Sauces are on the mild side, so if you like your food fiery, inform your waiter. A kachumber salad—topped with yogurt and spices—is a refreshing accompaniment to entrées. Fresh-from-the-tandoor baked breads (like hot, chewy naan) also merit consideration. For dessert, try kheer, a cooling rice pudding garnished with chopped nuts. There's a full bar, including a nice choice of wines.

Clyde's

3236 M St. NW. ☎ **202/333-9180.** Reservations recommended. Burgers, ribs, omelets, salads, sandwiches $5.50–$10.95; lunch specials $6.95–$10.95; brunch specials $4.25–$8.95; dinner specials $8.95–$15.95. AE, DC, DISC, MC, V. Mon–Thurs 11:30am–2am, Fri 11:30am–3am, Sat 9am–3am, Sun 9am–2am; brunch Sat–Sun 9am–4pm. AMERICAN.

Clyde's has been a favorite watering hole for an eclectic mix of Washingtonians since 1963. You'll see university students, Capitol Hill types, affluent professionals, Washington Redskins, romantic duos, and well-heeled "ladies who lunch" bogged down with shopping bags from Georgetown's posh boutiques.

The restaurant consists of a warren of pubby bars and cozy dining areas. The Back Room has wide-plank oak floors, dark oak walls, and amber globe lamps overhead. Ornate brass filigree antique elevator doors divide this room from the Main Bar, which is always mobbed at night. The smaller Atrium Bar has a train theme, with railroad lamps flanking an 1880s mother-of-pearl-inlaid painting of the *Rocky Mountain Limited.* The sunnier Omelette Room, up front, lit by authentic gaslight sconces, features an exhibition kitchen under a copper hood. And the light and airy brick-walled Patio Room is a lush jungle setting with dozens of plants, trees, vines, and ferns flourishing under a skylight ceiling. Big papier-mâché toucans and parrots amid the lush foliage add to the tropical ambience.

At weekend brunch you can get terrific omelets prepared to order or eggs Benedict with thinly sliced smoked salmon. Throughout the day the menu lists burgers, homemade soups, delicious Maryland lump crabmeat sandwiches, award-winning chili, hickory-smoked barbecued ribs, and salads—plus daily specials such as fresh-made fettuccine (tossed with Cajun andouille sausage, tomatoes, and herbs) or thin-sliced London broil served with roasted potatoes and a vegetable. A special snack menu offered from 4 to 7pm features "Afternoon Delights" ($2.50 to $4) such as beer-batter shrimp with orange-mustard sauce. Beverage choices range from premium wines by the glass, to Clyde's famous lager, to a milkshake made with Ben & Jerry's ice cream. For dessert, a rich mousse made from Belgian Callebaut chocolate merits attention.

⑤ Houston's

1065 Wisconsin Ave. NW (just below M St.). ☎ **202/338-7760.** Reservations not accepted. Main courses $6.25–$17.95 (most under $12). AE, MC, V. Sun–Thurs 11:15am–11pm, Fri–Sat 11:15am–1am. AMERICAN.

Arrive before or after peak lunch and dinner hours to avoid long lines at the very popular Houston's, where the barbecued ribs are tender and juicy enough to eat with a knife and fork, the large and delicious burgers are made from fresh-ground chuck, and the soups, salads, and desserts are prepared from scratch. A very simpatico ambience further enhances this restaurant's appeal. Exposed brick walls are hung with framed mirrors and an old American flag, and there are rough-hewn wood rafters overhead. Most seating is in roomy red leather booths at oak tables, lighting—from dark-green enamel lamps with amber bulbs and flickering gaslight sconces—is subdued, and the background music is mellow rock and country.

The same menu is offered throughout the day. A hickory-grilled cheeseburger is served with a choice of iron skillet beans, couscous,

Family-Friendly Restaurants

Dirksen Senate Office Building South Buffet Room *(see p. 133)*
Getting here involves a subway ride through the belly of the Capitol;
there's a reduced price for children, and, for dessert, a make-your-own-
sundae bar.

Flight Line *(see p. 136)* At this airy, very pleasant cafeteria the kids
can dig into burgers and pizza, while adults enjoy many other options, even wine. Before you arrive, pick up astronaut freeze-dried
ice cream for the kids at any museum shop, an intriguing dessert.

Union Station Food Court *(see p. 139)* Something for everyone,
and the setting is very pleasant.

Houston's *(see p. 125)* Burgers, barbecue, and an ice-cream-topped
brownie for dessert.

Sholl's Cafeteria *(see p. 107)* Pleasant surroundings, a wide choice
of freshly made high-quality fare, and low, low prices. You can't beat
it with a stick.

fries, or coleslaw. You can choose two of these side dishes with an
order of barbecued chicken breast or ribs. If you're in the mood for
something heartier, there's prime rib with a baked potato, creamed
spinach, and house or Caesar salad; something lighter might be a grilled
chicken salad tossed with honey-lime vinaigrette and garnished with a
light peanut sauce. The bar serves drinks made with premium liquor
brands only and fresh-squeezed juices. For dessert, an immense chewy
brownie topped with vanilla ice cream and Kahluá is hard to surpass.

La Ruche

1039 31st St. NW (a block below M St.). ☎ **202/965-2684.** Reservations
recommended. Main courses $6.50–$8.50 at lunch, $9–$14.50 at dinner; prix-fixe
brunch $9.95. AE, MC, V. Mon–Fri 11:30am–midnight, Sat 10am–1am, Sun 10am–
11pm; brunch Sat–Sun 10am–3pm. COUNTRY FRENCH.

This is a pretty plant-filled restaurant with cushioned wicker-seated
chairs, flower-bedecked tables (candlelit at night), and white walls
adorned with framed art posters, French street signs, and baskets. The
French countryside ambience is furthered by an outdoor courtyard café
with umbrella tables amid lots of plants.

   Inside, your eye is likely to be caught by the pastry case filled with
exquisite fresh-baked desserts ranging from a gâteau amande chocolat
layered with meringue and whipped cream to a classic tarte aux
pommes. Many people take an afternoon break from Georgetown
rambles just for dessert and coffee here. Throughout the day menu
offerings include a hearty potage parisien with fresh chopped leeks,
potatoes, and cream; salade niçoise; a wedge of Brie with apple and
French bread; croque-monsieur (toasted French bread with ham and
cheese); and escargots aux champignons—all the traditional specialties
of a Paris brasserie. In addition, there are daily "spécialités du chef
Jean-Claude," which might include mussels niçoises, bouillabaisse,
Algerian couscous, and a duck à l'orange served with tomatoes

provençal, haricots verts, and sautéed potatoes. There's a full bar, and wines are offered by the bottle, glass, and carafe. A three-course Early "Bee" dinner served from 5 to 7pm costs $13.95, including tea or coffee. And the prix-fixe brunch includes a mimosa, entrée, and pastry.

INEXPENSIVE

✪ Dean & Deluca

3276 M St. NW. ☎ **202/342-2500.** Croissants, muffins, and breakfast pastries $1.95–$3; sandwiches, salads, and hot dishes $4–$5.95. AE, MC, MOST, V. Cafe, Sun–Thurs 9am–8pm, Fri–Sat 9am–10pm, with extended hours in summer. Store, Sun–Thurs 10am–8pm, Fri–Sat 10am–9pm. INTERNATIONAL.

Occupying an 1865 markethouse, this renowned fine food emporium (I think of its aesthetically presented culinary offerings as "museum quality") adjoins an awning-covered brick-walled and brick-floored café with forest-green and cream wicker-weave bamboo bistro chairs at marble-topped tables. It's rather European in feel; you can even buy *Le Figaro* at the counter. Come by in the morning for scrumptious buttery almond and chocolate croissants, scones, and fresh-baked muffins with espresso or cappuccino. Later in the day there are sandwiches (such as tomato, homemade mozzarella, and basil drizzled with extra-virgin olive oil on fresh-baked focaccia bread), soups, an array of tempting salads, and a daily hot dish such as polenta with wild mushroom sauce or bowtie pasta quattro formaggi. But you needn't limit yourself to counter offerings; you can buy anything at the store and eat it in the cafe. There is a vast selection of cheeses and pâtés, oven-roasted vegetables, exquisite salads, olives, fresh produce, dried fruits, charcuterie meats, fresh-baked breads and cakes, and gourmet ice creams. You don't just eat at Dean & Deluca—you engage in a romance with food. Fine wines are available by the glass.

Georgetown Bagelry

3245 M St. NW. ☎ **202/965-1011.** Sandwiches $3–$5.50. No credit cards. Mon–Sat 6am–9pm, Sun 6am–6pm. SANDWICHES.

Here, ex–New Yorker and bagel maven Erik Koefoed turns out about 5,000 bagels a day—plain, sesame, poppyseed, onion, garlic, salt, garlic-salt, caraway, rye, onion rye, pumpernickel, oatmeal-raisin, cinnamon-raisin, whole-wheat, and bran. And that's not to mention bialys. You can get them spread with cream cheese and lox or an array of other fillings such as homemade chicken salad, hummus and sprouts, even hot pastrami. Homemade brownies, carrot cakes, fruit salad, and other desserts are also inexpensive. Come by early in the morning to enjoy an oven-fresh bagel with fresh-squeezed orange juice and coffee over the morning paper (it's sold here, too). It's nice to sit by the big windows and watch Georgetown coming to life.

✪ Patisserie Café Didier

3206 Grace St. NW (off Wisconsin Ave. just below M St.). ☎ **202/342-9083.** Main courses $7.95–$8.50; breakfast pastries, muffins, croissants, and desserts $1.10–$4.95. DC, DISC, MC, V. Tues–Sat 8am–7pm, Sun 8am–5pm. CONTINENTAL/PATISSERIE.

This is the most delightful place in town for continental breakfasts, light lunches, and afternoon teas. Dieter Schorner, former pastry chef at New York's haute-cuisine bastions Le Cirque and La Côte Basque, came to D.C. in 1988, and his marvelous creations have graced many of this city's most fashionable parties. For National Symphony Orchestra Director Mstislav Rostropovich's 60th birthday, he fashioned a cello-shaped birthday cake complete with bow and strings of pulled sugar—plus 800 miniature replicas for guests!

His cafe is charming—light and sunny, with 18th-century lithographs on pale-peach walls, fresh flowers adorning the tables, plants in terra-cotta pots, and a flower box in the window. The tempting pastries are displayed in a glass case—oven-fresh croissants worthy of Paris, classic tarte tatins, mini-fruit tartlets and eclairs, and sumptuous creations such as a rich Swiss chocolate cake lavishly iced and filled with chocolate ganache. And while you're decadently eating cake for breakfast, why not enjoy it with real hot chocolate made from scratch with chunks of Belgian chocolate? Cappuccino, espresso, and cafe au lait are also options. At lunchtime, you can enjoy homemade soups (for example, saffron-flavored cream of mussel) served with a basket of fresh-baked breads, quiches, soufflés (shrimp, spinach, cheese, mushroom), sandwiches (perhaps tarragon chicken salad on a baguette or croissant), salads, small European-style pizzas, cold platters (seafood, saucisson, chicken, cheese plates), and hot items such as crabcakes, lamb couscous, or grilled trout served with fresh vegetables and new potatoes.

⑤ The Tombs

1226 36th St. NW (at Prospect St.). ☎ **202/337-6668.** Reservations not accepted. Burgers, sandwiches, salads $4.95–$7.75; main courses mostly $5.25–$10.95. AE, DISC, MC, V. Mon–Thurs 11:30am–2am, Fri 11:30am–3am, Sat 11am–3am, Sun 9:30am–2am; brunch Sun 10am–3pm. AMERICAN.

For good food, moderate prices, and simpatico ambience, you can't beat this classic college watering hole, which occupies a converted 19th-century Federal-style house. Its name derives from a London pub in T. S. Eliot's *Old Possum's Book of Practical Cats*. Innlike and cozy, with low ceilings, brick floors, and a working fireplace, it's a favorite hangout of both local residents and Georgetown University students (Bill Clinton was a frequent patron during his college years) and faculty. They congregate at the central bar and surrounding tables, but I prefer to sit in the less rambunctious room called "the Sweeps." Down a few steps, its exposed brick walls are hung with vintage rowing-motif prints, along with oars from Yale, Columbia, and other college teams. Seating is in comfortable red leather banquettes.

The menu offers a wide selection of burgers and sandwiches served with steak fries, chili, and salads, along with a few more serious entrées such as sliced London broil with a baked potato and vegetable. From 5pm on there are low-priced nightly specials—perhaps broiled salmon fillet stuffed with spinach, topped with herbed cream sauce, and served with rice and vegetables. There are similar specials at lunch. Beer prices are low to accommodate the student crowd, lager is a specialty, and a few premium wines are offered by the glass each night. And the fresh-baked desserts are stupendous. Try the densely moist chocolate brownie topped with ice cream and a dollop of real whipped cream. A special brunch menu offering items such as eggs Maryland (somewhat like eggs Benedict but prepared with crabmeat) is featured on Sunday. Arrive at off-peak hours to avoid a wait for tables.

○ Zed's

3318 M St. NW. ☎ **202/333-4710.** Reservations accepted for large parties only. Main courses $5.95–$8.95 at lunch, mostly $6.95–$12.95 at dinner. AE, MC, V. Sun–Thurs 11am–11pm, Fri–Sat 11am–1am. ETHIOPIAN.

Although this spicy cuisine has long been popular in Washington, it's not always easy to find restaurants offering truly authentic, high-quality Ethiopian fare. Such a one is Zed's, a charming little place with Ethiopian paintings, posters, and artifacts adorning pine-paneled walls and tables set with fresh flowers. Ethiopian music enhances the ambience. Zed's three dining floors are particularly cozy at night by candlelight.

Everything here is made from scratch using spices imported from Ethiopia. The food is eaten *sans* utensils—a sourdough crêpelike bread called injera is used to scoop up food. Items listed as *watt* are hot and spicy; *alitchas* are milder and more delicately flavored. I love both the chicken dishes here. Doro watt is chicken stewed in a tangy hot red-chili-pepper sauce; it comes with a hard-boiled egg that has simmered in the sauce. Equally scrumptious is infillay—strips of tender chicken breast flavored with seasoned butter and honey wine and served with a delicious chopped spinach and rice side dish. Also highly recommended are the flavorful lamb dishes and deep-fried whole fish. And vegetables have never been tastier. You get a choice of one with each entrée, but consider ordering extras such as garlicky chopped collard greens, red lentil purée in spicy red-pepper sauce, or a purée (served chilled) of roasted yellow split peas mixed with onions, peppers, and garlic. Other marvelous side dishes are cooked bulgur wheat blended with herbed butter and marvelous lemony fresh-made tomato or potato salads spiked with hot green chili peppers. There's a full bar, and, should you have the inclination, there are Italian pastries for dessert.

7 Adams-Morgan

EXPENSIVE

Cities

2424 18th St. NW. (near Columbia Rd.). ☎ **202/328-7194.** Reservations recommended. Main courses $10–$18. AE, DC, MC, V. Mon–Thurs 6–11pm, Fri–Sat 6–11:30pm. Bar, Sun–Thurs 5pm–2am, Fri–Sat 5pm–3am. INTERNATIONAL.

Housed in a century-old former five-and-dime store, Cities is a restaurant-cum-travelogue. Every six or seven months, following a comprehensive research expedition by the owner and chef, the restaurant is revamped to reflect the cuisine, character, and culture of a different city. Even the music reflects the city under consideration, and waiters are in native dress or some facsimile thereof. When the highlighted city was Paris, the decor replicated a Montparnasse-style brasserie, with French street lamps, flower boxes, murals of Parisian park and cafe scenes, and French bistro menus on the walls. My Parisian meal began with an appetizer of escargots served with shiitake mushrooms and sautéed spinach in a garlicky Pernod-flavored butter sauce with a gratinée of fresh Gruyère and parmesan. That was followed by an entrée of poulet grillé served in a fan of slices on a bed of leeks in butter-cream-chèvre reduction sauce with classic pommes frites. And dessert was a marquise au chocolat—layers of crunchy hazelnut meringue filled with hazelnut-butter cream on a crème anglaise marbleized with raspberry and garnished with fresh raspberries, mint, and crème chantilly. *Formidable!* Of course, by the time you read this, the cuisine and setting will be entirely different—that's part of the fun. Not to worry—Cities' fare is always excellent. There's a small but expertly conceived wine and champagne list enhanced by alcoholic beverages representing the city cuisine, and premium wines are offered by the glass.

The adjoining bar, open-air in summer and one of the most simpatico spots for imbibing in the Adams-Morgan district, is also redecorated with every city change. It offers a light-fare menu with items in the $4.50 to $7.50 range. For Paris, these included a croque-monsieur, plat de fromages, and pâté served with cornichons, radishes, and bread.

✪ Petitto's

2653 Connecticut Ave. NW. (between Calvert St. and Woodley Rd.). ☎ **202/ 667-5350.** Reservations recommended. Main courses $11–$17.75. AE, CB, DC, DISC, MC, V. Mon–Sat 6–10:30pm, Sun 6–9:30pm. Dolce Finale, Mon–Thurs 5pm–12:30am, Fri–Sat 5pm–1:30am. Metro: Woodley Park–Zoo. NORTHERN ITALIAN.

The superb Petitto's features the cuisine of Rome and Abruzzi—plus a few southern specialties—in a very charming setting. There are three dining rooms in this converted turn-of-the-century town house, each with its own working fireplace. Suffused lighting is provided by hanging lamps wrapped in creamy silk scarves, and operatic arias (sometimes live) serve as appropriate background music. In good weather you can dine alfresco at umbrella tables on the street.

A "symphony of pasta" sampler platter (three varieties)—perhaps falasche alla Petitto (homemade spinach and egg noodles tossed with mushrooms, prosciutto, and peas in a cream sauce), pomme tossed with chunks of bacon and hot peppers in a lusty red sauce, and seashell pasta with lump crabmeat and mushrooms in oil and garlic—is available as an appetizer or entrée. Nonpasta entrées change weekly, but always include excellent fresh seafood dishes such as cacciucco—an array of shellfish (lobster, scallops, mussels, clams, and squid). Breads—pan-fried in olive oil, flavored with garlic and Parmesan, or toasted with tomato, Parmesan, and basil—are famed house specialties, but you might forgo them in a good cause: leaving room for dessert. Recommended choices include zuppa inglese (a sponge cake layered with custard, real whipped cream, and fresh raspberries, saturated with Chambord liqueur) and the creamiest ever orange cheesecake topped with fresh fruit. A moderately priced and well-chosen list of Italian wines is augmented by costlier vintages (including French and California selections).

Dolce Finale, in Petitto's cozily candlelit, brick-walled wine cellar, features a variety of cappuccinos, wines, grappas, liqueurs, fruits and cheeses, and an array of sumptuous desserts. It can be visited separately from the restaurant.

MODERATE

Peyote Cafe

2319 18th St. NW (between Belmont and Kalorama rds.). ☎ **202/462-8330.** Reservations recommended. Sandwiches, salads, burgers $3.50–$9.95; main courses $5.95–$14.95 at dinner, mostly $3.95–$5.95 at brunch. AE, CB, DC, MC, V. Mon–Fri 5pm–1am, Sat–Sun 11:30am–1am. Bar, Sun–Thurs to 2am, Fri–Sat to 3am. Metro: Woodley Park–Zoo. SOUTHWESTERN/TEX-MEX.

Sharing an Adams-Morgan town house with Roxanne (see below), the Peyote Cafe, occupying the downstairs level, evokes a southwestern roadside eatery with Texas-themed ornament lights (shaped like cowboy boots, lizards, cacti) over the bar, neon beer signs, Sante Fe peach walls decorated with coyotes and armadillos, and a jukebox stocked with country-western tunes. You can dine at the bar or seated on high chairs at round tables.

It's a casual place, but there's nothing casual about the kitchen. The cafe's chili is Lone Star State quality—thick and stewlike with tender chunks of sirloin, tomatoes, and pinto beans, its spicy sauce spiked with Dos Equis beer. Similarly spiked is the chile con queso, a melted-cheese-and-jalapeño dip you eat with tortilla chips. Everything here is good, but two entrées are especially irresistible. One is the Tex-Mex mixed grill (pork chop, chicken breast, and chorizo sausage) served with skin-on mashed potatoes (the best ever, topped with ancho-chili gravy), corn on the cob, and chunky homemade applesauce. The other is tacos al carbón—flour tortillas stuffed with grilled pork, melted asadero cheese, shredded lettuce, homemade pico de gallo, guacamole, and sour cream. At brunch, served weekends, the regular menu is supplemented by entrées like New Orleans pain perdu—rum-soaked French toast topped with pecans, fresh berries, whipped cream, and powdered sugar. There's a full bar, and specialty drinks run the gamut from frozen margaritas to liqueur-coffee concoctions topped with fresh whipped cream. For dessert, cheesecake studded with chunks of dark and white chocolate and topped with dark cocoa, cherry sauce, chocolate fudge, and fresh strawberries makes an opulent finale.

Roxanne/On the Rox

2319 18th St. NW (between Belmont and Kalorama rds.). ☎ **202/462-8330.** Reservations recommended. Sandwiches, salads, burgers $3.95–$9.95; main courses $7.95–$15.95 at dinner, $4.95–$9.95 at brunch. AE, CB, DC, MC, MOST, V. Mon–Fri 5pm–1am, Sat–Sun noon–1am. Bar, Sun–Thurs to 2am, Fri–Sat to 3am. Metro: Woodley Park–Zoo. SOUTHWESTERN.

Up a flight of stairs from the Peyote Cafe (see above), Roxanne offers similar fare (some menu items are identical). Decorated in soft southwest-evocative pastels (adobe, peach, turquoise, and ocher), its banquette upholstery utilizes Native American motifs, cacti grow on the sills of a bay window up front, and a colorful iguana relief sculpture adorns an exposed brick wall. Though Roxanne is cozy, weather permitting, head to the candlelit rooftop deck area (called On the Rox). Warmed by big heaters, the Rox is open most of the year. It's a delightful setting for alfresco brunches and dinners.

The food is worthy of its romantic, starlit venue. There are two specially scrumptious appetizers: Spicy chicken wings are served with a celestial cilantro- and lime-flavored chunky peanut sauce. And plump poached shrimp and scallops, marinated in a mix of avocado, Serrano chilies, lime, and cilantro, are served enfolded in warm flour tortillas with grenadine-rimmed tequila-soaked orange slices; the mix of flavors is ambrosial. Entrées include the Tex-Mex grill described at Peyote Cafe, always a great choice. Crisp-skinned grilled Muscovy duck, moist and tender, is served over garlicky wilted spinach studded with roasted pumpkin seeds in a green mole sauce; it comes with blue-corn crêpes. I also like the thin-crust pizzas and pasta dishes here. Like the Peyote, Roxanne adds brunch items (such as blue-cornmeal pancakes served with honey-maple butter) on weekends. Drinks and desserts are also the same (see above). I usually don't want dessert after such filling fare. One exception is a refreshing gratin of lightly grilled fresh berries in sabayon sauce topped with powdered sugar.

INEXPENSIVE

⑤ Mixtec

1792 Columbia Rd. ☎ **202/332-1011.** Reservations not accepted. Main courses $4.75–$9.95, full breakfasts $6.25–$8.75. MC, V. Mon–Tues 7am–11:30pm, Fri–Sat 7am–1am, Sun 7am–11pm. Metro: Woodley Park–Zoo. MEXICAN REGIONAL.

This Adams-Morgan eatery serves up authentic regional cuisines of Mexico in a cheerful setting, with an open kitchen and white walls hung with color photographs of menu items. Colorful *faroles* (paper lanterns) are suspended overhead, and Mexican music provides south-of-the-border ambience. Dozens of brightly painted cut-tin creations (birds, fish, butterflies) adorn an adjoining dining room.

Delicious made-from-scratch corn and flour tortillas enhance whatever they're stuffed with. Start out with an appetizer of queso fundido—a bubbling hot dish of broiled Chihuahua cheese topped with shredded spicy chorizo sausage and flavored with jalapeños and cilantro. The freshly prepared guacamole is also excellent. An interesting side dish is cebollitas al carbón—spring onions lightly grilled in olive oil and flavored with fresh lime juice. And tacos al carbón, pieces of spicy grilled beef, come wrapped in small corn tortillas with three sauces—a purée of green tomatillos flavored with onion and garlic, a hot red-chili sauce, and a salsa cruda of chopped tomatoes, onions, jalapeños, and cilantro. All these dishes are in the $2.50–$4.50 range, and if you order a few of them you'll enjoy a hearty meal and diverse culinary thrills. Full entrées served with rice and beans include the house specialty, mole mexicano—broiled chicken in a rich sauce of five peppers (the kitchen spices dishes with 200 different varieties!), sunflower and sesame seeds, onions, garlic, almonds, cinnamon, and chocolate. There's a nice choice of Mexican beers and fresh fruit juices. For dessert, try homemade flan flavored with brandy and orange and lemon peel.

Come here, too, for hearty Mexican breakfasts such as Mexican steak and eggs with refried beans, tortillas, and soutéed tomatoes or potatoes.

8 Capitol Hill/Union Station

INEXPENSIVE

Chesapeake Bagel Bakery

215 Pennsylvania Ave. SE. ☎ **202/546-0994.** Salads $1.50–$4.50, bagel and croissant sandwiches $1.40–$5. No credit cards. Mon–Fri 6:30am–8pm, Sat 7am–6pm,
Sun 7am–5pm. Metro: Capitol South. SANDWICHES/SALADS.

For a good quick meal near the Capitol, its hard to beat this pleasant
minicafeteria with impressionist art posters adorning gallery-white
walls. The bagels are baked from scratch on the premises, and the
aroma is divine. There are 12 varieties running the gamut from cinnamon raisin to pumpernickel, and sandwich fillings include cream
cheese, walnuts, raisins, and carrots; cream cheese and Nova; chicken
salad; chopped liver; and hummus and sprouts, among others. There
are also sandwiches on fresh-baked croissants—for example, roast beef
with lettuce and mayo or a ham, turkey, Swiss combo with sliced
tomato and sprouts. A cup of coffee is 80¢, and for dessert there are
brownies, blondies, carrot cake, and such.

There's a Dupont Circle location at 1636 Connecticut Ave. NW,
between Q and R Streets (☎ **202/328-7985**), and another at 818 18th
St. NW (☎ **202/775-4690**). The menus are pretty much the same.

9 At Sightseeing Attractions

THE CAPITOL

You can rub elbows with senators and representatives if you dine in the
Capitol—a good choice when you're touring the building.

❸ Dirksen Senate Office Building South Buffet Room

1st and C sts. NE. ☎ **202/224-4249.** Reservations not accepted. Prix-fixe buffet
$7.75 adults, $5.25 children under 12, plus 15% gratuity. MC, V. Mon–Fri 11:30am–
2:30pm. Metro: Capitol South or Union Station. AMERICAN.

This is a marvelous lunchtime choice, featuring lavish all-you-can-eat
meals. To get here, you can take a free subway that runs through the
underbelly of the Capitol, a fun trip—ask Capitol police for directions.
You can also go directly to the Dirksen Building, of course, in which
case your closest Metro is Union Station. The marble-colonnaded art
deco setting for these buffets is most attractive, with seating in comfortable leather chairs at white-linen-covered, flower-bedecked tables.
You can help yourself to unlimited viands from the carvery station
(perhaps roast beef or leg of lamb), about eight additional hot entrées,
vegetables, potatoes, rice, pasta, a full salad and fruit bar, a make-your-
own-sundae bar, soft drinks, and tea, coffee, or milk.

House of Representatives Restaurant

Room H118, at the south end of the Capitol. ☎ **202/225-6300.** Reservations not
accepted. Main courses $4.75–$15.95. AE, DC, DISC, MC, V. Mon–Fri 8–11am and
1–2:30pm (when Congress is in session); closed when Congress is not in session.
Metro: Capitol South. AMERICAN REGIONAL.

Most impressive of all Capitol eateries open to the public, the House Restaurant consists of two beautifully appointed dining rooms. In one, walls are hung with gilt-framed Federal mirrors, historic prints, and a Bierstadt landscape, and lighting emanates from crystal sconces and graceful Georgian chandeliers. The other has high ceilings with beautiful crown moldings, floor-to-ceiling windows framed by swagged satin draperies, and a large gilt-framed Brumidi fresco of George Washington receiving Cornwallis's letter of surrender at Yorktown.

Bean soup has been a feature menu choice here since 1904, when Speaker of the House Joseph G. Cannon ordered it only to find that it had been omitted from the menu because the day was too hot for hearty soups. "Thunderation," roared Cannon, "I had my mouth set for bean soup. . . . From now on, hot or cold, rain, snow, or shine, I want it on the menu every day!" And so it has been ever since. Prices are very reasonable for such a lofty setting. A breakfast of two eggs, homemade biscuits, sausage patty, fresh-squeezed orange juice, and coffee is about $5. At lunch, the famous bean soup is $1.50. Other choices might include grilled Pacific salmon, Maryland crabcakes, or New York strip steak. There are also deli sandwiches, salads, and burgers, and daily specials always include one low-cholesterol/low-salt entrée. Seven wines (representing various regions of the country) are offered by the glass daily. For dessert, a butterscotch sundae is a treat, though apple pie seems more appropriate. Who knows, you might even get to see your congressperson.

Refectory

First floor, Senate side of the Capitol. ☎ **202/224-4870.** Reservations not accepted. Main courses $3.50–$9.95. MC, V. Mon–Fri 8am–4pm (later if the Senate is in session). Metro: Capitol South. AMERICAN.

Another good choice for Capitol meals, this charming dining room with vaulted ceilings and wainscoted walls offers light fare. Continental breakfast fare includes fresh-baked muffins. Lunch runs the gamut from a roast-beef sandwich with mashed potatoes and gravy to a cold chunky chicken salad plate with seasonal fruits. There are also sandwiches (including the three-decker senator's club), burgers, and salads. Try hot pecan pie or a hot-fudge sundae for dessert.

THE CORCORAN

✪ Café des Artistes at the Corcoran

17th St. NW (between E St. and New York Ave.). ☎ **202/638-1590.** Reservations recommended (not accepted for brunch). Main courses $5.95–$9.95; buffet gospel brunch $15.95 adults, $8.50 children under 12. AE, CB, DC, DISC, MC, V. Wed–Mon 10am–5pm, Thurs till 8:30pm; brunch Sun 11am–2pm. Metro: Farragut West or Farragut North. AMERICAN/CONTINENTAL.

This museum cafe couldn't be more lovely. Under a lofty skylight ceiling, it's ensconced by fluted Doric columns and neoclassic marble statuary. Flower-bedecked tables are set amid tall palms in terra-cotta pots. Fare includes sandwiches (such as smoked turkey with herbed stuffing, applewood bacon, and cranberry orange relish on country bread) and salads such as smoked trout tossed with romaine lettuce, croutons, and crumpled goat cheese in a horseradish vinaigrette.

Do stop by on Sunday for a buffet brunch, with live gospel music. The fare highlights créole and southern dishes such as jambalaya and cheese grits, along with waffles, egg dishes, blintzes, breakfast meats, fresh fruit, and salads.

KENNEDY CENTER

Encore Cafe

New Hampshire Ave. NW (at Rock Creek Pkwy.) ☎ **202/416-8560.** Most items $4.50–$6. AE, MC, V. Daily 11am–8pm. Metro: Foggy Bottom. AMERICAN.

An inexpensive choice is this attractive cafeteria with windows all around providing gorgeous city views. Typical entrées here: baked trout with mashed potatoes and a medley of fresh vegetables, Spanish paella, and chilled salmon fillet with pecan-studded wild rice. Sandwiches, homemade soups, pizza, salads, wine, and beer are available, and there are fresh-baked pastries such as apple-cinnamon cobbler for dessert. From 5 to 8pm you can order a fresh-carved prime-rib dinner here, with baked potato and vegetable, for $10.95.

Roof Terrace Restaurant

New Hampshire Ave. NW (at Rock Creek Pkwy.). ☎ **202/416-8555.** Reservations recommended. Roof Terrace, main courses $10–$14 at lunch $22–$25 at dinner; prix-fixe buffet brunch $22.95, prix-fixe three-course dinner $34. Hors d'Oeuvrerie, light-fare items $8–$12. AE, CB, DC, MC, V. Roof Terrace, matinee days only 11:30am–3pm; nightly 5:30–9pm, Sun 11:30am–3pm. Hors d'Oeuvrerie, daily 5pm–half an hour after the last show. *Note:* The Roof Terrace is occasionally closed when the show schedule is scant; call before you go. Metro: Foggy Bottom. AMERICAN REGIONAL.

A meal in this fine dining room adds a glamorous note to an evening at the theater. It's extremely plush, with ornate crystal candelabra chandeliers suspended from a lofty ceiling, immense windows providing panoramic views of the Potomac, and Louis XV–style chairs at white-linen-covered tables. Potted palms and big floral arrangements further adorn the luxe ambience.

Menus change seasonally. During my most recent visit, dinner appetizers included crabcakes served with herbed aïoli, smoked duck with asparagus strudel, and a grilled vegetable and goat-cheese terrine. Among the entrées were walnut- and herb-roasted rack of lamb and grilled salmon steak with potato-leek crust. The signature dessert here is chocolate Concorde cake—chocolate meringue topped with chocolate ganache and chocolate mousse. At lunch, lighter fare—such as a Mediterranean vegetable frittata with roasted tomato salsa—is an option. And Sunday brunch features a vast buffet. Many premium wines are offered by the glass.

After-theater munchies and cocktails are served in the adjoining and equally plush **Hors d'Oeuvrerie.** I love to stop here after a show for a glass of wine and late supper—perhaps a smoked duck on mustard cress drizzled with red lentil oil or cold lobster and papaya salad. It's gourmet snack fare. Desserts and coffee are also available.

LIBRARY OF CONGRESS

Ⓢ Cafeteria

James Madison Memorial Building of the Library of Congress, 101 Independence Ave. SE. ☎ **202/707-8300.** Main courses $2.50–$4, sandwiches $2–$3.80. No credit cards. Mon–Fri 9–10:30am and 12:30–2pm; light fare Mon–Fri 2–3:30pm. Metro: Capitol South. AMERICAN.

This building has a classy sixth-floor cafeteria that is open to the public. The decor is tasteful (wall-to-wall carpeting, Breuer chairs at oak-framed white tables, a wall of windows for panoramic city views), the food fresh and homemade. Hot entrées change daily; they might include old-fashioned beef stew, Swedish meatballs over noodles, homemade pizza, or crabcakes with tartar sauce. A stir-fry station and Chinese dishes are daily options. Selections from the salad bar begin at 29¢ an ounce for such things as greens, tomatoes, pasta salads, Greek salad, Caesar salad, egg salad, mushrooms, chick-peas, beans, cheeses, and sprouts. Vegetables might include broccoli, noodles with mushrooms, mashed and au gratin potatoes, sautéed dilled tomatoes, and spinach soufflé. There are also sandwiches, fresh-baked pies and cakes, and a full array of breakfast foods.

Ⓢ Montpelier Room

James Madison Memorial Building of the Library of Congress, 101 Independence Ave. SE. ☎ **202/707-8300.** Reservations recommended for parties of four or more. Prix-fixe lunch $8.50. MC, V. Mon–Fri 11:30am–2pm. Closed Aug to mid-Sept. Metro: Capitol South. AMERICAN.

Adjoining the James Madison cafeteria (details above), the Montpelier Dining Room offers a marvelous midday buffet. It's a lovely carpeted room, with panoramic views (including the Capitol dome) from white-draped windows on two sides, tables adorned with fresh flowers, oak-paneled walls, and an elegant dessert display table with a floral centerpiece. The fixed-price lunch served here is one of the best deals in town. Menus change daily. During my recent visit it included cream of broccoli soup, prime rib, lyonnaise potatoes, honeyed carrots, bread and butter, beverage, and salad bar; desserts were $1.75 extra. Wine and beer are available by the glass. Friday is the Montpelier's prime-rib day.

NATIONAL AIR AND SPACE MUSEUM

Flight Line

Independence Ave. (at 4th St. SW). ☎ **202/371-8750.** Main courses, sandwiches, salads $2.65–$6.95. MC, V. Daily 10am–5pm. Metro: L'Enfant Plaza. AMERICAN.

This major Mall museum features a 39,400-square-foot restaurant complex consisting of Flight Line, an 800-seat cafeteria on the main level, and The Wright Place (see below), an elegant full-service dining room on the mezzanine. The two eateries occupy a conservatorylike glass building, with floor-to-ceiling windows on both levels offering panoramic views of the Mall and Capitol. Surrounding terraces are lushly planted and landscaped with seasonal flowers.

Flight Line, under a Tinker-Toy assemblage of white-steel tubing, is carpeted in forest green and handsomely furnished with marble-topped pine tables. Needless to say, with all those windows it's bright and sunny inside. The self-service fare is reasonably priced, fresh, and tasty. It's displayed on an immense octagonal food counter with buffet stations for salads, hot entrées (such as baked lasagne, meatloaf, and fried chicken), hot soups and chili, burgers, vegetables, fresh-baked breads and pastries, pastas and pizzas, fresh fruit, sandwiches, wine and beer, even bottled waters.

The Wright Place

Independence Ave. (at 4th St. SW). ☎ **202/371-8777.** Reservations recommended. Main courses $7.50–$11.50, sandwiches and salads $6.75–$9.50. AE, DISC, MC, V. Daily 11:30am–3pm. Metro: L'Enfant Plaza. AMERICAN.

Upstairs from Flight Line (see above), this is a plush, full-service restaurant enclosed by a chrome railing and planters of greenery. Tables are adorned with fresh flowers, and pale-gray walls are hung with vintage aviation photographs from the museum's collection. The city views here, being higher up, are especially great. The menu changes seasonally. Entrées run the gamut from sandwiches (such as pulled pork with barbecue sauce on a kaiser roll, served with battered crispy fries) to a hearty Brunswick stew served with salad and fresh-baked corn muffins. Gourmet pizzas with toppings such as grilled chicken pesto are additional options. Wine and microbrewery beers are available, and there's a low-priced children's menu with foods such as a grilled-cheese sandwich, fries, and milk. Yummy fresh-baked desserts—like key lime pie and warm apple cobbler with a scoop of vanilla ice cream—change daily.

NATIONAL GALLERY OF ART

Concourse Buffet

On the Mall (between 3rd and 7th sts. NW). ☎ **202/347-9401.** Main courses $4–$5.50. AE, MC, V. Mon–Fri 10am–3pm, Sat 11am–4pm, Sun 11am–4:30pm. Metro: Archives or Judiciary Square. AMERICAN.

Set in the concourse connecting the two buildings of the National Gallery is this cheerful cafeteria with seating amid planters and potted palms. Good acoustics keep the noise level bearable, and efficient operations keeps the lines moving quickly. Selections include homemade soups and tasty salads, and a choice of four fresh vegetables each day. In addition, there are croissant sandwiches, pizza, frozen yogurts with varied toppings, burgers and hot dogs, a carvery for deli sandwiches, even a few hot entrées each day—perhaps roast beef with mashed potatoes, Idaho rainbow trout, or Italian vegetable quiche. Fresh-baked desserts and wine and beer are available.

National Gallery Restaurants

On the Mall (between 3rd and 7th sts. NW). ☎ **202/347-9401.** Cascade Espresso Bar, menu items $3.75–$8.95. Terrace and Garden cafés, main courses $5.95–$10. AE, MC, V. Cascade Espresso Bar, Mon–Sat noon–4:30pm, Sun noon–5:30pm. Terrace Café, Mon–Sat 11:30am–3pm, Sun noon–4pm. Garden Café, Mon–Sat 11:30am–3pm, Sun noon–4pm (extended hours in summer). Metro: Archives or Judiciary Square. INTERNATIONAL.

There are two charming full-service restaurants within the National Gallery itself, both of which provide restful settings and good food.

And an attractive lunch spot with waiter service is nothing to scorn when you've been trudging around museums all day. The **Terrace Café,** in the East Building, overlooks the Mall, and the fern- and flower-bordered **Garden Café,** in the West Building, is under a sky-light with tables around a marble fountain with a late Renaissance bronze *Venus and Cupid.*

The Terrace and Garden cafes have similar menus listing about five items each day. They change from time to time (often reflecting current exhibits), but might typically include a plate of chilled poached salmon served on a bed of spinach pasta with a basket of bread; a salmagundi salad (greens with Cheddar cheese, eggs, black olives, anchovies, and Virginia ham); a cheese-and-fruit plate served with pâté and a glass of wine; a Caesar salad topped with grilled chicken; and English spring lamb stew. Fresh-baked pastries and fresh fruit are among your dessert options at both eateries, as are wine, beer, and cappuccino/espresso.

The **Cascade,** an espresso/cappuccino/wine bar, features sandwiches served with fresh fruit, salads, fruit and cheese plates, and exquisite desserts. It overlooks an indoor waterfall, and patrons sit at marble tables amid potted palms.

NEAR THE NATIONAL ZOO

Uptown Bakers

3313 Connecticut Ave. NW (just north of Macomb St.). ☎ **202/362-6262.** Sand-wiches $4–$6.50, pastries $1.50–$2.75. No credit cards. Mon–Sat 7am–9pm, Sun 7am–7:30pm. Metro: Cleveland Park. SANDWICHES/PASTRIES.

Although there are eateries in the zoo, their fast-food menus are less than inspiring. A better bet is an alfresco lunch at one of the zoo's nice picnic areas. Get the fixings at Uptown Bakers—sandwiches on scrumptious fresh-baked breads (baguette, raisin-nut, sourdough, olive, herb, challah, and many more) with yummy fillings such as smoked ham with chutney and honey mustard; roasted eggplant and red peppers with pesto vinaigrette; and Caesar salad with grilled chicken. Focaccia pizzas, too. Uptown's coffee is a blend of Amazon and French roast beans. And oven-fresh desserts run the gamut from the world's best cinnamon buns to an apple tart with brown sugary streusel topping.

SUPREME COURT

Supreme Court Cafeteria

1st St. NE (between E. Capitol St. and Maryland Ave.). ☎ **202/479-3246.** Main courses and sandwiches $2.90–$4.95. No credit cards. Mon–Fri 7:30–10:30am and 11:30am–2pm (closed to public noon–12:15pm and 1–1:10pm). Metro: Capitol South. AMERICAN.

Like the Capitol restaurants, the Supreme Court cafeteria is run in the belief that members of each branch of government have to eat but can't always get out to do so. It's likely you'll see a justice or two in the ground-floor cafeteria here. It's a very pleasant eatery. The walls are hung with large photographs of the Supreme Court building in vari-ous stages of construction, architectural renderings, and interior shots;

soft lighting emanates from ornate brass candelabra chandeliers; and seating is in banquettes and mahogany chairs that are roomy enough to accommodate the largest judge.

Dining options include an excellent salad bar (items are 26¢ per ounce), good pizzas (perhaps topped with five cheeses and roasted garlic), soups, a make-your-own sandwich bar, and homemade pies and cakes. Entrées—ranging from chicken fajitas with black beans and Spanish rice to meatloaf with mushroom sauce and garlic mashed potatoes—change daily.

UNION STATION

Since its renovation in the late 1980s, Union Station has become an extremely popular dining choice for both locals and tourists. It offers dozens of restaurants and food vendors in different price ranges, and when you're through dining you can browse the diverse shops (see Chapter 9) or take in a movie at the nine-screen cinema complex on the lower level. Other events here might include strolling singers, orchestral performers, choral groups, and art exhibits. There's validated parking for 1,600 cars (entrance on H Street or Massachusetts Avenue), and of course, the Union Station Metro takes you right to the door.

On the lower level is a vast **Food Court,** offering an incredible array of low- to medium-priced options. It's all cafeteria-style, with food vendors selling blintzes, falafel, stuffed baked potatoes, burgers, fresh seafood, enchiladas, sushi, fresh-squeezed juices, salad-bar items, fresh baked goods, homemade ice cream, chili, pastrami sandwiches, pizzas, barbecue, and much more. Ordinarily I don't like food courts because they're big, noisy, and sterile-looking. This one, however, in line with the lofty quality of the station's renovation, is a totally different story. It's a really attractive facility, enhanced by extensive use of oak and pine, colorful canvas umbrellas over some tables, subtle lighting, live plants, and an exquisite marble floor. In addition, the vast space is divided into a number of seating areas, creating a more intimate ambience.

Union Station's most upscale restaurant is:

B. Smith's

Union Station, 50 Massachussetts Ave. NE. ☎ **202/289-6188.** Reservations recommended. Main courses mostly $8.95–$15.95 at lunch and brunch, $11.95–$19.95 at dinner. AE, DC, MC, V. Daily 11:30am–4pm; Sun 5–10pm, Mon–Thurs 5–11pm, Fri–Sat 5pm–midnight. Free validated parking for two hours. Metro: Union Station. TRADITIONAL SOUTHERN.

The creation of former model Barbara Smith, this eponymous restaurant occupies palatial Union Station's most exalted precinct—the Presidential Suite, where, in the heyday of rail travel, presidents officially greeted visiting monarchs and dignitaries. Entered off the East Hall through an elegant bar (an after-work hangout for Washingtonians), the magnificent main dining room is shaped like the White House Oval Office, with 29-foot ceilings, imposing mahogany doors, white marble floors, gold-leafed moldings, Ionic columns, and decorative faux-leather panels adorned with arabesques. There's additional seating in the adjoining loggia, with its 35-foot vaulted granite domes and arched floor-to-ceiling windows. Background music is mellow (Nat King Cole, Ray Charles, Sarah Vaughan); Wednesday, Thursday, and Saturday nights there's laid-back live jazz. B. Smith's is the scene of many celebrity-studded events.

Chef Robert Holmes spent 14 years—eventually as head chef—in Paul Prudhomme's kitchen at K-Paul's in New Orleans. Hence, one of his best appetizers is a jalapeño-nuanced Louisiana crabcake served with buttery toasted wheat bread, Tabasco mayonnaise, and crunchy slaw. Crisply fried green tomatoes sprinkled with tangy aged ricotta and served with a flavorful roasted red pepper vinaigrette is another good beginning. Among the main dishes, I love Holmes's sautéed Virginia trout piled high with crabmeat/vegetable "stuffing" and served atop mesclun with rice and a medley of roasted vegetables. And barbecued ribs come with roasted corn on the cob, creamy church-picnic-style potato salad, and pickled vegetables. A basket of mini biscuits, corn and citrus-poppyseed muffins, and sourdough rolls accompanies all entrées. Yummy desserts here include dense pecan diamonds topped with praline ice cream, and an almost all-American wine list features many by-the-glass selections.

Also noteworthy here:

ⓢ America

Union Station, 50 Massachusetts Ave. NE. ☎ **202/682-9555.** Reservations recommended. Main courses $6.95–$17.95 (most items are $10 or less). AE, DC, MC, V. Sun–Thurs 11:30am–midnight, Fri–Sat 11:30am–1am. Bar stays open a few hours later. Metro: Union Station. AMERICAN.

I always enjoy eating at this New York transplant, with seating on three levels and cafe tables spread out into the Main Hall. Its essentially art deco interior includes WPA-style murals, a large painting of the American West, and a whimsical frieze depicting surfers, athletes, astronauts, and superheroes in outer space. I especially like sitting by the balcony rail so I can see the action below. A vast American-classic menu consisting of hundreds of items is offered throughout the day. Some choices: delicious baked macaroni and cheese, sandwiches (Philadelphia cheese steak, New Orleans oyster po'boy, and Georgia pulled pork barbecue, among others), burgers, salads, egg dishes and omelets, and entrées running the gamut from Maryland crabcakes to Rhode Island roast turkey with stuffing and orange-cranberry compote. A list of about 20 desserts includes peanut butter pie, strawberry shortcake, and ultra-rich "death-by-chocolate" cake. All bar drinks are available, including a wide selection of domestic beers, wines by the glass, and microbrews; nonalcoholic beverages range from milkshakes to lemonade.

Center Cafe

Union Station, 50 Massachusetts Ave. NE. ☎ **202/682-0143.** Reservations accepted for large parties only. Main courses $8.95–$14.95. AE, CB, DC, MC, V. Sun–Thurs 11:30am–10:30pm (bar, to 11:30pm), Fri–Sat 11:30am–midnight (bar, to 12:30am). Metro: Union Station. AMERICAN/MEXICAN/ASIAN.

This handsome two-level oval mahogany restaurant, the hub of the Main Hall, offers a diverse menu of salads, sandwiches, quesadillas, and fancy pizzas. Entrées include crabmeat-filled lobster ravioli in herbed tomato-cream sauce, blue-corn enchiladas stuffed with chicken and chilies, and hacked roast Oriental chicken served with spicy peanut sauce and sesame noodles. Good desserts here, too, such as mixed-berry cobbler topped with a sweet biscuit and whipped cream.

Sfuzzi

Union Station, 50 Massachusetts Ave. NE. ☎ **202/842-4141.** Reservations recommended. Main courses $8–$11 at lunch, $10–$20 at dinner; brunch Sun $14. AE, CB, DC, MC, V. Mon–Sat 11:30am–3pm, Sun 11am–3pm; nightly 5:30–10pm. Metro: Union Station. ITALIAN.

An elegant multilevel restaurant in an alcove off the Main Hall, Sfuzzi serves California-influenced Italian fare. Entrées range from pizzas with gourmet toppings (smoked chicken, wild oregano, goat cheese) to grilled salmon in basil-citrus sauce with green beans and herbed potatoes. There are also many pasta dishes such as fettuccine tossed with grilled chicken, artichokes, and sun-dried tomatoes in Parmesan cream sauce. There's a full bar, and an extensive wine list includes many by-the-glass selections. A prix-fixe Sunday brunch includes an extensive antipasto bar, an entrée, and dessert.

7

What to See & Do in Washington, D.C.

People often come to Washington for a weekend expecting to see all the sights. Talk about life in the fast lane! The Smithsonian Institution alone consists of more than a dozen museums plus the National Zoo. Then there are the monuments and memorials, the White House, the Capitol, the Supreme Court, the Library of Congress, the FBI, the Kennedy Center, the Holocaust Museum, the National Archives, and Washington National Cathedral—major sights one and all. About a dozen other very interesting attractions vie for your sightseeing time, and it's nice to get over to Georgetown, take a stroll on the canal, or visit nearby Mount Vernon, Arlington, and Alexandria.

There's so much to see that you should consider spending at least a week. Even then, remember that you can't see everything, and it's more rewarding to see a few attractions thoroughly than to race through dozens. To make the most of your time, read the following listings and plan a reasonably relaxed sightseeing itinerary focusing on the sights that interest you most. As you plan, keep in mind geographic proximity (don't waste energy zigzagging back and forth across town); days and hours attractions are open; and applicable warnings about arriving early to avoid long lines or secure necessary tickets. "Special Tickets for VIP Congressional Tours" in (Chapter 2) tells you how to obtain tickets ahead of time for VIP tours to some attractions.

Since even close friends whom I've personally counseled to take it easy while sightseeing in Washington have wound up exhausting themselves, I suspect that my advice to program relaxation into your touring day will go unheeded. For the record, I suggest an occasional long leisurely lunch and visits to relaxing outdoor attractions. Tour the beautiful gardens at Dumbarton Oaks, take a river cruise, or plan a picnic at the Arboretum–anything that gets you off your museum-weary feet for a while. Speaking of those feet, you'll be on them a lot in Washington. Comfortable shoes are essential to bearing up under the rigors of sightseeing; during sweltering summer days running shoes, shorts, and a T-shirt (or whatever minimum attire you feel comfortable with) is the ideal outfit.

Most museums offer highlight tours (call in advance for exact hours)—a good way to get a useful overview in a short time.

The good news: Almost everything is free.

SUGGESTED ITINERARIES

If You Have 1 Day

Make the Mall your destination, visiting whichever museums best suit your interests. Rest up, have a leisurely dinner (this advice goes for every day's itinerary), and visit the Lincoln Memorial at night.

If You Have 2 Days

Spend your first day as suggested above. Start your second day with a tour of the Capitol, followed by a tour of the Supreme Court. After a relaxing lunch, spend the afternoon visiting the Washington Monument, walking around the Tidal Basin, and seeing the Jefferson Memorial. If the weather makes this plan unfeasible, continue visiting Mall museums (you won't even have scratched the surface in one day). Have dinner in Georgetown and browse the shops.

If You Have 3 Days

Spend your first two days as outlined above.

In the morning of your third day, tour the White House and the National Archives. In the afternoon, visit the Vietnam Veterans Memorial, and, if you haven't already done so, the Lincoln Memorial. Or in bad weather, tour the Washington National Cathedral or some of the non-Mall art museums (for example, the Phillips Collection, National Portrait Gallery, Museum of American Art, or the Corcoran). See Chapter 10 for evening suggestions.

If You Have 5 Days or More

Spend your first three days as suggested above.

On the fourth day, get an early start taking the FBI tour, and spend the rest of the morning at Ford's Theatre. Spend the afternoon in outdoor activities—the zoo or a hike along the C&O Canal. Alternatively, you might visit the U.S. Holocaust Memorial Museum (not recommended for children under 12); this will require most of a day to see. See Chapter 10 for evening suggestions.

On the fifth day, plan an entire day visiting Alexandria, Virginia. Or spend the morning touring Mount Vernon and the afternoon seeing the sights you've missed. See Chapter 10 for evening suggestions.

1 The Top Attractions

Although these are the sights most tourists choose to visit in Washington, they may or may not strike you as major, and nowhere is it written that you must see them all. You might want to consider other sights and outdoor activities (listed later in this chapter) when planning your itinerary.

What's Special About Washington, D.C.

Government Buildings
- The White House and the Capitol, two of America's most-visited shrines.
- The Supreme Court, Cass Gilbert's marble-columned temple.
- The National Archives, displaying original parchments of the Constitution, Declaration of Independence, and Bill of Rights.

Monuments
- Monuments to Presidents Washington, Lincoln, and Jefferson.
- The Vietnam Veterans Memorial, a poignant tribute.

After Dark
- The John F. Kennedy Center for the Performing Arts—our national cultural facility.
- The Arena Stage, repertory theater at its very best.
- Wolf Trap Farm Park, bucolic setting for a prestigious summer performing-arts festival.

Zoo
- National Zoo, home to several thousand animals.

Architectural Highlights
- Library of Congress—the ornate Italian Renaissance–style Thomas Jefferson Building (1897).
- Smithsonian "Castle" (1849), Victorian red-turreted and towered James Renwick building, the first in the famed museum complex.
- Union Station (1907), modeled after Rome's Baths of Diocletian and Arch of Constantine.
- Old Post Office Pavilion (1899), in Romanesque style, crowned by a 315-foot clock tower.
- Old Stone House (1765), probably the city's oldest surviving pre-Revolutionary building.
- The Renwick Gallery (1859), a landmark building of the French Second Empire style.

Parks & Gardens
- West Potomac Park, site of the famous cherry tress.
- C&O Canal, built in the 1800s when inland water routes were vital to transportation; today a major D.C. recreational area.
- The National Arboretum , which houses the National Bonsai Collection.
- Rock Creek Park, a 1,754-acre playground in the heart of the city.

For Kids
- The National Air and Space Museum, where exhibits range from the 1903 Wright Brothers' plane to the *Apollo 11* Command Module.
- The Museum of Natural History Discovery Room, for a hands-on learning experience.
- The FBI building, where exhibits range from the DNA lab to weapons used by notorious 1930s gangsters.

THE THREE MAJOR HOUSES OF GOVERNMENT

Three of the most visited sights in Washington are the buildings housing the executive, legislative, and judicial branches of the U.S. government. All stunning edifices, they offer considerable insight into the workings of our system.

❖ The White Houses

1600 Pennsylvania Ave. NW (visitor entrance gate on E. Executive Ave.). ☎ **202/456-7041** or 202/755-7798. Admission free. Tues–Sat 10am–noon. Closed some days for official functions; check before leaving your hotel by calling the 24-hour number. Metro: McPherson Square.

"I never forget," said Franklin Delano Roosevelt in one of his fireside chats, "that I live in a house owned by all the American people." Not only do Americans own the White House, they're welcome to visit, making it almost unique among world residences of heads of state. The White House has been the scene of many great moments in American history. It is the central theater of government, where decisions on national and international policies are made. And, of course, it's also the private home of the president and his family, their personal doings and dramas as much a focus of national interest as any happenings in the political arena. Its interior is a repository of art and furnishings, reflecting the tastes of our chief executives and first ladies from the early years of the American Republic. Highlights of the tour include the following rooms:

The gold-and-white **East Room,** scene of great and gala receptions, weddings of presidents' daughters (Lynda Bird Johnson, for one), and other dazzling events. Here, heads of state have been entertained, seven presidents who died in office lay in state, and Nixon delivered his resignation speech. The room is decorated in the early 20th-century style of the Theodore Roosevelt renovation; it has parquet Fontainebleau oak floors and white-painted wood walls with fluted pilasters and classically themed relief inserts. Note the famous Gilbert Stuart portrait of George Washington that Dolley Madison saved from the British torch during the War of 1812.

The **Green Room** (named in the 19th century for its green upholstery), today used as a sitting room, was Thomas Jefferson's dining room. He designed a revolving door with trays on one side, so servants could leave dishes on the kitchen side. Then he would twirl the door, and guests could help themselves. Thus he retained his privacy. Walls here are covered in green watered-silk fabric, and some of the early 19th-century furnishings are attributed to the famous cabinetmaker Duncan Phyfe. There are notable paintings by Gilbert Stuart and John Singer Sargent.

The oval **Blue Room,** where presidents and first ladies have officially received guests since the Jefferson administration, is today decorated in the French Empire style chosen by James Monroe in 1817. It was, however, Van Buren's decor that began the "blue room" tradition. The walls, on which hang portraits of five presidents (including Rembrandt Peale's portrait of Thomas Jefferson and G. P. A. Healy's of Tyler), are covered in reproductions of early 19th-century French and American wallpaper. A settee and seven of the original gilded armchairs Monroe ordered from French cabinetmaker Pierre-Antoine Bellangé remain. Grover Cleveland, the only president ever to wed in the White House, was married in the Blue Room; the Reagans, Nancy wearing symbolic yellow, here greeted the 53 Americans liberated after being held hostage in Iran for 444 days; and every year it's the setting for the White House Christmas tree.

Several portraits of past presidents—plus Albert Bierstadt's *View of the Rocky Mountains* and a Gilbert Stuart portrait of Dolley Madison—hang in the **Red Room.** It's used as a reception room, usually for afternoon teas. The satin-covered walls and most of the Empire furnishings are red, with white wainscoting and crown moldings.

The white-walled, gold-accented **State Dining Room** is a superb setting for state dinners and luncheons. Its architecture is modeled after late 18th-century neoclassical English houses. Theodore Roosevelt, a big-game hunter, had a large moose head over the fireplace and other trophies on the walls. Below G. P. A. Healy's portrait of Lincoln is an inscription written by John Adams on his second night in the White House (FDR had it carved into the mantel): "I Pray Heaven to Bestow The Best of Blessings on THIS HOUSE and on All that shall hereafter Inhabit it. May none but Honest and Wise Men ever rule under This Roof."

History   Since its cornerstone was laid in 1792, the White House has gone through numerous changes. It was designed by Irishman James Hoban, so it isn't surprising that it resembles the house of the duke of Leinster of Dublin. The South Portico was added in 1824, the North Portico in 1829. Electricity was first installed during Benjamin Harrison's presidency in 1891.

In 1902, repairs and refurnishings of the White House cost almost $500,000. No other great change took place until Harry Truman added his controversial "balcony" inside the columns of the South Portico. Also in 1948, after the leg of Margaret Truman's piano cut through the dining room ceiling, nearly $6 million was allotted for reconstruction of the building. The Trumans lived at Blair House across the street for close to four years while the White House interior was taken apart and put back together again, piece by piece. Steel girders and concrete shored up the place. It's as solid as Gibraltar now.

In 1961 Mrs. John F. Kennedy formed a Fine Arts Committee to help restore the famous rooms to their original grandeur.

Seeing the White House   More than 1.2 million people line up annually to see the Executive Mansion. Your best bet is to obtain tickets in advance from your congressperson or senator for the VIP tours at 8:15, 8:30, and 8:45am (see Chapter 2 for details). This will ensure your entrance, even during the tourist season when more than 6,000 people try to squeeze in during the two hours each day the White House is open. It will also entitle you to a more extensive—and guided tour; during the regular visiting hours, there are guides on hand to answer questions, but no actual tour is given. A good idea, before you take any tour, is to pick up a book called *The White House: An Historic Guide,* available in District bookstores and at many of the top sights. Then you'll know what to look for in each room, and your experience

The White House Visitor Center

The White House Visitor Center, Pennsylvania Avenue between 14th and 15th streets NW (☎ **202/208-1631,** 202/456-7041 for recorded information), opened in 1995 to provide extensive interpretive data about the White House (as well as other Washington tourist attractions) and serve as a ticket-distribution center. It is under the joint auspices of the White House Historical Association, the National Park Service, and the U.S. Department of the Interior. Here visitors can view a 26-minute video about the White House called "Within These Walls" which provides interior views of the presidential precincts and features footage with both the president and Hillary Clinton. On-premises exhibits include:

Architectural History of the White House (including the grounds and extensive renovations to its structure and interior that have taken place since the first cornerstone was laid in 1792);

Symbol and Image, showing how the White House has been portrayed by photographers, artists, journalists, political cartoonists, and others;

First Families, with displays about the people who have lived here (such as prankster Tad Lincoln who once stood in a window above his father and waved a Confederate flag at a military review);

The Working White House, focusing on the vast staff of servants, chefs, gardeners, Secret Service people, and others who maintain this institution;

Ceremony and Celebration, depicting notable White House events from a Wright Brothers' aviation demonstration in 1911 to a performance by Baryshnikov during the Carter administration;

White House Interiors, Past and Present, including photographs of the ever-changing Oval Office as decorated by administrations from Taft through Clinton; and

Herbert Hoover: A Life of Leadership (the building housing the facility was named for Hoover).

The Center is open Memorial Day to Labor Day 7am to 5pm Tuesday through Saturday, 8am to 5pm Sunday and Monday; hours the rest of the year are 8am to 5pm daily. It is closed Thanksgiving, Christmas, and New Year's Day.

will be greatly enhanced. You can order it in advance (as well as another book, *The Living White House,* which gives more biographical information about the presidents and their families) from the **White House Historical Association,** 740 Jackson Place NW, Washington, D.C. 20503 (☎ **202/737-8292**). Send $5.75 for a paperback or $7.50 for a hardcover edition of either book.

The White House is open to tourists mornings only, Tuesday through Saturday. Most of the year, if you don't have VIP tour tickets, you just line up at the southeast gate at E Street and Executive

Avenue (just south of the White House) where uniformed guards are on hand to assist visitors.

From about mid-March (sometimes a bit earlier) through Labor Day weekend, tickets are required. They are distributed, free of charge, at the White House Visitor Center (see box on p. 147 for details). Tickets are timed for tours between 10am and noon, issued on the day of the tour only on a first-come, first-served basis starting at 7am. One person may obtain up to six tickets. The number of tickets for each day is limited (approximately 4,500 are distributed), and the ticket counter closes when the supply for that day is gone. Hence, it is essential that you arrive early (even before 7am, to ensure admission). Tickets are valid only for the day and time issued. Tours depart from bleachers on the Ellipse—the park area south of the White House. After obtaining your tickets, you'll probably have quite a bit of time to spare before your scheduled tour time; consider enjoying a leisurely breakfast at Reeve's or the Old Ebbitt Grill, both close by (see Chapter 6 for details). From June 1 through August 31, the National Park Service offers free musical performances at the Ellipse for waiting visitors.

Note: During those months when tickets are not required, you still need to arrive early. Also, all visitors—even those with Congressional tour passes—should call 202/456-7041 before setting out in the morning; occasionally the White House is closed to tourists on short notice because of unforeseen events.

✪ The Capitol

At the east end of the Mall, entrance on E. Capitol St. and 1st St. NW. ☎ **202/ 225-6827.** Admission free. Daily 9am–4:30pm (tours 9am–3:45pm). The Rotunda is open till 8pm Memorial Day–Labor Day most years (this is decided each year). Closed Jan 1, Thanksgiving Day, and Dec 25. Parking at Union Station. Metro: Capitol South.

As our most tangible national symbol since its first wing was completed in 1800, and the place where all our laws are debated, the Capitol is perhaps the most important edifice in the United States. It's also one of the most beautiful. Historian Allan Nevins called it "the spirit of America in stone." For 135 years it sheltered not only both houses of Congress but the Supreme Court, and for 97 years the Library of Congress as well.

On the massive bronze doors leading to the **Rotunda** are portrayals of events in the life of Columbus. The Rotunda—a huge circular hall some 96 feet across and under a 180-foot dome—is the hub of the Capitol. Nine presidents have lain in state here; when Kennedy's casket was displayed, the line of mourners stretched 40 blocks. On the circular walls are eight immense oil paintings of events in American history, such as the presentation of the Declaration of Independence and the surrender of Cornwallis at Yorktown. In the dome is an allegorical fresco masterpiece by Constantino Brumidi, *Apotheosis of Washington,* a symbolic portrayal of George Washington surrounded by Roman gods and goddesses watching over the progress of the nation. A trompe l'oeil frieze overhead depicts events in American history from Columbus through the Wright brothers' flight at Kitty Hawk. There's also a life-size marble statue of Lincoln.

Capitol Hill

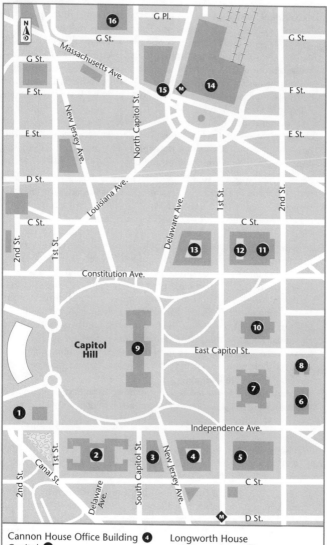

Cannon House Office Building **4**
Capitol **9**
Dirksen Senate Office Building **12**
Folger Shakespeare Library **8**
Government Printing Office **16**
Hart Senate Office Building **11**
Library of Congress
  Thomas Jefferson Building **7**
  James Madison Building **5**
  John Adams Building **6**

Longworth House
  Office Building **13**
National Postal Museum **15**
Rayburn House Office Building **2**
Russell Senate Office Building **13**
Supreme Court **10**
Union Station **4**
U.S. Botanic Garden **1**

National Statuary Hall was originally the chamber of the House of Representatives. In 1864 it became Statuary Hall, and the states were invited to send two statues each of native sons and daughters to the hall. As the room filled up, statues spilled over into the Hall of Columns, corridors, and anywhere that might accommodate the bronze and marble artifacts. Many of the statues honor individuals who have had important roles in American history, such as Henry Clay, Ethan Allen, and Daniel Webster.

The south and north wings are occupied by the House and Senate chambers, respectively. The House of Representatives chamber is the largest legislative chamber in the world. The president delivers his annual State of the Union address there.

Seeing the Capitol   As at the White House, VIP tour tickets from a congressperson or senator for the morning tours (departing at intervals between 8 and 8:45am) are a definite advantage (see Chapter 2 for details). Also request visitors' passes for each member of your party to view a session of the House and/or Senate. If you don't get advance tickets, free 30-minute guided tours leave from the Rotunda every 15 minutes (more often in spring and summer) between 9am and 3:45pm. And if you don't receive visitors' passes in the mail (not every senator or representative sends them), they're obtainable at your senators' office on the Constitution Avenue side of the building or your representative's office on the Independence Avenue side (noncitizens can just present a passport at the first-floor appointment desk on the Senate side or at the third-floor House gallery and ask for a pass). You'll know when the House or Senate is in session when you see flags flying over their respective wings of the Capitol. Or you can check the weekday "Today in Congress" column in the *Washington Post* for details on times of House and Senate committee meetings. This column also tells you which sessions are open to the public, allowing you to pick one that interests you.

✪ Supreme Court

East of the Capitol on 1st St. NE (between E. Capitol St. and Maryland Ave). ☎ **202/ 479-3000.** Admission free. Mon–Fri 9am–4:30pm. Closed weekends and all federal holidays. Metro: Capitol South or Union Station.

In these oft-turbulent times, I find it reassuring to visit the massive Corinthian marble palace that houses the Supreme Court, its serene classical dignity reinforced by the pledge etched in a frieze over the colonnaded entrance: "Equal Justice Under Law." The Court's subtle

Impressions

The Capitol is the first temple dedicated to the sovereignty of the people, embellishing with Athenian taste the course of a nation looking far beyond the range of Athenian destinies. —Thomas Jefferson

It is our national center. It belongs to us, and whether it is mean or majestic, whether arrayed in glory or covered with shame, we cannot but share its character and its destiny. —Frederick Douglass

excitement is well described by Justice Oliver Wendell Holmes, Jr., who wrote, "We are very quiet . . . but it is the quiet of a storm center." The highest tribunal in the nation, the Supreme Court is charged with deciding whether actions of Congress, the president, the states, and lower courts are in accord with the Constitution and with interpreting that document's enduring principles and applying them to new situations and changing conditions. It has the power of "judicial review"—authority to invalidate legislation or executive action that conflicts with the Constitution. Out of the 6,500 cases submitted to it each year, the Supreme Court hears only about 120 cases, many of which deal with issues vital to the nation. The Court's rulings are final, reversible only by another Supreme Court decision, or in some cases, an Act of Congress or a Constitutional amendment.

Until 1935 the Supreme Court met in the Capitol. Architect Cass Gilbert designed the stately Corinthian marble palace that houses the Court today. The building was considered rather grandiose by early residents: One justice remarked that he and his colleagues ought to enter such pompous precincts on elephants.

If you're in town when the Court is in session, try to see a case being argued. The Court meets Monday through Wednesday from 10am to 3pm (with a lunch-hour recess from noon to 1pm) from the first Monday in October through late April, alternating, in approximately two-week intervals, between "sittings" to hear cases and deliver opinions and "recesses" for consideration of business before the Court. Mid-May to early July, you can attend brief sessions (about 15 minutes) at 10am on Monday, when the justices release orders and opinions. You can find out what cases are on the docket by checking the *Washington Post's* "Supreme Court Calendar." Arrive at least an hour early—even earlier for a highly publicized case—to line up for seats, about 150 of which are allotted to the general public.

At 10am the entrance of the justices is announced by the marshal, and all present rise and remain standing while the justices are seated following the chant: "The Honorable, the Chief Justice and Associate Justices of the Supreme Court of the United States. Oyez! Oyez! Oyez! [French for "Hear ye!"] All persons having business before the Honorable, the Supreme Court of the United States, are admonished to draw near and give their attention, for the Court is now sitting. God save the United States and this Honorable Court!" There are many rituals here. Unseen by the gallery is the "conference handshake"; following a 19th-century tradition symbolizing a "harmony of aims if not views," each Justice shakes hand with each of the other eight when they assemble to go to the bench. The Court has a record before it of prior proceedings and relevant briefs, so each side is allowed only a 30-minute argument.

If the Court is not in session during your visit, you can attend a free **lecture** in the courtroom about Court procedure and the building's architecture. Lectures are given from 9:30am to 3:30pm every hour on the half hour.

After the talk, explore the Great Hall and go down a flight of steps to see the 20-minute film on the workings of the Court. The ground floor is a good vantage point to view one of two grand spiral staircases here similar to those at the Vatican and the Paris Opéra. There are also interesting exhibits and a gift shop on this level, and good meals are served in the adjoining cafeteria (see "At Sightseeing Attractions," in Chapter 6, for details).

TRIUMVIRATE OF PRESIDENTIAL MEMORIALS

Only three American presidents have been singled out for recognition with great monuments in Washington, D.C.: George Washington, Abraham Lincoln, and Thomas Jefferson.

The first monument to be built (to Washington) was begun in 1848, the last (to Jefferson) was dedicated in 1943 during cherry-blossom time. There are wreath-laying ceremonies on Washington's, Lincoln's, and Jefferson's birthdays at their respective monuments.

✪ Washington Monument

Directly south of the White House (at 15th St. and Constitution Ave. NW). ☎ **202/ 426-6839.** Admission free. Easter Sunday–Labor Day, daily 8am–midnight; the rest of the year, daily 9am–5pm. Last elevators depart 15 minutes before closing. Closed July 4 (open till noon only) and Dec 25. Metro: Smithsonian; then a 10-minute walk.

The 555-foot stark marble obelisk that shimmers in the sun and glows under floodlights at night is the city's most visible landmark. It is, like the Eiffel Tower in Paris or London's Big Ben, a symbol of the city.

The idea of a tribute to George Washington first arose 16 years before his death at the Continental Congress of 1783. An equestrian statue was planned, and Washington himself approved the site for it— on the Mall, west of the future Capitol and south of the "President's Palace." However, more than a century elapsed before a very different monument was completed. The new nation had more pressing problems, and funds were not readily available. It wasn't until the early 1830s, with the 100th anniversary of Washington's birth approaching, that any action was taken. Then there were several fiascos. A mausoleum was provided for Washington's remains under the Capitol Rotunda, but a grand-nephew, citing Washington's will, refused to allow the body to be moved from Mount Vernon. In 1830 Horatio Greenough was commissioned to create a memorial statue for the Rotunda. He came up with a bare-chested, seated Washington, draped in classical Greek garb; a shocked public claimed he looked as if he were "entering or leaving a bath," and so the statue was relegated to the Smithsonian. Finally, in 1833 prominent citizens organized the Washington National Monument Society. Treasury Building architect Robert Mills's design (originally with a circular colonnaded Greek temple base, but later discarded for lack of funds) was accepted. The cornerstone was laid on July 4, 1848; for the next 37 years, watching the monument grow—or not grow—was a local pastime. The Civil War and lagging funds brought construction to a halt at an awkward 150 feet. The unsightly stump remained until 1876 when President Grant approved federal monies to complete the project. Rejecting plans for ornate embellishment that ranged from English Gothic to Hindu pagoda designs, authorities put the U.S. Army Corps of Engineers to work on the obelisk. Dedicated in 1885, it was opened to the public in 1888.

The 360° views are spectacular. To the east are the Capitol and Smithsonian buildings; to the north, the White House; to the west, the Lincoln and Vietnam memorials, and Arlington National Cemetery beyond; and to the south, the gleaming-white shrine to Thomas Jefferson and the Potomac River. It's a marvelous orientation to the city.

June through September, 30-minute talks are given by rangers throughout the day. During tourist season, arrive before 8am to avoid long lines. Climbing the 897 steps is verboten, but a large elevator whisks visitors to the top in just 70 seconds. If, however, you're avid to see more of the interior, **"Down the Steps" tours** are given, subject to staff availability, weekends at 10am and 2pm (more often in summer). For details, call before you go or ask a ranger on duty. On this tour you'll learn more about the building of the monument and get to see the 193 carved stones inserted into the interior walls. They range from a piece of stone from the Parthenon to plaques presented by city fire departments.

Light snacks are sold at a snack bar on the grounds, where you'll also find a few picnic tables. There's free two-hour parking at the 16th Street Oval.

✪ Lincoln Memorial

Directly west of the Mall in Potomac Park (at 23rd St. NW, between Constitution and Independence aves). ☎ **202/426-6895.** Admission free. Park staff on duty 8am–midnight daily. Metro: Foggy Bottom; then about a 15-minute walk.

The Lincoln Memorial attracts some 6 million visitors annually. It's a beautiful and moving testament to a great American, its marble walls seeming to embody not only the spirit and integrity of Lincoln, but all that has ever been good about America. Visitors are silently awed in its presence.

The monument was a long time in the making. Although it was planned as early as 1867, two years after Lincoln's death, it was not until 1912 that Henry Bacon's design was completed, and the memorial itself was dedicated in 1922.

A beautiful neoclassical templelike structure, similar in architectural design to the Parthenon in Greece, the memorial has 36 fluted Doric columns representing the states of the Union at the time of Lincoln's death, plus two at the entrance. On the attic parapet are 48 festoons

Impressions

May the spirit of which animated the great founder of this city descend to future generations.   —John Adams

Every dedicated American could be proud that a dynamic experience of democracy in his nation's capital had been made visible to the world.
    —Martin Luther King, Jr., after the 1963 march on Washington

Washington, D.C., Attractions

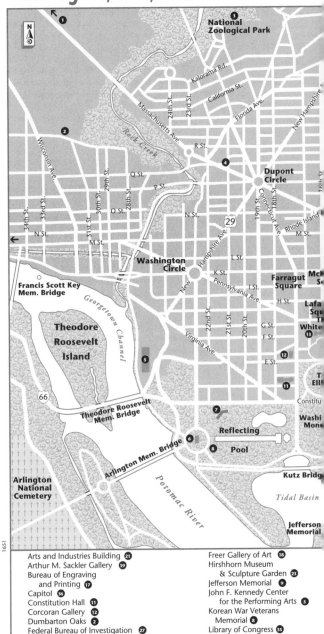

N

National
Zoological Park

Kalorama Rd.

California St.

Florida Ave.

Massachusetts Ave

New Hampshire

Rock Creek

Wisconsin Ave.

R St.

Q St.

P St.

Dupont
Circle

O St.

N St.

Connecticut Ave.

Rhode Island

34th St.

33rd St.

31st St.

30th St.

29th St.

28th St.

Washington
Circle

N St.

M St.

29

M St.

19th St.

18th St.

L St.

K St.

Farragut
Square

McI
Sq

Francis Scott Key
Mem. Bridge

Georgetown Channel

New

Pennsylvania Ave.

I St.

H St.

Lafa
Squ

Theodore
Roosevelt
Island

Virginia Ave.

22nd St.

21st St.

20th St.

G St.

F St.

E St.

White

66

Theodore Roosevelt
Mem. Bridge

Reflecting

Pool

Constitu

Washi
Mon

Arlington Mem. Bridge

Potomac River

Kutz Bridg

Arlington
National
Cemetery

Tidal Basin

Jefferson
Memorial

1651

U St.
T St.
S St.
R St.

Vernon Ave.

Rhode Island Ave.

Florida Ave.

13th St.
12th St.
11th St.
10th St.
9th St.
8th St.
7th St.
6th St.
5th St.
4th St.

P St.
O St.
N St.

M St.

Mt. Vernon Place

New Jersey Ave.

K St.
I St.
Massachusetts Ave.
K St.

North Capitol

Union Station

New York Ave.

14

G St.
30
29
F St.
28
27
3rd St.
2nd St.
1st St.

31
32

E St.

2nd St.
3rd St.

sylvania Ave.

26

Louisiana Ave.

D St.

C St.

itution Ave.

15
22
25

The Mall
23
24

The Capitol
36
37
33
East Capitol
34
35

18
21
ependence 19 20 Ave.

Maryland Ave.

C St.

Virginia Ave.

South Capitol

New Jersey Ave.

395

❓ Did You Know?

- Architect Pierre L'Enfant's bill for designing Washington came to $95,000; years later he finally accepted Congress's offer of $2,500.
- In 1835 Pres. Andrew Jackson paid off the national debt; it was the first—and last—time in U.S. history that the federal books have been balanced.
- Ambassadors to Washington in the early days were given "hardship pay" for enduring the inconveniences of living there.
- The classic novel *Little Lord Fauntleroy* was written by Frances Hodgson Burnett on I Street in 1886.
- A famous beverage was concocted for a Missouri lobbyist, Col. J. K. Rickey; originally rye whiskey was used, but later some "barbarous New Yorkers" substituted gin—hence, "Gin Rickey."

symbolic of the number of states in 1922 when the monument was erected. Hawaii and Alaska are noted in an inscription on the terrace. To the west, the Arlington Memorial Bridge crossing the Potomac recalls the reunion of North and South. To the east is the beautiful Reflecting Pool, lined with American elms and stretching 2,000 feet toward the Washington Monument and the Capitol beyond.

The memorial chamber, under 60-foot ceilings, has limestone walls inscribed with the Gettysburg Address and Lincoln's Second Inaugural Address. Two 60-foot murals by Jules Guerin on the north and south walls depict, allegorically, Lincoln's principles and achievements. On the south wall, an Angel of Truth freeing a slave is flanked by groups of figures representing Justice and Immortality. The north-wall mural depicts the unity of North and South and is flanked by groups of figures symbolizing Fraternity and Charity. Most powerful, however, is Daniel Chester French's 19-foot-high seated statue of Lincoln in deep contemplation in the central chamber. Its effect is best evoked by these words of Walt Whitman: "He was a mountain in grandeur of soul, he was a sea in deep undervoice of mystic loneliness, he was star in steadfast purity of purpose and service and he abides." It is appropriate to the heritage of Lincoln that on several occasions those who have been oppressed have expressed their plight to America and the world at the steps of his shrine. Most notable was a peaceful demonstration of 200,000 people on August 28, 1963, at which another freedom-loving American, Dr. Martin Luther King, Jr., proclaimed "I have a dream."

An information booth and bookstore are on the premises. June through September, 30-minute ranger programs are presented throughout the day. The rest of the year, ranger talks are given on request.

✪ Jefferson Memorial

South of the Washington Monument on Ohio Dr. (at the south shore of the Tidal Basin). ☎ **202/426-6822.** Admission free. Park staff on duty 8am–midnight daily. Transportation: Tourmobile.

Pres. John F. Kennedy, at a 1962 dinner honoring 29 Nobel Prize winners, told his guests they were "the most extraordinary collection of talent, of human knowledge, that has ever been gathered together at the White House, with the possible exception of when Thomas Jefferson dined alone." Jefferson penned the Declaration of Independence, spoke out against slavery, and was George Washington's secretary of state, John Adams's vice president, and our third president. And he still found time to establish the University of Virginia and to pursue wide-ranging interests including architecture, astronomy, anthropology, music, and farming.

The site for the Jefferson Memorial, in relation to the Washington and Lincoln memorials, was of extraordinary importance. The Capitol, the White House, and the Mall were already located in accordance with L'Enfant's plan, and there was no spot for such a project if the symmetry that guided L'Enfant was to be maintained. So the memorial was built on land reclaimed from the Potomac River, now known as the Tidal Basin. Franklin Delano Roosevelt had all the trees between the Jefferson Memorial and the White House cut down, so that he could see it every morning and draw inspiration from it.

It's a beautiful memorial, a columned rotunda in the style of the Pantheon in Rome, which Jefferson so admired. On the Tidal Basin side the sculptural group above the entrance depicts Jefferson with Benjamin Franklin, John Adams, Roger Sherman, and Robert Livingston, who worked on drafting the Declaration of Independence. The domed interior of the memorial contains the 19-foot bronze statue of Jefferson standing on a 6-foot pedestal of black Minnesota granite. The sculpture is the work of Rudulph Evans, who was chosen from more than 100 artists in a nationwide competition. Jefferson is depicted wearing a fur-collared coat given to him by his close friend, the Polish general, Tadeusz Kosciuszko. Inscriptions from Jefferson's writing engraved on the interior walls expand on Jefferson's philosophy, which is best expressed in the circular frieze quotation: "I have sworn upon the altar of God eternal hostility against every form of tyranny over the mind of man."

June through September, 35-minute ranger programs are presented throughout the day. The rest of the year, rangers give short talks to visitors on request. Spring through fall, a refreshment kiosk at the Tourmobile stop offers snack fare. A bookshop is on the premises. There's free one-hour parking.

SMITHSONIAN INSTITUTION

Once referred to as "the nation's attic,"—a description that seemed somewhat musty—the Smithsonian Institution was later redubbed, "the nation's showcase." That doesn't totally explain the Smithsonian either, for its collection of more than 140 million objects pertains to the entire world and its history, as well as its peoples and animals (past and present) and our attempts to probe into the future. The sprawling institution comprises nine immense Smithsonian buildings located between the Washington Monument and the Capitol on the Mall; other buildings devoted to specialized exhibits are within walking

A "Liberal and Enlightened Donor"

Wealthy English scientist James Smithson (1706–1829), the illegitimate son of the Duke of Northumberland, never explained why he willed his vast fortune to the United States—a country he had never visited. Speculation is that he felt a new nation, lacking established cultural institutions, stood in greatest need of his bequest. Smithson died in Genoa, Italy, in 1829. Congress accepted his gift in 1836; two years later a shipment of 105 bags of gold sovereigns (about half a million dollars' worth—a considerable sum in the 19th century) arrived at the United States Mint in Philadelphia. For the next eight years Congress debated the best possible use for these funds. Finally, in 1846, James Polk signed an act into law establishing the Smithsonian institution and providing "for the faithful execution of said trust, according to the will of the liberal and enlightened donor." It authorized a board to receive "all objects of art and of foreign and curious research, and all objects of natural history, plants, and geological and mineralogical specimens . . . for research and museum purposes."

In addition to the original Smithson bequest—which has been augmented by many subsequent endowments—the Smithsonian is also supported by annual congressional appropriations. Today it comprises a complex of 14 museums, nine of them on the Mall, plus the National Zoological Park. Its holdings—in every area of human interest—total more than 140 million objects and specimens, running the gamut from a 3.5-billion-year-old fossil to part of a 1902 Horn & Hardart Automat. Additionally, the Smithsonian has sponsored thousands of scientific expeditions that have pushed into remote frontiers in deserts, mountains, polar regions, and jungles.

An interesting note: Alexander Graham Bell was the regent charged with bringing Smithson's remains to the United States from Italy in 1904. The remains were reinterred in a chapel-like room of the Smithsonian "Castle."

distance of the Mall; and farther out are the National Zoological Park (the zoo) and the Anacostia Museum. Thousands of scientific expeditions sponsored by the Smithsonian have pushed into remote frontiers in the deserts, mountains, polar regions, and jungles. Traveling exhibits are sent to other museums, schools, and libraries. And all this is a mere hint of the Smithsonian's scope and involvement.

The Smithsonian Institution began with a $500,000 bequest from James Smithson, an English scientist who had never visited this country. When he died in 1829, he willed his entire fortune to the United States "to found at Washington . . . an establishment for the increase and diffusion of knowledge. . . ." In 1846 Congress created a corporate entity to carry out Smithson's will, and the federal government agreed to pay 6% interest on the bequeathed funds in perpetuity.

Since then, other munificent private donations have swelled Smithson's original legacy many times over. Major gallery and museum construction through the years stands as testament to thoughtful donors. In 1987 the **Sackler Gallery** (Asian and Near Eastern art) and the **National Museum of African Art** were added to the Smithsonian's Mall attractions. The **National Postal Museum** opened in 1993. And future plans call for moving the **National Museum of the American Indian** (currently in New York) here by the end of the decade.

If you're at the Smithsonian at lunchtime or just want to rest your feet and refuel, check "Restaurants at Sightseeing Attractions" (Chapter 6) for descriptions of the restaurants in the various museums here.

More Information, Please If you want to know what's happening at any of the Smithsonian museums, just get on the phone; **Dial-a-Museum** (☎ **202/357-2020**), a recorded information line, will bring you news of daily activities and special events. For other information call 202/357-2700.

Smithsonian Information Center

1000 Jefferson Dr. SW. ☎ **202/357-2700.** Daily 9am–5:30pm. Closed Dec. 25. Metro: Smithsonian.

For years, visitors were left to explore the intimidatingly vast Smithsonian complex with only a scanty orientation. But that all changed with the 1989 opening of the high-tech Smithsonian Information Center, located in the "Castle" on the Mall. It is appropriately housed in the original Victorian red sandstone Smithsonian building, named for its resemblance to a Norman castle. Today the Castle is fronted by a lovely flower garden and entered via the ornate Oriental-motif Children's Room. Designed at the turn of the century for exhibits displayed at a child's eye level, this charming room has a gold-trimmed ceiling decorated to represent a grape arbor with brightly plumed birds and blue sky peeking through the trellis. Furnishings are peacock-themed, and large Chinese paintings adorn the walls.

The main information area, however, is the Great Hall, where a 20-minute video overview of the institution runs throughout the day in two theaters. There are two large schematic models of the Mall (as well as a third in braille), and two large electronic maps of Washington allow visitors to locate 69 popular attractions and Metro and Tourmobile stops. Interactive videos, some of them at children's heights, offer comprehensive information about the Smithsonian and other capital attractions and transportation (the menus seem infinite).

The entire facility is handicapped-accessible, and information is available in a number of foreign languages. Daily Smithsonian events are displayed on monitors; and the information desk's multilingual staff can answer all your questions and help you plan a Smithsonian sightseeing itinerary. James Smithson's crypt is also on the premises.

You can pick up brochures here. A stop at the center is highly recommended, especially for first-time visitors to the Smithsonian. Most of the museums are within easy walking distance of the facility.

Note: The Information Center opens one hour earlier than the museums.

✪ National Museum of American History

On the north side of the Mall (between 12th and 14th sts. NW), with entrances on Constitution Ave. and Madison Dr. ☎ 202/357–2700. Admission free. Daily 10am–5:30pm. Summer hours, sometimes extended, are determined annually. Closed Dec 25. Metro: Smithsonian or Federal Triangle.

The National Museum of American History deals with "everyday life in the American past" and the external forces that have helped to shape our national character. Its massive contents run the gamut from a Revolutionary War general's tent to Archie Bunker's chair.

Exhibits on the **first floor** (enter on Constitution Avenue) explore the development of farm machines, power machinery, transportation, timekeeping, phonographs, and typewriters. The Palm Court on this level, a turn-of-the-century re-creation, includes the interior of Georgetown's Stohlman's Confectionery Shop as it appeared around 1900 and part of an actual 1902 Horn & Hardart Automat. You can have your mail stamped "Smithsonian Station" at a post office that had been located in Headsville, West Virginia, from 1861 to 1971, when it was brought lock, stock, and barrel to the museum. An important first-floor exhibit, "A Material World," deals with the changing composition of artifacts—from predominantly natural materials such as wood and stone, to manufactured materials such as steel, to the vast range of synthetics we have today. Also on this level is "Engines of Change: The American Industrial Revolution 1790–1860," which tells the story of America's transformation from an agricultural to an industrial society. "Information Age: People, Information & Technology," looks at the ways information technology has changed society during the past 150 years. And "Science in American Life" analyzes the impact of science on society from the 1870s to the present.

If you enter from the Mall, you'll find yourself on the **second floor** facing the original Star-Spangled Banner, 30 by 42 feet, that inspired Francis Scott Key to write the U.S. national anthem in 1814 (*Note: it may be down for repairs during 1996*). "After the Revolution," a major exhibition, focuses on the everyday activities of ordinary 18th-century Americans—their work, family life, and communities. "Field to Factory: Afro-American Migration, 1915–40," is an in-depth study of America's social and demographic history from an African-American perspective. And "American Encounters" on this level commemorates the Columbus quincentennial. Perhaps the most fascinating exhibit is the Foucault Pendulum, a copy of the original model that was exhibited in Paris in 1851 with the accompanying teaser, "You are invited to witness the earth revolve." The heavy pendulum, suspended from the roof, swings monotonously from one side to the other, never varying in its arc, yet knocking over, one by one, a series of red pointers that form a circle around it. How? The pendulum has an unvarying arc, but the earth revolves beneath it. Also on the second floor you will find the first ladies' gowns displayed in an exhibit called "First Ladies: Political Role and Public Image."

A vast collection of ship models, uniforms, weapons, and other military artifacts is located on the **third floor,** where major exhibits focus on the experiences of GIs in World War II (and the postwar world) as well as the wartime internment of Japanese Americans. Other areas include Money and Medals, Textiles, Printing and Graphic Arts, and Ceramics. Here, too, is the first American flag to be called Old Glory (1824).

Inquire at the information desks about highlight tours, demonstration center hands-on activities for children and adults, films, lectures, and concerts. There are several museum shops (most noteworthy is the Smithsonian bookstore, offering books and objects on all aspects of Americana), and a cheerful cafeteria is on the premises.

○ National Museum of Natural History

On the north side of the Mall (between 9th and 12th sts. NW), with entrances on Madison Dr. and Constitution Ave. ☎ **202/357-2700.** Admission free. Daily 10am–5:30pm, with extended hours in summer some years. Closed Dec 25. Metro: Smithsonian or Federal Triangle.

The National Museum of Natural History contains more than 120 million artifacts and specimens—everything from one of the largest African elephants ever bagged by a hunter in our time (it dominates the Rotunda on the Mall—entrance level) to the legendary Hope Diamond.

Free highlight **tours** are given daily at 10:30am and 1:30pm, but if you have the time, the self-guided audio tour provides the most comprehensive commentary on exhibits. It's available at the Rotunda information desk for a nominal fee. A **Discovery Room,** filled with creative hands-on exhibits for children, is on the first floor; it's open Monday to Friday noon to 2:30pm, Saturday and Sunday 10:30am to 3:30pm. Children under 12 must be accompanied by an adult. Free passes are available from 15 minutes prior to opening at the Discovery Room. If you have kids, this is a "must."

On the **Mall Level,** off the Rotunda, evolution is traced back billions of years in Fossils, comprising such exhibits as a 3.5-billion-year-old stromatolite (blue-green algae clump) fossil—one of the earliest signs of life on earth—and a 70-million-year-old dinosaur egg. "Life in the Ancient Seas" features a 100-foot-long mural depicting primitive whales, a life-size walk-around diorama of a 230-million-year-old coral reef, and more than 2,000 fossils that chronicle the evolution of marine life. Dinosaurs, of course, loom large—giant skeletons of creatures that dominated the earth for 140 million years before their extinction about 65 million years ago. Suspended from the ceiling over Dinosaur Hall are exhibits on ancient birds, including a life-size model of the pterosaur, which had a 40-foot wingspan. Also residing above this hall is an ancient shark—or at least the jaw of one, the *Carcharodon megalodon,* that lived in our oceans 5 million years ago. A monstrous 40-foot-long predator, its teeth were 5 to 6 inches long, and it could have consumed a Volkswagen "bug" in one gulp! Here, too: the World of Mammals and Exploring Marine Ecosystems, the latter including a spectacular living coral reef in a 3,000-gallon tank. A second 1,800-gallon tank houses a subarctic sea environment typical of the Maine coast. And an exhibit called "Giant Squid" focuses on the world's largest invertebrates.

On the **second floor** is the Gem and Mineral Hall, where—along with the Hope Diamond—such dazzling gems as the 182-carat Star of Bombay sapphire that belonged to Mary Pickford and Marie Antoinette's diamond earrings are on display. Nearby are geological specimens ranging from meteorites to moon rocks. Kids will enjoy the Orkin Insect Zoo's Plexiglas cages housing tarantulas, centipedes, and the like—not to mention a crawl-through model of an African termite mound (many other fascinating entomological displays here range from cave insects to swamp bugs). Numerous skeletons—from the gigantic extinct Stellar sea cow to the tiny pocket mouse—are displayed in "Bones." Additional exhibits include "South America: Continent and Culture," with objects from the Inca civilization, among others, and "Origin of Western Culture"—from about 10,000 years ago to A.D. 500.

There's a plant-filled cafeteria off the Rotunda. Museum shops feature books on natural history and anthropology for adults and children, jewelry, crafts, fossil reproduction kits, shells, and more. On the second floor is a gem and mineral store.

Note: Due to renovations, the Gem and Mineral Hall, some museum shops, and the restaurant may be closed during your visit.

✪ National Air and Space Museum

On the south side of the Mall (between 4th and 7th sts. SW), with entrances on Jefferson Dr. or Independence Ave. ☎ **202/357-2700;** 202/357-1686 for IMAX ticket information. Admission free. Daily 10am–5:30pm (some years the museum has extended hours during summer). Closed Dec 25. Metro: L'Enfant Plaza (Smithsonian Museums exit).

The National Air and Space Museum chronicles the story of man's mastery of flight—from Kitty Hawk to outer space—in 23 galleries filled with exciting exhibits. Plan to devote at least three or four hours exploring these exhibits and, especially during the tourist season and on holidays, arrive before 10am to make a rush for the film-ticket line when the doors open. The not-to-be-missed **IMAX films** shown in the Samuel P. Langley Theater here, on a screen five stories high and seven stories wide, are immensely popular; tickets tend to sell out quickly. There are five or more films playing each day, most with nature or space-exploration themes. See as many as you have time for. Tickets cost $4 for adults, $2.75 for ages 2 to 21 and seniors over 55; they're free for children under 2. You can also see IMAX films most evenings after closing (call for details and ticket prices). At the same time, purchase tickets (same prices) for a show at the **Albert Einstein Planetarium.**

In between shows, you can view the exhibits; free 1¹/₂-hour highlight **tours** are given daily at 10:15am and 1pm. Recorded tours, narrated by astronauts, are also available for rental. Interactive computers and slide and video shows enhance the exhibits throughout.

Highlights of the **first floor** include famous airplanes (such as the *Spirit of St. Louis*) and spacecraft (the *Apollo 11* Command Module); the world's only touchable moon rock; numerous exhibits on the history of aviation and air transportation; galleries in which you can design your own jet plane and study astronomy; and rockets, lunar-exploration vehicles, manned spacecraft, and guided missiles. A major exhibit on the *Enola Gay,* the plane that dropped the atomic bomb on Hiroshima, includes parts of the vehicle and videotaped interviews with crew members. And "How Things Fly," a gallery that opened in 1996 to celebrate the museum's 20th anniversary, includes wind and smoke tunnels, a boardable Cessna 150 airplane, and dozens of interactive exhibits that demonstrate principles of flight, aerodynamics, and propulsion. All the aircraft, by the way, are originals.

Kids love the "walk-through" Skylab orbital workshop on the **second floor.** Other galleries here highlight the solar system, U.S. manned space flights, sea-air operations, aviation during both world wars, and artists' perceptions of flight. An important exhibit is "Beyond the Limits: Flight Enters the Computer Age," illustrating the primary applications of computer technology to aerospace.

A very attractive cafeteria and a rather elegant restaurant, **Flight Line** and the **Wright Place,** respectively, are on the premises (see "At Sightseeing Attractions" in Chapter 6 for details). And the museum shop sells everything from model kits to freeze-dried astronaut ice cream.

National Museum of American Art

8th and G sts. NW. ☎ **202/357-2700.** Admission free. Daily 10am–5:30pm. Closed Dec 25. Metro: Gallery Place.

NMAA owns more than 37,500 works representing two centuries of our national art history. About 1,000 of these works are on display at any given time, along with special exhibitions highlighting various aspects of American art. The collection, along with the National Portrait Gallery (described below), is housed in the palatial quarters of the 19th-century Greek Revival Old Patent Office Building, partially designed by Washington Monument architect Robert Mills and Capitol dome architect Thomas U. Walter. Fronted by a columned portico evocative of the Parthenon, it was originally a multipurpose facility housing an eclectic mix of items ranging from the original Declaration of Independence to a collection of shrunken heads.

Twentieth-century art occupies the most exalted setting, the third-floor Lincoln Gallery, with vaulted ceilings and marble columns. In this room, 4,000 revelers celebrated Lincoln's second inaugural in 1865. On view are works of post–World War II artists (de Kooning, Kline, Noguchi, and others). Other 20th-century works on this floor include paintings commissioned during the New Deal era.

Mid- to late-19th-century artists—such as Winslow Homer, Mary Cassatt, Albert Pinkham Ryder, and John Singer Sargent—are on the second floor, as is the Hiram Powers Gallery housing the contents of the 19th-century neoclassic sculptor's Florence studio. Here, too: works by such early American masters as Charles Willson Peale, Benjamin West, and Samuel F. B. Morse.

A unique work of folk art on the first floor is James Hampton's visionary religious piece (completely covered in aluminum and gold foil), *Throne of the Third Heaven of the Nation's Millennium General Assembly.* Other first floor displays include the $1.4-million Herbert

Waide Hemphill, Jr., Folk Art Collection (19th and 20th centuries) and an Art of the West Gallery featuring paintings by John Mix Stanley and Charles Bird King, along with George Catlin's Native American portraits from the collection he showed in Paris in the 1840s (the museum owns 445 of them).

When you enter, pick up a map and calendar of events and ask about current temporary exhibits at the information desk. Free walk-in tours are given at noon weekdays and at 2pm Saturday and Sunday. There is a lovely courtyard cafe on the premises.

The National Portrait Gallery

8th and F sts. NW. ☎ **202/357-2700.** Admission free. Daily 10am–5:30pm. Closed Dec 25. Metro: Gallery Place.

The "heroes and villains, thinkers and doers, conservatives and radicals" who have made "significant contributions to the history, development, and culture of the United States" are represented here in paintings, sculpture, photography, and other forms of portraiture. Although the museum didn't open until 1968, the concept of a national portrait gallery first arose in the mid-19th century when Congress commissioned G. P. A. Healy to paint a series of presidential portraits for the White House. And American portraiture dates back even further, as evidenced by the Rembrandt Peale portraits of George and Martha Washington on display here, not to mention those predating the Revolution (of Pocahontas, among others). It's great fun to wander the corridors here, sometimes putting faces to famous names for the first time.

In addition to the Hall of Presidents (on the second floor), notable exhibits include Gilbert Stuart's famed "Lansdowne" portrait of George Washington, a portrait of *Mary Cassatt* by Degas, 19th-century silhouettes by French-born artist August Edouart, Jo Davidson's sculpture portraits (including a Buddha-like Gertrude Stein), and a self-portrait by John Singleton Copley. On the mezzanine, the Civil War is documented in portraiture, including one of the last photographs ever taken of Abraham Lincoln. Take a look at the magnificent Great Hall on the third floor. Originally designed as a showcase for patent models, it later became a Civil War hospital, where Walt Whitman came frequently to "soothe and relieve wounded troops."

Pick up a calendar of events at the information desk to find out about the museum's comprehensive schedule of temporary exhibits, lunchtime lectures, concerts, films, and dramatic presentations. Walk-in tours are given at varying hours—usually between 10am and 3pm.

Renwick Gallery of the National Museum of American Art

Pennsylvania Ave. and 17th St. NW. ☎ **202/357-2700.** Admission free. Daily 10am–5:30pm. Closed Dec 25. Metro: Farragut West or Farragut North.

A department of the National Museum of American Art, the Renwick, a showcase for American creativity in crafts, is housed in a historic mid-1800s landmark building of the French Second Empire style. The original home of the Corcoran Gallery, it was saved from demolition by First Lady Jacqueline Kennedy in 1963, when she recommended that it be renovated as part of the Lafayette Square restoration. In 1965 it became part of the Smithsonian and was renamed for its architect, James W. Renwick, who also designed the Smithsonian Castle. Although the setting—especially the magnificent Victorian Grand Salon with its wainscoted plum walls and 38-foot skylight ceiling—evokes another era, the museum's contents are mostly contemporary. The rich and diverse display of objects here includes both changing crafts exhibitions and contemporary works from the museum's permanent collection. Typical exhibits run the gamut from "Uncommon Beauty: The Legacy of African-American Craft Art" to "Masterpieces of Louis Comfort Tiffany." The above-mentioned Grand Salon on the second floor, furnished in opulent 19th-century style, displays paintings by 18th- and 19th-century artists.

The Renwick offers a comprehensive schedule of crafts demonstrations, lectures, and films. Inquire at the information desk. And check out the museum shop near the entrance for books on crafts, design, and decorative arts, as well as craft items, many of them for children.

✪ Hirshhorn Museum and Sculpture Garden

On the south side of the Mall (at Independence Ave. and 7th St. SW.). ☎ **202/357-2700.** Admission free. Daily 10am–5:30pm, Sculpture Garden 7:30am–dusk. Closed Dec. 25. Metro: L'Enfant Plaza (Smithsonian Museums exit).

This museum of modern and contemporary art is named after Latvian-born Joseph H. Hirshhorn, who, in 1966 donated his vast art collection—more than 4,000 drawings and paintings and some 2,000 pieces of sculpture—to the United States "as a small repayment for what this nation has done for me and others like me who arrived here as immigrants." At his death in 1981, Hirshhorn bequeathed an additional 5,500 artworks to the museum, and numerous other donors have since greatly expanded his legacy.

Constructed 14 feet above the ground on sculptured supports, the museum's contemporary cylindrical concrete-and-granite building shelters a verdant plaza courtyard where sculpture is displayed. The light and airy interior follows a simple circular route that makes it easy to see every exhibit without getting lost in a honeycomb of galleries. Natural light from floor-to-ceiling windows makes the inner galleries the perfect venue for viewing sculpture, second only, perhaps, to the magnificently beautiful tree-shaded sunken Sculpture Garden across the street (don't miss it). Paintings and drawings are installed in the outer galleries, artificially lit to prevent light damage.

A rotating show of about 600 pieces is on view at all times. The collection features just about every well-known 20th-century artist and provides a comprehensive overview of major trends in Western art from the late 19th century to the present. Among the best-known pieces are Rodin's *The Burghers of Calais,* four bas-reliefs by Matisse known as *The Backs,* and an important collection of the works of Henry Moore.

Pick up a free calendar when you come in to find out about free films, lectures, concerts, and temporary exhibits. Free docent **tours** are given mornings and early afternoons (call for schedule). Art books, posters, and prints are sold at the museum shop.

✪ Arthur M. Sackler Gallery

1050 Independence Ave. SW. ☎ **202/357-2700.** Admission free. Daily 10am–5:30pm. Closed Dec. 25. Metro: Smithsonian.

Opened in 1987, the Sackler, a museum of Asian art, presents traveling exhibitions from major cultural institutions in Asia, Europe, and the United States. In the recent past, these have focused on such wide-ranging areas as 15th-century Persian art and culture, ancient Buddhist and Hindu sculpture from Sri Lanka, Chinese porcelain, 19th-century Japanese woodblock prints, and the opulent court arts of Indonesia. Supplementing these exhibitions is art from the permanent collection, which includes Chinese bronzes from the Shang (1700–1028 B.C.) through the Han (206 B.C.–A.D. 220) dynasties; Chinese jade figures spanning the millennia from 3000 B.C. to the 20th century; Chinese paintings and lacquerware (from the 10th through the 20th century); 20th-century Japanese ceramics and works on paper; ancient Near Eastern works in silver, gold, bronze, and clay; and stone and bronze sculptures from South and Southeast Asia. Since the museum's opening, Sackler's original gift has been enhanced by significant collections such as the Vever assemblage of 11th- to 19th-century Persian and Indian paintings, manuscripts, calligraphies, miniatures, and bookbindings.

Architecturally the Sackler is linked to the adjoining National Museum of African Art in a complex housing both facilities. Although 96% of the buildings' exhibition space is subterranean, there are two above-ground pavilions, both designed to harmonize with neighboring landmark buildings. The pyramidal silhouette of the Sackler is related to the Victorian Arts and Industries Building, and its exterior is faced with dark-beige Rockville granite. Subterranean areas are enlivened by dramatic descents, vast north-facing skylights, a spacious concourse, and lush plantings. Roofing material is copper, treated to oxidize green as it ages. The Sackler shares its staff and research facilities with the adjacent Freer Gallery and is connected to it via an underground exhibition space.

While you are visiting, be sure to browse the vast gallery shop, which offers books on Asian art, children's books, posters, and art reproductions, along with marvelous gifts—Indian mirrorwork fabrics, Balinese masks, jade jewelry, bonsai kits, and much more. For information about museum programs (including many wonderful experiences for children and families), highlight tours (highly recommended), films, events, and temporary exhibits, inquire at the information desk.

National Museum of African Art

950 Independence Ave. SW. ☎ **202/357-2700** or 202/357-4600. Admission free. Daily 10am–5:30pm. Closed Dec. 25. Metro: Smithsonian.

This is the only national art museum in the United States devoted to research in, and the collection and exhibition of, African art. Founded in 1964, and part of the Smithsonian since 1979, it moved to the Mall in 1987 to share a subterranean space with the Sackler Gallery (see above) and the Ripley Center. Its above-ground domed pavilions reflect the arch motif of the neighboring Freer.

Although the museum collects and exhibits ancient and contemporary art from the entire African continent, its permanent collection of more than 7,000 objects (shown in rotating exhibits) highlights the traditional arts of the vast sub-Saharan region. Most of the collection dates from the 19th and 20th centuries. Also among the museum's holdings are the Eliot Elisofon Photographic Archives, comprising 300,000 photographic prints and transparencies and 120,000 feet of film on African arts and culture. Permanent exhibits include a display of Royal Benin art from Nigeria (1300–1897), "The Ancient Nubian City of Kerma, 2500–1500 B.C. (ceramics, jewelry, and ivory animals), "The Art of the Personal Object" (everyday items such as chairs, headrests, snuff boxes, bowls, and baskets), and "Purpose and Perfection: Pottery as a Woman's Art in Central Africa." Specific objects or themes are explored in depth in a small exhibition space called the Point of View Gallery.

Inquire at the desk about special exhibits, workshops (including excellent children's programs), storytelling, lectures, docent-led tours, films, and demonstrations. A comprehensive events schedule here (together with exhibitions) provides a unique opportunity to learn about the diverse cultures and visual traditions of Africa.

Enid A. Haupt Garden

10th St. and Independence Ave. SW. ☎ **202/357-2700.** Admission free. Memorial Day–Labor Day, daily 7am–8pm; the rest of the year, daily 7am–5:45pm. Closed Dec 25. Metro: Smithsonian.

With its central parterre and 1870s cast-iron furnishings, elaborate flower beds and borders, plant-filled turn-of-the-century urns, and lush baskets hung from 19th-century-style lampposts, this tranquil, beautiful oasis on the Mall is named for its donor, a noted supporter of horticultural projects. Although on ground level, it's really a rooftop garden above the subterranean Sackler and African art museums. The magnolia-lined parterre has multicolored swags and ribbon beds adapted from the 1876 Philadelphia Centennial Exposition's horticultural hall. The swags are composed of 30,000 green and yellow Alternanthera, supplemented by seasonal displays of spring pansies, begonias, or cabbage and kale. An "Island Garden" near the Sackler Gallery, entered via a 9-foot moongate, has benches backed by English boxwoods under the shade of weeping cherry trees; half-round pieces of granite in its still pool are meant to suggest ripples. A "Fountain Garden" outside the African art museum provides granite seating walls shaded by hawthorn trees, with tiny water channels fed by fountains and a waterfall or "chadar" inspired by the gardens of Shalimar. Three small terraces, shaded by black sour gum trees, are located near the Arts and Industries Building. And five majestic linden trees shade a seating area around the Downing Urn, a memorial to American landscapist Andrew Jackson Downing. Additional features include wisteria-covered dome-shaped trellises, clusters of trees (Zumi crabapples, ginkgoes, and American hollies), a weeping European beech, and rose gardens. Elaborate cast-iron carriage gates made according to a 19th-century design by James Renwick, flanked by four pillars made from the same red

Seneca sandstone used to construct the Castle, have been installed at the Independence Avenue entrance to the garden.

National Postal Museum

2 Massachusetts Ave. NE (at 1st St.). ☎ **202/357-2700.** Admission free. Daily 10am–5:30pm. Closed Dec 25. Metro: Union Station.

This recent addition to the Smithsonian complex (opened in 1993) appropriately occupies the palatial beaux-arts quarters of the City Post Office Building designed by brilliant architect Daniel Burnham. Created to house and display the Smithsonian's national philatelic and postal history collection of more than 16 million objects, it is, somewhat surprisingly, a great deal of fun to visit. Dozens of intriguing interactive exhibits range from Nickelodeon "films" about train wrecks and robberies to a video game that challenges visitors to get 20 bags of mail from Philadelphia to New Orleans in the 1850s via train, boat, or stagecoach. The game is programmed so that 17,000 problems can arise en route! The museum documents America's postal history from 1673 (about 170 years before the advent of stamps, envelopes, and mailboxes) to the present.

In the central gallery, titled "Moving the Mail," three planes that carried mail in the early decades of the 20th century (including a converted World War I bomber) are suspended from a 90-foot atrium ceiling. Here, too: a railway mail car, an 1851 mail/passenger coach, a Ford Model A mail truck, and a replica of an airmail beacon tower. In "Binding the Nation," historic correspondence (letters from slaves and Native Americans, from a Revolutionary War soldier to his wife, from immigrants keeping in touch with their relatives back home, and from pioneers during America's westward expansion) illustrate how mail served to bind families together in the developing nation. Several exhibits deal with the famed Pony Express, a service that lasted less than two years but was romanticized to legendary proportions by Buffalo Bill and others. In the Civil War section you'll learn about Henry "Box" Brown, a slave who had himself "mailed" from Richmond to a Pennsylvania abolitionist in 1856. "Customers and Communities" explores how a growing America dealt with the vast increase in mail volume generated by an expanding population—via pneumatic tubes that carried mail underground, mail metering, ZIP Codes, and technological advance. Here you can try to decipher addresses on dead letters, and find out how marketers view the demographics of your ZIP Code. Entertaining exhibits include whimsical folk art mailboxes on rural routes and an array of mail frauds such as an advertisement for a "solar clothes dryer" that turned out to be a clothespin! "The Art of Cards and Letters" gallery displays personal correspondence from World War I through Operation Desert Storm, as well as greeting cards and postcards. There are, of course, stamps on display here too (in the "Stamps and Stories" gallery), ranging from the rare and valuable to fakes and forgeries. An 800-square-foot gallery, opening shortly after press time, will focus on federal duck stamps (first issued in 1934 to license waterfowl hunters), with displays on the hobby of duck hunting and the ecology of American water birds. In addition, the museum houses a vast research library for philatelic researchers and scholars, a stamp store, and a museum shop.

Freer Gallery of Art

On the south side of the Mall (at Jefferson Dr. and 12th St. SW.). ☎ **202/357-2700.** Admission free. Daily 10am–5:30pm. Closed Dec 25. Metro: Smithsonian (Mall or Independence Avenue exit).

A gift to the nation of 9,000 works from Charles Lang Freer, a collector of Asian art and American art from the 19th and early 20th centuries, the Freer Gallery opened in 1923. Freer's original interest was, in fact, American art, but his good friend James McNeill Whistler encouraged him to collect Asian works as well. Eventually the latter became predominant. Freer's gift included funds to construct a museum and an endowment to add objects of the highest quality to the Asian collection only, which has been greatly augmented over the years. It includes Chinese and Japanese sculpture, printing, lacquer, metalwork, and ceramics; early Christian illuminated manuscripts; Japanese screens and woodblock prints; Chinese jades and bronzes; Korean ceramics; Iranian manuscripts, metalwork, and miniatures; ancient Near Eastern metalware; and Indian sculpture and paintings.

Among the American works are more than 1,200 pieces (the world's largest collection) by Whistler, including the famous Peacock Room permanently installed here. Originally a dining room designed by an architect named Thomas Jeckyll for the London mansion of F. R. Leyland, the Peacock Room contained a Whistler painting called *The Princess from the Land of Porcelain.* But after his painting was installed, Whistler was dissatisfied with the room as a setting for his work. When Leyland was away from home, Whistler painted over the very expensive gilded leather interior, embellishing it with paintings of golden peacocks. A permanent rift ensued between Whistler and Leyland. After Leyland's death, Freer purchased the room, painting and all, and had it shipped to his home in Detroit. Other American painters represented in the collections are Childe Hassam, Thomas Wilmer Dewing, Dwight William Tryon, Abbott Henderson Thayer, and John Singer Sargent. (*Note:* About 90% of the American works are in their original frames, many of them designed by Stanford White or Whistler.)

Housed in an Italian Renaissance–style granite-and-marble building, the Freer has lovely skylit galleries. In 1993, a 4¹/₂-year, $26-million expansion and renovation project was completed. The main exhibit floor centers on a garden court open to the sky. A museum shop features books relating to the collection and reproductions from it; wonderful gifts here, too. An underground exhibit space connects the Freer to the neighboring Sackler Gallery. The museum's Meyer Auditorium is the setting for free chamber music concerts, dance performances, Asian feature films, and other programs. Inquire about these, as well as children's programs, at the information desk.

Arts and Industries Building

900 Jefferson Dr. SW (on the South Side of the Mall). ☎ **202/357-2700.** Admission free. Daily 10am–5:30pm. Closed Dec 25. Metro: Smithsonian.

Completed in 1881 as the first national museum, this redbrick-and-sandstone structure was the scene of President Garfield's Inaugural Ball. Since 1976 it has housed exhibits from the 1876 United States International Exposition in Philadelphia—a celebration of America's 100th birthday that featured the latest advances in technology. The Exposition was re-created here in 1976 for the Bicentennial. The entrance floor is like a turn-of-the-century mall with display cases of Victorian furnishings, fashions, clocks, musical instruments, tools, photographic equipment, and medicines. In areas off the magnificent central Rotunda there's machinery that probably evoked oohs and aahs in the 19th century—steam and gas engines, printing presses, corn mills, refrigerator compresses, and tool builders, as well as a considerable display of weaponry and vehicles. Some machines are rather large, such as a steam locomotive. There are also state exhibits highlighting California wines, Kansas corn and wheat, Tennessee lumber, and so forth, as well as international displays.

Singers, dancers, puppeteers, and mimes perform in the Discovery Theater (October to July, Tuesday to Saturday—call **202/357-1500** for show times and ticket information; admission is charged). Don't miss the charming Victorian-motif shop on the first floor that sells books, jam and jellies, china, needlepoint patterns and samplers, antique reproduction dolls, and more. Weather permitting, there's a 19th-century carousel in operation across the street.

○ National Zoological Park

Adjacent to Rock Creek Park, main entrance in the 3000 block of Connecticut Ave. NW. ☎ **202/673-4800** or 202/673-4717. Admission free. Apr 15–Oct 15, daily (weather permitting): grounds, 8am–8pm; animal buildings, 9am–4:30pm. Oct 16–Apr 14, daily: grounds, 8am–6pm; animal buildings, 9am–4:30pm. Closed Dec 25. Metro: Cleveland Park or Woodley Park–Zoo.

Established in 1889, the National Zoo is home to several thousand animals of some 500 species, many of them rare and/or endangered. A leader in the care, breeding, and exhibition of animals, it occupies 163 beautifully landscaped woodland acres and is one of the country's most delightful zoos. Star resident is Hsing-Hsing, a rare giant panda donated by the People's Republic of China. He's best observed at feeding times, 11am and 3pm, and he's generally livelier at the morning feeding.

Enter the zoo at the Connecticut Avenue entrance; you will be right by the Education Building, where you can pick up a map and find out about feeding times and special activities taking place during your visit.

Zoo animals live in large open enclosures—simulations of their natural habitats—along two easy-to-follow numbered paths, **Olmsted**

Impressions

Take an umbrella, an overcoat, and a fan, and go forth. —Mark Twain

It has a damp, wheezy, Dickensian sort of winter hardly equalled by London, and a steaming tropical summer not surpassed by the basin of the Nile.
                                                              —Alistair Cooke

Birth of a Baby Elephant

Kumari, a star resident of the Elephant House, was the first elephant to be born at the zoo. She arrived December 14, 1993, weighing in at 264 pounds. Her 18-year-old mother, Shanthi, weighed 8,900 pounds by Kumari's delivery, having gained 1,000 pounds during her 22-month pregnancy! Shanthi had earned the right to a bit of compulsive overeating; she had a pretty traumatic childhood. Born in Sri Lanka, she was orphaned at a young age when her herd raided a village. As villagers chased the elephants away, Shanthi fell into a well, where a leopard attacked her. She was then reared at an elephant orphanage until 1977, when she was presented as a bicentennial gift from the children of Sri Lanka to the children of the United States. Her name means "peace," and Kumari's means "princess."

After Shanthi was selected for breeding, Elephant House curator John Lehnhardt visited every North American zoo with a breeding male Asian elephant to find her a suitable mate. He selected Indy, at the Burnet Park Zoo in Syracuse, New York; in 1991, Shanthi was taken to live there with him. She became pregnant early in 1992 and was returned to the National Zoo later that year. She had a remarkably easy delivery: Kumari was born in only 26 minutes, to the accompaniment of trumpeting and rumbling by delighted fellow Elephant House residents. Kumari's birth represents a ray of hope because wild Asian elephants, crowded by expanding human populations, are in serious danger of extinction—there are only about 40,000 left.

Walk and the **Valley Trail.** You can't get lost, and you won't unintentionally miss anything. Signs indicate the presence of baby animals born on the premises. Follow the Valley Trail past tapirs and antelope (grass grazers) to the **Wetlands Exhibit,** where, from a boardwalk path, you can view brown pelicans, herons, and other waterfowl amid water lilies and cattails. Proceed via the **Australia Pavilion** to Hsing-Hsing, who is bracketed with kangaroos, camels, and antelopes at the center of the park. Just across the way are the four largest land mammals—hippos, rhinos, giraffes, and elephants. Continue north on Olmsted Walk to the **Great Ape House;** it adjoins, via an overhead Orangutan Transport System, the **Think Tank**—an intriguing facility focusing on the biology and evolution of animal thinking. Up ahead is the **Reptile Discovery Center**—home to Indonesian Komodo dragons, the world's largest lizards. In the same area, the **Invertebrate Exhibit** is the only one of its kind in the country; on display are starfish, sponges, giant crabs, anemones, insects, and other spineless creatures (a section here on animals that pollinate plants deserves special attention). Lions and tigers live nearby in a moated circular habitat surrounding a pond. Next door is the **Bat Cave.** Continuing south on the U-shaped Olmsted Walk stop for awhile to watch the always-amusing antics of prairie dogs in a small earth mound. Across the way, back on the Valley Trail, is **Amazonia,** a lush rain forest habitat that includes a cascading tropical "Amazon River" and a tropical biology laboratory. Occupying a futuristic building under a 50-foot dome, it is home to 358 species of plants, dozens of animals and tropical birds, and immense naturalistic aquariums that simulate deep river pools. Continue uphill past the spectacled bears to see seals and sea lions cavorting in their pool.

Zoo facilities include stroller-rental stations, a number of gift shops, a bookstore, and several paid-parking lots. The lots fill up quickly, especially on weekends, so arrive early or take the Metro.

Snack bars and ice-cream kiosks are scattered throughout the park. Most notable is the **Panda Cafe,** with umbrella tables overlooking the outdoor habitat of Hsing-Hsing; fast food is featured. The largest facility is the **Mane Restaurant,** near the Beach Drive entrance. A pleasant alternative is an alfresco lunch at one of the zoo's very nice picnic areas. Buy picnic fare at **Uptown Bakers** (details in Chapter 6) or at the zoo eateries.

Anacostia Museum

1901 Fort Place SE (off Martin Luther King Ave.). ☎ **202/287-3382** or 202/357-2700. Admission free. Daily 10am–5pm. Closed Dec 25. Metro: Anacostia; then take a W1 or W2 bus directly to the museum.

This unique Smithsonian establishment was created in 1967 as a neighborhood museum serving African Americans in the Anacostia community. Expanding its horizons over the years, it is today a national resource devoted to the identification, documentation, protection, and interpretation of the African-American experience, focusing on Washington, D.C., and the Upper South. The permanent collection includes about 5,000 items, ranging from videotapes of African-American church services to art, sheet music, and historic documents. In addition, the Anacostia produces a varying number of shows each year and offers a comprehensive schedule of free educational programs and activities in conjunction with exhibit themes. For instance, to complement an exhibition called "The African American Presence in American Quilts," the museum featured a video about artist/quiltmaker Faith Ringgold, quilting workshops for adults and children, talks by local quilting societies, and storytelling involving quilts.

Call for an events calendar (which always includes children's activities) or pick one up when you visit.

OTHER TOP ATTRACTIONS

✪ Library of Congress

1st St. SE (between Independence Ave. and E. Capitol St.). ☎ **202/707-5458.** Admission free. Mon–Fri 8:30am–9:30pm, Sat 8:30am–6pm. Call ahead for tour information. Closed Sun and most major holidays. Metro: Capitol South.

Note: Due to ongoing renovations, the tour procedure will vary for some time. Call **202/707-8000** before you go for up-to-the-minute tour information.

This is the nation's library, established in 1800 "for the purchase of such books as may be necessary for the use of Congress." Over the years, it has expanded to serve all Americans—from the blind, for whom books are recorded on cassette and/or translated into braille, to research scholars and college students. Its first collection of books was destroyed when the British burned the Capitol (where the library was then housed) during the War of 1812. Thomas Jefferson then sold the institution his personal library of 6,487 books as a replacement, and this became the foundation of what would grow to be the world's largest library. Today the collection contains a mind-boggling 1.8 million

The Library of Congress: The "Nation's Attic"

Just what is filling up building after building of the Library of Congress? A complete list would comprise an entire book, but the following will give you some idea of the scope of this vast and eclectic collection:

- The world's largest cartographic collection—more than four million maps and atlases, some of them dating back to the mid-14th century.
- Major collections of 18-century American newspapers.
- Nine million photographs and negatives, including original prints by many noted photographers.
- Rare Stradivarius violins, violas, and cellos.
- A 1445 copy of the Gutenberg bible, the first book made with movable type (one of three perfect copies in existence, it's one of the world's most valuable books).
- The largest collection of incunabula (books printed before 1500) in the Western Hemisphere.
- Close to 700,000 motion-picture reels, among them the earliest motion-picture print made by Thomas Edison in 1893.
- Thomas Jefferson's rough draft of the Declaration of Independence.
- Transcription discs for thousands of hours of radio programming, beginning in 1926.
- More than $3^1/_2$ million pieces of music.
- The magic books of Harry Houdini.
- Over 80,000 volumes of Russian literature.
- Two drafts of Lincoln's Gettysburg Address.
- A valuable collection of prints and sketches by James Whistler.
- The papers of Sigmund Freud, many presidents, Alexander Graham Bell, Orville and Wilbur Wright, and others.
- The contents of Lincoln's pockets on the night he was shot.
- Over 1.3 million recordings of music and the spoken word, ranging from a recording of the voice of Kaiser Wilhelm II to modern CDs.

Impressions

*I went to Washington as everybody goes there prepared to see everything
done with some furtive intention, but I was disappointed—pleasantly
disappointed.*   —Walt Whitman

items, with new materials being acquired at the rate of 10 items per
minute! Its three buildings house, among many other things, 16.5 million books in all languages, $4^{1}/_{2}$ million maps and atlases dating back
to the middle of the 14th century; Stradivari violins; the letters of
George Washington; more than 15 million prints and photographs;
over 2 million recordings; a million-plus movies and videotapes, among
them the earliest motion-picture print (made by Thomas Edison in
1893); Thomas Jefferson's rough draft of the Declaration of Independence; the papers of everyone from Freud to Groucho Marx; sketches
by Alexander Graham Bell; the magic books of Houdini; and the contents of Lincoln's pockets the night he died. The library also maintains
the Dewey decimal system; offers a year-round program of concerts,
lectures, and poetry readings; and houses the Copyright Office.

As impressive as the scope of the library's effects and activities is its
original home—the ornate Italian Renaissance–style **Thomas Jefferson
Building,** erected between 1888 and 1897 to hold the burgeoning collection and establish America as a cultured nation with magnificent
institutions equal to anything in Europe. Fifty-two painters and sculptors worked for eight years on its interior, utilizing more than 1,500
fully developed architectural drawings. There are floor mosaics from
Italy, allegorical paintings on the overhead vaults, more than 100 murals, and numerous ornamental cornucopias, ribbons, vines and gar-
lands within, as well as 42 granite sculptures and yards of bas-reliefs on
the outside. Especially impressive are the exquisite marble Great Hall
and the Main Reading Room, the latter under a 160-foot dome. Originally intended to hold the fruits of at least 150 years of collecting, the
building was, in fact, filled up in 13. It is now supplemented by the
James Madison Memorial Building and the **John Adams Building.**

Guided tours depart weekdays at 10:30 and 11:30am and 1:30 and
3:30pm. Free tickets are available at the Information Desk in the foyer
of the James Madison Building, where (in room LM-139) a 22-minute
orientation film is shown every half hour weekdays from 9am to 9pm,
Saturdays from 9am to 5:30pm.

Pick up a calendar of events when you visit. The Madison Building
offers interesting exhibits and features classic, rare, and unusual films
in its Mary Pickford Theater. It also houses a noteworthy restaurant
and cafeteria (see "At Sightseeing Attractions" in Chapter 6 for details),
though picnic tables out front here and at the Thomas Jefferson
Building provide a tempting alternative.

✪ National Archives

Constitution Ave. NW (between 7th and 9th sts.). ☎ **202/501-5000** for information on exhibits and films, 202/501-5400 for research information. Admission free.

Exhibition Hall, Apr–Labor Day, daily 10am–9pm; day after Labor Day–Mar, daily 10am–5:30pm. Call for research hours. Closed Dec 25. Metro: Archives.

Keeper of America's documentary heritage, the National Archives displays our most cherished treasures in appropriately awe-inspiring surroundings. Housed in the Rotunda of the Exhibition Hall are the Nation's three charter documents—the Declaration of Independence, the Constitution of the United States, and its Bill of Rights—which are on view daily to the public. Every night these three "Charters of Freedom" are lowered 20 feet into a 50-ton vault for safekeeping, and every morning they are once again raised for exhibition. Throughout the day, armed guards stand on duty in the hall.

High above and flanking the documents are two larger-than-life murals painted by Barry Faulkner. One, entitled *The Declaration of Independence,* shows Thomas Jefferson presenting a draft of the Declaration to John Hancock, the presiding officer of the Continental Congress; the other, entitled *The Constitution,* shows James Madison submitting the Constitution to George Washington and the Constitutional Convention. In the display cases on either side of the Declaration of Independence are changing exhibits, presently, "American Originals"—26 cases of compelling documents relating to American history ranging from the Louisiana Purchase Treaty signed by Napoléon to President Ronald Reagan's 1987 speech at the Berlin Wall. Exhibits will rotate over a three-year period. The 1297 version of the Magna Carta, one of the bases for fundamental English privileges and rights, is on display in the Rotunda indefinitely. And there are temporary exhibits in the Circular Gallery (at this writing, "The Perfect Gift," featuring more than 200 gifts given to American presidents from Hoover to Clinton.

The Archives serves as much more than a museum of cherished documents. Famous as a center of genealogical research—Alex Haley began his work on *Roots* here—it is sometimes called the "nation's memory." This federal institution is charged with sifting through the accumulated papers of a nation's official life—billions of pieces a year–and determining what to save and what to destroy. The Archives' vast accumulation of census figures, military records, naturalization papers, immigrant passenger lists, federal documents, passport applications, ship manifests, maps, charts, photographs, and motion-picture film (and that's not the half of it) spans two centuries. And it's all available for the perusal of anyone 16 or over (call for details). If you're casually thinking about tracing your roots, stop in first at Room 400 where a staff member can tell you whether it's worth the effort and how to go about it.

Even if you have no research project in mind, the National Archives merits a visit. The neoclassical building itself, designed by John Russell Pope in the 1930s (also architect of the National Gallery and the Jefferson Memorial) is an impressive example of the beaux-arts style. Seventy-two columns create a Corinthian colonnade on each of the four facades. Great bronze doors herald the Constitution Avenue entrance, and allegorical sculpture centered on *The Recorder of the Archives* adorns the pediment. On either side of the steps are male and female figures symbolizing guardianship and heritage, respectively. Guardians of the Portals at the Pennsylvania Avenue entrance represent the past and the future, and the theme of the pediment is destiny.

Free docent **tours** are given weekdays at 10:15am and 1:15pm by appointment only; call 202/501-5205 for details. Pick up a schedule of events (lectures, films, genealogy workshops) when you visit.

✪ National Gallery of Art

On the north side of the Mall (between 3rd and 7th sts. NW), with entrances at 6th St. and Constitution Ave. or Madison Dr., also at 4th and 7th sts. between Madison Dr. and Constitution Ave. ☎ **202/737-4215.** Admission free. Mon–Sat 10am–5pm, Sun 11am–6pm. Closed Jan 1 and Dec 25. Metro: Archives or Judiciary Square.

Most people don't realize it, but the National Gallery of Art is not really part of the Smithsonian complex (though it is, in some arcane way, related to it); hence its listing here apart from the other Mall museums.

Housing one of the world's foremost collections of Western painting, sculpture, and graphic arts from the Middle Ages through the 20th century, the National Gallery has a dual personality. The original West Building, designed by John Russell Pope (architect of the Jefferson Memorial and the National Archives), is a neoclassic marble masterpiece with a domed rotunda over a colonnaded fountain and high-ceilinged corridors leading to delightful garden courts. It was a gift to the nation from Andrew W. Mellon, who also contributed the nucleus of the collection, including 21 masterpieces from the Hermitage—two Raphaels among them. The ultramodern East Building, designed by I. M. Pei and opened in 1978, is composed of two adjoining triangles with glass walls and lofty tetrahedron skylights. The pink Tennessee marble from which both buildings were constructed was taken from the same quarry; it forms an architectural link between the two structures.

The West Building: On the main floor of the West Building, about 1,000 paintings are always on display. To the left (as you enter off the Mall) is the Art Information Room, housing the Micro Gallery, where those so inclined can design their own tours of the permanent collection and enhance their knowledge of art via user-friendly computers. Continuing to the left of the Rotunda are galleries of 13th-through 18th-century Italian paintings and sculpture, including what is generally considered the finest Renaissance collection outside Italy and the only da Vinci painting outside Europe, *Ginevra de' Benci.* Paintings by El Greco, Ribera, and Velázquez highlight the Spanish galleries; Grünewald, Dürer, Holbein, and Cranach can be seen in the German; Van Eyck, Bosch, and Rubens in the Flemish; and Vermeer, Steen, and Rembrandt in the Dutch. To the right of the Rotunda, galleries display 18th- to 19th-century French paintings (including one of the world's greatest impressionist collections), paintings by Goya, works of late 19th-century Americans—such as Homer, Whistler, and Sargent—and of somewhat earlier British artists, such as Constable, Turner, and Gainsborough. Room decor reflects the period and country of the art shown: For example, Italian gallery walls are travertine marble, while Dutch galleries are paneled in somber oak. Down a flight of stairs are prints and drawings, 15th- through 20th-century sculpture (with many pieces by Daumier, Degas, and Rodin), American naive 18th- and 19th-century paintings, Chinese porcelains, small Renaissance bronzes, 16th-century Flemish tapestries, and 18th-century decorative arts.

The East Building: The scene of major changing exhibits, the East Building also houses an important collection of 20th-century art—including a massive aluminum Calder mobile under a seven-story skylight and, outside the front entrance, an immense bronze sculpture by Henry Moore.

In addition to its permanent collection, the National Gallery hosts a wide range of important temporary exhibits. Recent shows have ranged from "Jan Vermeer" to "Thomas Eakins: The Rowing Pictures."

Pick up a floor plan and calendar of events at an information desk to find out about exhibits, films, tours, lectures, and concerts. Highly recommended are the free highlight **tours** (call for exact times) and audio tours. There are several dining options here (see "At Sightseeing Attractions" in Chapter 6 for details).

✪ Federal Bureau of Investigation

J. Edgar Hoover FBI Building, E St. NW (between 9th and 10th sts.). ☎ **202/324-3447.** Admission free. Mon–Fri 8:45am–4:15pm. Closed Jan 1, Dec 25, and other federal holidays. Metro: Metro Center or Federal Triangle.

More than half a million annual visitors learn why crime doesn't pay by touring the headquarters of the FBI. The attraction is especially popular with kids. To beat the crowds, arrive for the one-hour **tour** before 8:45am or write to a senator or congressperson for a scheduled reservation as far in advance as possible (details in Chapter 2).

The tour begins with a short videotape presentation about the priorities of the bureau—organized crime, white-collar crime, terrorism, foreign counterintelligence, illicit drugs, and violent crimes. En route, you'll learn about this organization's history (it was established in 1908) and its activities over the years. You'll see some of the weapons used by big-time gangsters like Al Capone, Dillinger, Bonnie and Clyde, and "Pretty Boy" Floyd; an exhibit on counterintelligence operations; and photos of the 10 most wanted fugitives—438 of them (including 7 women) have made the list since its inception in 1950; 406 have been captured (128 apprehended through direct citizen cooperation). Two were recognized at this exhibit by people on the tour, and nine have been located via the FBI-assisted TV show, "America's Most Wanted."

Other exhibits deal with white-collar crime, the use of fingerprints for identification, terrorism, and agent training. On display are more than 4,200 weapons, most confiscated from criminals; they're used for reference purposes. An illicit drug exhibit shows paraphernalia and demonstrates how the FBI tries to combat illicit drugs via educational as well as investigational methods.

You'll also visit the DNA lab, the Firearms Unit (where it's determined whether a bullet was fired from a given weapon), the Material Analysis Unit (where from a tiny piece of paint the FBI can determine the approximate make and model of a car), the unit where hairs and fibers are examined, and a Forfeiture and Seizure Exhibit—a display of jewelry, furs, and other proceeds from illegal narcotics operations. The tour ends with a bang—lots of them in fact—when an agent gives a sharpshooting demonstration. He also talks about the FBI's firearms policy and gun safety.

John F. Kennedy Center for the Performing Arts

New Hampshire Ave. NW (at Rock Creek Pkwy.). ☎ **202/467-4600** or 800/ 444-1324 for information or tickets. Admission free. Daily 10am–midnight. Metro: Foggy Bottom. Bus: 80 or 81 from Metro Center.

Opened in 1971, the Kennedy Center is both our national performing arts center and a memorial to John F. Kennedy. Carved into the center's river facade are several Kennedy quotations, including ". . . the New Frontier for which I campaign in public life can also be a New Frontier for American art." Set on 17 acres overlooking the Potomac, the striking $73-million facility, designed by noted architect Edward Durell Stone, houses an opera house, a concert hall, two stage theaters, a theater lab, and a film theater. The best way to see the Kennedy Center—including areas you can't visit on your own—is to take a free 50-minute guided **tour,** given daily between 10am and 1pm. Once again, you can beat the crowds by writing in advance to a senator or congressperson for tickets for a 9:30 or 9:45am VIP tour (details in Chapter 2).

The tour begins in the Hall of Nations, which displays the flags of all nations diplomatically recognized by the United States. Throughout the center you'll see gifts from more than 40 nations, including all the marble used in the building (3,700 tons), which was donated by Italy. First stop is the Grand Foyer—scene of many free concerts and programs and the reception area for all three theaters on the main level; the 18 crystal chandeliers are a gift from Sweden. You'll also visit the Israeli Lounge (where 40 painted and gilded panels depict scenes mentioned in the Bible); the Concert Hall, home of the National Symphony Orchestra; the Opera House; the African room (decorated with beautiful tapestries from African nations); the Eisenhower Theater; the Hall of States, where flags of the 50 states and four territories are hung in the order they joined the Union; the Performing Arts Library; and the Terrace Theater, a Bicentennial gift from Japan. Your guide will point out many notable works of art along the way, such as a Barbara Hepworth sculpture (a gift of England), Henri Matisse tapestries (gifts of France), and an alabaster vase from 2600 B.C. found in a pyramid (a gift of Egypt). If rehearsals are going on, visits to the theaters are omitted.

If you'd like to attend performances during your visit, call the toll-free number above and request the current issue of *Kennedy Center News Magazine,* a free publication that describes all Kennedy Center happenings and prices.

After the tour, walk around the building's terrace for a panoramic 360° view of Washington and plan a meal in one of the Kennedy Center restaurants (details in "At Sightseeing Attractions" in Chapter 6). See Chapter 10 for specifics on theater, concert, and film offerings. There is parking below the Kennedy Center during the day at $3 for the first hour, $5 for two hours, $6.50 for three hours, with a maximum of five hours for $8; nighttime parking (after 5pm) is a flat $6.

✪ Washington National Cathedral

Massachusetts and Wisconsin aves. NW (entrance on Wisconsin Ave.). ☎ 202/537-6200. Suggested donation $2 for adults, $1 for children under 12. May 1–Labor Day Mon–Fri 10am–9pm, Sat 10am–4:30pm, Sun 7:30am–4:30pm; the rest of the year Mon–Sat 10am–4:30pm, Sun 7:30am–4:30pm. Metro: Tenleytown; then about a 20-minute walk. Bus: Any N bus up Massachusetts Avenue from Dupont Circle.

Pierre L'Enfant's 1791 plan for the capital city included "a great church for national purposes," but possibly because of early America's fear of mingling church and state, more than a century elapsed before the foundation for Washington National Cathedral was laid. Its actual name is the Cathedral Church of St. Peter and St. Paul. Though it's Episcopal in denomination, it has no local congregation and seeks to serve the entire nation as a house of prayer for all people. It has been the setting for every kind of religious observance from Jewish to Serbian Orthodox.

A church of this magnitude (it's the sixth largest cathedral in the world!) took a long time to build. Its principal (but not original) architect, Philip Hubert Frohman, worked on the project from 1921 until his death in 1972. The foundation stone (a stone from a field in Bethlehem set into a larger piece of American granite) was laid in 1907 using the mallet with which George Washington set the Capitol cornerstone. Construction was interrupted by both world wars and periods of financial difficulty. It was completed with the placement of the final stone atop a pinnacle on the west front towers on September 29, 1990—83 years to the day of its inception.

English Gothic in style (with several distinctly 20th-century innovations, such as a stained-glass window commemorating the flight of *Apollo 11* and containing a piece of moon rock), the cathedral is built in the shape of a cross, complete with flying buttresses and gargoyles. It is, together with the Capitol and the Washington Monument, among the most dominant structures on the Washington skyline. Its 57-acre landscaped grounds have two lovely gardens; four schools, including the College of Preachers; and an herb garden, greenhouse, and shop called Herb Cottage.

Over the years the cathedral has seen a lot of history. Services to celebrate the end of World Wars I and II were held here. It was the scene of President Wilson's funeral (he and his wife are buried here), as well as President Eisenhower's. Helen Keller and her companion, Anne Sullivan, were buried in the cathedral at her request. And during the Iranian crisis, a round-the-clock prayer vigil was held in the Holy Spirit Chapel throughout the hostages' captivity. When they were released, the hostages came to a service here, and tears flowed at Col. Thomas Shaefer's poignant greeting, "Good morning, my fellow Americans. You don't know how long I've been waiting to say those words."

The best way to explore the cathedral and see its abundance of art, architectural carvings, and statuary is to take a 45-minute **tour.** They leave continually—from the west end of the nave—Monday to Saturday 10am to 3:15pm and Sunday 12:30 to 2:45pm. Among the highlights are dozens of stained-glass windows with themes ranging from the lives of Civil War Generals Lee and Jackson to the miracles of Christ; three exquisite rose windows; the nave, stretching a tenth of a mile to the high altar; Wilson's tomb; the delightful Children's Chapel; St. John's Chapel, where needlepoint kneelers memorialize great Americans; the Holy Spirit Chapel, painted by Andrew Wyeth's father, N. C. Wyeth; and crypt chambers like the Bethlehem Chapel, first section of the cathedral to be constructed.

Allow time to tour the grounds or "close," and to visit the Observation Gallery where 70 windows provide panoramic views. Tuesday- and Wednesday-afternoon tours are followed by a high tea in the Observation Gallery; reservations are required and a fee is charged. And you can, of course, attend **services** at the cathedral (Monday to Saturday at 7:30am, noon, and 4pm; Sunday at 8, 9, and 11am and 4 and 6:30pm). September to June there's a folk guitar mass on Sunday at 10am.

The cathedral hosts numerous events: organ recitals, choir performances, an annual flower mart, calligraphy workshops, and jazz, folk, and classical concerts. The 53-bell carillon is played on Saturday at 12:30pm. Organ recitals are usually given on the great organ following Sunday-evening services at 5pm. Call for additional events.

A large gift shop on the premises sells replicas of cathedral statuary, religious books and art, Christmas cards, and more.

○ Bureau of Engraving and Printing

14th and C sts. SW. ☎ **202/874-3188** or 202/874-2330. Admission free. Mon–Fri 9am–2pm. Closed Dec 25–Jan 1 and federal holidays. Metro: Smithsonian (Independence Avenue exit).

This is where they make the paper money—$103 *billion* of it each year. A staff of 2,300 work around the clock churning it out at the rate of 22.5 million notes a day. Everyone's eyes pop as they walk past rooms overflowing with money. But although the money is the big draw, it's not the whole story. The bureau prints many other products, including 30.5 billion postage stamps per year, presidential portraits, and White House invitations.

As many as 5,000 people line up each day to get a peek at all that moolah, so early arrival—especially during the peak tourist season—is essential (unless you have secured VIP tickets from your senator or congressperson; details in Chapter 2). From April 1 through September 30 (when you must obtain a ticket that specifies a tour time), the ticket booth opens at 8am. Be there! The rest of the year no ticket is needed; you just have to line up. *Note:* June 1 through August 31, there are evening tours from 4 to 7:30pm as well. Tickets are required; the booth opens at 3:30pm.

The 40-minute **self-guided tour,** enhanced by audiovisual aids, begins with a short introductory film. Then you'll see, through large windows, all the processes that go into the making of paper money—the inking, stacking (each stack of dollar bills contains $320,000), cutting, and examination for defects. Most printing here is done from engraved steel plates in a process known as "intaglio"—the hardest to counterfeit, because the slightest alteration will cause a noticeable change in the portrait in use. Additional exhibits include bills no longer in use, counterfeit money, and a $100,000 bill designed for official transactions (since 1969, the largest denomination printed for the general public is $100).

After you finish the tour, allow time to explore the **Visitor Center** (open 8:30am to 3:30pm, 4 to 8:30pm for summer evening tours), where exhibits include informative videos, money-related electronic games, and a display of $1 million. Here, too, you can buy unique gifts ranging from bags of shredded money to copies of documents such as the Gettysburg Address.

○ The Vietnam Veterans Memorial

Just across from the Lincoln Memorial, (east of Henry Bacon Dr. between 21st and 22nd sts. NW). ☎ **202/634-1568.** Admission free. Rangers on duty 8am–midnight daily. Ranger-led programs are given throughout the day June through Labor Day. Metro: Foggy Bottom.

To my mind, the saddest sight in Washington is the Vietnam Veterans Memorial—two long, black granite walls inscribed with the names of the men and women who gave their lives, or remain missing, in the longest war in our nation's history. Even if no one close to you died in Vietnam, it's emotionally wrenching to watch visitors grimly studying the directories at either end to find out where their husbands, sons, and loved ones are listed. The slow walk along the 492-foot wall of names—close to 60,000 people, many of whom died very young—is a powerful evocation of the tragedy of all wars. And whatever your views on the war, it's also affecting to see how much the monument means to Vietnam vets who visit it. Because of the raging conflict over U.S. involvement in the war, its veterans had received virtually no previous recognition of their service.

The memorial was conceived by Vietnam veteran Jan Scruggs and built by the Vietnam Veterans Memorial Fund, a nonprofit organization that raised $7 million for the project. The VVMF was granted a 2-acre site in tranquil Constitution Gardens to erect a memorial that would make no political statement about the war and would harmonize with neighboring memorials. By separating the issue of the wartime service of individuals from the issue of U.S. policy in Vietnam, VVMF hoped to begin a process of national reconciliation.

Yale senior Maya Ying Lin's design was chosen in a national competition open to all citizens over 18 years of age. It consists of two walls in a quiet, protected park setting, angled at 125° to point to the Washington Monument and the Lincoln Memorial. The walls' mirrorlike surface reflects surrounding trees, lawn, and monuments. The names are inscribed in chronological order, documenting an epoch in American history as a series of individual sacrifices from the date of the first casualty in 1959 to the date of the last death in 1975.

The wall was erected in 1982. In 1984 a life-size sculpture of three Vietnam soldiers by Frederick Hart was installed at the entrance plaza. He describes his work this way: "They wear the uniform and carry the equipment of war; they are young. The contrast between the innocence of their youth and the weapons of war underscores the poignancy of their sacrifice. . . . Their strength and their vulnerability are both evident." Near the statue a flag flies from a 60-foot staff. Another sculpture, the Vietnam Veterans Women's Memorial, depicting three Service women tending a wounded soldier was installed on Veterans Day 1993.

✪ United States Holocaust Memorial Museum

100 Raoul Wallenberg Pl. (formerly 15th St. SW; near Independence Ave., just off the Mall). ☎ **202/488-0400.** Admission free. Daily 10am–5:30pm. Closed Yom Kippur and Dec 25. Metro: Smithsonian.

"Out of our memory . . . of the Holocaust we must forge an unshakable oath with all civilized people that never again will the world stand silent, never again will the world . . . fail to act in time to prevent the terrible crime of genocide. . . . " These words of Jimmy Carter are inscribed on a wall outside the museum.

Washington's multitude of museums celebrate the knowledge, the glory, and the creative achievements of human civilization. This museum, mandated by an Act of Congress in 1980 and opened in 1993, reminds us of what can happen when civilization goes awry. It serves the dual purpose of commemorating the dead and educating the living to the dangers of prejudice and fanaticism and the fragility of freedom.

Just over 50 years ago, a seemingly civilized Western nation legalized racism, brutally trampled on human rights, and engaged in the genocide of millions. Here the story is told in full. Even the building housing the museum is designed to reflect the bleakness of the Nazi era—to disorient the visitor with false perspectives and eerily somber spaces. An outer wall is reminiscent of an extermination camp's exterior brickwork, and towers evoke the guard towers of Auschwitz.

Upon entering, you will be issued an identity card of an actual victim of the Holocaust. By 1945, 66% of those whose lives are documented on these cards were dead. As you go up to the fourth floor (where the events of 1933 to 1939 are portrayed), a video in the elevator features an American soldier describing his experiences liberating a camp. The Holocaust story begins with the rise of Nazism—book burnings, the Nuremberg Laws of 1935 that isolated Jews from German society, and the terror of "Kristallnacht" in 1938, when hundreds of Jewish synagogues and businesses were destroyed. A winding path takes you to a border crossing where the near impossibility of escape is dramatized. No countries will admit you; you're forced to return to the horror. Also highlighted are the non-Jewish victims of the Nazis, among them Gypsies, the physically and mentally handicapped, homosexuals, and political and religious dissidents.

On the third floor (documenting the years 1940 to 1944), constricting walls symbolize the narrowing choices of people caught up in the Nazi machine. You'll board a Polish freightcar of the type used to transport Jews from the Warsaw ghetto to Treblinka and hear recordings of survivors telling what life in the camps was like. A reconstructed Auschwitz barracks, the yellow stars Jews were forced to wear, instruments of genocide, and a gas-chamber door are among the thousands of artifacts bearing silent witness to this grim era. Like your identity card, displays foster identification with individuals who perished. In one of the towers, a montage of 1,500 family photographs documents the beauty and vitality of everyday lives of people in the Jewish town of Ejszyszki, Lithuania, before the Holocaust; later you'll learn that 90% of them were murdered by Nazi death squads during two days in 1941.

On the second floor, the focus turns to a more heartening story: how non-Jews throughout Europe—by exercising individual action and responsibility—saved Jews at great personal risk. In Denmark, 90% of the Jews were hidden and saved! The saga continues with exhibits on the liberation of the camps, life in DP camps, emigration to Israel and America, and the Nuremberg trials. The tour ends in the hexagonal Hall of Remembrance—a place to meditate on what you've experienced and light a candle for the victims.

Dozens of educational interactive videos further enhance understanding, as do films, lectures, cultural events, and temporary exhibits. The exhibits are designed so you can shield children (or yourself) from the most graphic material. This museum is not like any other you've ever visited. It's a deeply affecting encounter with evil—an opportunity to learn the lessons of history and the role of individual responsibility in protecting freedom and preserving human rights.

Allow at least four or five hours to see the exhibits. I would not recommend bringing children under 12 to this museum, and even then, it's advisable to prepare them for what they'll see. There's a cafeteria and museum shop on the premises.

Because so many people want to visit the museum, tickets specifying a visit time are required. Reserve them via Ticketmaster (☎ 202/432-SEAT or 800/551-SEAT). There's a small service charge. You can also get them at the museum box office, (14th Street entrance); it opens at 10am daily, and lines form early. If for some reason you can't obtain tickets, there are some portions of the museum you can see without them.

✪ Union Station

50 Massachusetts Ave. NE. ☎ **202/371-9441.** Admission free. Daily 24 hours. Shops, Mon–Sat 10am–9pm, Sun noon–6pm. Metro: Union Station.

In Washington, D.C., the very train station where you arrive is itself a noteworthy sightseeing attraction. Union Station, a monument to the great age of rail travel built between 1903 and 1907, was painstakingly restored in the 1980s to its original grandeur at a cost of $160 million. The station was designed by noted architect Daniel H. Burnham, an enthusiast of French beaux-arts neoclassicism and a member of the McMillan Commission—an illustrious task force assembled in 1900 to beautify the Mall and make the city an appropriately imposing world capital. The committee's philosophy was summed up by Burnham, who counseled, "Make no little plans. They have no magic to stir men's blood, and probably themselves will not be realized." The committee's "big plans" included Union Station, modeled after the Baths of Diocletian and Arch of Constantine in Rome.

When it opened in 1907, this was the largest train station in the world. Its Ionic-colonnaded exterior is of white granite, and 100 eagles are portrayed in the facade. Out front are a replica of the Liberty Bell and a monumental statue of Columbus. Six carved allegorical fixtures in niches over the entranceway represent Fire, Electricity, Freedom, Imagination, Agriculture, and Mechanics. The station's interior, entered through graceful 50-foot Constantinian arches, is finished with extravagant materials–acres of white marble flooring with red "Champlain dots," bronze grilles, elaborate coffered ceilings (embellished with a half-million dollars' worth of 22-carat gold leaf!), and rich Honduran mahogany. The Main Hall is a massive rectangular room with a 96-foot barrel-vault ceiling, its balcony adorned with 36 Augustus Saint-Gaudens sculptures of Roman legionnaires. Off the Main Hall is the East Hall, one of the most beautiful areas of the station, with scagliola marble walls and columns, a gorgeous hand-stenciled skylight ceiling, and stunning murals of classical scenes inspired by ancient Pompeian art. Today it's the station's plushest shopping venue.

In its heyday, many important events took place at this "temple of transport." President Wilson welcomed General Pershing here in 1918 on his return from France. South Pole explorer Rear Admiral Byrd was also feted at Union Station on his homecoming. Franklin D. Roosevelt's funeral train, bearing his casket, was met by thousands of mourners in 1945. And in the 1960s, the Kennedys greeted King Hassan II of Morocco and Ethiopian Emperor Haile Selassie here.

But soon after, with the decline of rail travel, the station fell on hard times. Rain damage caused parts of the roof to cave in, and the entire building—with floors buckling, rats running about, and mushrooms sprouting in damp rooms—was sealed in 1981. That same year, Congress enacted legislation to preserve and faithfully restore this national treasure.

Today, Union Station is once again a vibrant entity—a transportation/dining/shopping/entertainment center patronized by locals and visitors alike. Every square inch of the facility has been cleaned, repaired, and/or replaced according to original designs. An elliptical mahogany kiosk has been erected in the center of the Main Hall, inspired by a Renaissance baldacchino, to accommodate a bi-level café and a visitor information center. About 100 retail shops on three levels offer a wide array of merchandise. The skylit Main Concourse, extending the entire length of the station, has become the primary shopping area as well as a ticketing and baggage facility. And a nine-screen cinema complex and beautiful food court have been installed on the lower level. The remarkable restoration, which involved hundreds of European and American artisans utilizing historical research, bygone craft techniques, and modern technology, is meticulous in every detail. I'm sure Burnham would be greatly pleased if he could walk the majestic corridors of Union Station today. His own 1907 declaration foretells the spirit of the renovation ". . . a noble, logical diagram once recorded will never die, but long after we are gone will be a living thing, asserting itself with ever-growing insistency. . . . Let your watchword be order and your beacon beauty."

For information on Union Station restaurants and shops, see Chapter 6 ("At Sightseeing Attractions") and Chapter 9.

✪ Ford's Theatre and Lincoln Museum

511 10th St. NW (between E and F sts.). ☎ **202/426-6924.** Admission free. Daily 9am–5pm. Closed Thanksgiving and Dec 25. Metro: Metro Center.

On April 14, 1865, President Lincoln was in the audience of Ford's Theatre, one of the most popular playhouses in Washington. Everyone was laughing at a funny line from Tom Taylor's celebrated comedy, *Our American Cousin,* when actor John Wilkes Booth grabbed center stage by shooting the president. Booth escaped by jumping to the stage, mounting his horse in the back alley, and galloping off. Doctors carried Lincoln to the house of William Petersen, across the street, and the president died there the next morning. (See below for details.)

After Lincoln's assassination, the theater was closed by order of Secretary of War Edwin M. Stanton. For many years afterward it was used as an office by the War Department. In 1893, 22 clerks were killed when three floors of the building collapsed. It remained in disuse until the 1960s, when it was remodeled and restored to its appearance on the night of the tragedy. Except when rehearsals or matinees are in progress (call before you go), visitors can see the theater and trace Booth's movements on that fateful night. Free 15-minute talks on the history of the theater and the story of the assassination are given throughout the day (call for exact times). Be sure to visit the **Lincoln Museum** in the basement, which has exhibits on Lincoln's life and times. In addition to Lincoln memorabilia, exhibits depict the clothes Lincoln was wearing the night he was killed, the Derringer pistol used by Booth, the killer's diary outlining his rationalization for the deed, and other artifacts. A bookstore is on the premises. See Chapter 10 for information on theatrical presentations here.

The House Where Lincoln Died

516 10th St. NW. ☎ **202/426-6924.** Admission free. Daily 9am–5pm. Closed Thanksgiving and Dec 25. Metro: Metro Center.

This is where Lincoln was carried after the shooting. Furnished with period pieces, it looks much as it did on that fateful April night. You'll see the front parlor where an anguished Mary Todd Lincoln spent the night with her son, Robert. Her emotional state was such that she was banned from the bedroom because she was creating havoc. In the back parlor Secretary of War Edwin M. Stanton held a Cabinet meeting and began questioning witnesses. From this room, Stanton announced at 7:22am on April 15, 1865, "Now he belongs to the ages."

Twelve years after Lincoln's death, the house was sold to Louis Schade, who published a newspaper called the *Washington Sentinel* in its basement for many years. In 1896 the government bought the house for $30,000, and it is now maintained by the National Park Service.

2 More Attractions

✪ Phillips Collection

1600 21st St. NW (at Q St.). ☎ **202/387-0961.** Admission Sat–Sun, $6.50 adults, $3.25 seniors and students, free for children under 18; contribution suggested Tues–Fri. Tues–Sat 10am–5pm, Sun noon–7pm. Closed Mon, Jan 1, July 4, Thanksgiving Day, and Dec 25. Metro: Dupont Circle (Q Street exit).

Conceived as "a museum of modern art and its sources," this intimate establishment houses—in an elegant 1890s Georgian Revival mansion plus an added wing—the exquisite collection of Duncan and Marjorie Phillips, avid collectors and proselytizers of modernism. Carpeted rooms, with leaded- and stained-glass windows, oak paneling, plush chairs and sofas, and frequently, fireplaces create a comfortable, home-like setting for viewing art. The original building was once the Phillipses' elegant abode, though always doubling as a museum. When their collection totaled 600 paintings, they moved out and had it reno-vated entirely as a museum. Today the collection includes more than 2,500 works. Among the highlights are superb examples of Daumier, Dove, and Bonnard paintings; some splendid small Vuillards; five van Goghs; Renoir's *Luncheon of the Boating Party;* seven Cézannes; and six works by Georgia O'Keeffe. Ingres, Delacroix, Manet, El Greco, Goya, Corot, Constable, Courbet, Giorgione, and Chardin are among the "sources" or forerunners of modernism represented. Modern notables include Rothko, Hopper, Kandinsky, Matisse, Klee, Degas, Rouault, Picasso, and many others. It's a collection no art lover should miss. An ongoing series of temporary shows is presented, with works from the Phillips supplemented by loans from other museums and private collections.

Free **tours** are given on Wednesday and Saturday at 2pm, and a full schedule of events includes gallery talks, lectures, and free concerts in the ornate music room (every Sunday at 5pm, September to May; early arrival is advised at these popular performances). Thursdays the museum stays open until 8:30pm for **Artful Evenings** with music, gallery talks, and a cash bar; admission is $5.

On the lower level are a charming little restaurant serving light fare and a comprehensive museum shop.

Corcoran Gallery of Art

17th St. NW (between E St. and New York Ave.). ☎ **202/638-3211** or 202/638-1439. Admission free. Wed and Fri–Mon 10am–5pm, Thurs 10am–9pm. Closed Tues, Jan 1, and Dec 25. Metro: Farragut West or Farragut North.

The first art museum in Washington, and one of the first in the country, the Corcoran Gallery was housed from 1874 to 1896 in the redbrick and brownstone building that is now the Renwick. The collection outgrew its quarters and was transferred in 1897 to its present beaux-arts building, designed by Ernest Flagg. It features a double atrium with two levels of fluted columns and a grand staircase.

The collection itself—shown in rotating exhibits—focuses chiefly on American art. A prominent Washington banker, William Wilson Corcoran was among the first wealthy American collectors to realize the

> ### ❓ Did You Know?
>
> - When the *Washington Post* sponsored a public music competition, John Philip Sousa was asked to compose a march for the awards ceremony; the result was *The Washington Post March,* for which Sousa earned the grand sum of $35.
> - The only presidential inauguration ceremony to be held in the White House was that of Franklin D. Roosevelt, in 1941.
> - Herbert Hoover was the first president to have a telephone on his desk.
> - The desk in the Oval Office, carved from the British ship *Resolute,* was a gift to Rutherford B. Hayes from Queen Victoria.
> - The first first lady to fly to a foreign country was Eleanor Roosevelt, in 1934.

importance of encouraging and supporting this country's artists. Enhanced by further gifts and bequests, the collection comprehensively spans American art from 18th-century portraiture to 20th-century moderns like Nevelson, Warhol, and Rothko. Nineteenth-century works include Bierstadt's and Remington's imagery of the American West; Hudson River School artists like Cole, Church, and Durand; genre paintings; expatriates like Whistler, Sargent, and Mary Cassatt; and two giants of the late 19th century—Homer and Eakins. Displayed on the second floor is the white marble female nude, *The Greek Slave,* by Hiram Powers, considered so daring in its day that it was shown on alternate days to men and women.

The Corcoran is not, however, an exclusively American art museum. On the first floor is the collection from the estate of Sen. William Andrews Clark—an eclectic grouping of Dutch and Flemish masters, European painters, French impressionists, Barbizon landscapes, Delft porcelains, a Louis XVI salon doré transported in toto from Paris, and more. Clark's will stated that his diverse collection—which any curator would undoubtedly want to disperse among various museum departments—must be shown as a unit. He left money for a wing to house it which opened in 1928. Other non-American aspects of the museum's collection include a room of exquisite Corot landscapes, another of medieval Renaissance tapestries, and numerous Daumier lithographs donated by Dr. Armand Hammer.

Free 30-minute **tours** are given at 12:30pm (and on Thursday also at 7:30pm). The museum shop has a terrific selection of art reproductions, books, jewelry, and art nouveau glassware, among other things. Pick up a schedule of events—temporary exhibits, gallery talks, concerts, art auctions, and more. There's a charming restaurant on the premises (details in "At Sightseeing Attractions" in Chapter 6).

National Museum of Women in the Arts

1250 New York Ave. NW (at 13th St.). ☎ **202/783-5000.** Suggested contribution, $3 adults, $2 children. Mon–Sat 10am–5pm, Sun noon–5pm. Closed Jan 1, Thanksgiving Day, and Dec 25. Metro: Metro Center.

Celebrating "the contribution of women to the history of art," this relatively new museum (opened 1987) is Washington's 72nd but a national first. Founders Wilhelmina and Wallace Holladay, who donated the core of the permanent collection–more than 200 works by women spanning the 16th through the 20th century—became interested in women's art in the 1960s. After discovering that no women were included in H. W. Janson's *History of Art,* a standard text (this, by the way, did not change until 1986!), the Holladays began collecting art by women, and the concept of a women's art museum (to begin correcting the inequities of underrepresentation) soon evolved. (Though women comprise nearly 50% of the working artists in the United States; more than 95% of the works hanging in museums are by men!)

Since its opening, the collection has grown to more than 2,000 works by artists including Rosa Bonheur, Frida Kahlo, Helen Frankenthaler, Barbara Hepworth, Georgia O'Keeffe, Camille Claudel, Lila Cabot Perry, Mary Cassatt, Elaine de Kooning, and Käthe Kollwitz, along with many other lesser known but notable artists from earlier centuries. I was interested to discover here, for instance, that the famed Peale family of 19th-century portrait painters included a very talented sister, Sarah Miriam Peale. The collection is complemented by an ongoing series of changing exhibits.

The museum is housed in a magnificent Renaissance Revival landmark building designed in 1907 as a Masonic temple by noted architect Waddy Wood. It's entered via an opulent Great Hall with Turkish white marble floors, silk-brocaded walls, gilded moldings, and Belgian crystal chandeliers suspended from an ornately detailed ceiling. A recently purchased adjoining building will expand the exhibit space and include a rooftop sculpture garden. The museum's library has more than 15,000 volumes. The charming and sunny Mezzanine Cafe serves light lunches Monday through Saturday—soups, salads, and sandwiches.

United States Botanic Garden

100 Maryland Ave. (at the east end of the Mall). ☎ **202/225-8333.** Admission free. Daily 9am–5pm. Metro: Federal Center SW.

Originally conceived by Washington, Jefferson, and Madison, and opened in 1820, the Botanic Garden is a lovely oasis—a series of connected glass-and-stone buildings and greenhouses (they call it a "living museum under glass") filled with pots of brightly colored flowers, rock beds of ferns, Spanish moss, palms, and shrubs. Tropical, subtropical, and desert plants highlight the collection. The Conservatory, inspired by 17th-century French orangeries, is entered via a room with two reflecting pool fountains under a skylight. Further within are a section filled with cactus, a lush tropical jungle with tranquil pools, and benches in shady corners that create the illusion of carefully tended woods. Poinsettias bloom at Christmas, chrysanthemums in fall; spring is heralded by lilies, tulips, hyacinths, and daffodils; and a large collection of orchids is on display year-round. Of topical interest is the Dinosaur Garden of cycads (primitive conifers that resemble palms), ferns, mosses, and liverworts that existed in the Jurassic era—an age that predated flowering plants. The Summer Terrace, with umbrella tables amid plants and flower beds overlooking the Capitol's reflecting pool, is a lovely spot for a picnic lunch. The complex also includes adjacent Bartholdi Park, about the size of a city block, with a stunning cast-iron classical fountain created by Frédéric Auguste Bartholdi, designer of the Statue of Liberty. Charming flower gardens bloom amid tall ornamental grasses here, benches are sheltered by vine-covered bowers, and a touch and fragrance garden contains such herbs as pineapple-scented sage. For information on special shows (perhaps a rose show or Japanese flower-arranging display), tours, lectures, and classes call the above number. You can also call 202/225-7099 for a recording of events and to find out what's in bloom.

✪ Dumbarton Oaks

1703 32nd St. NW (entrance to the collections on 32nd St., between R and S sts.; garden entrance at 31st and R sts.). ☎ **202/338-8278** or 202/342-3200. Garden, $3 adults, $2 children under 12 and senior citizens; collections, free. Garden (weather permitting), Nov–Mar, daily 2–5pm; Apr–Oct, daily 2–6pm. Collections, Tues–Sun 2–5pm. Closed Federal holidays and Dec 24.

Many people associate Dumbarton Oaks, a 19th-century Georgetown mansion named for a Scottish castle, with the 1944 international conference that led to the formation of the United Nations. Today the 16-acre estate is a research center for studies in Byzantine and pre-Columbian art and history, as well as landscape architecture. Its yards, which wind gently down to Rock Creek Ravine, are magical, modeled after European gardens. The pre-Columbian museum, designed by Philip Johnson, is a small gem, and the Byzantine collection is a rich one.

This unusual collection originated with Robert Woods Bliss and his wife, Mildred. In 1940 they turned over the estate, their extensive Byzantine collection, a library of works on Byzantine civilization, and 16 acres (including 10 acres of exquisite formal gardens) to Mr. Bliss's alma mater, Harvard, and provided endowment funds for continuing research in Byzantine studies. In the early 1960s they also donated their pre-Columbian collection and financed the building of a wing to house it, as well as a second wing for Mrs. Bliss's collection of rare books on landscape gardening. The Byzantine collection includes illuminated manuscripts, a 13th-century icon of St. Peter, mosaics, ivory carvings, a 4th-century sarcophagus, jewelry, and more. The pre-Columbian works, displayed chronologically in eight marble- and oak-floored glass pavilions, feature Olmec jade and serpentine figures, Mayan relief panels, textiles from 900 B.C. to the Spanish Conquest, funerary pottery, gold necklaces made by the lost-wax process, and sculptures of Aztec gods and goddesses.

The historic music room, furnished in French, Italian, and Spanish antiques, was the setting for the 1944 Dumbarton Oaks Conversations about the United Nations. It has a beamed, painted 16th-century-French-style ceiling and an immense 16th-century stone fireplace. Among its notable artworks is El Greco's *The Visitation*.

Don't miss the formal gardens, which include an Orangery, a Rose Garden (final resting place of the Blisses amid 1,000 rose bushes), wisteria-covered arbors, herbaceous borders, groves of cherry trees, and magnolias. You can picnic nearby in Montrose Park.

National Geographic Society's Explorers Hall

17th and M sts. NW. ☎ **202/857-7588.** Admission free. Mon–Sat 9am–5pm, Sun 10am–5pm. Closed Dec 25. Metro: Farragut North (Connecticut Ave. and L St. exit) or Farragut West.

The National Geographic Society was formed in 1888 to further "the increase and diffusion of geographic knowledge." At Explorers Hall, dozens of fascinating displays—most of them utilizing interactive videos—put that knowledge literally at your fingertips. In Geographica, on the north side of the hall, you can touch a tornado, find out what it's like inside the earth, explore the vast Martian landscape, and study the origin of humankind. A seven-minute video presentation narrated by Leonard Nimoy introduces visitors to the National Geographic Society. After hearing "Spock" speak, you can test your geographic knowledge at computer kiosks. The major exhibit here is Earth Station One, an interactive amphitheater (centered on an immense free-floating globe) that simulates an orbital flight. My favorite activity, however, is peering into a video microscope that zooms in clearly on slides showing such specimens as a hydra (a simple multicellular animal) or mosquito larva. Many of the video exhibits have overtones of environmental awareness.

Also on display: a scale model of Jacques Cousteau's diving saucer in which he descended to 25,000 feet; the flag and dog sledge, among other equipment, of Adm. Robert E. Peary, first man to reach the North Pole, along with a recording he made (his 1909 expedition was funded by the National Geographic Society); an *Aepyornis maximus* egg, from Madagascar's extinct 1,000-pound flightless "elephant bird"; and the world's largest freestanding globe (34 feet around the equator, with a scale of 1 inch per 60 miles). There's a full-size replica of a giant Olmec stone head dating to 32 B.C. from La Venta, Mexico. A 3.9-billion-year-old moon rock is on view in a small planetarium, and video excerpts from the society's TV specials are shown in the National Geographic Television Room. In addition, there's an ongoing program of temporary exhibits.

The National Geographic Store sells a wide array of publications, maps, globes, games, and videos. Within walking distance of the White House, this is a great place to take the kids, but they should be at least 9 or 10 years old. Younger children will not understand most of the exhibits.

The Folger Shakespeare Library

201 E. Capitol St. SE. ☎ **202/544-7077.** Admission free. Mon–Sat 10am–4pm. Closed Federal holidays. Metro: Capitol South.

"Shakespeare taught us that the little world of the heart is vaster, deeper, and richer than the spaces of astronomy," wrote Ralph Waldo Emerson in 1864. A decade later, Amherst student Henry Clay Folger was profoundly affected upon hearing a lecture by Emerson similarly extolling the Bard. Folger purchased an inexpensive set of Shakespeare's plays and went on to amass the world's largest collection of his printed works, today housed in the Folger Shakespeare Library. By 1930, when Folger and his wife, Emily (whose literary enthusiasms matched his own), laid the cornerstone of a building to house the collection, it comprised 93,000 books, 50,000 prints and engravings, and thousands of manuscripts. The Folgers made it all a gift to the American people.

The building itself is classical in style, its Georgian marble facade decorated with nine bas-relief scenes from Shakespeare's plays. A statue of Puck stands in the west garden, and quotations from the Bard and from contemporaries such as Ben Jonson adorn the exterior walls. An Elizabethan garden on the east side of the building is planted with flowers and herbs of the period, many of them mentioned in the plays.

The facility, today housing some 250,000 books, 100,000 of which are rare, is an important research center not only for Shakespearean scholars, but for those studying any aspect of the English and continental Renaissance. And the oak-paneled Great Hall, reminiscent of a Tudor long gallery, is a popular attraction for the general public. It has an intricate plaster ceiling decorated with Shakespeare's coat of arms, fleurs-de-lis, and other motifs. On display are rotating exhibits from the permanent collection—books, paintings, playbills, Renaissance musical instruments, and more.

At the end of the Great Hall is a theater designed to suggest an Elizabethan innyard theater where plays, concerts, readings, and Shakespeare-related events take place (see Chapter 10 for details).

Free walk-in **tours** are given at 11am.

United States Navy Memorial

701 Pennsylvania Ave. NW. ☎ **202/737-2300** or 800/831-8892. Admission free. Mon–Sat 9:30am–5pm, Sun noon–5pm. Closed Thanksgiving, New Year's Day, and Dec. 25. Metro: Archives/Navy Memorial.

Authorized by Congress in 1980 to honor the men and women of the United States Navy, this memorial is comprised of a 100-foot-diameter circular plaza bearing a granite world map flanked by fountains and waterfalls salted with waters from the seven seas. In summer, military bands perform on the plaza. A statue of *The Lone Sailor* watching over the map represents all who have served in the navy. And two sculpture walls adorned with bronze bas-reliefs commemorate navy history and related maritime services.

The building adjoining the memorial houses a naval heritage center. In its "Quarterdeck" entrance area, a wall frieze depicts battles from Yorktown to Operation Desert Storm, and a statue called *The Homecoming* shows the joyous reunion of a navy family. Along a spiral staircase, a timeline of ship development spanning 200 years of naval history is etched into a glass wave-motif wall. Museum highlights include interactive video kiosks proffering a wealth of information about navy ships, aircraft, and history; the Navy Memorial Log Room, a computerized record of past and present navy personnel; the Presidents Room, honoring six U.S. presidents who served in the navy and two who were secretaries of the navy; the Ship's Store, filled with nautical and maritime merchandise; and a wide-screen 70mm Surroundsound film called *At Sea* (by the makers of *To Fly*), which lets viewers experience the grandeur of the ocean and the adventure of going to sea on a navy ship. The 35-minute film plays every hour on the hour between 10am and 4pm; admission is $3.75 for adults, $3 for seniors and students 18 and under.

Guided **tours** are available from the front desk, subject to staff availability. Free concerts take place in spring and summer Tuesday evenings at 8pm and on selected days at noon; call for details.

The Korean War Veterans Memorial

Just across from the Lincoln Memorial (east of French Drive, between 21st and 23rd Sts. NW). ☎ **202/634-1568.** Admission free. Rangers on duty 8am–midnight daily. Metro: Foggy Bottom.

This privately funded new memorial, focusing on an American flag, honors those who served in Korea, a three-year conflict (1950–1953) that produced almost as many casualties as Vietnam. It consists of a circular "Pool of Remembrance" in a grove of trees and a triangular "Field of Service"—the latter highlighted by statues of 19 infantrymen, with several emerging from the woods creating the impression there are legions to follow. In addition, a 164-foot-long black granite wall depicts the array of combat and combat support troops that served in Korea (nurses, chaplains, airmen, gunners, mechanics, cooks, and others); a raised granite curb lists the 22 nations that contributed to the UN's effort there; and a commemorative area honors KIAs, MIAs, and POWs.

3   Especially for Kids

Visiting the capital with parents or classmates is an intrinsic part of American childhood. Washington is a great place for family vacations, but how much fun you have depends on your approach and planning. Let the kids help in planning daily itineraries, a project that allows everyone to become acquainted with the sights and build up excitement over what you'll be seeing. The more you know about each place, the easier it is to communicate and create enthusiasm; it's also helpful when taking tours if you can supplement the guide's commentary with child-oriented explanations. This might mean doing a wee bit of homework (reading up a bit on the various attractions), but your efforts will enhance everyone's trip.

FAVORITE CHILDREN'S ATTRACTIONS

Check for special children's events at museum information desks when you enter; better yet, call the day before to find out what's available. Here's a rundown of the biggest kid-pleasers in town (for details, see the full entries earlier in this chapter):

National Air and Space Museum. Spectacular IMAX films (don't miss), planetarium shows, missiles, rockets, and a walk-through orbital workshop.

National Museum of Natural History. A Discovery Room just for youngsters, an insect zoo, shrunken heads, and dinosaurs.

National Museum of American History. The Foucault Pendulum, locomotives, Archie Bunker's chair, and an old-fashioned ice-cream parlor.

Federal Bureau of Investigation. Gangster memorabilia, crime-solving methods, espionage devices, and a sharpshooting demonstration. You can't miss.

Bureau of Engraving and Printing. Kids enjoy looking at immense piles of money as much as you do.

National Zoological Park. Kids always love a zoo, and this is an especially nice one.

Ford's Theatre and Lincoln Museum and the **House Where Lincoln Died.** Booth's gun and diary, the clothes Lincoln was wearing the night he was assassinated, and other such grisly artifacts. Kids adore the whole business.

National Geographic Society's Explorers Hall. A moon rock, the egg of an extinct "elephant bird" (if it hatched it would weigh 1,000 pounds), numerous interactive videos. The magazine comes alive.

Washington Monument. Easy to get them up there, hard to get them down. If only they could use the steps, they'd be in heaven.

Lincoln Memorial. Kids know a lot about Lincoln and enjoy visiting his memorial. A special treat is visiting it after dark (same for the Washington Monument and Jefferson Memorial).

Arts and Industries Building. 19th-century steam engines, ship models, farm machinery, old clocks, and performances just for children in the Discovery Theater.

National Archives. See the original Declaration of Independence, Constitution, and Bill of Rights.

White House, Capitol, and **Supreme Court.** Kids enjoy learning how our government works.

Call the **Kennedy Center** and **National Theatre** to find out about children's shows; see Chapter 10 for details.

ADDITIONAL TIPS

As to the rest, plan with your children's ages and interests in mind.

An occasional purchase at a museum shop can quickly revive flagging interest, and most of the museums have wonderful toys and children's books, not to mention items like freeze-dried astronaut ice cream.

The Friday "Weekend" section of the *Washington Post* lists numerous activities (mostly free) for kids: special museum events, children's theater, storytelling programs, puppet shows, video-game competitions, and so forth.

A hotel with a swimming pool is an excellent child-refresher; it also allows time alone for adults. Consider this feature when making reservations; it may be worth a few extra bucks.

Ride the Metro, and let the kids purchase the tickets and insert their own farecards. It will be a high point, especially if they've never been on a subway before.

Enjoy some of the outdoor activities discussed later in this chapter; go bicycling or rowing; take a guided nature hike or a Potomac boat ride.

Have fun!

4   Organized Tours

BY BUS

Even if you have just a few days to spend in Washington, I think you can do better on your own. However, a guided motorcoach tour can provide a good city overview.

The **Gray Line** (☎ **202/289-1995**) offers a variety of tours, among them: "Washington After Dark" (3 hours), focusing on night-lit national monuments and federal buildings; the "Washington, D.C., All-Day Combination Tour," which includes major Washington sights plus Arlington National Cemetery, Mount Vernon, and Alexandria; and the full-day "Interiors of Public Buildings," visiting Ford's Theatre, the Jefferson Memorial, the Museum of American History, the Capitol, the Supreme Court, the National Air and Space Museum, and the National Archives. There are also trips as far afield as Colonial Williamsburg, Harper's Ferry, Gettysburg, and Charlottesville. Tours depart from Gray Line's Union Station terminal, with pickups at most major hotels. Headsets and tour tapes in foreign languages are available for afternoon tours. For details and tour prices, call the above number or inquire at your hotel desk.

A local company, **All About Town, Inc.,** 519 6th St. NW (☎ **202/393-3696**), offers a similar range of tours. Pickup is offered at major hotels. Call for details or, once again, inquire at your hotel desk.

Consider, too, **Tourmobile** and **Old Town Trolley** tours (see "Getting Around" in Chapter 4 for details).

BY BOAT

Since Washington is a river city, why not see it by boat. **Spirit of Washington Cruises,** Pier 4 at 6th and Water streets SW (☎ **202/554-8000**), offers a variety of such trips daily from early March to December. Lunch and dinner cruises include a 20-minute high-energy musical revue. Call for departure times and make reservations in advance. The following trips are offered at this writing; check when you arrive, because they tend to change with some frequency.

Evening Dinner Cruises (7 to 10pm daily) include dancing to live music and a lavish buffet meal. The fare is $45.40 Sunday to Thursday, $50.55 on Friday, $54.95 on Saturday.

Lunch and Brunch Cruises are two-hour narrated excursions on the Washington Channel. The meal consists of a seafood buffet, dessert, and tea or coffee. The fare is $27.45 Tuesday to Friday, $31.45 Saturday and Sunday.

Moonlight Dance Cruises feature dance music, complimentary hors d'oeuvres, cocktails (a cash bar), and dancing under the stars. Music is 1940s to Top 40, geared to adults, not teens (you must be at least 21 to participate). The boat heads to Alexandria. Cost for this $2^{1}/_{2}$-hour late-night cruise is $21.95.

The Mount Vernon Cruise, a popular half-day excursion, takes in D.C. sights en route to Mount Vernon plantation, George Washington's beautiful estate on the Potomac. The trip is about 1¹/₂ hours each way. The round-trip fare is $21.50 for adults, $19.25 for seniors, $12.75 for children 6 to 11, free for children 5 and under. Prices include entrance to Mount Vernon. It's a good idea to book in advance.

The *Spirit of Washington* is a luxury harbor cruise ship with climate-controlled, carpeted decks and huge panoramic windows designed for sightseeing. There are three well-stocked bars on board. Mount Vernon cruises are aboard an equally luxurious sister ship, the *Potomac Spirit.*

BY BOAT ON WHEELS

A company called **D.C. Ducks** (☎ 202/966-3825) features unique land and water tours of Washington aboard the red, white, and blue DUKW, an amphibious army vehicle (boat with wheels) from World War II that accommodates 30 passengers. Ninety-minute guided tours aboard the open-air canopied craft include a land portion taking in major sights—the Capitol, Lincoln Memorial, Washington Monument, the White House, and Smithsonian museums—and a 30-minute Potomac cruise. Boarding and ticket purchase take place at 1323 Pennsylvania Ave. NW. There are departures during tour season (April to November) Monday to Friday at 10am, noon, 2pm, and 4pm; Saturday and Sunday hourly between 10am and 4pm. Tickets cost $16 for adults, $14 for seniors over 64, and $8 for children under 13.

SCANDAL TOURS

You've seen the Smithsonian and the Lincoln Memorial. Now it's time to bypass the monuments and head right into the gutter. **Scandal Tours,** the creation of a brilliantly talented D.C. political-comedy group called Gross National Product, is a guided bus tour of Washington's sleaziest sites. ABC News anchor Peter Jennings called it "a worm's-eye view of Washington."

Highlights include the White House, where the focus is on presidential sex scandals; the Old Executive Office Building, where Ollie North and Fawn Hall shredded their way into history; the Tidal Basin, where Former Congressman Wilbur Mills and "Argentine firecracker" Fanne Foxe cavorted in the moonlight (she fell into the water, he got in hot water); the Capitol steps, scene of a night of passion for John and Rita Jenrette (Congressman Jenrette was later entrapped by Abscam and, still later, caught shoplifting in a department store); the FBI ("Janet Reno" talks about J. Edgar Hoover, "another man in a dress"); the Vista Hotel, where former mayor Marion Barry repeatedly protested the "bitch set me up"; Watergate (of course); and Gary Hart's town house, from which he emerged with Donna Rice one morning to find himself at the evening of his political career. Tour participants are greeted by a GNP troupe member in the guise of a political figure (perhaps "Nancy Reagan" in signature red dress), while other GNP actors aboard the bus portray Clinton, Gennifer Flowers, Sen. Bob Packwood, and other personalities in the forefront of the political arena. Historical figures are not spared—the company even has some dish on George Washington! "The great thing is the constant source of material," says GNP creator John Simmons. "You have power, money, and sex all along the Potomac. It's an unbeatable product—bad things happening to people it's hard to feel sorry for."

The 90-minute tours depart every Saturday at 1pm (call for reservations and departure point). The cost is $27 per person. Or you can buy "Scandal Tour In-A-Box" for $12.95 and take the tour yourself by car. To order or make your reservations, call **301/587-4291.** *Note:* You can also see GNP perform weekend nights at the Arena Stage or The Bayou in Georgetown (details in Chapter 10).

5 Park Activities

Like most cities, Washington has manicured pockets of green amid its high-rise office buildings and superhighways. Unlike most cities, it's also extensively endowed with vast natural areas—thousands of parkland acres; two rivers; a 185-mile-long, tree-lined canalside trail; an untamed wilderness area; and a few thousand cherry trees—all centrally located within the District. And there's much more just a stone's throw away.

ROCK CREEK PARK

Created in 1890, ✪ **Rock Creek Park** was purchased by Congress for its "pleasant valleys and ravines, primeval forests and open fields, its running waters, its rocks clothed with rich ferns and mosses, its repose and tranquillity, its light and shade, its every-varying shrubbery, its beautiful and extensive views." A 1,750-acre valley within the District of Columbia, extending 12 miles from the Potomac River to the Maryland border (another 2,700 acres), it's one of the biggest and finest city parks in the nation. Parts of it are still wild; it's not unusual to see a deer scurrying through the woods in more remote sections.

The park's offerings include the Carter Barron Amphitheatre (see Chapter 10), playgrounds, an extensive system of beautiful wooded hiking trails, and sports facilities.

For full information on the wide range of park programs and activities, visit the **Rock Creek Nature Center,** 5200 Glover Rd. NW (☎ 202/426-6829), Wednesday to Sunday 9am to 5pm; or **Park Headquarters,** 5000 Glover Rd. (☎ 202/282-1063), Monday to Friday 7:45am to 4:15pm. The Nature Center itself is the scene of numerous activities—weekend planetarium shows for kids (minimum age 4) and adults, nature films, crafts demonstrations, live animal demonstrations, and guided nature walks, plus a daily mix of lectures, films, and other events. A calendar is available on request. Self-guided nature trials begin here. All activities are free, but for planetarium shows you need to pick up tickets a half hour in advance. There are also nature exhibits on the premises. The Nature Center is closed on federal holidays.

You can see a water-powered 19th-century gristmill (one of more than 20 mills that operated along Rock Creek from 1664 to 1925) grinding corn and wheat into flour at Tilden Street and Beach Drive (☎ 202/426-6908). It's called **Pierce Mill** (a man named Isaac Pierce built it), and it's open to visitors Wednesday to Sunday 8am to 4:30pm. Pierce's old carriage house is today the **Art Barn** (☎ 202/244-2482), where works of local artists are exhibited; it's open Thursday to Sunday 11am to 4:30pm (closed federal holidays and the month of August).

Call 202/673-7646 or 202/673-7647 for details, locations, and group reservations at any of the park's 30 **picnic areas,** some with fireplaces. A brochure available at Park Headquarters or the Nature Center also provides details on picnic locations.

There are 15 soft-surface (clay) and 10 hard-surface **tennis courts** (five enclosed for indoor play October to May 1) at 16th and Kennedy Streets NW (☎ 202/722-5949). April to mid-November you must make a reservation in person at Guest Services on the premises to use them. Fees vary with court surface and time of play; call for details. Six additional clay courts are located off Park Road just east of Pierce Mill.

Poetry readings and workshops are held during the summer at the one-time residence of High Sierra poet Joaquin Miller, Beach Drive north of Military Road. Call 202/282-1063 for information.

The 18-hole **Rock Creek Golf Course** and clubhouse, 16th and Rittenhouse Streets NW (☎ 202/882-7332), are open year-round, daily dawn to dusk. A fee is charged. Clubs, lockers, and carts can be rented.

There are stables at the **Rock Creek Park Horse Center,** near the Nature Center on Glover Road NW (☎ 202/362-0117). Trail rides are offered Tuesday through Thursday at 3pm, Saturday at noon and 1:30pm, Sunday at noon, 1:30, and 3pm. Call for rates, reservations, and information on riding instruction.

Although you must rent bikes elsewhere, there's an 11-mile **bike path** from the Lincoln Memorial through the park into Maryland, all of it paved. On weekends and holidays a large part of it is closed to vehicular traffic.

Joggers will enjoy the 1½-mile **Perrier parcourse** with 18 calisthenics stations en route. It begins near the intersection of Cathedral Avenue and Rock Creek Parkway. There's another Perrier parcourse, with only four stations, at 16th and Kennedy Streets NW.

Finally, 20 miles of **hiking trails,** from easy to strenuous, traverse the park. You can go on your own or participate in guided hikes. Details and maps are available at Park Headquarters or the Nature Center.

There's convenient **free parking** throughout the park. To get to the Nature Center by public transport, take the Metro to Friendship Heights and transfer to an E2 or E3 bus to Military Road and Oregon Avenue/Glover Road.

POTOMAC PARK

West and East Potomac parks, their 720 riverside acres divided by the Tidal Basin, are most famous for their spring display of **cherry blossoms** and all the hoopla that goes with it.

West Potomac Park has 1,300 trees bordering the Tidal Basin, 10% of them Akebonos with delicate pink blossoms, the rest Yoshinos with white cloudlike flower clusters. It's the focal point of many of the week-long celebrations, which include the lighting of the 300-year-old **Japanese Stone Lantern** near Kutz Bridge, presented to the city by the governor of Tokyo in 1954. The trees bloom for a little less than two weeks beginning somewhere between March 20 and April 17; April 5 is the average date. See the calendar of events in Chapter 2 for further details on cherry blossom events.

Though West Potomac Park gets more cherry blossom publicity, East Potomac Park has more trees (1,800 of them) and more varieties (11). Here, too, are **picnic grounds;** 24 **tennis courts,** including five indoors and three lit for night play (☎ 202/554-5962); one 18-hole and two 9-hole **golf courses** (☎ 202/863-9007); a large **swimming pool** (☎ 202/727-6523); and **biking** and **hiking** paths by the water.

West Potomac Park encompasses Constitution Gardens; the Vietnam, Korean, Lincoln, and Jefferson Memorials; a small island where ducks live; and the Reflecting Pool.

CHESAPEAKE & OHIO CANAL
NATIONAL HISTORICAL PARK (C&O CANAL)

One of the great joys of living in Washington is the ✪ **C&O Canal** and its unspoiled 184¹/₂-mile towpath. One leaves urban cares and stresses behind while hiking, strolling, jogging, cycling, or boating in this lush, natural setting of ancient oaks and red maples, giant sycamores, willows, and wildflowers. I've never walked the canal without making an exciting discovery—a proud mother duck with a new family in tow; raspberries suddenly abundantly in season; a brilliant flowering tree amid the greenery; a quaint canalside home; a sudden appreciation of light shimmering on the water. The canal is a happy place. However, it wasn't always just a leisure spot for city people. It was built in the 1800s, when water routes were considered vital to transportation. Even before it was completed, however, the B&O Railroad, which was constructed at about the same time and along the same route, had begun to render it obsolete. Today, perhaps, it serves an even more important purpose as a cherished urban refuge.

Canal Activities Headquarters for canal activities is the **Office of the Superintendent,** C&O Canal National Historical Park, P.O. Box 4, Sharpsburg, MD 21782 (☎ 301/739-4200). Also knowledgeable is the National Park Service office at **Great Falls Tavern Visitor Center,** 11710 MacArthur Blvd., Potomac, MD 20854 (☎ 301/299-3613). At this 1831 tavern you can see museum exhibits and a film about the canal; there's also a bookstore on the premises. And April to November, Wednesday to Sunday, the **Georgetown Information Center,** 1057 Thomas Jefferson St. NW (☎ 202/653-5844), can also provide maps and information. Call ahead for hours at all the above.

Hiking any section of the flat dirt towpath—or its more rugged side paths—is a pleasure. There are **picnic tables,** some with fire grills, about every 5 miles beginning at Fletcher's Boat House (about 3.2 miles out of Georgetown) on the way to Cumberland. There are also numerous camping areas, starting at Swain's Lock, 16 miles from Georgetown. Use of campsites is on a first-come, first-served basis. Enter the towpath in Georgetown below M Street via Thomas Jefferson Street. If you hike 14 miles, you'll reach **Great Falls,** a point where the Potomac becomes a stunning waterfall plunging 76 feet. Or drive to Great Falls Park on the Virginia side of the Potomac.

Stop at **Fletcher's Boat House,** described in "Active Sports," below (☎ 202/244-0461), to rent **bikes** or **boats** or purchase bait and tackle (or a license) for **fishing.** A snack bar and picnic area are on the premises. It's also accessible by car.

Much less strenuous than hiking is a **mule-drawn 19th-century canal boat trip** led by Park Service rangers in period dress. They regale passengers with canal legend and lore and sing period songs. These boats depart Wednesday through Sunday from mid-April to early November; call 202/653-5844 or 301/299-3613 for departure times. Tickets are available at the Georgetown Information Center or the Great Falls Tavern (address and phone for both above). The fare is $5 for adults, $3.50 for children under 12 and seniors over 62.

Call any of the above information numbers for details on riding, rock climbing, fishing, birdwatching, concerts, ranger-guided tours, ice skating, camping, and other canal activities.

UNITED STATES NATIONAL ARBORETUM

A research and educational center focusing on trees and shrubs, the ✪ **U.S. National Arboretum,** 3501 New York Ave. NE (☎ 202/245-2726), is one of the great joys of Washington. Its 9¹/₂ miles of paved roads meander through 444 hilly acres of rhododendrons, azaleas (the most extensive plantings in the nation), crabapples, magnolias, hollies, peonies, irises, dogwoods, day lilies, boxwoods, cherry trees, aquatic plants, and dwarf conifers. The highlight for me is the **National Bonsai and Penjing Museum**—a $4.5-million Bicentennial gift from Japan of 53 beautiful miniature trees, some of them more than three centuries old. Each one is an exquisite work of art. The exhibit was augmented by a gift of 35 Chinese Penjing trees in 1986, and again in 1990 by the American Bonsai Collection of 56 North American plants; in 1993 a conservatory for tropical bonsai was erected. This area also includes a **Japanese Garden** and a garden of plants of American origin. The **Herbarium** contains 600,000 dried plants for reference purposes. The **Herb Garden,** another highlight, includes a historic rose garden (100 old-fashioned fragrant varieties), a contemporary interpretation of a 16th-century English-style "knot" garden, and 10 specialty gardens—a dye garden, a medicinal garden, and a culinary garden among them. Along Fern Valley Trail is the Franklin Tree—a species now extinct in the wild—discovered in 1765 by a botanist friend of Benjamin Franklin. And a magnificent sight is the arboretum's **acropolis**—22 of the original U.S. Capitol columns designed by Benjamin Latrobe in a setting created by the noted English landscape artist Russell Page. The **American Friendship Garden,** opened in 1990, is a collection of ornamental grasses—reminiscent of prairie landscapes—and perennials, with brick walkways, terraces, and a statue of Demeter, the Greek goddess of agriculture. Its colorful spring bulb plants comprise a wide variety of narcissi, tulips, irises, and crocuses enhanced by small flowering and fruiting trees and interesting shrubs. Carefully placed teak benches provide a place for quiet contemplation. This garden also features an extensive collection of perennials and bulb plants. And the **Asian Collections** in a landscaped valley include rare plants from China and Korea.

Magnolias and early bulbs bloom in late March or early April; rhododendrons, daffodils, and flowering cherry trees in mid-April; azaleas and peonies in May; lilies and hibiscus in summer. In autumn the arboretum is ablaze in reds and oranges as the leaves change color.

The arboretum is open daily 8am to 5pm, the bonsai collection 10am to 3:30pm. Everything is closed December 25. Take bus B2 from the Stadium Armory Metro station to Bladensburg Road and R Street NE. Or hop in a taxi; it's only a few dollars. If you drive, **parking** is free (you can drive through if you wish). Frequent tours, lectures, and workshops (including bonsai classes) are offered, and a comprehensive guidebook is available in the gift shop.

THEODORE ROOSEVELT ISLAND

A serene 88-acre wilderness preserve, Theodore Roosevelt Island is a memorial to our 26th president, in recognition of his contributions to conservation. An outdoor enthusiast and expert field naturalist, Roosevelt once threw away a prepared speech and roared, "I hate a man who would skin the land!" During his administration, 150 million acres of forest land were reserved, and five national parks, 51 bird refuges, and four game refuges were created.

Theodore Roosevelt Island was inhabited by Native American tribes for centuries before the arrival of English explorers in the 1600s. Over the years it passed through many owners before becoming what it is today—an island preserve of swamp, marsh, and upland forest that's a haven for rabbits, chipmunks, great owls, fox, muskrat, turtles, and groundhogs. It's a complex ecosystem in which cattails, arrow arum, and pickerelweed growing in the marshes create a hospitable habitat for abundant bird life. And willow, ash, and maple trees rooted on the mudflats create the swamp environment favored by the raccoon in its search for crayfish. You can observe these flora and fauna in their natural environs on 2^1/$_2$ miles of foot trails.

In the northern center of the island, overlooking an oval terrace encircled by a water-filled moat, stands a 17-foot bronze statue of Roosevelt. From the terrace rise four 21-foot granite tablets inscribed with these tenets of his philosophy: "There are no words that can tell the hidden spirit of the wilderness, that can reveal its mystery, its melancholy, and its charm" and "The Nation behaves well if it treats the natural resources as assets which it must turn over to the next generation increased and not impaired in value."

To get to the island, take the George Washington Memorial Parkway exit north from the Theodore Roosevelt Bridge. The **parking** area is accessible only from the northbound lane; from there, a pedestrian bridge connects the island with the Virginia shore. You can also rent a canoe at Thompson's Boat Center (see "Boating" in "Active Sports," below) and paddle over, or walk across the pedestrian bridge at Rosslyn Circle, two blocks from the Rosslyn **Metro** station. **Picnicking** is permitted on the grounds near the memorial.

For further information, contact the District Ranger, Theodore Roosevelt Island, George Washington Memorial Parkway, c/o Turkey Run Park, McLean, VA 22101 (☎ 703/285-2598).

6 Active Sports

BICYCLING   Both **Fletcher's Boat House** and **Thompson's Boat Center** (see "Boating," below for addresses and hours) rent bikes, as does **Big Wheel Bikes,** 1034 33rd St. NW, right near the C&O Canal just below M Street (☎ 202/337-0254). Hours are 10am to 6pm daily, and till 8pm weekdays from April to September. There's another Big Wheel shop on Capitol Hill at 315 7th St. SE (☎ 202/543-1600); call for hours. Photo ID and a major credit card are required to rent bicycles.

The *Washington Post* Friday "Weekend" section lists cycling trips. See also Rock Creek Park, the C&O Canal, and the Potomac Parks in "Activities," earlier in this chapter, for details on their biking facilities.

BOATING   **Thompson's Boat Center,** 2900 Virginia Ave. at Rock Creek Parkway NW (☎ 202/333-4861 or 202/333-9543), rents canoes, sailboats, rowing shells, and rowboats. They also offer sculling and sweep-rowing lessons. Photo ID and a $20 deposit are required. They're open mid-April to early October, Monday to Friday 7am to 6pm, Saturday and Sunday 8am to 5pm. You can't rent a boat after 5pm. For bike rentals ($10 deposit required) the shop is open March to mid-November, same hours.

Late March to mid-September, you can rent paddleboats on the north end of the Tidal Basin off Independence Avenue (☎ 202/479-2426). Hours are 10am to 7pm daily.

Fletcher's Boat House, Reservoir and Canal Roads (☎ 202/244-0461), is right on the C&O Canal, about a 3.2-mile wonderfully scenic walk from Georgetown. It's been owned by the same family since 1850! Open March to mid-November, daily 7:30am to dusk, Fletcher's rents canoes and rowboats and sells fishing licenses, bait, and tackle. ID is required (a driver's license or major credit card). A snack bar and restrooms here are welcome after that hike. And there are picnic tables (with barbecue grills) overlooking the Potomac. You don't have to walk to Fletcher's; it's accessible by car (west on M Street to Canal Road) and has plenty of free parking.

CAMPING   See the C&O Canal in "Park Activities," earlier in this chapter.

FISHING   The Potomac River around Washington provides an abundant variety of fish—some 40 species, all perfectly safe to eat. Good fishing is possible from late February to November, but mid-March to June (spawning season) is peak. Perch and catfish are the most common catch, but during bass season a haul of 20 to 40 is not unusual. The Washington Channel offers good bass and carp fishing year-round.

A **fishing license** is required. You can obtain one at various locations around the city, among them **Fletcher's Boat House** (address and telephone number above) and the **Chinatown Coffee House,** 616 H St. NW (☎ 202/783-6212). Cost for nonresidents is $7.50 for a year, $3 for a 14-day permit.

GOLF There are dozens of public courses within easy driving distance of the D.C. area, but within the District itself East Potomac Park and Rock Creek Park have the only public courses. The 18-hole **Rock Creek Golf Course** and clubhouse, at 16th and Rittenhouse Streets NW (☎ 202/882-7332), are open to the public daily year-round from dawn to dusk. You will find a snack bar and lockers on the premises, and you can rent clubs and carts. A fee is charged.

East Potomac Park has one 18-hole, par-72 and two 9-hole courses. For details, call 202/554-7660.

HIKING Check the *Washington Post* Friday "Weekend" section for listings of hiking clubs; almost all are open to the public for a small fee. Be sure to inquire about the difficulty of any hike you plan to join and the speed with which the group proceeds; some hikes are fast-paced, allowing no time to smell the flowers.

On your own, there are numerous hiking paths. The **C&O Canal** offers 184$^{1}/_{2}$ miles alone; it would be hard to find a more scenic setting than the 9$^{1}/_{2}$ miles of road at the **arboretum** (see "Park Activities," earlier in this chapter); **Theodore Roosevelt Island** has more than 88 wilderness acres to explore, including a 2$^{1}/_{2}$-mile nature trail (short but rugged); and in **Rock Creek Park** there are 15 miles of hiking tails for which maps are available at the Visitor Information Center or Park Headquarters.

HORSEBACK RIDING The **Rock Creek Park Horse Center,** near the Nature Center on Glover Road NW (☎ 202/362-0117), offers rental horses for trail rides and riding instruction, there are 14 miles of woodland bridle paths to explore. Call for ride times. No riding experience is required.

ICE SKATING My favorite place for winter skating is on the **C&O Canal,** its banks dotted with cozy fires at which one can warm frozen extremities. Call **301/299-3613** for information on ice conditions. Guest Services, Inc., operates the **National Sculpture Garden Ice Rink** on the Mall at 7th Street and Constitution Avenue NW (☎ 202/371-5342), the **Pershing Park** outdoor rink at 14th Street and Pennsylvania Avenue NW (☎ 202/737-6938), and a huge hockey-size indoor facility, the **Fort Dupont Ice Arena,** at 3779 Ely Place SE, at Minnesota Avenue in Fort Dupont Park (☎ 202/581-0199). All three offer skate rentals. The Sculpture Garden and Pershing Park rinks are open approximately from December (some years earlier) to February, weather permitting; Fort Dupont, from Labor Day to the end of April. Call for hours and admission prices.

Note: The Pershing Park rink may be closed for repairs this year; call ahead.

JOGGING   A **parcourse jogging path,** a gift from Perrier, opened in Rock Creek Park in 1978. Its 1½-mile oval route, beginning near the intersection of Cathedral Avenue and Rock Creek Parkway, includes 18 calisthenics stations with instructions on prescribed exercises. There's another Perrier parcourse, with only four stations, at 16th and Kennedy streets NW. Other popular jogging areas are the **C&O Canal** and **Mall.**

SWIMMING   There are 45 swimming pools in the District run by the **D.C. Department of Recreation Aquatic Program** (☎ 202/576-6436). They include the Capitol East Natatorium, an indoor/outdoor pool with sun deck and adjoining baby pool at 635 North Carolina Ave. SE (☎ 202/724-4495 or 202/724-4496); the outdoor pool in East Potomac Park (☎ 202/727-6523); a large outdoor pool at 25th and N streets NW (☎ 202/727-3285); and the Georgetown outdoor pool at 34th Street and Volta Place NW (☎ 202/282-2366). Indoor pools are open year-round; outdoor pools, from Memorial Day to Labor Day. Call for hours and details on other locations.

TENNIS   There are 144 outdoor courts in the District (60 of them lighted for night play) at 45 locations. Court use is on a first-come, first-served basis. For a list of locations, call or write the **D.C. Department of Recreation,** 3149 16th St. NW, Washington, DC 20010 (☎ 202/673-7646). Most courts are open year-round, weather permitting. In addition, there are courts in **Rock Creek** and **East Potomac Parks** (see "Park Activities," earlier in this chapter, for details).

7 Spectator Sports

BALTIMORE ARENA   The 13,500-seat Baltimore Arena, 210 W. Baltimore St., a few blocks from the Inner Harbor in Baltimore (☎ 410/347-2020), is home to the **Baltimore Thunder** (indoor lacrosse). Between late September and June, the Baltimore Bandits (AHL) farm team for The Mighty Ducks, play about 40 games here. The **Washington Bullets** (NBA) play at least four games here each year, and the facility also hosts the Ice Capades every February, Harlem Globetrotters games, tractor pulls, and more. For tickets, call 410/481-SEAT, or 800/551-SEAT. Once again, take the MARC train from Union Station. To get here by car, take I-95 north to I-395 (stay in left lane) to the Inner Harbor exit and follow Howard Street to the arena.

ORIOLE PARK AT CAMDEN YARDS   The 48,000-seat Oriole Park at Camden Yards, 333 W. Camden St., between Howard and Conway streets, in Baltimore, Maryland (☎ 410/685-9800), opened in 1992. It's the home of baseball's **Baltimore Orioles.** Unlike recent ultra-modern sports stadiums, Oriole Park incorporates features of its urban environment, such as the old B&O Railroad yards near downtown Baltimore. A renovated brick warehouse serves as a striking visual backdrop beyond the right-field fence. For tickets, call

410/481-SEAT, or 800/551-SEAT. From Union Station in Washington, take a MARC train to Baltimore, which lets you off right at the ballpark. By car, take I-95 north to Exit 53.

THE PATRIOT CENTER   The Patriot Center, 4400 University Dr. in Fairfax, Virginia (☎ 703/993-3000), opened in late 1985 on the campus of nearby George Mason University. A 10,000-seat facility, it's used for Patriot (men's and women's GMU teams) college basketball games, Harlem Globetrotters games, gymnastic competitions, horse shows, and other events. To get here, take the Wilson Bridge to Braddock Road West (Route 623) and proceed about 8 miles to University Drive. For tickets, call 703/573-SEAT or 800/551-SEAT.

ROBERT F. KENNEDY MEMORIAL STADIUM/D.C. ARMORY
The 55,000-seat Robert F. Kennedy Memorial Stadium (and the 10,000-seat D.C. Armory complex), East Capitol Street between 19th and 20th Streets SE (☎ 202/547-9077 or 202/ 546-3337), is the D.C. home of the **Washington Redskins** (NFL). Events here also include wrestling, nationally televised boxing, roller derby, the circus, soccer games, and rodeos. To charge tickets call 202/432-SEAT or 800/ 551-SEAT.

USAIR ARENA   The **Washington Bullets** (NBA) and the **Washington Capitals** (NHL) play home games at the USAir Arena, Exit 15A or 17A off the Capital Beltway in Landover, Maryland (☎ 301/ 350-3400). The 19,000-seat arena is also used for Georgetown University basketball games (the Hoyas), Washington Warthogs (CISL) indoor soccer games, monster truck shows, wrestling, and annual events like the Washington International Horse Show, Campbell's Olympic Figure-Skating Championships, and World Professional Figure Skating Championships. Also big-name concerts. For tickets, call 202/432-SEAT or 800/551-SEAT.

Washington Scandals: A Walking Tour

Start: Watergate Hotel (Metro: Foggy Bottom).
Finish: The Supreme Court.
Time: Approximately 3 hours.
Best Times: Anytime.

Ask Americans if they think their elected leaders are by and large a straitlaced, high-minded bunch and you'll get a collective roll of the eyes. The reason, of course, is that scandalous news never stops pouring out of the nation's capital. Politics and dirty deeds seem to be inseparable; Washington lore is rich with stories of politicians arriving here burning with lofty ideals and ambition only to fall prey to one or another of the grubby demons of human nature. And the sins of the government are thrown into spectacular relief by the klieg lights of the capital's scandal press, which makes its living feeding the public's appetite for news from the gutter.

As Mark Twain put it, Washington houses the only "distinctly native American criminal class." In the spirit of that great American curmudgeon, this tour wades through 200-odd years of avarice, lust, and plain idiocy as cause for amusement and stimulus to a healthy skepticism. The framers of our constitution were indeed wise when they labored to build a government that would keep any individual from accruing too much power—as you'll now be reminded, power is often too great a burden for human frailties to bear.

From the Foggy Bottom Metro, make a U-turn to your right after exiting the Metro station; walk through a small park to New Hampshire Avenue. Follow it the equivalent of one block, to Virginia Avenue. You'll see the curving facade of the:

1. **Watergate Hotel/Apartment/Office Complex,** 2650 Virginia Avenue. Just after 1am on June 17, 1972, on the sixth floor of the Watergate, a security guard found a taped-over lock on an office door of the Democratic Party's national headquarters. Suspecting foul play, he called the police, who arrived at the scene to find five well-dressed men huddled under the furniture, all wearing rubber gloves and in possession of high-tech spy gear and 32 sequentially numbered $100 bills.

Thus began the Watergate scandal, perhaps the darkest shadow ever cast over the federal government. By the time the details of the "dirty tricks" perpetrated by the Committee to Reelect the President ("CREEP") emerged, 25 members of President Richard Nixon's staff had received jail terms at the hands of Judge "Maximum John" Sirica; Nixon himself, facing sure impeachment for reasons of perjury, obstruction of justice, misuse of federal funds, and politicization of federal agencies, had resigned (on August 9, 1974); and an outraged "throw-the-bums-out" attitude had settled over the nation.

Take a look inside the elegant Watergate Hotel if you feel so moved. Directly across Virginia Avenue is the:

2. **Howard Johnson's Hotel** where G. Gordon Liddy hung out to do his share of the dirty work on the Democrats. The former FBI agent and the counsel to CREEP was paid $235,000—in cash—for his Watergate work.

Now take Virginia Avenue to the traffic light at 25th Street and turn right, following the curve of the sidewalk around to the:

3. **Kennedy Center for the Performing Arts.** Walk inside and to the back of the Grand Foyer, where a large bust of John F. Kennedy (by Robert Berks) faces the Opera House. We now know that JFK, he of the high-minded idealism and inspirational vision of the presidency as a new "Camelot," was less than pure both in his practice of politics and in his personal life. His administration engaged in more than the usual amount of skulduggery, from the infamous Bay of Pigs invasion, to the enlistment of the Chicago mob's help during the 1960 elections, to secret assassination plots. "Operation Mongoose," the most notorious of the latter, targeted Cuba's Fidel Castro; various plans (in which the Mafia may also have played a role) to take out the Cuban leader turned on improbable devices such as poisoned pens, LSD-laced cigars, and exploding seashells.

And then there were the women: Jack Kennedy, like most of the men in his family, was a compulsive philanderer. He and wife Jackie may have looked the perfect couple, but their marriage was termed "an understanding" at best by a family friend. He may have slowed down after a fashion upon becoming president—he reportedly called a friend one day and said, "There are two naked girls in the room but I'm sitting here reading the *Wall Street Journal.* Does that mean I'm getting old?" Jackie took it all with resigned hauteur; upon finding a pair of panties in the White House bed, she turned to her husband and said, "Here, find out who these belong to—they're not my size." He carried on well-documented affairs with such notables as Jayne Mansfield, Kim Novak, Angie Dickinson, and Marilyn Monroe, who, according to columnist Earl Wilson, is supposed to have said after a night

Walking Tour—Washington Scandals

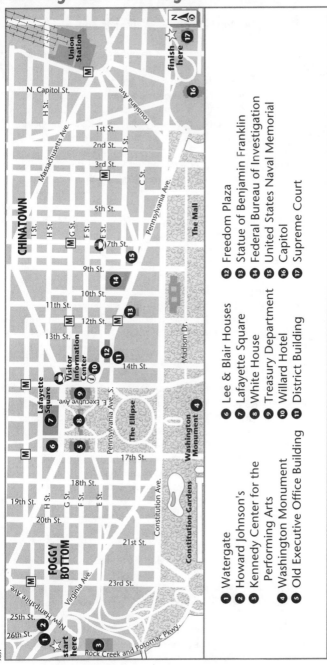

CHINATOWN

FOGGY BOTTOM

Union Station

N. Capitol St.
H St.
1st St.
2nd St.
3rd St.
D St.
C St.
5th St.
I St.
H St.
G St.
F St.
E St.
7th St.
9th St.
10th St.
11th St.
12th St.
13th St.
14th St.
17th St.
18th St.
19th St.
20th St.
21st St.
23rd St.
25th St.
26th St.

Massachusetts Ave.
Louisiana Ave.
Pennsylvania Ave.
New Hampshire Ave.
Virginia Ave.
Constitution Ave.

Lafayette Square
Visitor Information Center
E. Executive Ave. S.
Pennsylvania Ave.
The Ellipse
Madison Dr.
The Mall
Washington Monument
Constitution Gardens
Rock Creek and Potomac Pkwy.

start here
finish here

1 Watergate
2 Howard Johnson's
3 Kennedy Center for the Performing Arts
4 Washington Monument
5 Old Executive Office Building
6 Lee & Blair Houses
7 Lafayette Square
8 White House
9 Treasury Department
10 Willard Hotel
11 District Building
12 Freedom Plaza
13 Statue of Benjamin Franklin
14 Federal Bureau of Investigation
15 United States Naval Memorial
16 Capitol
17 Supreme Court

9651

G. Gordon Liddy & the Watergate Follies

The strength of our democracy is in public consensus and the constitutional safeguards that protect the integrity of that consensus; in the early 1970s, Richard Nixon's administration was willing to bypass any number of those safeguards in the name of gaining four more years. As columnist William White wrote, "We know that politics is extremely rough, but most people in it do, at some point, recognize a line, admittedly indefinable, but a line beyond which you just don't go."

G. Gordon Liddy was general counsel to CREEP (Committee to Reelect the President) at a time when the Nixon campaign was muscling major corporations for illegal contributions— and when the unfortunates on Nixon's infamous "enemies list" (ostensible political opponents who ranged from George McGovern to David Brinkley to Tony Randall) were treated as threats to national security and subjected to wiretapping, burglaries, and tax audits. Liddy was only slightly atypical in his belief that the American "fatherland" was smothering in permissive flab; in his eyes all was fair in the war for the soul of the country. He was fond of proving his discipline by holding his hand over an open flame. And when CREEP director Jeb Magruder muttered something about "getting rid" of some "enemy" in Liddy's presence, the good soldier grimly announced to a subordinate "I have been ordered to kill [the 'enemy']" (he was persuaded that wasn't what Magruder had in mind).

Liddy's first proposal to Presidential Counsel John Dean and Attorney General John Mitchell for doing in the Democrats was a wild million-dollar plan that involved kidnapping radical leaders as well as launching a floating whorehouse off Miami Beach in hopes of luring prominent Dems into compromising positions. When Mitchell told him to come back with something more "realistic," the plan to break into and bug the Democratic National Committee's offices in the Watergate Hotel was born. After two botched attempts and one successful entry (on May 27, 1972), Mitchell ordered

with Jack, "Well, I think I made his back feel better." (Monroe was later passed on to brother Bobby Kennedy; much as Jack did, Bobby would eventually unceremoniously dump her. Peter Brown and Patte Barham's *Marilyn: The Last Take* (Dutton, 1992) suggests that Monroe's death in 1962 was not a suicide but murder. Fed up with her treatment at the hands of the Kennedys, Monroe had begun to act on threats to go public about her relationships with them. The coroner in the case has said that the Nembutal that killed her could not have been a simple overdose

Liddy to go back for better information. Liddy's team broke in again on June 17, and the rest is history.

A portrait of the burglary, CREEP's other activities, and the remarkable G. Gordon Liddy began to emerge during the Watergate congressional hearings. John Dean testified that an aggrieved Liddy told him after the disastrous break-in that he would never talk and "If anyone wished to shoot him on the street he was ready." An incredulous public was astounded that Liddy's harebrained schemes even reached the President's ears. That this was indeed the case became fully apparent only when Nixon was finally prevailed upon, in August 1974, to release the taped White House conversations between himself and his chief of staff, Bob Haldeman, from June 23, 1972. As George F. Will put it, the tapes were "more of a smoking howitzer than a smoking gun." Here's a portion:

Nixon: Well, who's the ass—that did [authorize the break-in]? Is it Liddy? Is that the fellow? He must be a little nuts.

Haldeman: He is.

Nixon: I mean he just isn't well screwed on, is he? Is that the problem?

Haldeman: No, but he was under pressure, apparently, to get more information, and as he got more pressure, he pushed the people harder to move harder—

Nixon: Pressure from Mitchell?

Haldeman: Apparently.

Nixon: All right, fine, I understand it all. We won't second-guess Mitchell and the rest.

Nixon then went on to agree with Haldeman on a coverup scheme to tell the FBI to "lay off" its investigation of the break-in because any further breaks in the investigation "would be very unfortunate . . . for the country." As the contents of the tapes broke, it was clear that the President himself was complicit in all the "dirty tricks" perpetrated by his staff, complicit in the myriad ways his administration stepped over (one might say obliterated) that "indefinable line." He resigned from office four days later.

of pills—it was likely administered by injection in a spot unlikely to be discovered during autopsy. Brown and Barham suggest that Bobby Kennedy had something to do with it.)

Another blow to the Kennedy mystique came in 1988 when Judith Campbell Exner, stricken with terminal cancer, decided to clear her conscience. She revealed that during her 2½-year affair with JFK she functioned as courier between the president and the mob, delivering packages and arranging meetings between Kennedy and Chicago Mafia godfather Sam Giancana.

From the rooftop terrace of the Kennedy Center you can see several recognizable Washington landmarks, among them the:

4. **Washington Monument.** Today, even George Washington would not find himself above reproach. Although he married into plenty of money when he took Martha Dandridge Custis to wife (she owned 17,000 acres of land and a Williamsburg townhouse), the general disdained the modest salaries other revolutionary generals earned and accorded himself an expense account of $449,261.50—an emperor's ransom in those days—over his eight years' service. And he reportedly showed the worst possible taste in mistresses, most notably Mary Gibbons, who pumped Washington about his military plans during their trysts and then passed the information on to William Tryon, the royal governor of New York. Tryon capitalized on it by raiding American seaport towns and destroying much-needed supplies.

Return to Virginia Avenue. Turn right onto it (follow the pointing arm of the Benito Juarez statue). At 23rd Street turn right and walk to H Street. Turn right and follow it through the campus of George Washington University, including the university yard, between 20th and 21st Streets. Continue in the same direction on H Street. Make a left on 19th Street and a right on Pennsylvania Avenue. Just across 17th Street, you will notice the multi-columned:

5. **Old Executive Office Building.** When the Iran-Contra scandal began to break in November 1986, it was as deeply disturbing as any revelation from Washington since Watergate. The Reagan administration, in its zeal to topple the socialist Sandinista government in Nicaragua, had illegally sold arms to Ayatollah Khomeini's Iran to fund a ragtag army of "freedom fighters" in Nicaragua known as the "Contras." There were many parallels between the two scandals: Both revealed glimpses of a secret government accountable only to the president (and that in a very hazy way), financed with ill-gotten public funds, and used to carry out policies against the express wishes of the Congress. Watergate had its "plumbers" and the "dirty-tricks" committee; Iran-Contra had CIA director William Casey speaking approvingly to Oliver North of a permanent, "off the shelf, self-sustaining, stand-alone entity that could perform certain activities on behalf of the United States." In the sanctimonious North, Iran-Contra had its very own G. Gordon Liddy. North was the chief architect of the Iran-Contra policy, which political analyst Frances Fitzgerald called "as stupid as any since the Trojans took in that gigantic wooden horse." But during the congressional hearings into the matter in 1987, North somehow became a hero to many by virtue of his G.I.-Joe persona and such flag-waving statements as this one: "I am proud to work for that commander-in-chief. And if the commander-in-chief tells this lieutenant colonel to go stand in the corner and sit on his head, I will do so."

But history did not quite repeat itself. In the bowels of this enormous gray building, North and his pretty blond secretary, Fawn Hall, showed that the misfortunes endured by Nixon and his staff had not been in vain: Determined not to leave a smoking gun on the order of Nixon's White House tapes, they shredded evidence of the affair. Through their efforts and the stubborn resistance of Reagan and his officials to congressional questions about the imbroglio ("I can't recall" became a refrain throughout the hearings), most of the miscreants got off with a slap on the wrist or scot-free. Hall—who concisely captured the spirit of Iran-Contra when she told Congress, "Sometimes you have to go above the written law"—later tried to cash in on her involvement in the affair, signing with the William Morris talent agency. In 1994 she turned up again, on her way into a rehab center for treatment of cocaine addiction. Oliver North has made the most of his notoriety, publishing a book in 1991 and making a strong run for the U.S. senate in Virginia in 1994. Ronald Reagan's "Teflon" reputation was finally tarnished by Iran-Contra; either he lied in steadfastly denying involvement in the cloak-and-dagger theatrics of his subordinates, or he was troublingly out of touch with the policies perpetrated in his name. If it's the latter, perhaps when he said, "Every night I go to bed knowing that there are things that I am not aware of," he was justifiably paranoid.

Across Pennsylvania Avenue from the Old Executive Office Building (just past the Renwick Gallery), the brick house with the dormer windows is:

6. **Lee House** (built 1824), which, with the adjacent **Blair House** (built 1858), has served as the president's official guesthouse since 1943. Blair House was once the home of Montgomery Blair, the attorney of Dred Scott, a slave who wanted to be declared a free man because he had lived for a time with his master in a free territory. His case made its way to the Supreme Court in 1857, at which point it became a focal point in the struggle over slavery in the new territories between abolitionist and proslavery forces. With the nation looking to the court to solve a problem Congress could not, Chief Justice Roger B. Taney (a southerner) delivered the infamous majority opinion that a Negro had no rights that "a white man was bound to respect;" therefore, Scott's case had no merit. Abolitionists were outraged, and the nation moved within a hair's breadth of civil war.

In this house, Robert E. Lee was offered the command of the Union Army. Though he supported the Union, his greater loyalty was to his home state of Virginia. He turned the offer down, creating a furor in the federal capital.

Continuing along Pennsylvania Avenue, you'll cross Jackson Place and come to:

7. **Lafayette Square.** This small public park, its Pennsylvania Avenue side flanked by heroic statues of Rochambeau and Lafayette, has been the site of several dark incidents. In 1859 Daniel Sickles, a congressman from New York, discovered that his friend Philip Barton Key (whose father was Francis Scott Key, author of "The Star-Spangled Banner") had been carrying on an affair with his wife, Teresa. When Key next signaled Teresa from Lafayette Square outside the Sickles' window, the infuriated Sickles rushed outside and shot Key dead. The murder sparked the sort of sensational tabloid coverage commonplace today. When the case came to trial, Sickles's lawyer successfully made use of a "temporary insanity" defense, and his client was acquitted. Afterward, however, Sickles was anything but repentant: "Of course I intended to kill him," he told friends. "He deserved it."

In 1917 women's suffragists demonstrated in Lafayette Square and were arrested, charged with "obstructing traffic." Among them was Alice Paul, founder of the National Woman's Party in 1913 and author of the Equal Rights Amendment in 1923. Paul and the other women were jailed in the abandoned Occoquan Workhouse, where they had to sleep on the floor and were given worm-filled food. When they chose to go on a hunger strike, they were force-fed with tubes stuck up their nostrils and down their throats. Women's right to vote would not be ratified until 1920.

Lafayette Square continues to be a focal point for protests by individuals and groups that find the actions, or inaction, of the government scandalous in one way or another. Many consider it scandalous as well that the park is filled with homeless people, especially since it lies directly across the street from the:

8. **White House.** Many who've held the highest office in the land rose to the top precisely because they were ruthless and unprincipled, so it should come as no surprise that the White House's history is stained with scandal. John F. Kennedy was not the only president to enjoy illicit passion within these walls. Warren G. Harding, president from 1921 until his death in 1923, was reported to have enjoyed the favors of mistress Nan Britton in a closet near the Oval Office—the family dog once sniffed them out there. (Britton, 30 years Harding's junior, had a daughter she alleged was conceived with Harding on the couch of his office when he was a senator. After his death she tried unsuccessfully to get a portion of his estate for her child and in 1927 published a bestseller called *The President's Daughter.* It was dedicated to "all unwed mothers, and to their innocent children whose fathers usually are not known to the world.") Before he became president, Harding carried on a 15-year affair with Carrie Fulton Phillips, a German sympathizer and the wife of an old friend. The Hardings and the Phillipses socialized and even took trips together. When Harding ran for the presidency, the Secret Service

paid off the couple and continued to supply them with "hush money" until Harding's death.

Harding had much more serious trouble in his choice of friends than with women. During his short term, a long list of his close associates, most of them part of what was called the "Ohio gang," made fast money brokering shady deals in smoke-filled rooms. Though he publicly lauded prohibition, he was an eager participant in all-night White House poker games with his cronies, at which a full complement of illegal alcohol was available. Washington insider Alice Roosevelt Longworth, daughter of Teddy Roosevelt, considered him a "slob" who imbued his White House "with the air of a loose speakeasy." The most infamous scandal attributed to his venal associates was Teapot Dome, in which two Cabinet Secretaries earned enormous kickbacks from private oilmen in exchange for turning over two huge government oil reserves to them for peanuts. Not long before he died, Harding said, "I can take care of my enemies all right. But my friends, my God-damn friends. . . they're the ones who keep me walking the floor nights." It's no wonder he keeled over from a heart attack.

Franklin Delano Roosevelt allegedly had lovers in the White House: lifetime love Lucy Mercer and his secretary Missy Lehand. Lucy Mercer was with FDR when he died in Warm Springs, Georgia, but she discreetly departed before Eleanor arrived.

Through the years, certain White House wives have been known for their eccentricities in personality or spending. Mary Todd Lincoln, who was often ill-tempered and mentally unstable, got so carried away while redecorating the White House that she overran by $6,700 a hefty appropriation of $20,000. When he got wind of his wife's profligate spending, Honest Abe was incensed: "[The overrun] can never have my approval," he fumed. "I'll pay it out of my own pocket first—it would stink in the nostrils of the American people to have it said the President of the United States had approved a bill overrunning an appropriation of $20,000 for *flub dubs,* for this damned old house, when the soldiers cannot have blankets!"

Jackie Kennedy, who observed upon her arrival at the White House that "it looked as though furnished from discount stores," fought off rumors of her husband's womanizing with lavish spending on furnishings and her own wardrobe. Nancy Reagan, on the other hand, merely "borrowed" the designer clothes she wore.

Perhaps the most reviled of all presidential wives was Edith Bolling Wilson (a great granddaughter of Pocahontas), who, for all intents and purposes, ran the White House for a year and a half after Woodrow Wilson suffered a severe stroke in 1919. He was left partially paralyzed and was often bedridden, but the severity of his condition was kept secret from the American people.

Edith screened all his memos and callers, essentially determining matters of state herself. Unlike Mary Todd Lincoln and Jackie Kennedy, Edith Wilson was a frugal first lady; during World War I, she put sheep to graze on the White House lawn rather than pay someone to mow it.

Her books written from the viewpoint of Millie the family dog notwithstanding, George Bush's housewifely spouse, Barbara, was popular with the public. Chief of Staff John Sununu, the "fat little pirate" (so-called by a Bush staffer) who was Bush's right-hand man through the 1988 campaign and the early years of his presidency, was not. The bumptious, relentlessly abrasive former governor of New Hampshire ruffled feathers all over Washington. When it was revealed that he had a penchant for using government jets and limos for pleasure trips, his down-fall was swift and unceremonious. He resigned in December 1991; when the news was announced a senior White House of-ficial greeted a reporter's call by singing, "Ding, dong, the witch is dead. . . ."

Next to the White House, on Pennsylvania Avenue between East Executive Avenue and 15th Street, stands the:

9. **Treasury Department,** fronted by an Ionic colonnade under a pediment. The nation's first Secretary of the Treasury, the bril-liant, tempestuous Alexander Hamilton, saw his presidential am-bitions wrecked on the shoals of his affair with a married woman named Maria Reynolds. Reynolds's unscrupulous husband, James, didn't mind the affair at all; he began leaning on Hamilton for small sums to keep his mouth shut. Hamilton continued seeing Maria and paying off her husband for some years, until Mr. Reynolds, finding himself in hot water with the law, asked Hamilton to pull some strings for him. When Hamilton refused, Reynolds made good on his threat to publish the sordid details of the affair. Hamilton responded by publishing his own version of events. In a humiliating public confession on the level of televangelist Jimmy Swaggart's, he described his affair as "an amo-rous connection, detected . . . by the husband, imposing on me the necessity of a pecuniary composition with him, and leaving me afterwards under a duress for fear of disclosure. . . . There is nothing worse in the affair than an irregular and indelicate amour. . . . I have paid pretty severely for the folly and can never recollect it without disgust and self condemnation." As news of Hamilton's pamphlet spread, the statesman became the laughing-stock of his Federalist party; all hopes of higher office were lost to him. He was killed in a duel with Aaron Burr on July 11, 1804—not over love, but politics.

🍵 **TAKE A BREAK**   You'll pass the **Old Ebbitt Grill,** 675 15th Street NW, at G Street (☎ 202/347-4801), a landmark Washington restaurant, on your left en route to your next stop, the Willard. It has stood at two other nearby locations: One was two doors down from Rhodes Tavern, where it is said British generals toasted each other as they watched Washington burn during the War of 1812. Though its interior is ultra elegant—with beveled mirrors, gaslight sconces, etched-glass panels, and Persian rugs strewn on beautiful oak and marble floors—prices are moderate. The menu changes daily; lunch entrées might range from burgers to pasta dishes to a fried oyster sandwich or crabcake platter. Lunch is served Monday through Friday from 11am to 5pm and Saturday from 11:30am to 4pm; Sunday brunch is 9:30am to 4pm.

At the Treasury Department, turn right onto 15th Street and follow it to Pennsylvania Avenue. Cross 15th Street. Coming up on your left is the stately:

10. **Willard Hotel** at 1401 Pennsylvania Avenue NW. The Willard has been center stage for Washington's hardball politics and seamy deals for more than 100 years. In fact, it was in the lobby of the original Willard Hotel (razed in 1901 to make way for the present structure) that the term "lobbyist" was coined. Ulysses S. Grant, who partook of many a cigar and brandy at the Willard, was often pestered here by people seeking to influence government business; hence he began to refer to them as "lobbyists." Apparently his associates peddled their influence freely—by the end of Grant's administration, his vice president, Navy Department, Department of the Interior, and Diplomatic Service were all under the cloud of scandal. During and after the Civil War, government was almost completely beholden to business; robber barons would come to places like the Willard and buy votes from politicians for a few glasses of good whiskey, supplemented by satchels of cash. The wheelers and dealers got rich in the process; as labor organizer Mother Jones put it, "You steal a pair of shoes, you go to jail. You steal a railroad, and you go to the U.S. Senate."

When muckraking journalists began to publish exposés of government corruption in mass-market magazines in the first decade of the 20th century, things began to change. But the arrogance of industrialists who were used to getting their way is clear in the response of banker J. P. Morgan to a reform effort by President Theodore Roosevelt: "If we've done anything wrong," he said to the President, "send your man to see my man, and they will fix it up."

Take a minute to admire the Willard's sumptuously restored interior. Then, exit the hotel, cross 14th Street, and cross the avenue to the rather ornate building at the corner of 14th and Pennsylvania Avenue South, the:

11. **District Building,** headquarters of the mayor of Washington. He's baaaaaack! On January 2, 1995, "Mayor for life" Marion

Barry was sworn in for a fourth term, completing one of the most improbable comebacks in American political history.

Marion Barry was busted by FBI agents after being videotaped taking two long hits from a crack pipe at the capital's Vista Hotel on January 18, 1990. The arrest ended a year's worth of ugly rumor and speculation that Barry—who presided over the nation's capital as it was consumed by an epidemic of drug use and violence, becoming the "murder capital" of the country—was himself a user. Testimony presented at Barry's trial on 11 drug charges and three perjury counts showed the mayor to be the very picture of depravity; in columnist George Hackett's words, he was "a fidgety drug addict, eager to snort cocaine or smoke crack any time, almost any place." Charles Lewis, a former city employee convicted of drug dealing in 1989, told of the numerous times he and Barry had used drugs together, the favors the mayor granted to his drug pal (with Barry's help, Lewis rose from his modest city job to broker a personnel-management deal between the District and the Virgin Islands), and of the women Barry consorted with on his frequent drugs-and-sex junkets. One of these was a former model named Rasheeda Moore, who testified at the trial that she and Barry had used drugs together "at least 100 times." It was Moore who baited the trap the FBI set for him at the Vista. A sordid, enduring image from the videotape of the arrest is the slump-shouldered, handcuffed Barry being led away, cursing Moore.

Barry surrendered his job and eventually served a six-month sentence in a federal prison in Petersburg, Virginia, where he reportedly enjoyed the attentions of a prostitute in the prison's visiting room. Thirty to 50 other inmates and guests were in the room, including one Floyd Robertson, who said "It was blatant. . . . There's no way on God's green earth anybody with . . . common sense would be able to not know what was going on in that corner." The incident surprised no one who saw Barry appear on the *Sally Jessy Raphaël* show to talk about his sexual addiction. Of his compulsive womanizing, Barry said, "It was all part of the addiction. This disease is cunning, baffling, powerful. It destroys your judgment." Incredibly, the people of Washington, D.C.—despite his well-documented lapses in judgment, despite the fact that 14 members of his administration had been found guilty of fiscal wrongdoing—decided in November 1994 to return Marion Barry to his office in this building.

Opposite the District Building, on Pennsylvania Avenue, walk through:

12. Freedom Plaza. On the upper terrace of the plaza is part of Pierre Charles L'Enfant's original plan for the federal capital, rendered in black and white stone and bookended by a fountain at one end and an equestrian statue of General Pulaski at the other. L'Enfant laid out the city with sweeping diagonal boulevards, open plazas, and circles, but his impetuous behavior and penchant for ignoring orders, overspending his budgets, and disregarding landowners with prior claims led George Washington to relieve him of his duties after only a year. One of his coworkers, Benjamin Banneker, a freed slave who worked as a surveyor, made a copy of L'Enfant's blueprints from memory, and the city envisioned by the Frenchman was ultimately built—without just remuneration for its creator. L'Enfant became obsessed with making ever more fantastic claims against the government (he asked for $95,000; the federal government offered $35,000), and lived the rest of his life on the charity of friends. He died penniless in Maryland.

Proceed along Pennsylvania Avenue to 12th Street. On your right, in front of the Old Post Office, is a:

13. Statue of Benjamin Franklin, which pays homage to this Renaissance man of America's early years. Over the course of his life he was many things—printer, writer, scientist, patriot, and diplomat—but with his wit, urbanity, and joy in the pleasures of life, he was also a notorious rake. Although he wrote an essay called "Eight Reasons Older Women Are Preferable to Younger Women" later in his life, he had an illegitimate son with a younger woman and had the nerve to ask his (older) wife to raise the child. She did, and the biological mother moved into their home and worked as a maid. Franklin never tried to hide the affair or the child (perhaps that's why nothing much was made of it in the pages of history), and the boy, William, grew up to become governor of New Jersey.

Note: Though it's not an official refreshment stop, there are several restaurants in a food court inside the Old Post Office. Whether you stop in for a bite or not, its stunning Romanesque interior merits a look.

The building festooned with flags at Pennsylvania Avenue and 10th Street is the headquarters of the:

14. Federal Bureau of Investigation (FBI), which aggressively fills the block. The building takes its name from the Bureau's first director, J. Edgar Hoover. Hoover built the new agency into a law enforcement empire and became enormously powerful in the process, running his fief with scant interference through the tenures of eight presidents (1924–72). By the time he died in 1972, Hoover was feared and hated by millions for his agency's habit of bending civil liberties laws, especially when gathering information on suspected "subversives"—nonconformists of any stripe. After Hoover's death, rumors of misuse of FBI funds and other abuses of office began to percolate, but the final blow to Hoover's status as an American icon came with the publication of Anthony Summers's *Official and Confidential* (1993). The book's revelations about Hoover's homosexuality, transvestism, and 42-year-long relationship with Clyde Tolson (Hoover's right hand at the FBI) were notable on the one hand because, as columnist Frank Rich noted, "For connoisseurs of hypocrisy, it is hard to beat the spectacle of our No. 1 G-man—the puritanical, black-mailing spy on the sex lives of Martin Luther King and the Kennedys, the malicious persecutor of 'sex deviates'—getting all dolled up in . . . cunning little cocktail ensembles." But much more serious is Summers's finding that mobster Meyer Lansky and others in organized crime allegedly obtained pictures of Hoover and Tolson having sex and used them to blackmail Hoover into protecting them from major prosecutions.

Continue along Pennsylvania Avenue. On your left, between 8th and 9th Streets, is the:

15. United States Naval Memorial, depicting a lone sailor survey-ing the world's bodies of water. Around the outside of the monu-ment achievements in naval history are represented. The navy has found the 1990s rough going. A 22-year-old radioman named Allen Schindler was harassed "24 hours a day" by shipmates aboard the U.S.S. *Belleau Wood* after they found out he was gay; in October 1992,he was beaten to death by fellow sailor Terry Helvey. There have been several other instances of gay-bashing involving sailors in recent years. In December 1993, three young and promising officers stationed in Coronado, California, became entangled in an amorous triangle that ended in a double murder and suicide. But the most far-reaching scandal to touch the navy in many years is the deplorable behavior of naval aviators at their 1991 Tailhook Association convention in Las Vegas. In a scene that would have made *Animal House*'s parties look like polite wine-and-cheese affairs, a mob of drunken fliers assaulted and sexually molested 26 women, many of them naval officers, in the hallways of the Las Vegas Hilton. Many senior navy officials were in the hotel at the time, and, as one outraged victim said, "Not one of them said, 'Stop!'"

☕ **TAKE A BREAK** A great choice in this area is **Jaleo,** a Spanish regional/tapas restaurant at 480 7th Street NW, at E Street (☎ 202/628-7949). Housed in the Civil War–era Lansburgh Building, Jaleo is exuberantly colorful, with a casual-chic interior focusing on a large mural of a flamenco dancer based on John Singer Sargeant's painting, *Jaleo*. Background music ap-propriately ranges from the Gypsy Kings to Spanish guitar. A meal here consists of a variety of small dishes—perhaps patatas bravas (crisp-fried chunks of red potato topped with a piquant chili sauce and aïoli), marinated steamed mussels served on a bed of haricots verts, and eggplant flan with red pepper sauce. Most dishes are under $5. Jaleo is open for lunch Monday through Saturday from 11:30am to 2:30pm, with a limited tapas menu from 2:30 to 5:30pm; dinner is served nightly from 5:30pm.

Farther east, Pennsylvania Avenue runs directly into the:

16. Capitol. You're looking at its west, or back, side, the only part of the facade that remains from the original building, the cornerstone of which was laid by George Washington himself. Capitol architect Benjamin Latrobe died prematurely in an accident here; he was killed when construction superintendent John Lenthall removed a support arch that Latrobe deemed necessary, causing part of the building to collapse on top of the unfortunate Latrobe.

The House of Representatives (to the right of the dome) and the Senate (to the left) have produced their share of scoundrels. The Democrats, it's said, get in trouble with sex and the Republicans with money, but there have been some crossovers.

Where to begin? Perhaps the most unsavory senator of all (and it had nothing to do with sex or money, but with fear) was Joseph P. McCarthy (R-Wisconsin, 1947–57), who conducted a heavy-handed witch hunt of Communists and alleged Communists, resorting to "guilt-by-association" and scare tactics.

When it comes to drinking and womanizing, the person who most readily comes to mind is Massachusetts senator Ted Kennedy, whose life could be characterized as one long scandal— from Chappaquiddick and the tragic drowning of Mary Jo Kopeckne to the Palm Beach "incident" in which his nephew William Kennedy Smith was accused (and acquitted) of raping a woman at the family vacation compound on Easter weekend in 1991 (Ted Kennedy was at the estate at the time).

Gary Hart, Democratic senator from Colorado, was within reach of his party's presidential nomination in 1987 when he was caught by two pesky reporters from the *Miami Herald* leaving through the back door of his townhouse with shapely Donna Rice. A furor ensued over the former divinity professor's ethics; when reports uncovered evidence of yet more adulterous liaisons, he was forced to abandon his presidential ambitions for the dubious consolation of becoming the butt of David Letterman's jokes. ("Top Ten List of Gary Hart Pick-Up Lines: 'Can a Kennedy-esque guy buy you a drink?' 'Have you ever seen a frontrunner naked?'" etc.)

On October 7, 1974, Wilbur Mills, Arkansas congressman and Chairman of the House Ways and Means Committee, was stopped by police at Washington's cherry-tree–lined Tidal Basin at 2am for speeding and driving without headlights on. His date for the evening, professional stripper Fanne Foxe, also known as the "Argentine firecracker," panicked and plunged into the Basin, taking Mills's career straight into the drink with her.

South Carolina Congressman John Jenrette was already under investigation for selling underwater land in Florida when his name was linked to Abscam. He and a few of his associates were caught selling Congressional favors to men they thought were

Arab sheiks but were really FBI agents. In the tape that was made of a deal in action, Jenrette admitted, "I've got larceny in my heart." The equally pleasant crook and congressman Michael Meyer simply said, "Bullshit walks, money talks." To top off the whole mess, Jenrette and his wife Rita were spotted having sex one night on the steps of the Capitol's west side. Jenrette was later arrested for shoplifting shoes and ties, and the now ex— Mrs. Jenrette wrote a tell-all tome called *My Capitol Secrets,* then exposed herself even more fully to the public in *Playboy* magazine.

Barney Frank, Democratic congressman from Massachusetts, made the headlines in 1990 when it was disclosed that his boyfriend was running a male prostitution ring out of Frank's Capitol Hill townhouse.

And in the fall of 1991, taxpayers were horrified to learn that 252 members of the House of Representatives and 51 former members had overdrafts (many into the thousands of dollars) with the House Bank.

Walk around the Capitol and make your way to the imposing:

17. Supreme Court. In 1963 and 1964, the Warren Commission, led by Chief Justice Earl Warren (who served from 1953 to 1969), investigated the assassination of John F. Kennedy and determined that gunman Lee Harvey Oswald acted alone, a conclusion that few believe today. This could be the major cover-up of the century.

On October 15, 1991, Clarence Thomas, who had been chairman of the Equal Employment Opportunity Commission under President Ronald Reagan, became the 106th Supreme Court justice, but not without great controversy. At his confirmation hearing, a former aide, Anita Hill, leveled charges of sexual harassment against Thomas, who labeled it "high-tech lynching." Thomas and Hill came to the hearings with sparkling reputations for character and integrity: Hill calmly delivered her specific, graphic testimony, and Thomas responded with agonized denials. In the end, the only clarities revealed were that either Hill or Thomas was a monumental liar, and that these two people had been swept up by the relentless undertows of partisan politics and the media's scandal machine. Thomas was confirmed by the Senate by a two-vote margin.

Some say Hill's action made it easier for other women to come forward in sexual-abuse situations. Case in point: In November 1992, 10 women pressed charges of sexual harassment against Oregon senator Bob Packwood, who managed to keep the allegations quiet until after his reelection.

Stay tuned for upcoming scandals.

From here, you can get the Metro at either Capitol South or Union Station.

9

Shopping

The city's most delightful shopping area is historic Georgetown, with hundreds of boutiques, antique shops, and a neo-Victorian mall that provides excellent browsing. Its highlights are detailed in a walking tour. But first I've covered the most interesting and/or budget-oriented shops throughout the District, malls (in D.C. and the suburbs), and major department stores. Check the Georgetown shopping tour for additional shops in each category.

You could also spend a very pleasant day poking about Alexandria's charming boutiques and antique shops. And there are marvelous high-quality items for sale at all the Smithsonian museum shops— unique toys, craft items, educational games for children, posters, art reproductions, books, jewelry, and so forth, as well as at many other museums and attractions.

1 Shopping A to Z

ART REPRODUCTIONS, PRINTS & ENGRAVINGS

All the art museums detailed in Chapter 7 have noteworthy shops. Of special interest are the following:

Bureau of Engraving and Printing
14th and C sts. SW. ☎ **202/874-2743.** Metro: Smithsonian.

Good engravings here, including portraits of presidents and Supreme Court justices, scenes of Washington landmarks, and government seals, plus prints of the Gettysburg Address; the list goes on and on. The bureau also sells sheets of uncut currency. Write for a free catalog or stop by the on-site store. It's open Monday to Friday 8:30am to 3:30pm.

National Gallery of Art
North side of the Mall (between 3rd and 7th sts. NW). ☎ **202/737-4215.** Metro: Archives or Judiciary Square.

The shops here feature a wide choice of prints, posters, art reproductions, gifts, and art books. The West Building shop is the largest, shops in both buildings highlight items relating to temporary exhibitions, and a large shop in the concourse specializes in art and children's books. All are open Monday to Saturday 10am to 5pm, Sunday 11am to 6pm.

Washington, D.C., Shopping

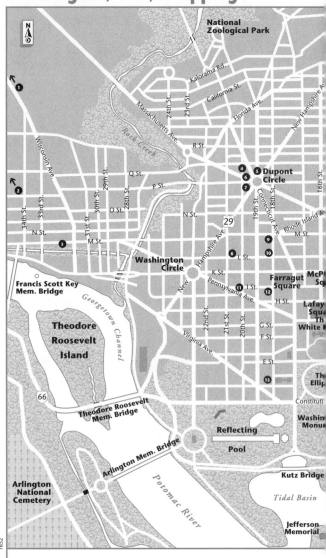

Borders Books & Music ⑩
Bureau of Engraving & Printing ⑯
Central Liquor ㉑
For Eyes Optical ⑧
Ginns ⑨
Government Printing Office
    Bookstore ㉓
Hecht's ⑱
Indian Crafts Shop ⑬

Kramerbooks & Afterwords ⑥
Mazza Gallerie ①
Melody Record Shop ④
National Gallery of Art ㉒
Olsson's Books & Records ⑦
Once Is Not Enough ②
Pavilion at the Old Post Office ⑲
Penn Camera Exchange ⑳
Shops at National Place ⑮

U St.

T St.

S St.

R St.

Vermont Ave.

Rhode Island Ave.

Florida Ave.

1

P St.

O St.

50

N St.

13th St.
12th St.
11th St.
10th St.
9th St.
8th St.
7th St.
6th St.
5th St.

4th St.

M St.

Mt. Vernon Place

K St.

I St.

New Jersey Ave.

K St.

North Capitol

...klin
...k

New York Ave.

G St. **18**

F St.

21

Massachusetts Ave.

23 Union Station

24

2nd St.

3rd St.

20

3rd St.

2nd St.

1st St.

E St.

...nsylvania Ave.

19

Louisiana Ave.

D St.

C St.

...stitution Ave.

22

The Capitol

East Capitol

The Mall

...dependence Ave.

Maryland Ave.

C St.

Virginia Ave.

South Capitol

New Jersey Ave.

395

17
↓

BOOKS/RECORDS/CDS/AUDIO-/VIDEOCASSETTES

Besides the stores listed here, you'll find others mentioned in "Malls" (below) and described in the Georgetown shopping tour later in this chapter.

Borders Books & Music

At the corner of 18th and L sts. NW. ☎ **202/466-4999** for books, 202/466-6999 for music. Metro: Farragut North.

This fabulous 30,000-square-foot two-level bookstore-cum-cultural center sells hardcover books at 10% off and discounts *New York Times* and *Washington Post* best-sellers and staff selections 30%. It also sells CDs, video- and audiotapes, and a wide selection of periodicals and out-of-state newspapers. And there are large remainder and children's book sections. Borders also schedules book signings, Saturday-morning storytelling for children ages 2 to 7 (at 10:30am), entertainment by and conversations with noted jazz musicians (e.g., Winton Marsalis), films, lectures, poetry readings, and art shows. The store has a pleasant café that offers yummy desserts (including Proustian madeleines), salads, sandwiches, cappuccino/espresso, and European sodas. You can borrow a book from the store to read while you eat. Open Monday to Friday 8am to 10pm, Saturday 9am to 9pm, Sunday 11am to 7pm.

Government Printing Office Bookstore

710 N. Capitol St. NW (between G and H sts.). ☎ **202/512-0132.** Metro: Union Station.

The GPO, founded in 1861, is now the world's largest printer, with close to 16,000 titles (books and pamphlets) in print. Every conceivable area is covered, from *Starting and Managing a Small Business on Your Own* to the *Everglades Wildguide.* If you're probing any new hobby, interest, or activity—or writing a term paper, trying to understand a medical problem, looking for a new career, or considering a major purchase—you'll probably find some helpful literature here. The collection makes for fascinating browsing. The GPO bookstore additionally sells books of photographs (such as *A Century of Photographs: 1846–1946,* selections from the Library of Congress) and sets of actual photographs (for example, a set of seven photos portraying marines in combat situations, suitable for framing); also CD-ROMs and diskettes, prints, lithographs, and posters. It's open Monday to Friday 8am to 4pm.

The GPO has another bookstore at 1510 H St. NW (☎ **202/ 653-5075**), open Monday to Friday 9am to 5pm. Metro: Farragut West.

Kramerbooks & Afterwords

1517 Connecticut Ave. NW (between Q St. and Dupont Circle). ☎ **202/387-1400.** Metro: Dupont Circle.

Ask 100 Washingtonians to name their favorite bookstore, and at least half will say Kramerbooks. This San Francisco–style bookstore combines with a popular restaurant (see Chapter 6 for details), so you can buy a book and read it over lunch. Employees here are all avid readers who display their current favorites on the counter and discuss literature with customers. It's also one of the few places anywhere you can buy a book at 7:30am—or at midnight for that matter. Kramerbooks carries quality paperbacks—fiction and nonfiction—as well as European and other foreign works of major importance. The store recently added 50% more space, including large children's, gardening, and travel-book sections. "I look for books of real and substantial quality," says owner David Tenney. Quality books must have an audience because Kramerbooks is one of the highest-grossing bookstores per square foot in the country. It's open Monday to Thursday 7:30am to 1am, and around the clock from Friday at 7:30am to Monday at 1am.

Melody Record Shop

1623 Connecticut Ave. NW. ☎ **202/232-4002.** Metro: Dupont Circle (Q Street exit).

CDs, cassettes, and tapes are discounted 10% to 20% here, new releases 20% to 40%. There's a wide variety of rock, classical, jazz, pop, show, and folk music, as well as a vast number of international selections. This is also a good place to shop for discounted electronic equipment such as cassette and CD players, as well as blank tapes and cas settes. A knowledgeable staff is a plus. Open Monday to Thursday 10am to 10pm, Friday and Saturday 10am to 11pm, Sunday noon to 8pm.

Olsson's Books & Records

1239 Wisconsin Ave. NW (between M and N sts.). ☎ **202/338-6712** for recordings, 202/338-9544 for books.

This independent quality bookstore chain offers discounts of 10% to 20% on many tapes and CDs (of which they stock an immense variety) and has about 60,000 to 70,000 books on its shelves covering almost every area except romance and porn. *Washington Post* hardcover best-sellers and Olsson's "buyers choice books" (literary and highbrow selections) are reduced 25%; other books are sold at regular prices. However, if you buy three Penguin books here at one time, you get 20% off any other Penguin paperback forever. At the Metro Center location, author readings are frequent events (past ones have included P. D. James, Garrison Keillor, Norman Mailer, Calvin Trillin, and Anthony Burgess), and there are occasional signings of recordings at all stores.

Additional locations include 1200 F St. at Metro Center (☎ 202/393-1853 for recordings, 202/347-3686 for books), 418 7th St. NW (☎ 202/638-7613 for recordings, 202/638-7610 for books), and 1307 19th St. NW, just off Dupont Circle (☎ 202/785-2662 for recordings, 202/785-1133 for books). All locations are open daily; call for hours.

Sidney Kramer Books

1825 I St. NW. ☎ **202/293-2685.** Metro: Farragut West.

This unique and attractive bookstore specializes "in the business of Washington"—politics, economics, defense, military history, area studies, and business management. Its clientele includes foreign ambassadors, generals, congresspersons, White House staffers, and other major governmental players. The people-watching is almost as good as the browsing. Kramer also offers comprehensive travel-book, fiction, and children's-book sections. Call for a free catalog. Open Monday to Friday 9am to 6:30pm, Saturday 10am to 5pm.

Super Crown

11 Dupont Circle NW (between New Hampshire Ave. and P St., on the northeast side of the Circle). ☎ **202/319-1374.** Metro: Dupont Circle.

With locations throughout the District and in suburbia, Crown Books offers 40% off *New York Times* hardcover best-sellers and 25% off paperback best-sellers. Other books and magazines are discounted 10% to 20%. Its largest D.C. outlet is this 12,000-square-foot "super" store, which has expanded sections for biographies, audio (books on tape), remaindered books, new authors, magazines (including many foreign periodicals), and children's books. Super Crown can special-order titles for you at its usual discounts. It has wide aisles with benches where people can sit and read. The store is open daily 9am to midnight. Check the phone book for other Crown Book store locations.

Tower Records

2000 Pennsylvania Ave. NW (at the corner of 21st and I sts.). ☎ **202/331-2400.** Metro: Foggy Bottom.

Without a doubt, this 23,000-square-foot store houses the largest selection of cassettes and CDs in town. There are large departments for jazz, rock, soul, classical, and any other type of music you might favor, plus a vast inventory of videocassettes (for sale and rental) and CD-ROMs (for sale). Another section houses books about music and alternative culture. The store also functions as a **Ticketmaster** outlet. A trendy ambience is created by flashing lights, ultramodern decor, and about 20 monitors showing rock videos, cartoons, and movies. All merchandise is sold below list, with substantial discounts on sale items. Ongoing contests—drawings for trips to reggae festivals in Jamaica, stereo equipment, concert tickets—add to the fun. It's open daily 9am to midnight.

CLOTHING

Check out "Department Stores" and "Malls" (below) for more traditional places to shop for clothes.

Sunny's Surplus

1416 H St. NW. ☎ **202/347-2774.** Metro: McPherson Square.

If you like the "M*A*S*H" look, this is the place. They carry a full line of military surplus (mostly new, some used), including jeans, T-shirts, work shoes and clothing, insulated underwear, heavy thermal socks, rainwear and winter garments, pea coats, camouflage fatigues, army blankets, navy wool insignia middy blouses, all camping accessories (tents, sleeping bags, mess kits, rubber rafts, canteens), even World War I Snoopy helmets. It's open Monday to Saturday 8:30am to 6:30pm.

Other branches are at 912 F St. NW (☎ 202/737-2032) and 3342 M St. NW (☎ 202/333-8550). Call for hours.

CRAFTS

Indian Crafts Shop

Department of the Interior, 18th and C sts. NW. ☎ **202/208-4056.** Metro: Farragut West.

This shop's wares are of a very high quality, and the price range is wide: I found many lovely small Navajo weavings for $16 to $18 (larger rugs can go up to $3,000), squash-blossom necklaces for $300 to $3,000, and attractive pieces of jewelry—Navajo, Zuni, and Hopi—in varied price ranges. The store also offers Navajo sand paintings, a large choice of Eskimo walrus-ivory carvings, and an outstanding selection of Hopi, Santa Clara, San Ildefonso, Jemez, Acoma, Taos, Cochiti, and Navajo pottery. *Note:* You need a photo ID to enter the building. It's open Monday to Friday 8:30am to 4:30pm.

There's another shop in Georgetown Park Mall, 3222 M St. NW, at Wisconsin (☎ 202/342-3918), open Monday to Saturday 10am to 9pm, Sunday noon to 6pm.

DEPARTMENT STORES

In addition to the below-listed, Washington boasts branches of prestigious New York and West Coast stores. **Lord & Taylor** is at 5255 Western Ave. NW (☎ 202/362-9600); **Saks Fifth Avenue** can be found at 5555 Wisconsin Ave. NW in Chevy Chase, Maryland (☎ 301-657-9000); and **Neiman-Marcus** is located in Mazza Gallerie on upper Wisconsin Avenue (☎ 202/966-9700). You'll find a branch of **Bloomingdale's** at Tysons Corner Center in McLean, Virginia (☎ 703/556-4600).See stores listed under "Malls" (below).

Hecht's

12th and G sts. NW. ☎ **202/628-6661.** Metro: Metro Center.

Hecht's stores have been in Washington for almost a century. But this much newer branch (built in 1985) is anything but fusty. It's a fun store with five floors of moderate- to higher-priced merchandise and lots going on. You might happen upon cooking and merchandise demonstrations here, a contest (win a trip to Paris or a Jaguar XJ6), or an in-store personality appearance; in the past these have included Tommy Hilfiger (for his fragrance), Martin Yan (of "Yan Can Cook"), Jason Priestley (promoting Pepe Jeans), Oscar de la Renta (for Volupté), even Bart Simpson. It's a full-service department store, featuring brand names in clothing and footwear for the whole family and contemporary and traditional home furnishings. A personal shopping service is complimentary, and all Hecht's stores have **Ticketmaster** outlets on the premises. There are 16 Hecht's stores in the D.C. area; check the phone book for additional locations. This branch is open Monday to Saturday 10am to 8pm, Sunday noon to 6pm.

DRUGSTORES

Washington's major drugstore chain, carrying diversified merchandise from frozen foods to charcoal briquettes to appliances, is **CVS** (with about 40 stores). Check the phone book for the most convenient locations.

EYEGLASSES

For Eyes Optical

2021 L St. NW. ☎ **202/659-0077** or 800/FOR-EYES. Metro: Farragut North.

This company offers hefty discounts on lenses, designer frames (Pierre Cardin, Elizabeth Arden, Armani, Gucci, Ralph Lauren/Polo, Dior), and designer sunglasses (Bausch & Lomb and others).

There are additional locations at 1725 K St. NW (☎ 202/463-8860) and 700 13th St. NW (☎ 202/737-2222). All stores are open Monday to Friday 9:30am to 6pm, Saturday 10am to 6pm.

FISH & SEAFOOD

Southwest Waterfront Fish Market

Between 11th and 12th Sts. SW, along Maine Ave. No phone. Metro: Waterfront.

The best home-cooked meal I ever had in Washington was fresh-caught red snapper from this fabulous fish market. About half a dozen merchants offer a wide selection of just-off-the-boat fish and seafood—shrimp, soft-shell crabs, crabmeat, lobster, red snapper, bluefish, and whatever else the day's catch brings. It's a picturesque outdoor market, and there's usually a boat selling produce as well. The market is open daily 7:30am to 9:30pm.

MALLS

The Fashion Centre at Pentagon City

1100 S. Hayes St. (at Army-Navy Dr. and I-395). ☎ **703/415-2400.** Metro: Pentagon City.

This Arlington, Virginia, mall has nothing to do with America's defense establishment. It's a plush four-level shopping complex with more than 160 shops, restaurants, and services adjoining a Ritz-Carlton hotel. Anchored by Macy's and Nordstrom, it also features branches of Ann Taylor, Abercrombie & Fitch, The Museum Company (for museum art reproductions), Banana Republic, Brentano's, Scribner's, The Disney Store, Record World, Joan & David (upscale men's and women's shoes), America (U.S. souvenirs), Crabtree & Evelyn, Godiva Chocolatier, Laura Ashley, Villeroy & Boch, Victoria's Secret, Nature Company, Lane Bryant, The Limited, Body Shop, Charter Clubs, Sam Goody, Britches, and The Gap (also Gap Kids). There are numerous clothing and shoe stores for the whole family, jewelers, and retailers of photographic equipment, beach wear, maternity clothes, luggage, gifts, toys, eyeglasses, whatever. Dining choices include several restaurants plus 13 food-court eateries. There are six movie theaters, the Metro stops right in the mall, and parking is provided for 4,500 cars. The mall is open Monday to Saturday 10am to 9:30pm, Sunday 11am to 6pm.

Mazza Gallerie

5300 Wisconsin Ave. NW (between Western Ave. and Jenifer St.). ☎ **202/686-9515.** Metro: Friendship Heights.

Billing itself as "Washington's answer to Rodeo Drive," this *très chic,* four-level mall has 48 boutiques under a skylit atrium, including a branch of Neiman-Marcus, a multilevel Ann Taylor, and Filene's Basement (discount designer labels). Other classy boutiques here are Stephane Kélian (upscale women's shoes), Laura Ashley (home furnishings), The Forgotten Woman (elegant clothes in large sizes), Pea in the Pod (gorgeous maternity wear), Pampillonia Jewelers (estate jewelry and one-of a kind creations), Krön Chocolatier, and Williams-Sonoma (gourmet cookware and foods). There's an excellent on-premises restaurant called Pleasant Peasant, a Brentano's bookstore, a triplex movie theater, numerous other clothing and shoe stores, jewelers, gourmet food shops, home furnishing stores, and an American Express travel agency/ currency exchange. The mall, located at the D.C./Maryland border, is open Monday to Friday 10am to 8pm, Saturday 10am to 6pm, Sunday noon to 5pm. There's two-hour free indoor parking.

The Pavilion at the Old Post Office

1100 Pennsylvania Ave. NW. ☎ **202/289-4224.** Metro: Federal Triangle.

This is as much of a tourist attraction as a retail complex. Opened in 1983 in one of the capital's oldest federal buildings—an actual 1899 government postal department—it's a vital part of the renovation of the entire Pennsylvania Avenue area. The tallest structure in the city, after the Washington Monument, its 10 floors soar 196 feet to a skylight ceiling and are crowned by a 315-foot clock tower. The atrium is lined with balconied corridors reminiscent of an Italian palazzo, while the exterior stonework, turrets, and massive arches were inspired by the Romanesque cathedrals of 12th-century France. In the tower are 10 great bells, a Bicentennial gift from England; they duplicate those at Westminster Abbey.

Today the building houses boutiques and restaurants, and its hub is a performing-arts stage, the scene of daily lunchtime, afternoon, and early-evening free entertainment. (Call the phone number above to find out what entertainment is scheduled on a given day.) While you're here, ride the glass elevator to the tower observation deck for a lofty 360° vista. You can walk down a flight and see the bells themselves. If you'd like to hear them, the bellringers practice on Thursday evenings between 7 and 9pm.

Most of the shops carry whimsical merchandise, ranging from Stars and Stripes (all red, white, and blue items) to Juggling Capitol for juggler's paraphernalia. Others offer African fashions for men and women, jewelry, souvenirs, and accessories.

Plan a meal here, too. Choices include a large food court for international and American fare. And Blossoms features a gorgeous brick-terraced cafe and immense salads, among other American/ continental entrées.

The Pavilion is open March to September, Monday to Saturday 10am to 8pm (the restaurants stay open to 9pm), Sunday noon to 6pm; the rest of the year, Monday to Saturday 10am to 6pm (the restaurants stay open to 8pm) and Sunday noon to 6pm.

The Shops at National Place

Entrance on F St. NW (between 13th and 14th sts.) or via the J. W. Marriott at 1331 Pennsylvania Ave. NW. ☎ **202/783-9090.** Metro: Metro Center.

A Rouse Company project (like Baltimore Harborplace and New York's South Street Seaport), this four-tiered, 125,000-square-foot retail complex houses close to 100 stores and eateries in the renovated National Press Building. With its terra-cotta floors, balconies, columns, and fountains, it's a most attractive setting for serious shopping. All the mall regulars are here—B. Dalton, The Sharper Image, The Limited, Banana Republic, and Victoria's Secret—to name a few. You can also shop for candy, leather goods, lingerie, clothing and shoes for the entire family, gifts, and records and tapes. You will find Au Bon Pain (croissant sandwiches and homemade desserts) and two branches of the American Café. And if you really want to get down to some serious eating, there are excellent restaurants in the adjoining Marriott (see Chapter 5). The mall is open Monday to Saturday 10am to 7pm, Sunday noon to 5pm.

Springfield Mall

Just off I-95 at Exit 169A (Franconia Rd.), Springfield, Va. ☎ **703/971-3000.** Metro: Van Dorn; then take bus no. 109 or 204. A Springfield Metro stop which will take you right to the premises is nearing completion at press time.

This major shopping complex is about 10 miles from the downtown D.C. area. It has 240 shops and restaurants (including a food court) and 10 movie theaters. Major stores here include branches of Macy's, J. C. Penney, and Montgomery Ward. Ann Taylor, Britches of Georgetown, The Limited, The Gap, The Disney Store, Sports Authority, and Victoria's Secret are also represented. There are more than a dozen shoe stores; other shops and boutiques carry clothing for the entire family, athletic footwear, audio equipment, telephones, bicycles, books, toys, jewelry, health foods, gourmet foods, sporting goods, maternity wear, records and tapes, and just about anything else you might need or desire. While you're here you can have your hair done (several salons vie for your patronage) or even have your eyes examined. There's free parking. And you can park the kids either at the movies or at one of two video-game arcades while you shop. The mall is open Monday to Saturday 10am to 9:30pm, Sunday noon to 5pm.

Tysons Corner Center

1961 Chain Bridge Rd., McLean, Va. (at the intersection of Rtes. 7 and 123). ☎ **703/893-9400.** Metro: West Falls Church; from there you can catch a shuttle that runs every half hour in both directions.

This well-known mall is about 15 minutes from the District (take the Beltway, I-495, to Exit 11B and follow the signs). Among the 230-plus shops here are four major department stores—Bloomingdale's, Nordstrom, Lord & Taylor, and Hecht's. Other notable emporia include Laura Ashley, The Nature Company, Williams-Sonoma (kitchenware), The Limited, a Sesame Street General Store, The Disney Store, Banana Republic, Brooks Brothers, A/X Armani Exchange, Abercrombie & Fitch, Britches of Georgetown, Ann Taylor, Crabtree & Evelyn, Woolworth's, and The Gap. Once again, there are more than a dozen shoe stores, hair salons, a spa, and a bank. More than 30 eateries including branches of Morrison's Fresh Cooking, America, and California Pizza Kitchen, and eight movie theaters make this a good choice for an afternoon shopping spree followed by a relaxing dinner and a film. There's free parking. The mall is open Monday to Saturday 10am to 9:30pm, Sunday noon to 6pm.

Tyson's Galleria

2001 International Dr., McLean, Va. ☎ **703/827-7700.** Metro: West Falls Church; from there you can catch a shuttle that runs every half hour in both directions.

This plush three-level shopping center, adjoining a Ritz-Carlton hotel, offers about 100 shops, galleries, restaurants, and services. Its lushly planted interior is an indoor park setting, with skylights, gleaming-white Carrara marble, and cascading fountains. Anchored by three fine department stores—Macy's, Saks, and Neiman-Marcus—Tyson's Galleria also houses The Sharper Image, Victoria's Secret, Godiva Chocolatier, a vast Pottery Barn, a two-level F.A.O. Schwarz, The Forgotten Woman, Versace Lapin (imported children's wear), Williams-Sonoma Grand Cuisine, Ann Taylor, and Liljenquist & Beckstead (upscale jewelry). Your whole shopping spectrum is well covered here. There are three full-service restaurants (including Legal Seafoods of Boston), as well as a lovely Garden Food Court complete with trellises and ivy plantings. There's parking for 3,200 cars. Tyson's Galleria is open Monday to Saturday from 10am to 9pm, Sunday noon to 6pm.

Union Station

50 Massachusetts Ave. NE. ☎ **202/371-9441.** Metro: Union Station.

Union Station, with about 100 high-quality shops, has become one of Washington's most frequented retail complexes. The setting is magnificent; there are lots of great eateries (details in Chapter 6); and the stores here offer a wide array of unique and high-quality merchandise.

The plushest emporia are in the **East Hall,** with wares displayed in handsome brass-trimmed mahogany kiosks amid tall palm trees, or in alcoves flanked by scagliola marble columns. Here you'll find, among others, Noble House (gift items), The Historical Research Center (trace your roots), KD2 Miniature Buildings (noted architectural replicas), Aurea (pre-Columbian jewelry and pottery, African amber necklaces, jewelry from India, and more, including museum reproductions), Christmas Spirit (upscale holiday merchandise), Post Impressions (collector stamps—everything from Civil War to Elvis stamps), Appalachian Spring (for items handcrafted in America—patchwork quilts, pottery, exquisite jewelry, and an incredible collection of kaleidoscopes), and Washington Pen (fine pens and accessories).

Notable **West Hall** shops include The Proper Topper (hats), Made in America (American-made and U.S.-related items, from military accessories to western sculpture), Political Americana (historic and political memorabilia), and, one of my favorite shops in the complex, the Nature Company, carrying all nature-environmental-themed items, including books, cassettes, artwork, toys, kites, leaf-collecting kits, bird feeders, backpacks, telescopes, and more.

The **Main Floor Level** of the Concourse is home to branches of B. Dalton, Victoria's Secret, Speedo, The Body Shop, Crabtree &

Evelyn, and The Limited. Also here: The Great Train Store (model trains, books, cassettes, and numerous other railroad-motif items); a toy store called Flights of Fancy; Brookstone, a kind of adult toy store selling upscale gadgetry; and Parfumerie Douglas, for international fragrances.

Women's clothing boutiques predominate on the **Concourse Mezzanine Level,** among them Pendleton, Jones of New York, Ann Taylor, Putumayo, Benetton, and an interesting shop called White House, which specializes in all-white clothing and accessory items. There are men's clothing stores here, too. And don't miss Imposters for fine jewelry reproductions (most are between $30 and $95, and it all looks real!).

There's quite a bit more, including electronics stores, a branch of Sam Goody, additional jewelry shops, accessory stores, nine movie the-aters, and a variety of services (car and limousine rental, tour desks, post office, shoe repair, shoeshine, currency exchange, and so on).

Union Station is open Monday to Saturday 10am to 9pm, Sunday noon to 6pm.

OFFICE SUPPLIES/STATIONERY

Staples

3307 M St. NW. ☎ **202/337-8183.**

This marvelous "super store" offers discounts of 40% to 70% on a wide selection of office supplies, business machines (computers, answering machines, copiers, fax machines, and more), and office furniture. The staff is well informed, and you can return anything within 30 days if not satisfied. It's open Monday to Friday 7am to 9pm, Saturday 9am to 6pm, and Sunday 10am to 6pm.

There are other locations at 1133 20th St. NW (between L and M streets; ☎ 202/331-8853), and 1250 H St. NW (☎ 202/638-3910). Call for hours.

PHOTOGRAPHIC EQUIPMENT

Penn Camera Exchange

915 E St. NW. ☎ **202/347-5777** or 800/347-5770. Metro: Metro Center.

Penn offers big discounts on all major brand-name equipment—such as Olympus, Canon, Minolta, Pentax, Leica, Vivitar, and Nikon. The store has been owned and operated by the camera-buff Zweig family since 1953; their staff is quite knowledgeable, their inventory wide-ranging. Many professional Washington photographers shop at Penn. Most of the merchandise is new and comes with a U.S. warranty, but you'll also find good buys on used equipment here. Check the Friday *Washington Post* ("Weekend" section) for announcements of special sales. Penn is open Monday to Friday 9am to 6pm, Saturday 10am to 5pm.

RESALE & THRIFT SHOPS

In addition to the below-listed, stop by **Christ Child Opportunity Shop** and **Secondhand Rose,** detailed in the Georgetown shopping tour later in this chapter.

Once Is Not Enough

4830 MacArthur Blvd. NW (near Reservoir Rd.). ☎ **202/337-3072.**

Washington society women must change their wardrobes frequently: What do they do with the lovely clothes they've worn only once or twice? Some of their garments find their way to this upscale consignment shop, which specializes in top-quality women's clothing. I've seen names here like Fendi, Louis Feraud, Chanel, Ungaro, Valentino, Yves St. Laurent, Bill Biass, Escada, and Galanos, to mention just a few. On my last visit I saw a black voile Chanel gown for $150 (it had retailed for $2,500), an Yves St. Laurent cocktail dress for $160 (it had retailed for $2,600), and a four-piece Valentino outfit worth thousands for $450. Many items were much less. And there are terrific bargains in used men's clothing, such as a $400 camel's-hair coat for $75 and a $2,000 Gianfranco Ferré suit for $180; Brooks Brothers and Armani suits, Sulka shirts, tuxedos, and Liberty ties are other frequent finds. Owner Inga Guen is a fashion consultant to many of Washington's socially elite and executive women. Open Monday to Saturday 10am to 5pm.

WINES & LIQUORS

Central Liquor

726 9th St. NW (between G and H sts.) ☎ **202/737-2800.** Metro: Gallery Place.

Central Liquor abounds in bottled booze—more than 35,000 items on display, including thousands of wines ranging from Gallo to Château Mouton Rothschild. Not just wines, but liquors, cordials, and other alcoholic potables are all discounted 10% to 25%, with special sales on loss leaders. Good deals are also offered when you buy by the case. It's open Monday to Thursday 9am to 9pm, Friday 9am to 10pm, Saturday 9am to midnight.

WALKING TOUR
GEORGETOWN SHOPPING

Start: M and 29th streets NW.
Finish: Wisconsin Avenue NW, Q Street.
Time: Allow one to three hours, depending on how much time you spend browsing—or actually shopping.
Best Times: During store hours.

In Georgetown you can combine shopping and browsing (there are hundreds of stores) with a meal at a good restaurant, crowd-watching over cappuccino at a cafe, even a little sightseeing. The hub is at Wisconsin Avenue and M Street, and most of the stores are on those two arteries. In addition to shops, you'll encounter street vendors hawking T-shirts and handmade jewelry.

If you drive into Georgetown—definitely not advised because parking is almost impossible—check out the side streets off Wisconsin Avenue above M Street for possible spots. The Georgetown Park Mall (see below) offers validated parking. There's also public transportation (by bus) to Georgetown.

Walking Tour—Georgetown Shopping

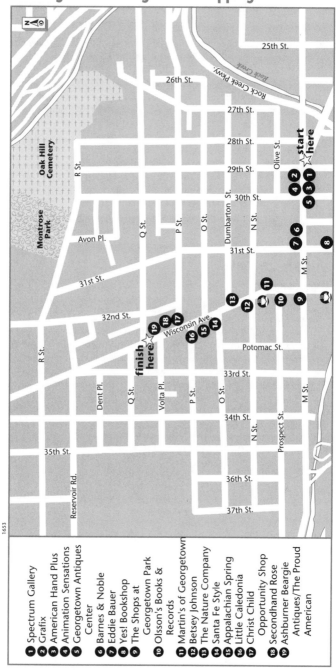

1. Spectrum Gallery
2. Grafix
3. American Hand Plus
4. Animation Sensations
5. Georgetown Antiques Center
6. Barnes & Noble
7. Eddie Bauer
8. Yes! Bookshop
9. The Shops at Georgetown Park
10. Olsson's Books & Records
11. Martin's of Georgetown
12. Betsey Johnson
13. The Nature Company
14. Santa Fe Style
15. Appalachian Spring
16. Little Caledonia
17. Christ Child Opportunity Shop
18. Secondhand Rose
19. Ashburner Beargie Antiques/The Proud American

Along M Street NW For the first part of this Shopping Tour, we'll head generally along M Street from 29th to 33rd Streets. Start at the:

1. **Spectrum Gallery,** 1132 29th St. NW, just below M Street (☎ 202/333-0954), a cooperative venture (since 1968) in which 32 professional Washington-area artists—painters, potters, sculptors, photographers, collagists, and printmakers—share in shaping gallery policy, maintenance, and operation. The art is reasonably priced. Open Tuesday to Saturday 11am to 6pm, Sunday noon to 5pm.

   Walk around the corner onto M Street to:

2. **Grafix,** 2904 M St. NW (☎ 202/342-0610), which carries a noteworthy collection of vintage posters (from 1895 on), 16th- to 20th-century maps, 19th-century prints, and other collectibles. Open Monday to Friday 11am to 6pm, Saturday 11am to 5pm.

3. **American Hand Plus,** 2906 M St. NW (☎ 202/965-3273), features exquisite contemporary handcrafted American ceramics and jewelry, plus international objets d'art. Open Monday to Saturday 11am to 6pm, Sunday 1 to 5pm.

4. **Animation Sensations,** 2914 M St. NW (☎ 202/337-5024). It's fun to peruse this collection of original animation cels and drawings, comic book/strip art, vintage movie posters, movie star autographs, Disney/Warner Brothers/Hanna-Barbera character figurines, and movie memorabilia. You'll find Disney, Peanuts, and other comic-inspired kids' clothing here, too. Open Monday to Saturday 11am to 7pm, Sunday noon to 5pm.

5. **Georgetown Antiques Center,** 2918 M St. NW, houses the **Cherub Antiques Gallery** (☎ 202/337-2224) specializing in art nouveau and art deco, art glass (signed Tiffany, Steuben, Lalique, and Gallé), perfume bottles, and Louis Icart etchings. Sharing the premises is **Michael Getz Antiques** (☎ 202/338-3811) offering American, English, and continental silver; porcelain lamps; and many fireplace accessories. Open Monday to Saturday 11am to 6pm, Sunday noon to 5pm; closed Sunday July and August.

   As we go to press a vast **6.** **Barnes & Noble** and a branch of **7.** **Eddie Bauer** are under construction on M Street between Thomas Jefferson and 31st streets.

   ☕ **TAKE A BREAK** At Washington Harbour (30th Street, a block South of M Street), is a delightful riverside development with an esplanade leading to a gorgeous fountain (the vista is a bit reminiscent of New York's Central Park's Bethesda Fountain) and a group of restaurants with indoor windowed and outdoor umbrella-table seating overlooking the Potomac. The best of these is **Sequoia,** with a menu eclectic enough to suit any dining mood (details in Chapter 6).

Turn left on 31st Street NW and continue past the canal; on your left is the:

8. **Yes! Bookshop,** 1035 31st St. NW (☎ 202/338-7874, or 800/YES-1516 for a free catalog). A wealth of literature (both books and books on tape) on personal growth and personal-transformation subjects can be found on the shelves of this rather unique store, along with books on health, natural medicine, men's and women's studies, mythology, creative writing, Jungian psychology, how to save the planet, ancient history, and Native American traditions. CDs and cassettes include non-Western music, instrumental music, New-Age music, and instruction in everything from quitting smoking to astral projection and hypnosis. They also sell a large number of instructional video-cassettes here. Open Monday to Saturday 10am to 8pm; Sunday noon to 7pm (later hours spring through fall).

9. **The Shops at Georgetown Park,** 3222 M St. NW, at Wisconsin Avenue (☎ 202/298-5577). This four-story complex of about 100 shops belongs, architecturally, to two worlds: outside, quietly Federal, in keeping with the character of the neighborhood; inside, flamboyantly Victorian, with a huge skylight, fountains, and ornate chandeliers. You could spend hours here exploring branches of the nation's most exclusive specialty stores. Represented are Ann Taylor, bebe (upscale women's clothing), Caché, J. Crew, Polo/Ralph Lauren, and Abercrombie & Fitch. Also featured are many gift/lifestyle boutiques such as Circuit City Express, Dapy, The Sharper Image, Crabtree & Evelyn, and the fascinating Gallery of History (framed collector historical documents). If you have kids take them to F.A.O. Schwarz, Learning-smith (billing itself as "the general store for the curious mind," it has many interactive facilities for children), and VOR for virtual- reality games and experiences. An Old Town Trolley ticket booth (see Chapter 4) is on the premises. There are several restaurants, including Clyde's, gourmet emporium/cafe Dean & Deluca (details in Chapter 6), and the porklike Canal Walk Café Food Court with a pointed sky overhead, lots of plants, and garden furnishings. An archeological exhibit of artifacts found during the complex's excavation can be viewed on Level 2. And Georgetown Park maintains a full-service Concierge Center offering gift wrapping, worldwide shipping, postal/fax/photocopy services, gift certificates, even sightseeing information. Validated parking is available at an underground garage on Wisconsin Avenue. Open Monday to Saturday 10am to 9pm, Sunday noon to 6pm.

☕ **TAKE A BREAK**   Stop in for croissants and cappuccino; a Camembert sandwich on baguette, or afternoon tea with sumptuous desserts at **Patisserie Café Didier,** 3206 Grace St. NW, off Wisconsin Avenue just below M Street.

Along Wisconsin Avenue NW   Walk back up Wisconsin
Avenue crossing M Street en route to:

10. **Olsson's Books & Records,** 1239 Wisconsin Ave. NW, between
M and N Streets (☎ 202/338-9544). Open Monday to Thurs-
day 10am to 11pm, Friday and Saturday 10am to midnight,
Sunday noon to 8pm. See details in Section 1 under "Books."

11. **Martin's of Georgetown,** 1304 Wisconsin Ave. NW (☎ 202/
338-6144). This shop has been proffering exquisite wares since
1929. Come in and feast your eyes on Martin's selection of
Lalique vases, Christofle silver, hand-painted Herend china, and
Limoges boxes, along with other fine lines of china, silver, crystal, flatware, and dinnerware. Martin's is a prestigious bridal
registry (both the Nixon and Johnson daughters were registered
here). Stuffed animals, baby gifts, picture frames, and other
quality gift items here, too. Open Monday to Saturday 10am
to 6pm.

☕ **TAKE A BREAK**   **Paolo's,** for California-style Italian
cuisine in a simpatico setting, is just down the street at 1303
Wisconsin Ave. NW, at N Street.

12. **Betsey Johnson,** 1319 Wisconsin Ave. NW (☎ 202/338-4090).
New York's flamboyant flower-child designer has a Georgetown
shop. She personally decorated the bubble-gum pink walls. Her
sexy, offbeat play-dress-up styles are great party and club clothes
for the young and the still-skinny young at heart. Open Monday
to Saturday 11am to 8pm, Sunday noon to 6pm.

13. **The Nature Company,** 1323–1325 Wisconsin Ave. NW
(☎ 202/333-4100), has a branch here. These ecologically themed
stores sell bird feeders, chimes, craft kits, decorative mineral specimens, cassettes of whale songs, beautiful T-shirts, camping and
hiking gear, wonderful books (many for kids) and toys, sundials,
delightful novelties, and much more. Frequent special events here
include storytelling, snake and bird shows, and exhibitions about
endangered species and the rain forest. The store also sponsors
cycling and birdwatching excursions. Open Monday to Thursday
11am to 7pm, Friday and Saturday 10am to 8pm, Sunday noon
to 6pm, with extended hours Memorial Day to the end of
December.

14. **Sante Fe Style,** 1413 Wisconsin Ave. NW (☎ 202/333-3747).
Here you'll find high-quality Southwest merchandise, mostly
handmade items from New Mexico and Arizona. The inventory
includes silver jewelry, picture frames, oxidized-iron animal decorations, barbed-wire art, antique Mexican and iron furniture,
pottery, Zapotec pillows from Oaxaca, rugs, colorful painted
sculptures made from barn-roof tin, birdhouses, southwest
cookbooks, and more. Open Monday to Saturday 10am to 6m,
Sunday noon to 5pm.

15. Appalachian Spring, 1415 Wisconsin Ave. NW, at P Street (☎ 202/337-5780), brings country crafts to citified Georgetown. They sell pottery, jewelry, newly made pieced and appliqué quilts in traditional and contemporary patterns, stuffed dolls and animals, candles, rag rugs, hand-blown glassware, an incredible collection of kaleidoscopes, glorious weavings, and simple country toys. Everything in the store is made by hand in the U.S.A. There's another branch in Union Station. Open Monday to Friday 10am to 8pm, Saturday 10am to 6pm, Sunday noon to 6pm.

16. Little Caledonia, 1419 Wisconsin Ave. NW (☎ 202/333-4700), is a rabbit warren of tiny rooms filled with indoor and outdoor furnishings (18th- and 19th-century mahogany reproductions are featured), dolls, Beatrix Potter ceramic figures, stuffed animals, children's books and toys, exquisite fabrics, housewares candles, fancy gift wrappings, Indian dhurrie rugs, tablecloths, wallpapers, lamps, and much, much more. A delight. Open Monday to Saturday 10am to 6pm, and Thanksgiving to Christmas Sunday noon to 5pm.

17. Christ Child Opportunity Shop, 1427 Wisconsin Ave. NW (☎ 202/333-6635). Proceeds from merchandise bought here go to children's charities. Among the first-floor items (donations all), I saw a wicker trunk for $5 and the usual thriftshop jumble of jewelry, clothes, shoes, hats, and odds and ends. Upstairs, higher quality merchandise is left on consignment; it's more expensive, but if you know antiques you might find bargains in jewelry, silver, china, quilts, and other items. Good browsing. Open Monday to Saturday 10am to 3:45pm; closed in August.

18. Secondhand Rose, 1516 Wisconsin Ave. NW, between P and Q streets (☎ 202/337-3378). This upscale second-floor consignment shop specializes in designer merchandise. Creations by Norma Kamali, Armani, Donna Karan, Calvin Klein, Yves Saint-Laurent, Ungaro, Ralph Lauren, and others are sold at about a third of the original price. Everything is in style, in season, and in excellent condition. On a recent visit I saw a gorgeous Scaasi black velvet and yellow satin ball gown for $400 (it was $1,200 new) and Yves Saint-Laurent pumps in perfect condition for $45. Secondhand Rose is also a great place to shop for gorgeous furs, designer shoes and bags, and costume jewelry. Open Monday to Saturday 10am to 6pm.

19. Ashburner Beargie Antiques, second floor of 1529 Wisconsin Ave. NW (☎ 202/337-4513), houses a large inventory of 17th-, 18th-, and early 19th-century European antiques and old master paintings. Sharing the premises (on the first floor; ☎ 202/625-1776) is **The Proud American,** somewhat of a misnomer, since—though its offerings include some American pieces— it specializes in 18th- and 19th-century European furnishings, decorative accessories, paintings, prints, and porcelains. Both shops are open Monday to Saturday 11am to 6pm.

10

Washington, D.C., After Dark

Don't go to bed early just because you're worn out from traipsing around museums and monuments all day. Take a nap before dinner and catch your second wind. Washington offers a wealth of nighttime activities. In addition to the listings below, check the Friday "Weekend" section of the *Washington Post,* which will also tell you about children's theater, sports events, flower shows, and all else. *Washingtonian* magazine and *The City Paper* are other good sources.

TICKETS

TICKETplace, located in George Washington University's Lisner Auditorium, 1730 21st St. NW, at H St. (☎ 202/TICKETS), is a service of the Cultural Alliance of Greater Washington. Here—on the day of performance only (except Sunday and Monday, see below)—you can buy half-price tickets (for cash only) to performances at most major Washington-area theaters and concert halls, not only for dramatic productions, but for opera, ballet, and other events as well. The facility also serves as a **Ticketmaster** outlet. TICKETplace is open Tuesday to Friday noon to 6pm and Saturday 11am to 5pm; half-price tickets to Sunday and Monday shows are sold on Saturday. Closest Metro: Foggy Bottom.

Full-price tickets for most performances in town can also be bought through **Ticketmaster** (☎ 202/432-SEAT) at **Hecht's Department Store,** 12th and G Streets NW. You can purchase tickets to Washington entertainments before you leave home by calling 800/551-SEAT. A similar ticket outlet is **Protix** (☎ 703/218-6500 or 800/955-5566).

1 Theater

Except for New York, I can't think of another U.S. city that offers more first-rate theatrical productions than D.C. Almost anything on Broadway will eventually come to—or have previewed in—Washington. There are also several nationally acclaimed repertory companies here and an excellent theater specializing in Shakespearean productions. Additional theater offerings, including those at the **Kennedy Center,** are listed under "Other Performing Arts" later in this chapter.

Arena Stage

6th St. and Maine Ave. SW. ☎ **202/488-3300.** Tickets $23–$42; discounts available for students, the disabled, groups, and senior citizens. And HOTTIX, a limited number of half-price tickets, are available 90 minutes before most performances (call for details). Metro: Waterfront.

Founded by the brilliant Zelda Fichandler, the Arena Stage, now in its fifth decade, is the home of one of the longest standing acting ensembles in the nation. Several works nurtured here have moved to Broadway, and many graduates—among them "L.A. Law"'s Jill Eikenberry and Michael Tucker, Ned Beatty, James Earl Jones, Robert Prosky, Jane Alexander, and George Grizzard—have gone on to commercial stardom.

The Arena's subscription-season productions (there are eight annually) are presented on two stages—the **Fichandler** (a theater-in-the-round), and the smaller, fan-shaped **Kreeger.** In addition, the Arena houses the **Old Vat,** a space used for new play readings and the special productions (for example, political satire group Gross National Product's recent show, *New World Order*).

A recent September-to-June season (sometimes shows are extended into summer) included productions of Sean O'Casey's *The Plough and the Stars,* Cheryl L. West's *Holiday Heart,* Thornton Wilder's *The Matchmaker* (starring Robert Prosky), August Strindberg's *The Dance of Death* directed by JoAnne Akalaitis, Hugh Wheeler's adaptation of *Candide* (with Leonard Bernstein's music and Stephen Sondheim's lyrics), and Noel Coward's *Blithe Spirit.* The theater has always championed new plays and playwrights and is committed to producing works of playwrights from diverse cultures. Douglas Wager is the Arena Stage's artistic director.

Ford's Theatre

511 10th St. NW (between E and F sts.). ☎ **202/347-4833** for listings; 703/218-6500 or 800/955-5566 to charge tickets. Tickets $24–$36; discounts available for families, also for senior citizens at matinee performances; both seniors and students with ID can get "rush" tickets an hour before performances. Metro: Metro Center or Gallery Place.

This is the actual theater where, on the evening of April 14, 1865, actor John Wilkes Booth shot President Lincoln. The assassination marked the end of what had been John T. Ford's very popular theater—it remained closed for more than a century. In 1968 Ford's reopened, completely restored to its 1865 appearance, based on photographs, sketches, newspaper articles, and samples of wallpaper and curtain material from museum collections. The presidential box is decorated and furnished as it was on that fateful night, including the original crimson damask sofa and framed engraving of George Washington.

Ford's season is more or less year-round (it's dark part of the summer). Several productions here went on to Broadway and off-Broadway. Recent shows have included *Five Guys Named Moe, Hot Mikado,* and Lynn Redgrave's one-woman show, *Shakespeare for My Father.*

A big event here is the nationally televised A Festival at Ford's, always a celebrity-studded bash.

Major Concert & Performance Hall Box Offices

Arena Stage ☎ **202/488-3300**

Constitution Hall ☎ **202/638-2661**

Ford's Theatre ☎ **202/347-4833**

John F. Kennedy Center for the Performing Arts ☎ **202/467-4600**

National Theatre ☎ **202/628-6161** or 800/447-7400

Shakespeare Theatre ☎ **202/393-2700**

Wolf Trap Farm for the Performing Arts ☎ **703/255-1868**

National Theatre

1321 Pennsylvania Ave. NW. ☎ **202/628-6161** or 800/447-7400. Tickets, $22.50–$60; discounts available for students, senior citizens, military personnel, and the handicapped. Metro: Metro Centers.

The luxurious, Federal-style National Theatre, elegantly renovated to the tune of $6.5 million in 1983, is the oldest continuously operating theater in Washington (since 1835) and the third-oldest in the nation. It's exciting just to see this stage on which Sarah Bernhardt, John Barrymore, Helen Hayes, and so many other notables have performed. The National is the closest thing Washington has to a Broadway-style playhouse. Managed by New York's Shubert Organization, it presents star-studded hits—often pre- or post-Broadway—all year round. A recent season included productions of *Annie Get Your Gun* starring Kathy Rigby, *My Fair Lady* starring Richard Chamberlain, *A Chorus Line, Kiss of the Spider Woman* starring Chita Rivera, and *Grease* with Rosie O'Donnell.

The National also offers free public-service programs: Saturday-morning children's theater (puppets, clowns, magicians, dancers, and singers), free summer films, and Monday-night showcases of local groups and performers. Call 202/783-3370 for details.

Shakespeare Theatre

450 7th St. NW (between D and E sts.). ☎ **202/393-2700**. Tickets $15–$45, $10 for standing-room tickets sold two hours prior to sold-out performances; discounts available for students and senior citizens. Metro: Archives or Gallery Place.

This internationally renowned classical ensemble company, which for two decades performed at the Folger Shakespeare Library, moved to larger quarters at the above address in 1992. Under the direction of Michael Kahn, it offers three Shakespearean productions and one other classical work each September-to-June season. The most recent season included *Macbeth* (starring Stacy Keach), *Henry V, All's Well That Ends Well*, and Ben Jonson's *Volpone* (starring Pat Carroll). Other well-known actors such as Jean Stapleton, Tom Hulce, Richard Thomas, and Kelly McGillis have joined the company for specific productions. This is top-level theater. Furthermore, the company offers admission-free summer Shakespearean productions at the Carter Barron Amphitheatre in Rock Creek Park, usually for two to three weeks in June; tickets are available the day of performance only, on a first-come, first-served basis. Call for details.

Source Theatre Company

1835 14th St. NW (between S and T sts.). ☎ **202/462-1073.** Tickets $18–$20, OFF HOURS shows $10, Washington Theatre Festival shows $8–$12.

Washington's major producer of new plays, the Source also mounts works of established playwrights—for instance, David Mamet's *The Woods* (not to mention *The Merchant of Venice*). It presents top local artists in a year-round schedule of dramatic and comedy plays (recently including Paul Rudnick's *Jeffrey*), both at the above address and, during the summer, at various spaces around town. The theater is also used for an OFF HOURS series of productions geared to a contemporary urban audience. Annual events here include the Washington Theatre Festival each July, a four-week showcase of 50 or so new plays. The Source produces many African-American works and welcomes original scripts from unknowns.

Studio Theatre

1333 P St. NW. ☎ **202/332-3300.** Tickets $18.50–$29.50, Secondstage shows $14. Discounts available for students and senior citizens. Metro: Dupont Circle or McPherson Square.

Under artistic director Joy Zinoman, the Studio has consistently produced interesting contemporary plays, nurtured Washington acting talent, and garnered numerous Helen Hayes Awards for outstanding achievement. Many plays come here from off-Broadway. Recent productions have included Ionesco's *Rhinoceros,* Frank McGuinness's *Someone Who'll Watch Over Me,* Herb Gardner's *Conversations with my Father,* and Thomas W. Jones II's *Bessie's Blues.* The Studio also houses **Secondstage,** a 50-seat space on the third floor where emerging artists, directors, and actors can showcase their work. The season runs from September through June (some productions run longer). Street parking is easy to find, and there's a pay lot at P street between 14th and 15th streets.

Woolly Mammoth Theatre Company

1401 Church St. NW (between P and Q sts.). ☎ **202/393-3939.** Tickets $17–$27. They offer a range of ticket discounts, including reduced prices for seniors and students, two-for-the-price-of-one admissions, and pay-what-you-can nights; inquire at the box office. An hour prior to performances, any remaining seats are catered at a reduced price. Free parking across the street. Metro: Dupont Circle, about five blocks away. You might prefer to take a cab from there, since the neighborhood is rather deserted and spooky at night; on request, they'll call a cab for you after the show.

Established in 1980, the Woolly Mammoth offers four productions each year-long season, specializing, according to a publicist, in "new, offbeat, and quirky plays." "I'm not interested in theater where people sit back and say, 'That was nice. I enjoyed that,'" says artistic director Howard Shalwitz. "I only look for plays that directly challenge the audience in some important way." Hence shows here have included Wallace Shawn's *The Fever,* which confronted America's materialist lifestyle in the face of massive suffering throughout the world; *Kvetch* by Steven Berkoff (a wild comedy about anxiety, sex, and the nagging inner voices that plague us all); and Nicky Silver's *The Food Chain* (a wrenching, desperate comedy about fat and thin people, sex with strangers, and the impact of Jewish mothers). This company has garnered nine Helen Hayes Awards, among other accolades, and is consistently reviewed by the *New York Times*.

2 Other Performing Arts

The following listings are a potpourri of places offering a mixed bag of theater, opera, classical music, headliners, jazz, rock, dance, and comedy. Here you'll find some of the top entertainment choices in the District.

MULTICULTURAL FACILITIES

The Folger

201 E. Capitol St. SE. ☎ **202/544-7077.** Metro: Capital South.

The **Folger Consort,** a medieval and Renaissance music ensemble, performs secular and sacred music, troubadour songs, madrigals, and court ensembles in 30 concerts given over seven weekends between October and May. Tickets are $14 to $28.

The Folger also presents a full October-to-June season each year of **theatrical programs** relating to Shakespeare and other literary greats. Some recent examples: Irish actor Donal Donnelly in *My Astonishing Self* (a one-man show as George Bernard Shaw), *Stand-up Shakespeare* (a musical revue), a production of *Richard III* by the Traveling Shakespeare Company, and The Reduced Shakespeare Company performing *The Complete Works of William Shakespeare (Abridged).* Tickets are $15 to $25.

In addition, an **evening lecture series** called "Places in the Mind," features writers, artists, actors, and performers (such as Spalding Gray and Elizabeth Hardwick) speaking on cities around the globe (tickets $10 to $25). On selected evenings, **readings** (tickets $6 to $12) feature poets such as Joseph Brodsky, Octavio Paz, Czeslaw Milosz, Adrienne Rich, and Allen Ginsberg. Another exciting program is the Friday-night **PEN/Faulkner series** of fiction readings by noted authors; Arthur Miller, Nadine Gordimer, Margaret Atwood, J. P. Donleavy, Pat Conroy, and John Irving have participated. And September to May, the Folger offers Saturday morning **programs for children** ranging from medieval treasure hunts to preparing an Elizabethan feast. Admission is $8 per child.

John F. Kennedy Center for the Performing Arts

At the southern end of New Hampshire Ave. NW and Rock Creek Pkwy. ☎ **202/467-4600** or 800/444-1324. Metro: Foggy Bottom. Bus: 80 or 81 from Metro Center.

Our national performing arts center, the hub of Washington's cultural and entertainment scene, is actually made up of five different theaters. You can find out what is scheduled during your stay before leaving home (and charge tickets) by calling the above toll-free number. Half-price tickets are available for full-time students, senior citizens, enlisted personnel, and the disabled (call 202/416-8340 for details).

Opera House   This plush red-and-gilt 2,300-seat theater is designed for ballet, modern dance, and musical comedy, as well as opera, and it's also the setting for occasional gala events such as the Kennedy Center Honors, which you've probably seen on TV (Lillian Gish, Cary Grant, Katharine Hepburn, and Paul Newman have been honorees). Other offerings have included performances by the Joffrey Ballet, the Bolshoi Ballet, the Kirov Ballet, the Royal Ballet, the American Ballet Theatre, and the Metropolitan Opera. Recent theater productions here have included Disney's *Beauty and the Beast,* Carol Channing in *Hello Dolly,* and *The King and I.*

Concert Hall   The National Symphony Orchestra has its home here and presents concerts from September to June. Tickets are available by subscription and single sales. Guest artists have included Itzhak Perlman, Vladimir Ashkenazy, Zubin Mehta, Pinchas Zukerman, André Previn, Jean-Pierre Rampal, and Isaac Stern. In addition, chamber music societies, orchestras, and choral groups from all over the world have performed in this space; there's an annual free Christmas concert, the *Messiah* sing-along; and rounding things out are headliner entertainers such as Johnny Mathis, Joel Grey, Dionne Warwick, Marvin Hamlisch, and Harry Belafonte.

Terrace Theater   Small chamber works, choral recitals, musicals, comedy revues, cabarets, and theatrical and modern-dance performances are among the varied provinces of the 500-seat Terrace Theater, a Bicentennial gift from Japan. It's been the setting for solo performances by violinist Eugene Fodor, pianists Santiago Rodriguez and Peter Serkin, soprano Dawn Upshaw, and jazz singer Barbara Cook. Performance artists Laurie Anderson and Michael Moschen have performed here, and jazz evenings have included tributes to Count Basie, Louis Armstrong, and Duke Ellington. Every spring the Terrace (along with the Theater Lab) hosts productions of six finalists in the American College Theatre Festival competition.

Eisenhower Theater   A wide range of dramatic productions can be seen here. Some recent examples: *Angels in America* (parts I and II), *Master Class* starring Zoe Caldwell as legendary diva Maria Callas, Edward Albee's *Three Tall Women,* and the Royal Shakespeare Company's *A Midsummer Night's Dream.* The Eisenhower is also the setting for smaller productions of the **Washington Opera** from December to February. Tickets for most theatrical productions are in the $18 to $40 range. Opera seats soar higher.

Theater Lab and More   By day, the Theater Lab is Washington's premier stage for children's theater. Evenings it becomes a cabaret, now in a long run of *Shear Madness,* a comedy whodunit (tickets are $19 to $23). Elsewhere at the center, there are family concerts by the National Symphony Orchestra several times each year, not to mention clowns, jugglers, dance troupes, improvisational theater, storytellers, and films. Many events are scheduled for Christmas, Easter, and the annual Kennedy Center Open House Arts Festival (September).

See also "Cinema," below, for details on the **American Film Institute,** yet another Kennedy Center facility.

Underground parking at the Kennedy Center is $6 for the entire evening after 5pm.

Warner Theatre

1299 Pennsylvania Ave. NW (entrance on 13th St., between E and F sts.). ☎ **202/783-4000,** 202/432-SEAT, or 800/551-SEAT to charge tickets. Play tickets $32.50–$60. Metro: Metro Center.

Opened in 1924 as the Earle Theatre (a movie/vaudeville palace)—and restored to its original appearance in 1992 at a cost of $10 million—this stunning neoclassical-style theater features a gold-leafed grand lobby and auditorium. Everything is plush and magnificent, from the glittering crystal chandeliers to the gold-tasseled swagged-velvet draperies. It's worth coming by just to see its ornately detailed interior. The Warner offers year-round entertainment, alternating dance performances (Twyla Tharp, Baryshnikov, Alvin Ailey, the Washington Ballet's Christmas performance of *The Nutcracker*) and Broadway shows (Maurice Hines in *Jelly's Last Jam,* Theodore Bikel in *Fiddler on the Roof,* the Pointer Sisters in *Ain't Misbehavin*) with headliner entertainment (Johnny Mathis, Sheryl Crow, Patti LaBelle, Anne Murray, Tony Bennett). Call to find out what's on during your visit.

Wolf Trap Farm Park for the Performing Arts

1551 Trap Rd., Vienna, Va. ☎ **703/255-1868;** PROTIX (703/218-6500) to charge tickets. Summer Festival $18–$39 seats, $10–$17 lawn; Barn tickets average $10–$18.

The country's only national park devoted to the performing arts, Wolf Trap, just 30 minutes by car from downtown D.C., offers a star-studded **Summer Festival Season** from late May to mid-September. Recent seasons have featured performances by the National Symphony Orchestra (it's their summer home), Ray Charles, Bonnie Raitt, the Kirov Ballet, Willie Nelson and Tammy Wynette (a double bill), Trisha Yearwood, the New York City opera, Tony Bennett, and Penn & Teller. Talk about eclectic! There's also an Irish music festival every May and a major jazz and blues festival every June. Performances take place in the 7,000-seat **Filene Center,** about half of which is under the open sky. You can also buy cheaper lawn seats on the hill, which is sometimes the nicest way to go. If you do, arrive early (the lawn opens 90 minutes before the performance), and bring a blanket and a picnic dinner; it's a tradition.

Year-round, jazz pop, country, folk, bluegrass, and chamber musicians perform in the pre-Revolutionary, 350-seat **German Barn** at 1635 Trap Rd., also the summer home of the Wolf Trap Opera Company. Call 703/938-2404 for information.

Take the Metro to West Falls Church; in summer only, the Wolf Trap Express Shuttle ($3.50 round-trip) runs from the Metro every 20 minutes starting two hours before the performance time and (return trip) 20 minutes after the performance ends or 11pm (whichever comes first). By car, take I-495 (the Beltway) to Exit 12W (Dulles Toll Road); stay on the local exit road (you'll see a sign) until you come to Wolf Trap. The park is also accessible from Exit 67 off I-66W.

MOSTLY HEADLINERS

The following facilities offer primarily big-name entertainers—they're large spaces only headliners can fill.

Baltimore Arena

201 W. Baltimore St., Baltimore, Md. ☎ **410/347-2020;** 410/481-SEAT or 800/551-SEAT for tickets.

This 13,500-seat arena, a few blocks from Baltimore's Inner Harbor, is home to several local sports teams. When they're not playing, there are big-name concerts and family entertainment shows here. The Arena hosted the Beatles back in the 1960s. More recently, they've presented *Nickelodeon Double Dare Live,* Ringling Brothers and Barnum & Bailey Circus, *Disney on Ice,* and headliners such as Neil Diamond, Reba McIntyre, Nine Inch Nails, Randy Travis, Paul Simon, Liza Minnelli, Luther Vandross, and George Jones.

To get here by car, take I-95 north to I-395 (stay in the left lane) to the Inner Harbor exit and follow Howard Street to the Arena. You can also take a MARC train from Union Station.

Constitution Hall

18th and D sts. NW. ☎ **202/638-2661** or 202/628-4780; 202/432-SEAT to charge tickets. Tickets $15–$50. Metro: Farragut West.

Somehow I don't associate Eddie Murphy with the Daughters of the American Revolution. Nevertheless, he's played this beautiful 3,746-seat Federal-style auditorium at the DAR's national headquarters. Others who've headlined here include Lee Greenwood, the Washington Civic Symphony, Patti LaBelle, Diana Ross, Jay Leno, Ray Charles, and Marilyn Horne.

Merriweather Post Pavilion

10475 Little Patuxent Pkwy. (just off Rte. 29 in Columbia, Md.). ☎ **410/730-2424;** PROTIX (☎ 202/481-6500 or 703/218-6500) to charge tickets. Tickets $17–$50 pavilion, $15–$23 lawn.

During the summer there's celebrity entertainment almost nightly at the Merriweather Post Pavilion, about 40 minutes by car from downtown D.C. There's reserved seating in the open-air pavilion (overhead protection provided in case of rain) and general-admission seating on the lawn (no refunds for rain) to see such performers as James Taylor, Tina Turner, Van Halen, the Beach Boys, Liza Minnelli, Sting, John Mellencamp, Julio Iglesias, Joan Rivers, Willie Nelson, Jimmy Buffett, Elton John, Al Jarreau, and Barry Manilow. If you choose the lawn seating, bring blankets and picnic fare (beverages must be bought on the premises).

Nissan Pavilion at Stone Ridge

7800 Cellar Door Dr. (off Wellington Rd. in Bristow, Va.). ☎ **703/754-6400** for concert information; 202/432-SEAT, or 800/551-SEAT to charge tickets.

With a capacity of 25,000 seats (10,000 under the roof, the remainder on the lawn), this immense new entertainment facility just 25 minutes from the Beltway features major acts varying from classical to country. During 1995, its first May-to-October season, performers included Emmylou Harris, Victor Borge, Regis and Kathie Lee, Ted Nugent, Yanni, Luther Vandross, Melissa Etheridge, Barry White, James Taylor, Van Halen, Jimmy Buffet, the Allman Brothers, and Elton John. The action is enhanced by giant video screens inside the pavilion and on the lawn. To get here, take I-66 to Exit 43B, follow Pavilion signs onto Route 29, continue half a mile and turn left onto Wellington Road; the Nissan Pavilion is about a mile down on your right.

The Patriot Center

George Mason University, 4400 University Dr., Fairfax, Va. ☎ **703/993-3000;** 703/573-SEAT to charge tickets.

This 10,000-seat facility hosts major headliners. Performers here have included Prince, Randy Travis, David Copperfield, Gloria Estefan, Tom Petty, Natalie Cole, Sting, Billy Idol, and Kenny Rogers. There are family events such as *Sesame Street Live* here, too. To get here by car, take the Wilson Bridge to Braddock Road West, and continue about 8 miles to University Drive.

Robert F. Kennedy Memorial Stadium

2400 E. Capitol St. SE. ☎ **202/547-9077** or 202/546-3337; 202/432-SEAT or 800/551-SEAT to charge tickets. Metro: Stadium-Armory.

It takes superstars to pack this 55,000-plus-seat facility. Michael Jackson, Bruce Springsteen, the Rolling Stones, U-2, Pink Floyd, Paul McCartney, the Grateful Dead, New Kids on the Block, and Bob Dylan are among those who've played here.

USAir Arena

Exit 15A or 17A off the Capital Beltway in Landover, Md. ☎ **301/350-3400** or 800/551-SEAT.

This 19,000-seat arena hosts a variety of concerts and headliner entertainment in between sporting events. Pavarotti, Michael Jackson, Janet Jackson, R.E.M., Peter Gabriel, Van Halen, Madonna, Elton John, Eric Clapton, Neil Diamond, Garth Brooks, Barbra Streisand, Aerosmith, and the Rolling Stones have all played here.

3 The Club & Music Scene

In addition to the big concert spaces detailed in "Other Performing Arts," above, and the free concerts listed in "More Entertainment," below, Washington has many more intimate places where great rock and jazz artists play. There are also lively bars, dance clubs (the latter offering some of the best singles action), and comedy clubs. There's even big-band music, square and folk dancing, and more, in a park. What else could you ask for?

COMEDY CLUBS & CABARET

Although big-name comedians perform around town at such places as **Constitution Hall,** and lesser-known comedians and groups at such places as **D.C. Space,** there are two clubs in town totally devoted to comedy:

Comedy Cafe

1520 K St. NW. ☎ **202/638-JOKE.** Comedy Cafe cover $5 Wed–Thurs, $10–$20 Fri–Sat, with a two-item minimum at all times; Fanatics no cover or minimum. Metro: McPherson Square or Farragut North.

The Comedy Cafe features both local talent and nationally known comics you might have seen in movies or on TV (for example, Larry Miller, Gabe Kaplan, *Saturday Night Live*'s Norm MacDonald, Chris Rock, David Alan Grier, and Jeff Foxworthy). Reservations are recommended, and it's a good idea to arrive early to get a good seat. There are two shows every Friday night (at 8:30 and 10:30pm) and three every Saturday night (at 7, 9, and 11pm). A reasonably priced menu offers full entrées (such as chicken teriyaki and New York strip steak), as well as sandwiches, burgers, hors d'oeuvres, desserts, and, of course, drinks. Wednesday (from 8:30pm) is open-mike night; that means people are auditioning or, occasionally, pros are working out new material. And on Thursday (same hours) four comics take the stage.

The Comedy Cafe is on the upper level. Below, under the same ownership, is **Fanatics,** a sports-themed club where there's a DJ weekend nights. Worldwide sporting events (they have satellite) are aired on 20 TV monitors, and there are games (pinball, video games, computerized bowling, and so forth). Open until 2am Sunday to Thursday, until 3am on Friday and Saturday.

The Improv

1140 Connecticut Ave. NW (between L and M sts.). ☎ **202/296-7008.** Cover $10 Sun–Thurs, $12 Fri–Sat, plus a two-item minimum (waived if you dine). Metro: Farragut North.

Offering a similar format to the above, the Improv features top performers on the national comedy-club circuit as well as comic plays and one-man shows. *Saturday Night Live* regulars Ellen Cleghorne (Queen Shenequa), David Spade, and Adam Sandler have all played here, as have comedy bigs Ellen De Generis, Jerry Seinfeld, David Alan Grier, and Rosie O'Donnell. Shows are about $1^1/_2$ hours long and include three comics (an emcee, feature act, and headliner). Show times are 8:30pm Sunday to Thursday, 8:30 and 10:30pm Friday and Saturday. Best way to snag a good seat is to have dinner here (make reservations), which allows you to enter the club as early as 7pm. Dinner entrées ($6.95 to $13.95) include prime rib, sandwiches, and pasta and seafood selections. Drinks average $3.25. You must be 18 to get in.

Marquee Cabaret

In the OMNI Shoreham Hotel, 2500 Calvert St. NW (at Connecticut Ave.). ☎ **202/234-0700.** Cover $7–$21 depending on the entertainment. Metro: Woodley Park–Zoo.

A hotel with a long history of providing great entertainment, the Shoreham today features talented ensembles in its plush art deco nightclub. In the 1930s, Lena Horne, Frank Sinatra, Marlene Dietrich, and Judy Garland performed at the hotel. And political satirist Mark Russell played the room for 20 years. For the last six years, a politically oriented and extremely funny musical comedy revue called *Mrs. Foggybottom & Friends* has been playing Thursday to Saturday at 9pm. On Monday at 8pm an improvisational comedy group called Now This takes the stage. Singers and comics fill in other nights. There's almost always something on. Reservations suggested.

DANCE CLUBS

Coco Loco

810 7th St. NW (between H and I sts.). ☎ **202/289-2626.** Cover $5–$10. Valet parking $4. Metro: Gallery Place.

This is D.C.'s hottest club, heralded by marquee lights. Wednesday through Saturday nights, come for a late tapas or mixed-grill dinner (see Chapter 6 for details) and stay for international music and dancing, with occasional live bands. Friday and Saturday nights, the entertainment includes a sexy 11pm floor show featuring the Coco Loco dancers—Brazilian exhibition dancers who begin performing in feathered and sequined Rio Rita costumes and strip down to a bare minimum. Laser lights and other special effects enhance the show, which ends with a conga line and a limbo contest, after which there's dancing until 2am weeknights, 3am weekends. Coco Loco draws an attractive crowd of all ages, including many experienced dancers. It's great fun.

Deja Vu

2119 M St. NW. ☎ **202/452-1966.** Cover Fri–Sat $3, no cover or drink minimum Sun–Thurs. Metro: Dupont Circle or Foggy Bottom.

This 10-room Victorian extravaganza, with a dance floor, eight bars, and two restaurants on the premises, is one of the liveliest places in D.C. The dance area has a wood-burning fireplace, which, along with stained-glass paneling, tropical plants, fountains, and plush furnishings, makes for a warm setting. A DJ plays Top-40 tunes and other dance music, and there are frequent celebratory events such as Mordi Gros; Halfway to Mordi Gros, and a Bastille Day Waiter's Race (participants run carrying a tray of drinks; first prize is a trip to Paris). You can dine here (reservations advised) at Blackie's House of Beef (steaks, prime rib, fresh seafood) or Lulu's New Orleans Cafe, offering créole-Cajun and seafood entrées as well as indoor and outdoor seating. Drinks average $3.25. You must be 21 to get into the club. Open Sunday to Thursday to 2am, Friday and Saturday to 3am.

Fifth Column

915 F St. NW. ☎ **202/393-3632.** Cover $5–$10. Metro: Gallery Place.

Fronted by massive neoclassical columns, the Fifth Column isn't decorator fancy but does have a rather grand interior—a former Equitable Bank with a soaring 45-foot arched ceiling over the dance floor. Especially plush is the velvet-walled upstairs VIP room with comfortable sofas and a working fireplace. Guests are admitted to the latter at the discretion of the man behind the velvet rope; bar prices are higher in this elevated precinct, but it's a cozy setting for sipping champagne. Also simpatico is the open-air patio out back. The music (mostly DJ/ occasional live entertainment, till 2am Monday to Thursday, to 3am Friday and Saturday) is a mix of progressive house, European house, acid jazz, techno, and underground. The club stays on top of trends, keeps an ear to New York and London, and often plays prerelease recordings. There are changing art shows on the walls. The crowd is 25 to 30 years old, upwardly mobile with a sprinkling of Arab princes and the occasional visiting celeb (Cher, the artist formerly known as Prince, Julia Roberts, Sylvester Stallone and *Beverly Hills 90210* stars Jennie Garth, Ian Zierling, and Jason Priestley). You must be 21 to get in (18 Monday and Wednesday to Friday nights). No drink minimum; the average drink is about $3.75.

Kilimanjaro

1724 California St. NW (between 18th St. and Florida Ave.). ☎ **202/328-3838** or 202/328-3839. No cover Wed, $5–$10 other nights; there's always a two-drink minimum.

This popular reggae/calypso/African-music club, owned by a Kenyan and a Bajan, is the hub of Washington's Caribbean music scene. The setting is fittingly exotic—dimly lit, with candles aglow in red-glass holders and zebra skins adorning the walls. There are two separate dance areas; on weekends, sometimes a different band plays in each (good acoustics here; there's no cacophony). Music varies between DJs and live performances. Some of the artists who've played Kilimanjaro are Shabba Ranks (from Jamaica), Hugh Masekela (South Africa), Lucky Dube (South Africa), Olu Dom (Brazil), Arrow (Trinidad), and Gregory Isaacs (Jamaica). You can dine here on such menu items as nyama ya mbuzi–East African–style charcoal-grilled goat. Drinks average $4.50. Open till 2am Sunday, Wednesday, and Thursday; till 4am Friday and Saturday; closed Monday and Tuesday. Best way to get here is by taxi. You must be 21 to get in.

Nightclub 9:30

930 F St. NW. ☎ **202/638-2008** or 202/393-0930. Cover $3–$20. Metro: Metro Center or Gallery Place.

This funky alternative music club features local and national live bands—punk, metal, house/industrial, reggae, rockabilly, and rap—including some well-known performers like John Spencer Blues Explosion, G Love & Special Source, Helmet, Jawbox, and Throwing Muses. Occasionally jazz artists—such as Buckshot LaFonque (Branford Marsalis's band)—play here as well. It's all very un-Washington, not just the music and the crowd but the grotty, black-walled interior with exposed pipes overhead. There are parties to introduce new artists and releases. And once in a great while, special shows feature really big names like Tony Bennett or the Black Crowes. The club is open five or six nights a week (it depends on bookings), usually until 12:30 to 1:30am Sunday to Thursday, until 3am Friday and Saturday; there's no minimum age for admission—a boon to young teens looking for trouble. No drink minimum; drinks average $3.75. Pizza and snack items are available.

River Club

3223 K St. NW. ☎ **202/333-8118.**

Isn't it romantic? This elegant art deco Georgetown nightspot evokes the sophisticated dine-and-dance clubs that flourished in the 1920s and

1930s, bringing unprecedented champagne-and-caviar glamour to the Washington nightlife scene. The clientele is glittery and gorgeous (wear your best), many with limos waiting out front. One often sees local and visiting celebrities here. I've spotted Redskins owner Jack Kent Cooke, Ted Kennedy, Ryan O'Neal, Jesse Jackson, Cher, Lynda Carter, Sen. John Warner, and Sylvester Stallone on various visits. You can hang out at the large bar up front or have dinner (the food's superb) at the tables surrounding the circular dance floor. It's a great place to dance.

Tuesdays through Thursdays, the River Club presents live entertainment ranging from '50s Motown to big band, jazz, and swing. Fridays and Saturdays a jazz pianist is featured early in the evening, followed by great dance music that progresses in decades (from big bad to contemporary tunes) as the evening wears on. If you can't manage witty repartee or kindle the spark of romance in this setting, you never will. Dinner entrées—ranging from roast rack of lamb to pepper-encrusted tuna with ginger-jasmin rice, snow peas, and orange-sesame sauce—are $16–$26. Open Tuesday to Thursday until 2am (food available through midnight), Friday and Saturday until 3am (food through 1am). Drinks average $5.50.

Spy Club

805 15th St. NW (between H and I sts. in Zel Alley). ☎ **202/289-1779.** Cover $8–$10. Metro: McPherson Square.

The Spy Club's dance floor is punctuated by "Gothic" columns. There are cozy nooks off the dance floor, including the Den (with overstuffed sofas, shaded table lamps, and a working fireplace), the Cubana Room (with palm trees and a roulette wheel), and the Billiards Room (set up with a pool table and backgammon boards). Thursday is college night, catering to a young crowd; a DJ provides an alternative mix. Friday and Saturday feature cutting-edge mixes of high-energy, house, techno, and European music, and the crowd is early 20s to about 35. The dress code prohibits sneakers or T-shirts, and weekend nights collared shirts are preferred. If you'd like to dine sometime during the evening, Notte Luna, a fine northern Italian restaurant, is right upstairs. Hours vary, but the club is generally open Thursday, Friday, and Saturday 10pm to 2:30am. Drinks average $4.

ROCK & JAZZ

The Bayou

3135 K St. NW (under the Whitehurst Fwy. near Wisconsin Ave.). ☎ **202/333-2897.** Cover $5–$25.

This lively nightclub, located on the Georgetown waterfront, features a mixed bag of live musical entertainment—mostly progressive, reggae, and alternative sounds. Performers are up-and-coming national groups, with occasional big names (e.g., Warren Zevon, The Kinks, Todd Rundgren) playing the club for old time's sake. In addition there are occasional comedy group shows such as political satirists Gross National Product. Show times vary.

The Bayou is a funky, cavelike club, with exposed brick and stone walls and seating on two levels. Sandwiches and pizza are available during the show. Drinks average $3.25; most food items are $5 or less. Except at special all-age shows, no one under 18 is admitted.

Blues Alley

1073 Wisconsin Ave. NW (in an alley below M St.). ☎ **202/337-4141**. Cover $13–$40, plus $7 food or drink minimum.

Blues Alley, in Georgetown, has been Washington's top jazz club since 1965, featuring such artists as Nancy Wilson, McCoy Tyner, Sonny Rollins, Flora Purim, Herbie Mann, Wynton Marsalis, Charlie Byrd, Ramsey Lewis, Rochelle Ferrell, and Maynard Ferguson. There are usually two shows nightly at 8 and 10pm; some performers also do midnight shows on weekends. Reservations are essential (call after noon); since seating is on a first-come, first-served basis it's best to arrive no later than 7pm and have dinner. Entrées on the steak and créole-seafood menu (for example, jambalaya, chicken créole, and crabcakes) are in the $14 to $19 range, snacks and sandwiches are $5.25 to $9, and drinks are $5.35 to $8. The decor is of the classic jazz club genre—exposed brick walls, beamed ceiling, and small candlelit tables. Sometimes well-known visiting musicians get up and jam with performers, and one night, when Jerry Lewis was in the audience, he got up on stage and told a few jokes.

Blues Alley will open a new adjoining club offering a wider spectrum of entertainers in the future.

4 The Bar Scene

Bottom Line

1716 I St. NW. ☎ **202/298-8488**. Metro: Farragut West.

The Bottom Line is a popular sports bar, owned by Dick Heidenberger and Jack Million, both former PAC rugby team players. Consequently, lots of PAC ruggers (the 1995 National Champions) and other athletes hang out here. Monday night, sporting events are televised at the bar, and free hot dogs are offered to customers. Tuesday to Saturday, there's dancing to music (Top-40 tunes, progressive rock, reggae) provided by a DJ from 8pm to closing. Some people describe the Bottom Line as a place to come and go nuts. There's a definite anything-goes attitude, enhanced by frequent zany promotions. One night, anyone who could sit on a block of ice for an hour had $100 donated to the charity of his or her choice–plus unlimited free drinks while ice-sitting. And, of course, there's a big holiday bash on Christmas, New Year's, Valentine's Day, St. Patrick's Day, and so forth—let's just say the party never stops. A reasonably priced menu—salads, omelets, sandwiches, Mexican fare, and burgers—is offered until 10 or 11pm. Drinks run $3 to $4. Open Monday to Thursday until 1:30am, to 2:30am Friday and Saturday.

Champions

1206 Wisconsin Ave. NW (just north of M St.). ☎ **202/965-4005**.

This Georgetown spot is D.C.'s premier hangout for athletes and sports groupies. The heaviest singles action takes place at the first-floor bar;

the upstairs bar and glassed-in deck are more laid-back. The attractive interior is chockablock with autographed sports photos, posters, and artifacts such as Carl Lewis's running shoes, Sugar Ray Leonard's boxing gloves, and Joe Louis's headgear. And many TV monitors air nonstop sporting events. Of course, you're likely to see your favorite sports stars (particularly of Washington area teams) at the bars or tables, and entertainment-world celebrities also drop by with some frequency. I once glimpsed Ryan O'Neal at the bar cheering the Celtics. Champions is always packed, and they don't take reservations, so unless you arrive early, you'll probably have to wait for a table. If you do get a seat, you might order such fare as nachos, burgers, a steak-and-cheese sandwich, or buffalo wings. And should you make your way through the crowd to the bar, you'll see that it's pasted over with $15,000 worth of baseball cards. Drinks average $3. A DJ is on hand nightly playing oldies and Top-40 tunes. Open Sunday to Thursday until 2am, Friday and Saturday until 3am.

Clyde's

3236 M St. NW. ☎ **202/333-9180.**

Located in Georgetown, this New York–style bar complete with checkered tablecloths, gaslight sconces, and white tile floors is mobbed every evening with an upscale crowd of young professionals, college students, political types, and Old Line Washingtonians. If you should want solid rather than liquid refreshment, there are several dining areas—my favorite is the candlelit patio with numerous plants and a skylight ceiling. Or you can adjourn to the Omelette Room where a chef working in an open copper-canopied kitchen turns out such omelets as the Bonne Femme—stuffed with bacon, sautéed potatoes, onions, sour cream, and chives—until the wee hours. (See further details on the food here in Chapter 6.) Clyde's opens at 11:30am and drinks are served until 2am Sunday to Thursday, 3am Friday and Saturday. Drinks average $3.50.

Old Ebbitt Grill

675 15th St. NW (between F and G sts.). ☎ **202/347-4801.** Metro: McPherson Square or Metro Center.

While I'm on the subject of simpatico hangouts, the Old Ebbitt, described in detail in Chapter 6, offers a good bit of glamour in its sumptuous turn-of-the-century bars and dining areas. A scene from Clint Eastwood's movie *In the Line of Fire* was shot here. Drinks average $3.50.

Sequoia

3000 K St. NW (at Washington Harbour). ☎ **202/944-4200.** No cover. Paid parking available at the Harbour.

Especially on weekend nights when the weather is balmy, this is Washington's hottest alfresco singles scene. Even if you don't meet anyone, Sequoia's awninged terrace bar overlooking the Potomac is a gorgeous place to spend an evening quaffing drinks. The restaurant is detailed in Chapter 6. The bar stays open until 1:30am Sunday to Thursday nights, till 2:30am Fridays and Saturdays.

5 More Entertainment

CINEMA

With the advent of VCRs, classic film theaters have almost become extinct. In addition to the **Mary Pickford Theater,** in the John Adams Building of the Library of Congress (see Chapter 7), there is only one choice in this category:

American Film Institute

At the Kennedy Center, New Hampshire Ave. NW and Rock Creek Pkwy. ☎ **202/828-4000** (information) or 202/785-4600 (box office). $6.50, $5.50 for members (AFI memberships are $20 a year), senior citizens, and students under 18 with ID. Metro: Foggy Bottom.

This marvelous facility features classic films, works of independent film makers, foreign films, themed festivals, and the like in a 224-seat theater designed to offer the highest standard of projection, picture, and sound quality. There's something on almost every Wednesday to Sunday evening and weekend afternoon. The AFI also sponsors audience-participation discussions with major directors, film stars, and screenwriters, for example, Linda Yellin, Sigourney Weaver, Gore Vidal, Nora Ephron, Faye Wray, and Jonathan Demme.

Underground parking at the Kennedy Center is $6 for the entire evening after 5pm.

FREE SHOWS

In D.C. some of the best things at night are free—or so cheap they might as well be free.

MILITARY BAND CONCERTS

The **U.S. Army Band, "Pershing's Own"** (☎ 703/696-3399), presents a mix of country, blues, Bach, choral music, jazz, pop, and show tunes every summer, all of it outdoors. There are performances at 8pm every Friday on the east steps of the Capitol and every Tuesday at the Sylvan Theatre on the grounds of the Washington Monument. Every June there's a major American history–themed pageant at the USAir Arena called *Spirit of America* (call 202/475-0685 to obtain free tickets). And beginning early in July (until mid- to late August) the band joins with the Third U.S. Infantry, "The Old Guard," on Wednesday at 7pm to present *Twilight Tattoo,* a military pageant, on the Ellipse; it features the Old Guard Fife and Drum Corps, rifle drills, flag presentations, and a musical salute to America's heritage. Arrive early to get a good seat at any of the above, and bring a picnic dinner and blanket to outdoor concerts. The season's highlight is a performance in August of Tchaikovsky's *1812* Overture with real roaring cannons. There are additional performances in winter at Brucker Hall in Arlington, Virginia. Call for details.

The **U.S. Navy Band** (☎ 202/433-2525 for a 24-hour recording, or 202/433-6090), performs a similar variety of music, alternately at 8pm Monday on the east steps of the Capitol and at 8pm Thursday at the Sylvan Theatre, June to August. There are also summer U.S.

Navy Band concerts Tuesday nights at 8pm at the U.S. Navy Memorial, 701 Pennsylvania Ave. NW. The navy band highlight: the *Children's Lollipop Concert* of child-oriented music (the third Thursday in August at the Sylvan Theatre at 8:30pm), with elaborate sets, costumes, balloons, clowns, and free lollipops for the audience. And the band also features the *Navy Summer Pageant,* a multimedia presentation tracing the history of the U.S. Navy, every Wednesday June to August at 9pm at the Washington Navy Yard Waterfront, 901 M St. SE. Advance reservations are required; call 202/433-2218.

The **U.S. Marine Band, "The President's Own"** (☎ 202/ 433-4011 for a 24-hour recording, or 202/433-5809), alternates performances June to August on the east steps of the Capitol on Wednesday at 8pm and at the Sylvan Theatre on Sunday at 8pm. It offers additional free concerts January, February, and October at the Marine Barracks, 8th and I Streets SE, including a chamber music series at 2pm every Sunday (no tickets required). Call for details.

Finally, there's the **U.S. Air Force Band, "America's International Musical Ambassadors"** (☎ 202/767-5658 for a 24-hour recording, or 202/767-4310). June through August, various units (jazz, show groups, country, orchestral) can be seen on the cast steps of the Capitol on Tuesday at 8pm and at the Sylvan Theatre on Friday at the same time. And a date in late August is set aside for Christmas in August (carols and other Christmas music).

HEADLINERS—MOSTLY JAZZ

Anheuser-Busch, together with local radio stations, sponsors two fabulous outdoor summer concert series in conjunction with the National Park Service.

Big names in jazz, pop, rock, Latin, and avant-garde music perform in the 4,200-seat **Carter Barron Amphitheatre,** Colorado Avenue and 16th Street NW, in Rock Creek Park (☎ 202/426-6837 or 202/ 619-7222) from mid-June to the end of August on Friday and Saturday nights at 8pm. Tickets are relatively inexpensive—about $16. They go on sale at Ticketmaster outlets (☎ 202/432-SEAT) at the beginning of the season and sell out fast. Seating is on a first-come, first-served basis, so arrive early and get in line. Who might you see here? Nancy Wilson, Ashford and Simpson, Ramsey Lewis, the O'Jays, Rochelle Ferrell, or B. B. King, among other stars. In addition, the National Symphony Orchestra presents several free summer concerts here, and the *Washington Post* also sponsors free Carter Barron concerts. Call for details.

Under the same sponsorship is a series of jazz concerts on the lawn in the **Fort Dupont Summer Theatre,** Randle Circle and Minnesota Avenue SE, in Fort Dupont Park (☎ 202/426-7723 or 202/ 619-7222), every Friday or Saturday at 8:30pm from sometime in July to the end of August. Bring a blanket and a picnic dinner; arrive early (by 6pm) to get a good spot on the lawn. Past performers here have included Stanley Turrentine, Roy Ayres, Herbie Mann, McCoy Tyner, Betty Carter, the Motown Revue, Flora Purim, and Ahmad Jamal. Admission is free.

OTHER OUTDOOR CONCERTS

Concerts at the Capitol, an American Festival, is sponsored jointly by the National Park Service and Congress. It's a series of free summer concerts with the National Symphony Orchestra that takes place at 8pm on the west side of the Capitol on Memorial Day, July 4, and Labor Day. Seating is on the lawn, so bring a picnic. Major guest stars in past years have included Ossie Davis (a narrator and host), Leontyne Price, Johnny Cash, Rita Moreno, Mary Chapin Carpenter, and Mstislav Rostropovich. The music ranges from light classical to country to show tunes of the Gershwin/Rodgers and Hammerstein genre. For further information call 202/619-7222.

Concerts on the Canal, sponsored by the Mobil Corporation, are free afternoon concerts at the Foundry Mall right on the C&O Canal between 30th and Thomas Jefferson Streets NW, just below M Street (☎ 703/866-7150). Featuring jazz, folk, Dixieland, bluegrass, country, and classical artists, they take place every other Sunday afternoon (4 to 6:30pm) from early June through August.

11

Easy Excursions from Washington, D.C.

If possible, consider spending a few days away from Washington, visiting pre-Revolutionary America and other close-to-the-capital attractions. All of the destinations discussed below can be visited on day trips, while you keep your Washington, D.C., hotel base.

1 Arlington National Cemetery

The land that today comprises Arlington County was originally carved out of Virginia as part of the territory ceded to form the nation's new capital district. In 1847 the land was returned to the state of Virginia, although it was known as Alexandria County until 1920, when the name was changed to avoid confusion with the city of Alexandria.

The county was named to honor Arlington House, built by George Washington Parke Custis (see below), whose daughter, Mary Ann Randolph Custis, married a young army officer named Robert E. Lee. The Lees lived in Arlington House until the onset of the Civil War in 1861. After the first Battle of Bull Run, at Manassas, several Union soldiers were buried here; the beginnings of the national cemetery date from that time. The Arlington Memorial Bridge at the base of the Lincoln Memorial symbolizes the reunion of North and South after the Civil War.

Note: Keep in mind that this is still an active cemetery and observe the proper decorum.

ESSENTIALS

GETTING THERE Arlington National Cemetery is just across the Potomac River from Washington, D.C. **By car,** from the Lincoln Memorial, drive across the Arlington Memorial Bridge. You can park in the huge lots (you're not allowed to drive around the cemetery). Or you can take the **Metro** to the Arlington National Cemetery stop on the Blue Line. If you're sightseeing on the **Tourmobile,** see "Getting Around" in Chapter 4.

GETTING AROUND Upon your arrival, head over to the **Visitor Center,** where you can purchase a Tourmobile ticket allowing you to stop at all major sights and then reboard whenever you like. Service is

Arlington National Cemetery

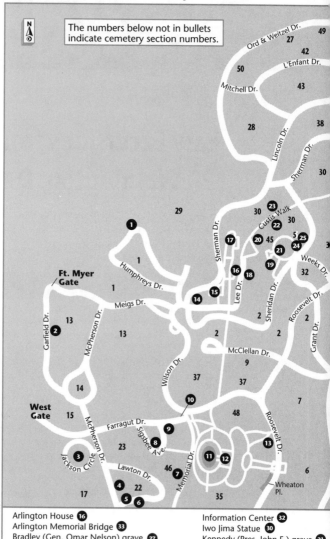

N

The numbers below not in bullets indicate cemetery section numbers.

Arlington House **16**
Arlington Memorial Bridge **33**
Bradley (Gen. Omar Nelson) grave **27**
Byrd (Rear Adm. Richard, Jr.) statue **31**
Challenger Memorial **10**
Confederate Section/
   Confederate Monument **3**
Douglas (Supreme Court Justice
   William O.) grave **22**
Dulles (Sec. of State John Foster)
   grave **6**
Evers (Medgar) grave **28**
Holmes (Supreme Court Justice
   Oliver Wendell) grave **23**

Information Center **32**
Iwo Jima Statue **30**
Kennedy (Pres. John F.) grave **21**
Kennedy (Sen. Robert F.) grave **19**
Lee (Robert E.) Museum **17**
L'Enfant (Pierre Charles) grave **18**
Louis (Joe) grave **13**
Marshall (Supreme Court Justice
   Thurgood) grave **25**
Memorial Amphitheater **11**
Murphy (Audie) grave **7**
Netherlands Carillon **29**
Old Amphitheater **14**
Paderewski (Ignace Jan) marker **9**

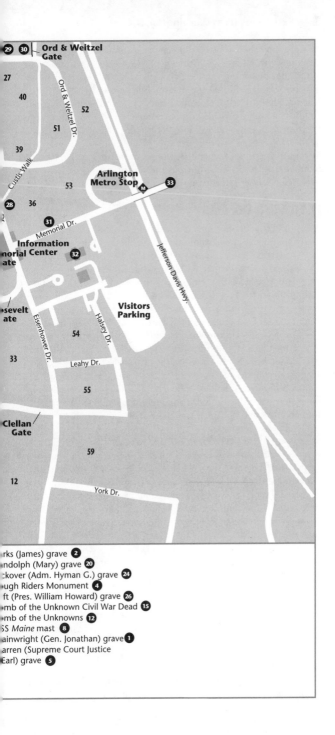

Ord & Weitzel Gate

29 **30**

27

40

52

51

39

Ord & Weitzel Dr.

Custis Walk

53

Arlington Metro Stop **M** **33**

28 36

31

Memorial Dr.

Information Center **Gate** **32**

Jefferson Davis Hwy.

Roosevelt Gate

Eisenhower Dr.

33

54

Halsey Dr.

Visitors Parking

Leahy Dr.

55

McClellan Gate

59

12

York Dr.

continuous, and the narrated commentary is informative. (See "Getting Around" in Chapter 4 for details.) However, if you've lots of stamina, consider doing the tour on foot (a free map is available at the Visitor Center). Riding the Tourmobile with crowds of tourists (usually in a holiday mood) usually makes me feel like I'm at Universal Studios. Walking provides a more contemplative experience. You could compromise by walking some of the distance and then riding some.

Arlington National Cemetery is open to visitors daily April to September 8am to 7pm, until 5pm the rest of the year. Call 703/692-0931 for further information.

WHAT TO SEE & DO

This famous cemetery occupies approximately 612 acres on the high hills overlooking the capital from the west side of the Memorial Bridge. One of America's most famous national shrines, it honors many national heroes and more than 240,000 war dead, veterans, and dependents. Many graves of the famous at Arlington bear nothing more than simple markers. Five-star Gen. John J. Pershing's is one of those. Secretary of State John Foster Dulles is buried here. So are Pres. William Howard Taft and Supreme Court Justice Thurgood Marshall.

The **Tomb of the Unknowns,** containing the unidentified remains of service members from both world wars, the Korean and Vietnam wars, is located here. It's an unembellished massive white-marble block, moving in its simplicity. Inscribed are the words: "Here rests in honored glory an American Soldier known but to God." Soldiers stationed at Fort Myer guard the tomb day and night. Changing of the guard is performed every half hour April to September and every hour on the hour October to March.

Arlington House (☎ 703/557-0613) was for 30 years (1831–61) the residence of Robert E. Lee. Lee married the great-granddaughter of Martha Washington, Mary Anna Randolph Custis, who inherited the estate upon the death of her father. It was at Arlington House that Lee received the news of Virginia's secession from the Union and decided to resign his commission in the U.S. Army. During the Civil War the estate was taken over by Union forces, and troops were buried there. A year before the defeat of the Confederate forces at Gettysburg, the estate was bought by the U.S. government. A fine example of Greek Revival architecture combined with many features of the grand plantation houses of the early 1800s, it has been administered by the National Park Service since 1933.

You can take a self-guided tour of the house; hosts in pre–Civil War dress give an orientation talk, hand out brochures, and answer questions. About 30% of the furnishings are original. Slave quarters and a small museum adjoin. Admission is free. It's open daily 9:30am to 4:30pm October to March, until 6pm April to September; closed January 1 and December 25.

Pierre Charles L'Enfant's Grave was placed near Arlington House at a spot that is believed to offer the best view of Washington, the city he designed.

Below Arlington House is the **Gravesite of John Fitzgerald Kennedy.** Simplicity is the key to grandeur here, too. John Carl Warnecke designed a low crescent wall embracing a marble terrace, inscribed with memorable words of the 35th U.S. president, including his famous utterance, "And so my fellow Americans, ask not what your country can do for you, ask what you can do for your country. . . ." Jacqueline Kennedy Onassis and Sen. Robert Kennedy are buried close by. The Kennedy graves attract streams of visitors. Arrive as close to 8am as possible to experience the mood of quiet contemplation the site evokes when it's not mobbed with tourists. Looking north, there's a spectacular view of Washington.

About $1^1/_2$ miles from the Kennedy Graves, the famous statue of the marines raising the flag on Iwo Jima—the **Marine Corps Memorial**— stands near the north (or Orde-Weitzel Gate) entrance to the cemetery as a tribute to marines who died in all wars. In summer there are military parades on the grounds on Tuesday evenings at 7pm.

Close to the Iwo Jima statue is the **Netherlands Carillon,** a gift from the people of the Netherlands, with 50 bells. Every spring thousands of tulip bulbs are planted on the surrounding grounds. Carillon concerts take place from 2 to 4pm on Saturday during April, May, and September; from 6 to 8pm on Saturday from June to August. (Sometimes the hours change; call 703/285-2598, before you go.) Visitors are permitted to enter the tower to watch the carillonneur perform and enjoy panoramic views of Washington.

2 Mount Vernon

No visit to Washington is complete without a trip to Mount Vernon, the estate of George Washington. Only 16 miles south of the capital, this southern plantation dates back to a 1674 land grant to Washington's great-grandfather.

ESSENTIALS

GETTING THERE If you're going **by car,** take any of the bridges over the Potomac into Virginia to the George Washington Memorial Parkway (Va. 400) going south; the parkway ends at Mount Vernon. **Tourmobile** buses (☎ 203/554-5100) depart daily, April to October, from Arlington National Cemetery and the Washington Monument. The round-trip fare is $17 for adults, $8.25 for children 3 to 11 (free for children under 3), and includes the admission fee to Mount Vernon (for details on the Tourmobile, see "Getting Around" in Chapter 4). You can also get there on a **Spirit of Washington Cruises** riverboat, which, from early March to December, travels down the Potomac from Pier 4, at 6th and Water streets SW (☎ 202/554-8000 for departure times). Round-trip fares—including the admission fee to Mount Vernon—are $21.50 for adults, $19.25 for seniors, $12.75 for children 6 to 11, and free for children under 6. Book in advance.

TOURING THE ESTATE

Mount Vernon (☎ 703/780-2000) was purchased for $200,000 in 1858 by the Mount Vernon Ladies' Association from John Augustine

Washington, great-grandnephew of the first president. Without the group's purchase, the estate might have crumbled and disappeared, for neither the federal government nor the Commonwealth of Virginia wanted to buy the property when it was offered for sale earlier. The restoration is an unmarred beauty; many of the furnishings are original pieces acquired by Washington, and the rooms have been repainted in the original colors favored by George and Martha.

Mount Vernon's mansion and grounds are stunning. Some 500 of the original 8,000 acres (divided into five farms) owned by Washington are still intact. Washington delighted in riding horseback around his property, directing planting and other activities; the Bowling Green entrance is still graced by some of the trees he planted. The American Revolution and his years as president took Washington away from his beloved estate most of the time. He finally retired to Mount Vernon in 1797, just two years before his death, to "view the solitary walk and tread the paths of private life with heartfelt satisfaction." He is buried on the estate. Martha was buried next to him in May 1802. Public memorial services are held at the estate every year on the third Monday in February, the date commemorating Washington's birthday; admission is free that day.

Mount Vernon has been one of the nation's most-visited shrines since the mid-19th century. Today more than a million people tour the property annually. There's no formal tour, but attendants stationed throughout the house and grounds provide brief orientations and answer questions. Best time to visit is off-season; during the heavy tourist months, avoid weekends and holidays if possible, and year-round, arrive early to beat the crowds.

The house itself is interesting as an outstanding prototype of colonial architecture, as an example of the aristocratic lifestyle in the 18th century, and of course, as the home of our first president. There are a number of family portraits, and the rooms are appointed as if actually in day-to-day use.

After leaving the house, you can tour the outbuildings—the kitchen, slave quarters, storeroom, smokehouse, overseer's quarters, coachhouse, and stables. A 4-acre exhibit area called "George Washington, Pioneer Farmer" includes a replica of Washington's 16-sided barn and fields of crops that he grew (corn, wheat, oats, and so forth). Docents in period costumes demonstrate 18th-century farming methods. A museum on the property exhibits Washington memorabilia, and details of the restoration are explained in the museum's annex; there's also a gift shop on the premises. You'll want to walk around the grounds (most pleasant in nice weather), see the wharf, the slave burial ground, the greenhouse, the tomb containing George and Martha Washington's sarcophagi (24 other family members are also interred here), the lawns, and the gardens.

Note: There's an ongoing schedule of special activities at Mount Vernon, especially in summer. These run the gamut from special garden and history tours (perhaps focusing on slavery or 18th-century farming) to colonial craft demonstrations and treasure hunts for children. Call to find out if anything is on during your visit.

Excursions from Washington, D.C.

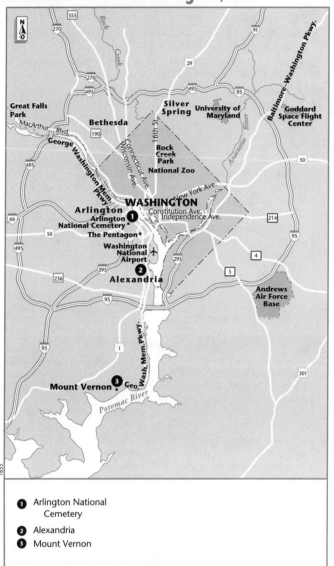

- **1** Arlington National Cemetery
- **2** Alexandria
- **3** Mount Vernon

The house and grounds are open to the public daily 8am to 5pm April to August; 9am to 5pm in March, September, and October; and 9am to 4pm November to February. Allow at least two hours to see everything. Admission is $8 for adults, $7.50 for senior citizens, $4 for children 6 to 11, under 6 free. A map is provided at the entrance.

WHERE TO DINE

At the entrance to Mount Vernon you'll find a **snack bar** serving light fare, and there are picnic tables outside. However, if a picnic is what you have in mind, drive a mile north on the parkway to **Riverside Park,** where you can lunch at tables overlooking the Potomac.

Mount Vernon Inn

Near the entrance to Mount Vernon. ☎ **703/780-0011.** Reservations recommended at dinner. Main courses $5.25–$7.25 at lunch, $12–$24 at dinner; prix-fixe dinner $14. AE, DISC, MC, V. Mon–Sat 11am–3:30pm and 5–9pm, Sun 11am–4pm. AMERICAN.

Lunch or dinner at the inn is an intrinsic part of the Mount Vernon experience. It's a quaintly charming colonial-style restaurant, complete with period furnishings and three working fireplaces. Waiters and waitresses are in 18th-century costume. Be sure to begin your meal with an order of homemade peanut and chestnut soup. Entrées range from colonial pye (a crock of meat or fowl and garden vegetables with a puffed pastry top) to a 20th-century-style burger and fries. There's a full bar, and premium wines are offered by the glass. At dinner, tablecloths and candlelight make this a plusher choice. Happily, a prix-fixe dinner means that it is also affordable. The meal includes soup (perhaps broccoli Cheddar) or salad, an entrée such as Maryland crabcakes or roast venison with peppercorn sauce, homemade breads, and dessert (like Bavarian parfait or English trifle).

3 Alexandria

Founded by a group of Scottish tobacco merchants, the seaport town of Alexandria came into being in 1749 when a 60-acre tract of land was auctioned off in half-acre lots. Colonists came from miles around, in ramshackle wagons and stately carriages, in sloops, brigantines, and lesser craft, to bid on land that would be "commodious for trade and navigation and tend greatly to the ease and advantage of the frontier inhabitants. . . ." The auction took place in **Market Square** (still intact today), and the surveyor's assistant was a capable lad of 17 named George Washington.

Today the original 60 acres of lots in George Washington's hometown (also Robert E. Lee's) are the heart of **Old Town,** a multimillion-dollar urban-renewal historic district. Many Alexandria streets still bear their original colonial names (King, Queen, Prince, Princess, Royal–you get the drift), while others like Jefferson, Franklin, Lee, Patrick, and Henry are obviously post-Revolutionary.

In this "mother lode of Americana," the past is being increasingly restored in an ongoing archeological and historical research program. And though the present can be seen in the abundance of quaint shops, boutiques, art galleries, and restaurants capitalizing on the volume of tourism, it's still easy to imagine yourself in colonial times—to smell the fragrant tobacco; hear the rumbling of horse-drawn vehicles over cobblestone; envision the oxcarts piled with crates of chickens,

Old Town Alexandria

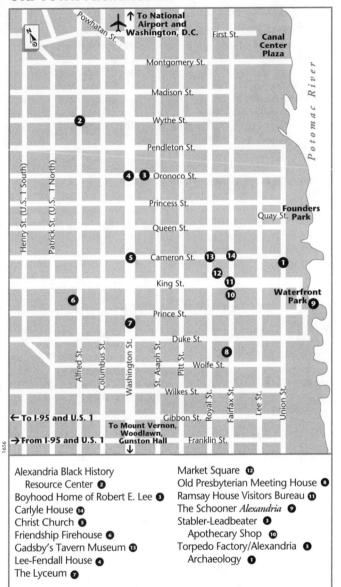

country-cured ham, and casks of cheese and butter; and picture the bustling waterfront where fishermen brought in the daily catch and foreign vessels unloaded exotic cargo.

ESSENTIALS

GETTING THERE   If you're traveling **by car,** take the Arlington Memorial or the 14th Street Bridge to the George Washington Memorial Parkway (Va. 400) south; it leads right to King Street, Alexandria's main thoroughfare. Parking permits are available from the Alexandria Convention & Visitors Bureau (see below). The easiest way to make the trip is on the **Metro,** and Old Town is so compact that you won't need a car once you arrive. Take the Metro Yellow Line to the King Street station, but be sure to get a transfer from your departure station. From King Street, take a blue-and-gold DASH bus (AT2 or AT5 eastbound) to the Visitors Bureau.

VISITOR INFORMATION   Before you do anything else, visit the **Alexandria Convention & Visitors Bureau** at Ramsay House, 221 King St., at Fairfax Street (☎ **703/838-4200, 703/838-5005** for a 24-hour Alexandria events recording), which is open daily from 9am to 5pm (closed January 1, Thanksgiving, and December 25). Here you can obtain a map/self-guided walking tour and brochures about the area; learn about special events that might be scheduled during your visit and get tickets for them; see a 13-minute video about Alexandria history; and receive answers to any questions you might have about accommodations, restaurants, sights, shopping, and whatever else. The bureau has materials in 20 languages.

   If you came by car, get a free **one-day parking permit** here for gratis parking at any two-hour meter for up to 24 hours. It can be renewed for a second day.

   Also available at Ramsay House: a money-saving **block ticket** for admission to five historic Alexandria properties—Gadsby's Tavern, Lee's Boyhood Home, the Carlyle House, Stabler-Leadbeater Apothecary Shop, and the Lee-Fendall House. The ticket, which can also be purchased at any of the buildings, costs $12 for adults, $5 for children ages 11 to 17; children under 11 enter free. You can also purchase block tickets for three sights. ($7 adults, $3 children) or two sights ($6 adults, $2 children), but I would recommend that you visit all five.

ORGANIZED TOURS   Though it's easy to see Alexandria on your own by putting yourself in the hands of guides at the various attractions, your experience may be enhanced by taking a comprehensive walking tour. **Doorways to Old Virginia** (☎ **703/548-0100**) has tours leaving from the Visitors Bureau at Ramsay House at 11am Monday through Saturday, and at 2pm Sunday (all weather permitting); tours cost $3 for adults and $1.50 for students 7 to 17. The Company also offers ghost tours weekend evenings all summer and through October, departing from Ramsay House at 9pm. Cost is $4 for adults, $3 for students.

CITY LAYOUT   Old Town consists of a very small area. Park your car for the day, don comfortable shoes, and start walking—it's the easiest way to get around. It's helpful to know, when looking for addresses, that Alexandria is laid out in a simple grid system. Union to Lee Street is the 100 block, Lee to Fairfax the 200 block, and so on up.

The cross streets (more or less going north and south) are divided north and south by King Street. King to Cameron is the 100 block north, Cameron to Queen the 200 block north, and so on. King to Prince is the 100 block south and so forth.

SPECIAL EVENTS

The below-listed are only the *major* events. If you're planning to participate in any of them, book your accommodations far ahead and contact the Visitors Bureau for details and necessary advance tickets. Whenever you come, you're sure to run into some activity or other— a jazz festival, tea garden or tavern gambol, quilt exhibit, wine tasting, or organ recital. It's all part of Alexandria's *ceád mile failte* (100,000 welcomes) to visitors.

JANUARY   The **birthdays of Robert E. Lee** and his father, Revolutionary War Col. **"Light Horse Harry" Lee,** are celebrated together at the Lee-Fendall House and Lee's Boyhood Home the fourth Sunday of the month. The party features period music, refreshments, and house tours.

FEBRUARY   Throughout the month, Alexandria celebrates **George Washington's Birthday.** Festivities typically include a colonial-costume or black-tie banquet followed by a ball at Gadsby's a 10-kilometer race, special tours, a Revolutionary War encampment at Fort Ward Park (complete with uniformed troops engaging in skirmishes), the nation's largest George Washington Day Parade (50,000 to 75,000 people attend each year), and 18th-century comic opera performances.

APRIL   Alexandria celebrates **Historic Garden Week in Virginia** with tours of privately owned local (usually historic) homes and gardens the fourth Saturday of the month.

JUNE   The **Red Cross Waterfront Festival,** the second week in June, honors Alexandria's historic importance as a seaport and the vitality of its Potomac shoreline today with a display of historic tall ships, ship tours, boat rides and races, nautical art exhibits, waterfront walking tours, fireworks, children's games, an arts and crafts show, food booths, and entertainment. This is the nation's largest Red Cross outdoor fund-raiser, attended by more than 120,000 people each year. Admission is charged.

JULY   Gather with the clans for **Virginia Scottish Games,** a two-day Celtic festival the fourth weekend of the month that celebrates Alexandria's Highland heritage. Activities include athletic events (such as the caber toss, in which competitors heave a 140-pound pole in the air), musicians (playing reels, strathspeys, and laments), fiddling and harp competitions, a parade of clan societies in tartans, a Celtic crafts fair, storytelling, Highland dance performances and competitions, booths selling Scottish foods and wares, dog trials featuring Scottish breeds, and a Scottish Country Dance Party. Tickets at the gate are about $9 for one day, $15 for the entire weekend; children 15 and under are admitted free with a paying adult. You can get a small discount on tickets purchased in advance at the Visitors Bureau.

AUGUST   A **Civil War Living History** program is featured the second Saturday of the month at Fort Ward, with authentically equipped and costumed military units demonstrating camp life with drills, music, a review of troops, and a torchlight tour. Admission is charged. For details, call 703/838-4848.

SEPTEMBER   Chili enthusiasts can sample "bowls of red" at the **War Between the States Chili Cookoff** in Waterfront Park. Contestants from almost every U.S. state and territory compete, and for a few dollars admission, you can taste all their culinary creations. Proceeds go to charity. Fiddling contests, jalapeño-eating contests, and country music are part of the fun. For details and exact dates, call 703/683-5340.

OCTOBER   Explore the ghosts and graveyards of Alexandria on a **Halloween Walking Tour** with a lantern-carrying guide in 18th-century costume. The tour focuses on eerie Alexandria legend, myth, and folklore. Admission is $4 for adults, $3 for students 7 to 17. For details, call 703/548-0100.

NOVEMBER   The **Historic Alexandria Antiques Show,** the third weekend of the month, features several dozen dealers from many states displaying an array of high-quality antiques—jewelry, silver, rare books, rugs, paintings, folk art, furniture, pottery, and decorative objects— in room settings. Admission is about $6 per day, including parking and a catalog. Proceeds are used for restoration of historic sites. Pricier activities include a gala opening party (about $75 admission) and a champagne brunch with a featured speaker (about $40). Call 703/838-4554 for details.

There's a **Christmas Tree Lighting** in Market Square the Friday after Thanksgiving; the ceremony—which includes choir singing, puppet shows, dance performances, and an appearance by Santa and his elves—begins at 7pm. The night the tree is lit, thousands of tiny lights adorning King Street trees also go on.

DECEMBER   Holiday festivities continue with the **Annual Scottish Christmas Walk,** the first Saturday in December. Activities include kilted bagpipers, Highland dancers, a parade of Scottish clans (with horses and dogs), caroling, fashion shows, storytelling, booths (selling crafts, antiques, food, hot mulled punch, heather, fresh wreaths, and holly), and children's games. Admission is charged to some events.

The **Old Town Christmas Candlelight Tour,** the second week in December, visits seasonally decorated historic Alexandria homes and an 18th-century tavern. There are colonial dancing, string quartets, madrigal and opera singers, and refreshments, too. Tickets—$12 for adults, $5 for students 6 to 17—are available at the Visitors Bureau.

There are so many holiday season activities, the Visitors Bureau issues a special brochure about them each year. Pick one up to learn about decorations, workshops, walking tours, tree lightings, concerts, bazaars, bake sales, crafts fairs, and much more.

WHAT TO SEE & DO

In addition to the annual events mentioned above, there's much to see and do.

About Admissions: If you have not purchased the money-saving block ticket described above, individual tickets to these first four attractions cost $3 for adults and $1 for children.

Note: Many Alexandria attractions are closed on Monday.

Gadsby's Tavern Museum

134 N. Royal St. (at Cameron St.). ☎ **703/838-4242.** Admission $3 adults, $1 children 11–17, free for children under 11; or buy the block ticket. Tours given Apr–Sept, Tues–Sat 10:15am–4:15pm, Sun 1:15–4:15pm; Oct–Mar, Tues–Sat 11:15am–3:15pm, Sun 1:15–3:15pm. Closed all federal holidays except Veterans Day.

Alexandria was at the crossroads of 18th-century America, and its social center was Gadsby's Tavern, which consisted of two buildings (one Georgian, one Federal) dating from circa 1770 and 1792, respectively. Innkeeper John Gadsby combined them to create "a gentleman's tavern," which he operated from 1796 to 1808; it was considered one of the finest in the country. George Washington was a frequent dinner guest (he and Martha danced in the second-floor ballroom), and the tavern was also visited by Thomas Jefferson, James Madison, and Lafayette. It was the scene of lavish parties, theatrical performances, small circuses, government meetings, and concerts. Itinerant merchants used the tavern to display their wares, and traveling doctors and dentists treated a hapless clientele (these were rudimentary professions in the 18th century) on the premises.

In the reception area, you'll see photographs of the tavern from the Civil War through the 20th century. The rooms have been restored to their 18th-century appearance with the help of modern excavations and colonial inventories. On the 30-minute tour, you'll get a good look at the Tap Room, a small dining room, the Assembly Room, the ballroom, typical bedrooms, and the underground icehouse, which was filled each winter from the icy river. Tours depart 15 minutes before and after the hour. Inquire about a special "living history" tour called Gadsby's Time Travels; it's given the last Sunday of each month. And cap off the experience with a meal at the restored colonial-style restaurant that occupies three tavern rooms (see "Where to Dine," below).

Boyhood Home of Robert E. Lee

607 Oronoco St. (between St. Asaph and Washington sts.). ☎ **703/548-8454.** Admission $3 adults, $1 children 11–17, free for children under 11; or buy the block ticket. Tours given Mon–Sat 10am–3:30pm, Sun 1–3:30pm. Closed Easter, Thanksgiving, and Dec 15–Jan 31 (except for the Sun closest to Jan 19, Robert E. Lee's birthday).

Revolutionary War cavalry hero Henry "Light Horse Harry" Lee brought his wife, Ann Hill Carter, and five children to this early Federal-style mansion in 1812, when Robert, destined to become a Confederate military leader, was just 5 years old. A tour of the house,

An American Dynasty: The Lees of Virginia

The history of one of the state's most noted families begins with Richard Lee, born in Shropshire, England, in 1613. As a younger son, his prospects were poor; so, after some legal and business education in London, he emigrated to Virginia in 1639 to serve as Clerk of the Quarter Court at Jamestown and to engage in fur trading. In 1649, Lee was appointed colonial Secretary of State. He frequently traveled to London in the interests of trade, became a successful planter, and amassed a vast fortune.

Many of Richard's descendants played major roles in American history. Richard Henry Lee (1732–94) and Francis Lightfoot Lee (1734–97) were signers of the Declaration of Independence. As a Virginia senator and a leader in the Continental Congress, Richard Henry proposed that "these United Colonies are, and of right ought to be, free and independent States." He was also influential in the adoption of the Bill of Rights.

Henry Lee (1756–1818), known as "Light Horse Harry," was a Revolutionary hero and a friend of George Washington. He played a leading part in the Virginia convention that ratified the Federal Constitution and served as governor of Virginia and in Congress. He penned the historic eulogy for George Washington: "First in war, first in peace, and first in the hearts of his countrymen."

Light Horse Harry was also the father of the most famous Lee— General Robert E. Lee (1807–70). As a loyal Virginian—though opposed to both slavery and secession— Lee resigned his Army commission when the state seceded in 1861. He had spent 32 years protecting the Union, and was Lincoln's choice to command Northern forces. However, after an agonizing personal struggle, Lee decided that he could not take up arms against his fellow southerners. On April 22, 1861 he assumed the rank of Major General of Virginia's military forces. In February of 1865—just two months before he surrendered at Appomattox—Lee was named general-in-chief of the Armies of the Confederate States.

built in 1795, provides a glimpse into the gracious lifestyle of Alexandria's gentry. George Washington was an occasional guest of two earlier occupants, John Potts (the builder of the house) and Col. William Fitzhugh. In 1804 the Fitzhughs' daughter, Mary Lee, married Martha Washington's grandson, George Washington Parke Custis, in the drawing room. And the Custises' daughter, Mary Ann Randolph, married Robert E. Lee.

General Lafayette honored Ann Hill Carter Lee with a visit to the house in October 1824 in tribute to her husband, "Light Horse Harry" Lee, who had died in 1818. Lafayette had been a comrade-in-arms with Lee during the American Revolution. The drawing room today is called the Lafayette Room to commemorate that visit.

On a fascinating tour, you'll see the nursery with its little canopied bed and toy box; Mrs. Lee's room; the Lafayette Room, furnished in period antiques, with the tea table set up for use; the morning room, where *The Iliad* translated into Latin reposes on a gaming table (both "Light Horse Harry" and Robert were classical scholars), and the winter kitchen. The furnishings are of the Lee period but did not belong to the family. The house was occupied by 17 different owners after the Lees left. It was made into a museum in 1967.

Lee-Fendall House

614 Oronoco St. (at Washington St.). ☎ **703/548-1789.** Admission $3 adults, $1 children 11–17, free for children under 11; or buy the block ticket. Tues–Sat 10am–3:45pm, Sun noon–3:45pm. Tours depart frequently throughout the day. Closed Jan 1, Thanksgiving, and Dec 24–25.

This handsome Greek Revival–style house is a veritable Lee family museum of furniture, heirlooms, and documents. "Light Horse Harry" Lee never actually lived here, though he was a frequent visitor, as was his good friend, George Washington. He did own the original lot, but sold it to Philip Richard Fendall (himself a Lee on his mother's side), who built the house in 1785. Fendall married three Lee wives, including Harry's first mother-in-law and, later, Harry's sister.

Thirty-seven Lees occupied the house over a period of 118 years (1785–1903), and it was from this house that Harry wrote Alexandria's farewell address to Washington, delivered when he passed through town on his way to assume the presidency. (Harry also wrote and delivered, but not at this house, the famous funeral oration to Washington that contained the immortal words: "First in war, first in peace, and first in the hearts of his countrymen.") During the Civil War, the house was seized and used as a Union hospital.

Thirty-minute guided tours interpret the 1850s era of the home and provide insight into Victorian family life. You'll also see the colonial garden with its magnolia and chestnut trees, roses, and boxwood-lined paths. Much of the interior woodwork and glass is original.

Carlyle House

121 N. Fairfax St. (at Cameron St.). ☎ **703/549-2997.** Admission $3 adults, $1 children 11–17, free for children under 11; or buy a block ticket. Tues–Sat 10am–4:30pm, Sun noon–4:30pm.

Not only is Carlyle House regarded as one of Virginia's most architecturally impressive 18th-century houses, but it also figured prominently in American history. In 1753 Scottish merchant John Carlyle completed the mansion for his bride, Sara Fairfax of Belvoir, a daughter of one of Virginia's most prominent families. It was designed in the style of a Scottish/English manor house and lavishly furnished. Carlyle, a successful merchant, had the means to import the best furnishings and appointments available abroad for his new Alexandria home.

When it was built, Carlyle House was a waterfront property with its own wharf. A social and political center, the house was visited by numerous great men of the time, including George Washington. But its most important moment in history occurred in April 1755 when Maj. Gen. Edward Braddock, commander-in-chief of His Majesty's forces in North America, met with five colonial governors here and asked them to tax colonists to finance a campaign against the French and Indians. Colonial legislatures refused to comply, one of the first instances of serious friction between America and Britain. Nevertheless, Braddock made Carlyle House his headquarters during the campaign, and Carlyle was less than impressed with him. He called the general "a man of weak understanding . . . very indolent . . . a slave to his passions, women and wine . . . as great an Epicure as could be in his eating, tho a brave man." Possibly these were the reasons his unfinanced campaign met with disaster. Braddock received, as Carlyle described it, "a most remarkable drubbing."

A **tour** of Carlyle House takes about 40 minutes. Two of the original rooms—the large parlor and the adjacent study—have survived intact; the former, where Braddock met the governors, still retains its original fine woodwork, paneling, and pediments. The house is furnished in period pieces; however, only a few of Carlyle's possessions remain. In an upstairs room an architecture exhibit depicts 18th-century construction methods with hand-hewn beams and hand-wrought nails. Tours are given every half hour on the hour and half hour.

Christ Church

118 N. Washington St. (at Cameron St.). ☎ **703/549-1450.** Admission free. Mon–Fri 9am–4pm, Sat 9am–noon, Sun 2–4:30pm. Closed all federal holidays.

This sturdy red-brick Georgian-style church would be an important national landmark even if its two most distinguished members had not been Washington and Lee. It has been in continuous use since 1773.

There have, of course, been many changes since Washington's day. The bell tower, church bell, galleries, and organ were added by the early 1800s, the "wineglass" pulpit in 1891. But much of what was changed later has since been restored to its earlier state. The pristine white interior with wood moldings and gold trim is colonially correct, though modern heating has obviated the need for charcoal braziers and hot bricks. For the most part, the original structure remains, including the hand-blown glass in the windows that the first worshipers gazed through when their minds wandered from the service. The town has grown up around the building that was first called the "Church in the Woods" because of its rural setting.

Christ Church has had its historic moments. Washington and other early church members fomented revolution in the churchyard, and Robert E. Lee met here with Richmond representatives to discuss assuming a command of Virginia's military forces at the beginning of the Civil War. You can sit in the pew where George and Martha sat with her two Custis grandchildren, or in the Robert E. Lee family pew.

It's a tradition for U.S. presidents to attend a service here on a Sunday close to Washington's birthday and sit in his pew. One of the most memorable of these visits took place shortly after Pearl Harbor when

". . . First in the Hearts of His Countrymen"

Though Alexandria calls itself George Washington's hometown, it was never his primary residence. He did spend a great deal of time here, though. As a 17-year-old surveyor, he helped lay out the town. As an adult, he had a home on Cameron Street, worshipped at Christ Church, trained his troops in Market Square, and bid them farewell at Gadsby's Tavern.

Born into a Virginia planter family in 1732, George Washington pursued his lifelong interest in military arts from an early age. At 22, he was already a lieutenant colonel fighting for the British in the French and Indian War. An aide to General Braddock, he escaped injury, though four bullets rent his coat and two horses were shot from under him. Like many Virginia planters, however, he began to feel exploited by the British government. On July 3, 1775, he assumed command of the Continental Army, a position he would hold for six years.

After the British surrender at Yorktown, Washington—respected as a great military hero— retired to his Potomac estate, Mount Vernon. However, he was unable to ignore the needs of the fledgling nation for which he had fought so valiantly. He agreed to preside over the 1787 Constitutional Convention. Washington also reluctantly accepted the presidency, taking office on April 30, 1789. His presidency was unique in that every action set traditions for the new republic. "As the first of everything . . . will serve to establish a Precedent," he wrote James Madison, "it is devoutly wished on my part that these precedents may be fixed on true principles."

Washington finally retired to Mount Vernon in 1797, two years before his death. He is buried there next to his wife Martha. Of all tributes to Washington, I like best that of Abigail Adams: "He never grew giddy, but ever maintained a modest diffidence of his own talents. . . . Possessed of power, possessed of an extensive influence, he never used it but for the benefit of his country. . . . If we look through the whole tenor of his life, history will not produce to us a parallel."

Franklin Delano Roosevelt attended services with Winston Churchill on the World Day of Prayer, January 1, 1942.

Of course, you're invited to attend a service. There's no admission, but donations are appreciated. A docent gives brief lectures to visitors. The old Parish Hall today houses a gift shop and an exhibit on the history of the church. Walk out to the weathered graveyard after you see the church. It was Alexandria's first and only burial ground until 1805; its oldest marked grave is that of Isaac Pearce, who died in 1771. The remains of 34 Confederate soldiers are also interred here.

Stabler-Leadbeater Apothecary Museum

105–107 S. Fairfax St. (near King St.). ☎ **703/836-3713.** Admission $2 for adults, $1 children 11–17, free for children under 11; or buy a block ticket. Mon–Sat 10am–4pm, Sun 1–5pm. Closed Jan 1, Thanksgiving, and Dec 25.

When its doors closed in 1933, this landmark drugstore was the second oldest in continuous operation in America. Run for five generations by the same Quaker family (beginning in 1792), its famous early patrons included Robert E. Lee (he purchased the paint for Arlington House here), George Mason, Henry Clay, John C. Calhoun, and George Washington. Gothic Revival decorative elements and Victorian-style doors were added in the 1840s.

Today the apothecary looks much as it did in colonial times, its shelves lined with original hand-blown gold-leaf-labeled bottles (the most valuable collection of antique medicinal bottles in the country, actually), old scales stamped with the royal crown, patent medicines, and equipment for blood-letting. The clock on the rear wall, the porcelain-handled mahogany drawers, and two mortars and pestles all date from about 1790. Among the shop's documentary records is this 1802 order from Mount Vernon: "Mrs. Washington desires Mr. Stabler to send by the bearer a quart bottle of his best Castor Oil and the bill for it."

There are docent tours Sundays from 1 to 5pm; other times a 10-minute recording will guide you around the displays. The adjoining gift shop uses its proceeds to maintain the apothecary.

Old Presbyterian Meeting House

321 S. Fairfax St. (between Duke and Wolfe sts.). ☎ **703/549-6670.** Admission free. Mon–Fri 9am–3pm; Sun services at 8:30 and 11am.

Presbyterian congregations have worshiped in Virginia since Jamestown days when the Rev. Alexander Whittaker converted Pocahontas. This brick church was built by Scottish pioneers in 1775. Although it wasn't George Washington's church, the Meeting House bell tolled continuously for four days after his death in December 1799, and memorial services were preached from the pulpit here by Presbyterian, Episcopal, and Methodist ministers. According to the Alexandria paper of the day, "The walking being bad to the Episcopal church the funeral sermon of George Washington will be preached at the Presbyterian Meeting House. . . ." Two months later, on Washington's birthday, Alexandria citizens marched from Market Square to the church to pay their respects to his memory.

Many famous Alexandrians are buried in the church graveyard, including John and Sara Carlyle, Dr. James Craik (the surgeon who treated—some say killed—Washington, dressed Lafayette's wounds at Brandywine, and ministered to the dying Braddock at Monongahela), and William Hunter, Jr., founder of the St. Andrew's Society of Scottish descendants (bagpipers pay homage to him the first Saturday each December). It is also the site of a Tomb of an Unknown Revolutionary War Soldier, and Dr. James Muir, whose distinguished ministry spanned the years 1789 to 1820, is buried beneath the sanctuary in his gown and bands.

The original Meeting House was gutted by a lightning fire in 1835 but restored around the old walls in the style of the day a few years later. The present bell, said to be recast from the metal of the old one, was hung in a newly constructed belfry in 1843, and a new organ was installed in 1849. The Meeting House closed its doors in 1889, and for 60 years it was virtually abandoned. But in 1949 it was reborn as a living Presbyterian U.S.A. church, and today the Old Meeting House looks much as it did following the restoration after the fire. The original parsonage, or manse, is still intact. There's no guided tour, but there is a recorded narrative in the graveyard.

The Lyceum

201 S. Washington St. (off Prince St.). ☎ **703/838-4994.** Admission free. Mon–Sat 10am–5pm, Sun 1–5pm. Closed Jan 1, Thanksgiving, and Dec 25.

This Greek Revival building houses a museum that depicts Alexandria's history from the 17th through the 20th century. It features changing exhibits and an ongoing series of lectures, concerts, and educational programs.

Information is also available here about Virginia state attractions, especially Alexandria attractions. You can obtain maps and brochures, and a knowledgeable staff will be happy to answer your questions.

But even without its many attractions, the brick and stucco Lyceum merits a visit. Built in 1839, it was designed in the Doric temple style to serve as a lecture, meeting, and concert hall. It was an important center of Alexandria's cultural life until the Civil War when Union forces took it over for use as a hospital. After the war it became a private residence, and still later it was subdivided for office space. In 1969, however, the City Council's use of eminent domain alone prevented The Lyceum from being demolished in favor of the proverbial parking lot.

Fort Ward Museum and Historic Site

4301 W. Braddock Rd. (between Rte. 7 [Leesburg Tpk.] and Seminary Rd.). ☎ **703/838-4848.** Admission free. Park, daily 9am–sunset; museum, Tues–Sat 9am–5pm, Sun noon–5pm. Closed Jan 1, Thanksgiving, and Dec 25. From Old Town, follow King Street west, go right on Kenwood Avenue, then left on West Braddock Road; continue for three-quarters of a mile to the entrance on the right.

A short drive from Old Town is a 45-acre museum, historic site, and park that takes you on a leap forward in Alexandria history to the Civil War. The action here centers, as it did in the early 1860s, on an actual Union fort that Lincoln ordered erected. It was part of a system of Civil War forts called the "Defenses of Washington." About 90% of the fort's earthwork walls are preserved, and the Northwest Bastion has been restored with six mounted guns (originally there were 36). A model of 19th-century military engineering, the fort was never attacked by Confederate forces. Self-guided tours begin at the Fort Ward ceremonial gate.

Visitors can explore the fort and replicas of the ceremonial entrance gate and an officer's hut. There's a museum of Civil War artifacts on the premises where changing exhibits focus on subjects such as Union arms and equipment, medical care of the wounded, and local war history.

There are picnic areas with barbecue grills in the park surrounding the fort. Concerts are presented on selected evenings June to mid-September in the outdoor amphitheater. And throughout the summer there are living-history programs on selected weekends (call for details).

Torpedo Factory

105 N. Union St. (near Cameron St.). ☎ **703/838-4565.** Admission free. Daily 10am–5pm; archaeology exhibit area, Tues–Fri 10am–3pm, Sat 10am–5pm, Sun 1–5pm.

This block-long, three-story building, once a torpedo shell-case factory, now accommodates some 155 professional artists and craftspeople who create and sell their own works on the premises. Here you can see artists at work in their studios—potters, painters, printmakers, photographers, sculptors, and jewelers, as well as those who make stained-glass windows and fiber art.

On permanent display here are exhibits on Alexandria history provided by **Alexandria Archaeology** (☎ 703/838-4399), which is headquartered here and engages in extensive city research. Their special exhibit area and lab are open to the public during the hours listed above with a volunteer or staff member on hand to answer questions. An ongoing exhibit, "Archaeologists at Work," highlights current excavation finds and methodology.

Schooner *Alexandria*

Waterfront Park (at the foot of Prince St.). ☎ **703/549-7078.** Admission (and tour) free. Donations requested. When in port (usually fall–spring), Sat–Sun noon–5pm.

The **Alexandria Seaport Foundation,** a nonprofit organization devoted to maritime heritage, acquired the Swedish three-masted, gaff-rigged, topsail schooner *Alexandria* in 1983. When it's in port (sometimes it participates in tall-ship festivals elsewhere), the schooner is docked at Waterfront Park and open to the public. A Baltic trader vessel built in 1929, the ship was remodeled for passenger use in the 1970s.

Friendship Firehouse

107 S. Alfred St. (between King and Prince sts.). ☎ **703/838-3891** or 703/ 838-4994. Admission free. Thurs–Sat 10am–4pm, Sun 1–4pm.

Alexandria's first firefighting organization, the Friendship Fire Company, was established in 1774. In the early days, the company met in taverns and kept its firefighting equipment in a member's barn. Its present Italianate-style brick building dates to 1855; it was erected after an earlier building was, ironically, destroyed by fire. Local tradition holds that George Washington was involved with the fire-house as a founding member, active firefighter, and purchaser of its first fire engine, although extensive research does not confirm these stories. Fire engines and fire fighting paraphernalia are on display.

Alexandria Black History Resource Center

638 N. Alfred St. (at Wythe St.). ☎ 703/838-4356. Admission free. Tues–Sat 10am–4pm.

In a 1940s building that originally housed the black community's first public library, the center exhibits historical objects, photographs, documents, and memorabilia relating to African-American Alexandrians from the 18th century forward. In addition to the permanent collection, the museum presents twice-yearly rotating exhibits, walking tours, and other activities.

SHOPPING

Old Town has hundreds of charming boutiques, antique stores, and gift shops selling everything from souvenir T-shirts to 18th-century reproductions. Some of the most interesting are at the sights (for example, Museum Shop at The Lyceum), but most are clustered on King and Cameron Streets and their connecting cross streets. Plan to spend a fair amount of time browsing in between visits to historic sites. A guide to antique stores is available at the Visitors Bureau.

WHERE TO DINE

There are so many fine restaurants in Alexandria that Washingtonians often drive over just to dine here and stroll the cobblestone streets.

EXPENSIVE

Landini Brothers

115 King St. (between Lee and Union sts.). ☎ 703/836-8404. Reservations recommended. Main courses $8.95–$11.95 at lunch. $12.50–$24.50 at dinner. AE, CB, DC, DISC, MC, V. Mon–Sat 11:30am–11pm. Sun 4–10pm. NORTHERN ITALIAN.

The classic, delicate cuisine of Tuscany is featured at this rustic, almost grottolike restaurant with stone walls, a flagstone floor, and rough-hewn beams overhead. Diners sit in wicker-seated chairs at white-linen-covered tables. It's especially charming at night by candlelight. There's additional seating in a lovely dining room upstairs. Everything is homemade—the pasta, the desserts, and the crusty Italian bread. At lunch you might choose a cold seafood salad or spinach and ricotta-stuffed agnolotti in buttery Parmesan cheese sauce, followed by a dessert of zuccotto (creamy frozen zabaglione). At dinner, get things under way with prosciutto and melon or shrimp sautéed in garlic with tangy lemon sauce. Then you might proceed to an order of prime aged beef tenderloin médaillons sautéed with garlic, mushrooms, and rosemary in a Barolo wine sauce. Or perhaps linguine with scallops, shrimp, clams, mussels, and squid in a garlic/parsley/red-pepper and white-wine sauce. Dessert choices include tira misu and custard-filled fruit tarts.

MODERATE

East Wind

809 King St. (between Columbus and Alfred sts.). ☎ **703/836-1515.** Reservations recommended. Main courses $5.95–$7.95 at lunch, $7.95–$13.95 at dinner; prix-fixe lunch $6.95. AE, CB, DC, DISC, MC, V. Mon–Fri 11:30am–2:30pm; Mon–Thurs 5:30–10pm, Fri–Sat 5:30–10:30pm, Sun 5:30–9:30pm. VIETNAMESE.

The decor of this Vietnamese restaurant is very appealing: Its sienna stucco and knotty-pine-paneled walls are adorned with works of Vietnamese artist Minh Nguyen, and there are planters of greenery, flowers on each pink-clothed table, and a large floral display up front. The owner personally visits the market each morning to select the freshest fish.

An East Wind meal might begin with an appetizer of cha gio (delicate Vietnamese egg rolls) or a salad of shredded chicken and vegetables mixed with fish sauce. One of my favorite entrées is bo dun—beef tenderloin strips marinated in wine, honey, and spices, rolled in fresh onions, and broiled on bamboo skewers. Also excellent are grilled lemon chicken or charcoal-broiled shrimp and scallops served on rice vermicelli. Vegetarians will find many selections on East Wind's menu. There's refreshing ginger ice cream for dessert. A good bargain is the prix-fixe lunch, which includes soup, an entrée, and coffee or tea.

Gadsby's Tavern

138 N. Royal St. (at Cameron St.). ☎ **703/548-1288.** Reservations recommended. Main courses $6.50–$9.95 at lunch/brunch, $14.95–$22.95 at dinner. Half-price portions available on some items for children 12 and under. DC, DISC, MC, V. Mon–Sat 11:30am–3pm, Sun 11am–3pm, nightly 5:30–10pm. COLONIAL AMERICAN.

In the spirit of history, pass through the portals where Washington reviewed his troops for the last time and dine at the famous Gadsby's Tavern. The setting authentically evokes the 18th century, with period music, wood-plank floors, hurricane-lamp wall sconces, and a rendition of a Hogarth painting over the fireplace (one of several). Servers are dressed in authentic colonial attire. George Washington dined and danced here often. At night, appropriate entertainment—a strolling minstrel or balladeer–adds to the ambience. A flagstone courtyard edged with flower beds serves as an outdoor dining area in nice weather.

All the fare is homemade, including the sweet Sally Lunn bread baked on the premises daily. You might start off with soup from the stockpot served with homemade sourdough crackers, continue with an entrée of baked ham and cheese pye (a sort of Early American quiche), hot roast turkey with bread/sage stuffing and giblet gravy on Sally Lunn bread, or George Washington's favorite—slow-roasted crisp duckling served with fruit dressing and Madeira sauce. For dessert, try the English trifle or creamy buttermilk-custard pye with a hint of lemon. Colonial "coolers" are also available—scuppernong, Wench's Punch, and such. The Sunday brunch menu adds items like thick slices of toast dipped in a batter of rum and spices, with sausage, hash browns, and hot cinnamon syrup. And a "desserts and libations" menu highlights items like Scottish apple gingerbread and bourbon apple pye, along with a wide selection of beverages. A strolling violinist entertains Sunday and Monday nights and at Sunday brunch. Tuesday to Saturday night an "18th-century gentleman" regales guests with song and tells the news of the day (200 years ago).

Panevino Ristorante

1755 Duke St. (in the Embassy Suites Hotel). ☎ **703/838-9600.** Reservations recommended. Main courses $6.75–$12.50 at lunch, $9.75–$14.95 at dinner (pizzas $6.75–$9.95); antipasti table $9.95; three-course early-bird dinner (5–8pm daily) $12.95; Fri night four-course seafood dinner $19.95; three-course Sat–Sun brunch $16.95. AE, CB, DC, MC, V. Daily 11am–11pm. Metro: King Street. CONTEMPORARY TUSCAN.

Directly across from the King Street Metro station, this is an ideal choice for a relaxing dinner before heading back to your Washington hotel. The menu is the same as at Panevino in Washington (see Chapter 6 for details), but the setting is lovelier. The airy windowed interior features terra-cotta walls adorned with a vast landscape mural of Tuscany, gorgeous tile work, and antique hutches filled with colorful Italian pottery. As at the Washington counterpoint, the central focus is a large rustic pine table laden with scrumptious daily-changing antipasti. However, this branch has covered open-air terraces on either side with trumpet vines growing up trellises, ficus trees in big flower-filled clay pots, and planters of ivy and geraniums. When the weather is pleasant, there's no nicer place. Opera singers entertain at brunch the first Sunday of every month, and there is a microbrewery-beer tasting the last Thursday of every month. A bar/lounge adjoins. One child under 12 per paying adult eats free. *Hint:* order Panevino's refreshing citrusy iced tea.

Radio Free Italy

5 Cameron St. (right behind the Torpedo Factory). ☎ **703/683-0361.** Reservations accepted for large parties only. Main courses $5.50–$10.95. AE, DC, DISC, MC, TRANSMEDIA, V. Daily 11:30am–midnight. CONTEMPORARY ITALIAN.

Anchor of the Food Pavilion, a pleasant waterfront dining complex, Radio Free Italy consists of a downstairs carry-out eatery and a fancier upstairs dining room with wraparound windows providing great views of the boat-filled harbor. The latter, with 62 theatrical halogen lights dramatically spotlighting tables at dinner, has a modernistic Italian black-and-white interior with exposed pipes overhead. Both levels offer outdoor waterfront seating in nice weather.

There are marvelous salads such as mixed chilled seafood—mussels, clams, calamari, scallops, and shrimp—marinated in lemon and olive oil. The antipasto sampler is also noteworthy. Oak-fired pizzas have California-style toppings such as grilled chicken, goat cheese, spinach, marinara, and quattro formaggio (Romano, fontina, Parmesan, and provolone). A bowl of mixed seafood is served on a bed of saffron linguine with three sauces—marinara, cream, and pesto. Yet another good entrée choice is fresh fettuccine tossed with pesto, sun-dried tomatoes, garlic-roasted mushrooms, and paper-thin slices of oak-roasted, peppercorn-studded sirloin. There's a full bar, with Italian wines available by the glass. Desserts include a decadently delicious tira misu.

✪ South Austin Grill

801 King St. (at S. Columbus St.). ☎ **703/684-8969.** Reservations not accepted. Main courses mostly $5.25–$10, lunch specials $4.95–$5.75. AE, DC, DISC, MC, V. Sun–Thurs 11:30am–11pm, Fri–Sat 11:30am–midnight. TEX-MEX.

The South Austin Grill opened in 1991 and immediately became one of my favorite Alexandria restaurants. This is great Tex-Mex food, totally authentic and brought to its highest culinary level. The two dining floors are cheerfully decorated with roomy booths painted in bright primary hues. Pastel walls are hung with Austin music club posters and other Texiana. A corner location permits lots of sunlight to stream in.

Start with some delicious chili con queso, flavored with finely minced jalapeño, tomato, and onion and spiked with Dos Equis beer. Also not to be missed are crabmeat quesadillas, stuffed with a mix of lump crabmeat, Monterey jack cheese, green onions, and poblano peppers; they're served with fresh guacamole. For an entrée, South Austin's lime-marinated, mesquite-grilled fajitas (beef or chicken) are out of this world; they come with rice, beans, guacamole, cheese, sour cream, and pico de gallo. Tacos al carbon—pork rubbed with red chilies, garlic, and spices, mesquite grilled, and served up in a tortilla with melted cheese—are also fabulous. Fresh-made iced tea comes with unlimited refills, Texas style, and margaritas are made from scratch. Leave a bit of room for sweet-potato flan—a scrumptious finale. Arrive off-hours to avoid a wait for seating.

INEXPENSIVE

The Deli on the Strand

211 The Strand (entrance on S. Union St. between Duke and Prince sts.). ☎ **703/548-7222.** Sandwiches $2.75–$6.95. AE, MC, V. Daily 8am–5pm, with extended hours spring–fall. DELI.

Why not a picnic, either combined with a visit to Fort Ward Park (described above), or right in Old Town at Founders Park, bordering the Potomac at the foot of Queen Street? The park doesn't have picnic tables, but there are benches and plenty of grass to sit on. Market Square is another possibility. Buy the fixings at the Deli on the Strand. They bake breads on the premises, so the aroma is divine, and you can get reasonably priced cold-cut sandwiches on fresh-baked rye and wheat bread, as well as muffins, and on weekends, bagels. Also available are homemade salads like seafood/pasta, cheeses, yummy desserts, beer, wine, and champagne. There are a few picnic tables outside under an awning.

✪ Hard Times Cafe

1404 King St. (near S. West St.). ☎ **703/683-5340.** Reservations not accepted. Main courses $3.95–$6.55. AE, MC, V. Mon–Thurs 11am–10pm, Fri–Sat 11am–11pm. Sun noon–10pm (hours extended in summer). AMERICAN/SOUTHWESTERN.

Will Rogers once said he "always judged a town by the quality of its chili." He would have loved Alexandria, where the fabulous Hard Times Cafe serves up top-secret-recipe homemade chilis and fresh-from-the-oven cornbread. It's a laid-back hangout where waiters and waitresses wear jeans and T-shirts; country music is always playing on the jukebox; and the Texas decor features Lone Star flags, a longhorn steer hide overhead, and historic photos of the Old West on the walls. The chili comes in three varieties—Texas, Cincinnati (cooked with sweeter spices, including cinnamon), and vegetarian. I favor the Texas style—coarse-ground chuck simmered for six hours with special spices in beef sauce. If chili isn't your thing, order grilled chicken breast, a burger, or salad. Side orders of steak fries cooked with the skins, Cheddar-filled jalapeños, and deep-fried onion rings are ample for two. Wash it all down with a bottle of Coors or Lone Star. The menu lists about 30 beers, including a Hard Times label and many selections from western "microbreweries." The Hard Times has garnered many a chili cookoff award, and CHILI-U.S.A.—a resolution before Congress "to make chili the official food of this great nation"—was conceived by Oklahoma lobbyists over a "bowl of red" here. There's additional seating upstairs; the Colorado flag overhead was brought in by a senator from that state.

Murphy's

713 King St. (between N. Washington and Columbus sts.). ☎ **703/548-1717.** Reservations accepted until 7:30pm only. Main courses $5.95–$10.95. AE, CB, DC, MC, V. Daily 11am–2am; brunch Sun 10am–3pm. IRISH/AMERICAN.

Murphy's is a self-described "grand Irish restaurant and pub," and it couldn't be more cozy and fun-loving. The bar serves up Irish liqueurs and whiskeys and Irish coffee, and has Guinness stout, Murphy's (from County Cork), Mooney's (a local microbrewery stout made especially for this restaurant), and 15 draft beers on tap. Fireplaces are ablaze on both floors during the winter, and Irish bands entertain nightly. This is the kind of bar where you can take the whole family; the kids will love it.

The food is fresh and tasty. Order up a meat-and-potato pie (filled with sage-spiced sausage, ground beef, pork, and mashed potatoes), a platter of fried oysters served with cottage fries (they're great), or hearty Irish stew. There's a low-priced children's menu, and desserts include brown-sugary homemade apple crisp topped with ice cream. At Sunday brunch, Murphy's offers a glass of champagne with a choice of entrées—perhaps bacon, eggs, sausage, home fries, homemade biscuit, and jelly—for $6.95.

The Tea Cosy

119 S. Royal St. (between King and Prince sts.). ☎ **703/836-8181.** Reservations not accepted. Tea cakes and sandwiches $1.95–$4.95, full afternoon tea $8.75, main courses $3.50–$8.25. DISC, MC, V. Sat–Thurs 10am–6pm, Fri 10am–7pm. BRITISH TEAROOM.

This pristine British tearoom is 100% authentic. It's a charming little place, with posters advertising Bovril and Colman's Mustard on white-washed walls, a beamed ceiling, and a magazine rack stocked with

British periodicals and newspapers. Tables are set with pretty floral-patterned place mats. A shop in the back sells archetypically British foodstuffs—digestive biscuits, ginger wine, Irish oatmeal, chutney, and such.

Come in for a full afternoon tea, including assorted tea sandwiches and oven-fresh scones (date/pecan, lemon, raisin, apricot, or cheese) served with jams and Devonshire cream. Assorted tea sandwiches, crumpets, shortbread, and trifle are also à la carte options. For heartier meals, your choices include steak-and-kidney pie, shepherd's pie, Cornish pasty, cheese-and-vegetable pasty, Scottish sausage rolls, and bangers and mash. Everything, including vegetables, is fresh and home-made. There are daily dessert specials such as apple-blackberry pie with custard. Possible libations: British ales and beers, hard cider, and a soft drink called orange quosh.

Index

Now Save Money on All Your Travels by Joining

Frommer's

T R A V E L   B O O K   C L U B

The Advantages of Membership:

1. Your choice of any **TWO FREE BOOKS.**

2. Your own subscription to the **TRIPS & TRAVEL** quarterly newsletter, where you'll discover the best buys in travel, the hottest vacation spots, the latest travel trends, world-class events and festivals, and much more.

3. A **30% DISCOUNT** on any additional books you order through the club.

4. **DOMESTIC TRIP-ROUTING KITS** (available for a small additional fee). We'll send you a detailed map highlighting the most direct or scenic route to your destination, anywhere in North America.

Here's all you have to do to join:

Send in your annual membership fee of $25.00 ($35.00 Canada/Foreign) with your name, address, and selections on the form below. Or call 815/734-1104 to use your credit card.

Send all orders to:

FROMMER'S TRAVEL BOOK CLUB

P.O. Box 473 • Mt. Morris, IL 61054-0473 • ☎ 815/734-1104

YES! I want to take advantage of this opportunity to join Frommer's Travel Book Club.

[ ] My check for $25.00 ($35.00 for Canadian or foreign orders) is enclosed.

    All orders must be prepaid in U.S. funds only. Please make checks payable to Frommer's Travel Book Club.

[ ] Please charge my credit card: [ ] Visa or [ ] Mastercard

    Credit card number: _____

    Expiration date: ___ / ___ / ___

    Signature: _____

    Or call 815/734-1104 to use your credit card by phone.

Name: _____

Address: _____

City: _____ State: _____ Zip code: _____

Phone number (in case we have a question regarding your order): _____

Please indicate your choices for TWO FREE books (*see following pages*):

    Book 1 - Code: _____   Title: _____

    Book 2 - Code: _____   Title: _____

For information on ordering additional titles, see your first issue of the *Trips & Travel* newsletter.

Allow 4–6 weeks for delivery for all items. Prices of books, membership fee, and publication dates are subject to change without notice. All orders are subject to acceptance and availability.   AC1

The following Frommer's guides are available from your favorite
bookstore, or you can use the order form on the preceding page
to request them as part of your membership in
Frommer's Travel Book Club.

FROMMER'S COMPLETE TRAVEL GUIDES

*(Comprehensive guides to sightseeing, dining and accommodations,
with selections in all price ranges—from deluxe to budget)*

FROMMER'S $-A-DAY GUIDES

(Dream Vacations at Down-to-Earth Prices)

FROMMER'S COMPLETE CITY GUIDES

(Comprehensive guides to sightseeing, dining, and accommodations in all price ranges)

Amsterdam, 8th Ed.	S176	Miami '95-'96	S149
Athens, 10th Ed.	S174	Minneapolis/St. Paul, 4th Ed.	S159
Atlanta & the Summer Olympic		Montréal/Québec City '95	S166
Games '96 (avail. 11/95)	S181	Nashville/Memphis, 1st Ed.	S141
Atlantic City/Cape May,		New Orleans '96 (avail. 10/95)	S182
5th Ed.	S130	New York City '96 (avail. 11/95)	S183
Bangkok, 2nd Ed.	S147	Paris '96 (avail. 9/95)	S180
Barcelona '93-'94	S115	Philadelphia, 8th Ed.	S167
Berlin, 3rd Ed.	S162	Prague, 1st Ed.	S143
Boston '95	S160	Rome, 10th Ed.	S168
Budapest, 1st Ed.	S139	St. Louis/Kansas City, 2nd Ed.	S127
Chicago '95	S169	San Antonio/Austin, 1st Ed.	S177
Denver/Boulder/		San Diego '95	S158
Colorado Springs, 3rd Ed.	S154	San Francisco '96 (avail. 10/95)	S184
Disney World/Orlando '96		Santa Fe/Taos/	
(avail. 9/95)	S178	Albuquerque '95	S172
Dublin, 2nd Ed.	S157	Seattle/Portland '94-'95	S137
Hong Kong '94-'95	S140	Sydney, 4th Ed.	S171
Las Vegas '95	S163	Tampa/St. Petersburg, 3rd Ed.	S146
London '96 (avail. 9/95)	S179	Tokyo '94-'95	S144
Los Angeles '95	S164	Toronto, 3rd Ed.	S173
Madrid/Costa del Sol, 2nd Ed.	S165	Vancouver/Victoria '94-'95	S142
Mexico City, 1st Ed.	S175	Washington, D.C. '95	S153

FROMMER'S FAMILY GUIDES

(Guides to family-friendly hotels, restaurants, activities, and attractions)

California with Kids	F105	San Francisco with Kids	F104
Los Angeles with Kids	F103	Washington, D.C. with Kids	F102
New York City with Kids	F101		

FROMMER'S WALKING TOURS

(Memorable strolls through colorful and historic neighborhoods, accompanied by detailed directions and maps)

Berlin	W100	San Francisco, 2nd Ed.	W115
Chicago	W107	Spain's Favorite Cities	
England's Favorite Cities	W108	(avail. 9/95)	W116
London, 2nd Ed.	W111	Tokyo	W109
Montréal/Québec City	W106	Venice	W110
New York, 2nd Ed.	W113	Washington, D.C., 2nd Ed.	W114
Paris, 2nd Ed.	W112		

FROMMER'S AMERICA ON WHEELS

(Guides for travelers who are exploring the U.S.A. by car, featuring a brand-new rating system for accommodations and full-color road maps)

Arizona/New Mexico	A100	Florida	A102
California/Nevada	A101	Mid-Atlantic	A103

FROMMER'S SPECIAL-INTEREST TITLES

Arthur Frommer's Branson!	P107	Frommer's Where to	
Arthur Frommer's New World		Stay U.S.A., 11th Ed.	P102
of Travel (avail. 11/95)	P112	National Park Guide, 29th Ed.	P106
Frommer's Caribbean		USA Today Golf	
Hideaways (avail. 9/95)	P110	Tournament Guide	P113
Frommer's America's 100		USA Today Minor League	
Best-Loved State Parks	P109	Baseball Book	P111

FROMMER'S BEST BEACH VACATIONS
(The top places to sun, stroll, shop, stay, play, party, and swim—with each beach rated for beauty, swimming, sand, and amenities)

California (avail. 10/95)	G100	Hawaii (avail. 10/95)	G102
Florida (avail. 10/95)	G101		

FROMMER'S BED & BREAKFAST GUIDES
(Selective guides with four-color photos and full descriptions of the best inns in each region)

California	B100	Hawaii	B105
Caribbean	B101	Pacific Northwest	B106
East Coast	B102	Rockies	B107
Eastern United States	B103	Southwest	B108
Great American Cities	B104		

FROMMER'S IRREVERENT GUIDES
(Wickedly honest guides for sophisticated travelers and those who want to be)

Chicago (avail. 11/95)	I100	New Orleans (avail. 11/95)	I103
London (avail. 11/95)	I101	San Francisco (avail. 11/95)	I104
Manhattan (avail. 11/95)	I102	Virgin Islands (avail. 11/95)	I105

FROMMER'S DRIVING TOURS
(Four-color photos and detailed maps outlining spectacular scenic driving routes)

Australia	Y100	Italy	Y108
Austria	Y101	Mexico	Y109
Britain	Y102	Scandinavia	Y110
Canada	Y103	Scotland	Y111
Florida	Y104	Spain	Y112
France	Y105	Switzerland	Y113
Germany	Y106	U.S.A.	Y114
Ireland	Y107		

FROMMER'S BORN TO SHOP
(The ultimate travel guides for discriminating shoppers—from cut-rate to couture)

Hong Kong (avail. 11/95)	Z100	London (avail. 11/95)	Z101